Hands-On RESTful Web Services with ASP.NET Core 3

Design production-ready, testable, and flexible RESTful APIs for web applications and microservices

Samuele Resca

BIRMINGHAM - MUMBAI

Hands-On RESTful Web Services with ASP.NET Core 3

Commissioning Editor: Richa Tripathi
Acquisition Editor: Alok Dhuri
Content Development Editor: Ruvika Rao
Technical Editor: Pradeep Sahu
Copy Editor: Safis Editing
Senior Editor: Rohit Singh
Project Coordinator: Francy Puthiry
Proofreader: Safis Editing
Indexer: Pratik Shirodkar
Production Coordinator: Alishon Mendonsa

First published: December 2019

Production reference: 1261219

Published by Packt Publishing Ltd.
Livery Place
35 Livery Street
Birmingham
B3 2PB, UK.

ISBN 978-1-78953-761-1

www.packtpub.com

To my family, Francesca, Gabriele, Angelica, Maurizio, Luisa, Guido, and Licia for their sacrifices and for being an example to follow.

To my partner, Luisa, for encouraging me in all my choices.

To all my friends, for always spreading good vibes.

Packt.com

Subscribe to our online digital library for full access to over 7,000 books and videos, as well as industry leading tools to help you plan your personal development and advance your career. For more information, please visit our website.

Why subscribe?

- Spend less time learning and more time coding with practical eBooks and Videos from over 4,000 industry professionals

- Improve your learning with Skill Plans built especially for you

- Get a free eBook or video every month

- Fully searchable for easy access to vital information

- Copy and paste, print, and bookmark content

Did you know that Packt offers eBook versions of every book published, with PDF and ePub files available? You can upgrade to the eBook version at www.packt.com and as a print book customer, you are entitled to a discount on the eBook copy. Get in touch with us at customercare@packtpub.com for more details.

At www.packt.com, you can also read a collection of free technical articles, sign up for a range of free newsletters, and receive exclusive discounts and offers on Packt books and eBooks.

Contributors

About the author

Samuele Resca is a software engineer working at Just Eat and primarily focused on web technologies. He is a Microsoft Most Valuable Professional in Visual Studio and development technologies. Samuele writes software engineering blog posts on Samuele Resca – Blog and The DEV Community, and he contributes to open source projects. He is continuously learning and developing around the web ecosystem with a focus on the .NET Core ecosystem, cloud computing, serverless computing, and reactive programming. Samuele is from Italy, and he currently lives in London.

> *First, I'd like to thank my whole family, in particular, my mother, Francesca; my dad, Gabriele; and my sister, Angelica, for being a role model to follow, and for welcoming me every time I come back to Italy. To Luisa, for always supporting me unconditionally, in every choice. I'd also like to thank Franco Melandri and Matteo Rizzatti for teaching me a lot and for all the knowledge they have shared with me.*

About the reviewer

Ankit Sharma is a software engineer currently working as a senior technical member with ADP in Hyderabad, India. He has over 5 years of extensive experience in Microsoft technologies including C#, ASP.NET, SQL Server, and UI technologies such as jQuery and Angular. He is a technical author and speaker and loves to contribute to the open source community. He writes articles for multiple platforms, which include c-sharpcorner, Dzone, Medium, and TechNet Wiki. For his dedicated contribution to the developer community, he has been recognized as a c-sharpcorner MVP, Dzone MVB, and Top contributor in Technology at Medium. He is also the author of the first ever book on Blazor – *Blazor Quick Start Guide*. You can tweet him at `@ankitsharma_007`.

Packt is searching for authors like you

If you're interested in becoming an author for Packt, please visit `authors.packtpub.com` and apply today. We have worked with thousands of developers and tech professionals, just like you, to help them share their insight with the global tech community. You can make a general application, apply for a specific hot topic that we are recruiting an author for, or submit your own idea.

Table of Contents

Section 4: Advanced Concepts for Building Services

Preface

.NET Core is a breath of fresh air for all the consumers of the Microsoft ecosystem. The old ASP.NET and .NET framework both have a long history. Over the years, the growth of the .NET framework and the long-time support constraints have resulted in odd implementations and hard-to-maintain web applications and web services.

Furthermore, the strong dependency between .NET framework and the Windows OS has led to substantial limitations in the cloud technology world.

.NET Core and ASP.NET Core are designed to evolve. They use abstract software development practices including open source, community-oriented approaches, as well as continuous improvement concepts. Today, ASP.NET Core is more flexible, fast, and powerful than ever. All the constraints developers had faced with .NET framework have been expelled and rewritten from scratch. Consequently, it is now possible to run .NET Core on every platform with no limitations. The framework is directly shipped with the .NET Core application. Therefore, it is possible to run it using a containerization approach. The documentation, the issues, and the roadmap are all available on GitHub. Microsoft is now following, by default, an open source way of working.

I've been interested in .NET Core since the first release of the old DNX runtime. This book will introduce you to the power of ASP.NET Core and how to use its strength and flexibility to run web services. Furthermore, the book aims to fight the prejudices that people have regarding the .NET ecosystem and seeks to increase the adoption of .NET Core.

Who this book is for

This book is intended for those who want to learn how to build RESTful web services with ASP.NET Core. To make the best use of the code samples included in the book, you should have basic knowledge of C#.

What this book covers

Chapter 1, *REST 101 and Getting Started with ASP.NET Core*, explains some fundamentals of RESTful APIs and how they can be useful when building an application.

Chapter 2, *Overview of ASP.NET Core*, shows the essential components of the .csproj file. It illustrates the main components of a project: the Startup class and the Program.cs file.

Chapter 3, *Working with the Middleware Pipeline*, explores middlewares, which are a central part of ASP.NET Core. This chapter walks you through the middleware pipeline and explains how it can handle requests and initialize different services based on them. Furthermore, the chapter covers the different out-of-the-box middlewares provided by ASP.NET Core and how to build a custom middleware.

Chapter 4, *Dependency Injection System*, introduces you to dependency injection principles and to the concepts behind dependency injection. It shows you how to use dependency injection to initialize components and options inside your application and how to use them inside your controllers.

Chapter 5, *Web Service Stack in ASP.NET Core*, describes how to create a web service stack in ASP.NET Core. It goes into depth on concerns such as controllers, action methods, action results, model binding, and model validation.

Chapter 6, *Routing System*, delves into the routing system, which handles HTTP requests. The chapter shows you how to deal with the default routing system of ASP.NET Core.

Chapter 7, *Filter Pipeline*, covers another essential topic in ASP.NET Core: filters. Filters are a vital component for achieving cross-cutting implementations in our services. The chapter introduces them; it shows how to implement our filters and explores some concrete use cases.

Chapter 8, *Building the Data Access Layer*, introduces the domain model part. The main topics are related to how to build the domain model and how to access data using **object-relational mapping (ORM)**.

Chapter 9, *Implementing the Domain Logic*, describes the mediator pattern approach to keeping logic isolated from other application components. The mediator pattern is one way to handle and manage our logic.

Chapter 10, *Implementing the RESTful HTTP Layer*, explains how to retrieve data from the mediator and use it inside our controllers.

Chapter 11, *Advanced Concepts of Building the API*, presents some advanced concepts around building APIs in ASP.NET Core. The chapter will cover topics around the soft deletion of resources, and it introduces some good practices for working with asynchronous code in ASP.NET Core.

Chapter 12, *The Containerization of Services*, gives you a quick introduction to containers and how they can be useful when running your application locally in a sandboxed environment.

Chapter 13, *Service Ecosystem Patterns*, focuses on the patterns involved when multiple services are part of the same ecosystem.

Chapter 14, *Implementing Worker Services Using .NET Core*, is dedicated to the new worker template of .NET Core. Workers provide a way to implement small services or daemons that can be used to perform background operations.

Chapter 15, *Securing Your Service*, talks about securing a service or an API. Besides that, it covers concepts including **Secure Sockets Layer (SSL)**, **Cross-Origin Resource Sharing (CORS)**, and authentication.

Chapter 16, *Caching Web Service Responses*, covers all the caching choices provided by ASP.NET Core.

Chapter 17, *Logging, Monitoring, and Health Checking*, shows some best practices for logging and monitoring your application.

Chapter 18, *Deploying Services on Azure*, shows some examples of how to host a web service in the cloud.

Chapter 19, *Documenting Your API Using Swagger*, introduces you to the OpenAPI standard and how to implement it in an ASP.NET Core application.

Chapter 20, *Testing Services Using Postman*, shows how to use Postman to test a web service.

To get the most out of this book

This book assumes that you have some knowledge of C# (or a similar object-oriented programming language, such as Java) and that you have some experience in building web applications.

This book doesn't require any specific tools, but you will need .NET Core installed on your machine (https://dotnet.microsoft.com/download). I strongly suggest that you have at least one code editor, such as Visual Studio Code, possibly with OmniSharp, or an **integrated development environment** (**IDE**) such as Visual Studio (on Windows or Mac), or Rider IDE (on Windows, Mac, or Linux).

I've written all the examples on macOS X using Rider IDE and Bash.

Download the example code files

You can download the example code files for this book from your account at www.packt.com. If you purchased this book elsewhere, you can visit www.packt.com/support and register to have the files emailed directly to you.

You can download the code files by following these steps:

1. Log in or register at www.packt.com.
2. Select the **SUPPORT** tab.
3. Click on **Code Downloads & Errata**.
4. Enter the name of the book in the **Search** box and follow the onscreen instructions.

Once the file is downloaded, please make sure that you unzip or extract the folder using the latest version of:

- WinRAR/7-Zip for Windows
- Zipeg/iZip/UnRarX for Mac
- 7-Zip/PeaZip for Linux

The code bundle for the book is also hosted on GitHub at https://github.com/PacktPublishing/Hands-On-RESTful-Web-Services-with-ASP.NET-Core-3. In case there's an update to the code, it will be updated on the existing GitHub repository.

We also have other code bundles from our rich catalog of books and videos available at https://github.com/PacktPublishing/. Check them out!

Download the color images

We also provide a PDF file that has color images of the screenshots/diagrams used in this book. You can download it here: https://static.packt-cdn.com/downloads/9781789537611_ColorImages.pdf.

Conventions used

There are a number of text conventions used throughout this book.

CodeInText: Indicates code words in text, database table names, folder names, filenames, file extensions, pathnames, dummy URLs, user input, and Twitter handles. Here is an example: "The headers part tells the client that the response should be processed using a specific content-type; in this case, application/json."

A block of code is set as follows:

```
<Project Sdk="Microsoft.NET.Sdk">
  <PropertyGroup>
    <OutputType>Exe</OutputType>
    <TargetFrameworks>netcoreapp3.0;net461</TargetFrameworks>
  </PropertyGroup>
</Project>
```

When we wish to draw your attention to a particular part of a code block, the relevant lines or items are set in bold:

```
<Project Sdk="Microsoft.NET.Sdk">
  <PropertyGroup>
    <OutputType>Exe</OutputType>
    <TargetFrameworks>netcoreapp3.0;net461</TargetFrameworks>
  </PropertyGroup>
</Project>
```

Any command-line input or output is written as follows:

```
dotnet build
dotnet run
```

Bold: Indicates a new term, an important word, or words that you see onscreen. For example, words in menus or dialog boxes appear in the text like this. Here is an example: "As you can see, it is running **Hello, World!**"

Warnings or important notes appear like this.

 Tips and tricks appear like this.

Get in touch

Feedback from our readers is always welcome.

General feedback: If you have questions about any aspect of this book, mention the book title in the subject of your message and email us at customercare@packtpub.com.

Errata: Although we have taken every care to ensure the accuracy of our content, mistakes do happen. If you have found a mistake in this book, we would be grateful if you would report this to us. Please visit www.packt.com/submit-errata, selecting your book, clicking on the Errata Submission Form link, and entering the details.

Piracy: If you come across any illegal copies of our works in any form on the Internet, we would be grateful if you would provide us with the location address or website name. Please contact us at copyright@packt.com with a link to the material.

If you are interested in becoming an author: If there is a topic that you have expertise in and you are interested in either writing or contributing to a book, please visit authors.packtpub.com.

Reviews

Please leave a review. Once you have read and used this book, why not leave a review on the site that you purchased it from? Potential readers can then see and use your unbiased opinion to make purchase decisions, we at Packt can understand what you think about our products, and our authors can see your feedback on their book. Thank you!

For more information about Packt, please visit packt.com.

Section 1: Getting Started

In this section, we will introduce you to all the macro concepts of REST APIs and ASP.NET Core. You will also learn about local development.

This section includes the following chapter:

- `Chapter 1`, *REST 101 and Getting Started with ASP.NET Core*

1
REST 101 and Getting Started with ASP.NET Core

Nowadays, almost all applications rely on web services. A lot of them operate using the RESTful method. The resource-centric approach and the simplicity of the REST style have become an industry standard. Therefore, it is essential to understand the theory behind the REST way of working and why it is important. This chapter will introduce you to the **Representational State Transfer (REST)** method. We will see what the definition of REST is and how to identify REST-compliant web services. We will also introduce .NET Core 3.1 and ASP.NET Core, the brand new version of the open-source, cross-platform framework provided by Microsoft.

In summary, this chapter covers the following topics:

- Overview of REST architectural elements
- A brief introduction to the .NET ecosystem
- Why you should choose .NET to build a RESTful web service

By the end of this chapter, you will have an overview of some useful tools and IDEs that you can use to start developing on .NET Core.

This chapter will cover some of the base concepts of .NET Core 3.1 and ASP.NET Core. You need to have either Windows, Linux, or macOS installed. The setup process will depend on which OS you are using. We'll look at the different tools that can be used to develop apps and web services in .NET Core.

REST

What is REST? **Representational State Transfer (REST)** is usually defined as a software architecture style that applies some constraints to a web service. It identifies a set of resource-centric rules that describe the roles and the interaction between the constraints of a distributed hypermedia system, instead of focusing on the implementation of the components. Although it is quite rare to find a REST service that does not use HTTP, the definition does not mention any of these topics and instead describes REST as media- and protocol-agnostic.

The preceding definition can be further explained with an example. Consider an e-commerce website. When you browse a list of products and click on one them, the browser interprets your click as a request to a specific resource; in this case, the details of the product you clicked on. The browser makes an HTTP call to the URI, which corresponds to the details of the product and asks for a specific resource using the URI. This process is shown in the following diagram:

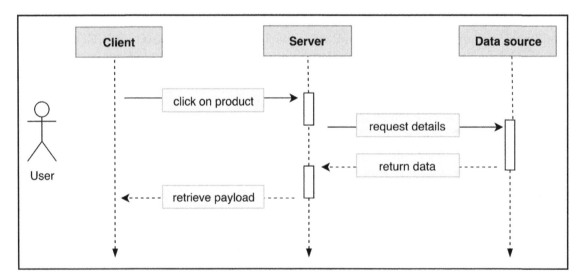

The concept of REST is pretty similar: the client asks the server for a specific resource, and this allows them to navigate and obtain other information about resources stored on the server.

The importance of being REST compliant

Before we discuss REST, we should understand the importance of web services in the modern application development world.

A typical modern application uses web services to obtain and query data. Any company that develop any product or solution uses web services to deliver and track information. This is because it can be difficult to replicate all the data and every behavior you need for every client who uses your application. Web services are also useful for providing access to third-party clients and services. Consider, for example, the **Application Programming Interfaces (APIs)** of Google Maps or Instagram: these platforms expose information through HTTP to share it with other companies and services.

The REST approach to web service architecture became increasingly popular because it is straightforward and clear. Unlike some old methods, such as the **Simple Object Access Protocol (SOAP)** or the **Windows Communication Foundation (WCF)**, REST services provide a clean way of querying data. Different information can be obtained using different URIs without the need for adding any overhead to requests.

Today, more than ever, our services need to be prepared to scale so that they can be adapted to consumers. In a world of different technologies and distributed teams around the globe, we should be able to transform our architecture to solve complex business challenges. HTTP and REST help us address these challenges.

REST requirements

Roy Thomas Fielding is the main person behind the formalization of the HTTP protocol and the REST style: he described them in his dissertation, *Architectural Styles and the Design of Network-based Software Architectures* (`https://www.ics.uci.edu/~fielding/pubs/dissertation/top.htm`). Moreover, Fielding's dissertation clearly defines the constraints of a REST system, as follows:

- Uniform interface
- Stateless
- Cacheable
- Client-server
- Layered system
- Code on demand

All of these, apart from code on demand, are essential when we wish to define a web service as REST-compliant. To explain these concepts, we will use the APIs provided by The New York Times: `https://developer.nytimes.com/`. To use these APIs, you need to go through a pre-authentication process. You can get an API key for this from the following link: `https://developer.nytimes.com/signup`.

Uniform interface

Uniform interface refers to the separation between the client and the server. This is advantageous because it means that the two systems are independent. The first principle of a uniform interface is that it should be *resource-based,* which means that we should start to think in a *resource-oriented way*. Therefore, every object or entity inside our system is a resource and a URI uniquely identifies each of them. Furthermore, if we think about the HTTP protocol, each resource is presented to the client in the form of XML or JSON to decouple the client from the server.

Let's use The New York Times APIs to understand this topic. Consider the following URI:

```
http://api.nytimes.com/svc/archive/v1/2018/6.json?api-key={your_api_key}
```

It contains some precise information about the resources we are asking for, including the following:

- The fact that we are getting information from the *archive* section of the newspaper data
- The specific month we are asking for; in this case, June 2018
- The fact that the resource will be serialized using *JSON format*

Manipulation of resources through representations

Let's take another API request provided by The New York Times:

```
https://api.nytimes.com/svc/books/v3/lists.json?api-key={your_api_key}&list
=hardcover-fiction
```

This provides a list of books based on a category; in this case, this category is `Hardcover Fiction`. Let's analyze the response:

```
{
    "status": "OK",
    "copyright": "Copyright (c) 2018 The New York Times Company. All Rights
      Reserved.",
    "num_results": 15,
```

```json
        "last_modified": "2018-06-28T02:38:01-04:00",
        "results": [
            {
                "list_name": "Hardcover Fiction",
                "display_name": "Hardcover Fiction",
                "published_date": "2018-07-08",
                "isbns": [
                    {
                        "isbn10": "1780898401",
                        "isbn13": "9780316412698"
                    }
                ],
                "book_details": [
                    {
                        "title": "THE PRESIDENT IS MISSING",
                        "contributor": "by Bill Clinton and James Patterson",
                        "author": "Bill Clinton and James Patterson",
                        "contributor_note": "",
                        "price": 0,
                        "age_group": "",
                        "publisher": "Little, Brown and Knopf"
                    }
                ],
                "reviews": [
                    {
                        "book_review_link": "",
                        "first_chapter_link": ""
                    }
                ]
            }
            . . . .
        ]
}
```

As you can see, this is a clear representation of the resource. The client has all the required information to process and modify data using APIs (if the APIs allow that).

Self-descriptive messages

Let's look at the response of the following call:

```
https://api.nytimes.com/svc/books/v3/lists.json?api-key={your_api_key}&list
=hardcover-fiction
```

As we mentioned previously, the response is a representation of the data, either stored in a data source or obtained from another system. In any case, some information is missing: how does the client know the format of the response? This kind of information is usually written in the response header. For example, here are all the headers of the previous request:

```
accept-ranges: bytes
access-control-allow-headers:Accept, Content-Type, X-Forwarded-For, X-
Prototype-Version, X-Requested-With
access-control-allow-methods: GET, OPTIONS
access-control-allow-origin: *
access-control-expose-headers: Content-Length, X-JSON
age: 0
connection: keep-alive
content-length: 14384
content-type: application/json; charset=UTF-8
date: Tue, 03 Jul 2018 12:47:08 GMT
server: Apache/2.2.15 (CentOS)
vary: Origin
via: kong/0.9.5
x-cache: MISS
x-kong-proxy-latency: 4
x-kong-upstream-latency: 29
x-ratelimit-limit-day: 1000
x-ratelimit-limit-second: 5
x-ratelimit-remaining-day: 988
x-ratelimit-remaining-second: 4
x-varnish: 63737329
```

The *headers* part tells the client that the response should be processed using a specific content-type; in this case, application/json. It also provides information about encoding, caching, and related meta information, such as the age header, which contains the time in seconds that the object has been in the proxy cache.

Hypermedia as the Engine of Application State

Services usually deliver a state to clients via body content, response codes, and response headers. Above all, *hypermedia-driven services (HATEOAS)* include the URI of other resources within their responses. The following example describes the concept of HATEOAS:

```
{
    "links": {
        "self": { "href": "http://example.com/people" },
        "item": [
            { "href": "http://example.com/people/1", "title": "Kendrick
```

```
            West" },
            { "href": "http://example.com/people/2", "title": "Anderson
            Rocky" }
        ]
    },
}
```

The previous response provides a list of people, together with the URIs that specify detailed information of each person. Therefore, the client knows the right URI of the request to use in order to get the information regarding each resource.

Stateless

Being stateless is a crucial characteristic of a REST service. Indeed, HTTP, as a stateless protocol, doesn't keep track of all the information about the connection between the client and the server once the communication ends.

A stateless protocol forces the client to fulfill the request with all the required information each time it needs some information from the server. Let's take one of the previous URIs:

```
https://api.nytimes.com/svc/books/v3/lists.json?api-key={your_api_key}&list
=hardcover-fiction
```

The client has to send the *API key* with each request to be authenticated by the server. Furthermore, it must store the API key information.

Statelessness is very important if we wish to take advantage of REST services. Nowadays, with the rise of highly distributed systems, it is difficult to deal with stateful services because this requires the states to be managed and replicated on different servers. A stateless approach helps delegate state management to the client.

Client-server separation

The main aim of REST services is to decouple the server and the client. This is very important because it helps keep unique business logic and data storage for each client application. Applications are usually distributed across a multitude of different clients, including the web, smartphones, smart TVs, and the IoT. A REST approach helps us prevent logic replication across clients. This means that the client does not have any business logic or storage, and the server does not deal with user interfaces or the presentation layer.

Layered system

The concept of a layered system is strictly related to the structure of the infrastructure of our application. RESTful services allow a loosely coupled approach because the information is transferred over a protocol – in most cases, HTTP – and each server has a single high-level purpose. Proxy servers, web servers, and database servers are usually isolated and they cover a purpose in our feature, if you have one server that provides all the required features, it is often hard to maintain and scale.

Richardson maturity model

The *Richardson maturity model* is a model that was developed by Leonard Richardson, and its purpose is to measure the maturity of APIs by providing some general criteria. The model has four classification steps, from **Level 0** to **Level 3**. The highest level corresponds to a more compliant service. This model isn't just for theoretical purposes; it also helps us understand some of the recommended methods for web service development. Let's take a look at an overview of these different levels. The following diagram shows the structure of the levels in the Richardson maturity model:

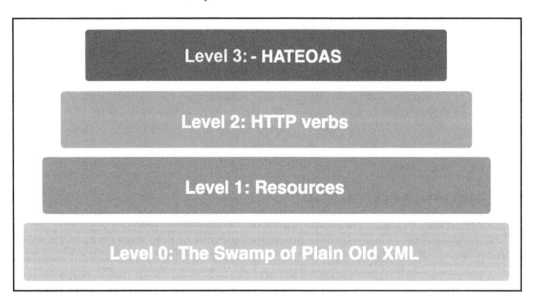

A generic service is at **Level 0: The Swamp of Plain Old XML** when it uses a generic protocol superficially (in the case of web services, this is HTTP). An example of this is a heavy SOAP web service. SOAP implementations use only one URI and only one HTTP verb, and they wrap each request message within a massive envelope.

As we mentioned previously, thinking in terms of resources is the best way to understand and design an API. Therefore, a generic service that's at **Level 1** uses multiple URIs associated with different resources. For example, if we think about an API of a general store, we could obtain the complete list of product categories by calling this sample URI:

```
GET https://api.mystore.com/v1/categories
```

At the same time, we can get the details of a single category by calling the following URI:

```
GET https://api.mystore.com/v1/categories/{category_id}
```

On the other hand, we can get a list of products related to a single category by calling the following URI:

```
GET https://api.mystore.com/v1/categories/{category_id}/products
```

As you can see, we can obtain different information by calling different URIs. There is no envelop, and all the requested information is contained in the URI.

Level 2, which is related to HTTP verbs, introduces the use of HTTP verbs to enhance the information that's transferred on request. Let's take the previous request URI as an example:

```
https://api.mystore.com/v1/categories/{category_id}/products
```

This can produce different results, depending on the HTTP verb. The following table shows the meanings of various HTTP verbs:

HTTP verbs	Performed operations	Example
GET	Retrieves information about a resource	GET /v1/categories/ HTTP/1.1 Host: api.mystore.com Content-Type: application/json

POST	Creates a new item related to the resource	POST /v1/categories/ HTTP/1.1
		Host: api.mystore.com
		Content-Type: application/json
		
		{
		  "categoryId": 1,
		  "categoryDescription": "Vegetables"
		}

PUT	Replaces an item related to the resource	```PUT /v1/categories/1 HTTP/1.1```
		```Host: api.mystore.com```
		```Content-Type: application/json```
		
		```{```
		``` "categoryId": 1,```
		``` "categoryDescription": "Fruits and```
		```Vegetables"```
		```}```

PATCH	Updates an item related to the resource	```PUT /v1/categories/1 HTTP/1.1```
		```Host: api.mystore.com```
		```Content-Type: application/json```
		
		```{```
		``` "categoryDescription": "Fruits and```
		```Vegetables"```
		```}```

DELETE	Deletes an item related to the resource	```DELETE /v1/categories/1 HTTP/1.1```
		```Host: api.mystore.com```
		```Content-Type: application/json```

Different HTTP verbs correspond to various data operations. As opposed to a **Level 0** service, which doesn't use any specifications of HTTP to deliver information, a **Level 2** service takes advantage of HTTP specifications to deliver as much information as possible. Finally, a system with a **Level 3** service implements the concept of HATEOAS. As we discussed in the previous section, a HATEOAS provides the resource's URI inside its response. A clear advantage of this approach is that the client doesn't need any information on its side to navigate through the web service's resources. Most importantly, if our web service adds the resource's URI, the client immediately has all the information they need.

Introducing ASP.NET Core

At the time of writing this book, .NET Core 3.1 is the **LTS** (short for **Long Term Support**) version of the framework powered by Microsoft and the community. ASP.NET Core is the highly modular web framework that runs over the .NET Core platform: it can be used to develop a wide range of web solutions, such as web applications, web assembly client applications and web API projects.

To learn about some of the basic concepts of ASP.NET Core, we need to understand the **Model View Controller (MVC)** pattern that is implemented in ASP.NET Core.

MVC separates our web application by grouping implementations into three different areas. In a web environment, the starting point is usually a web request that's made by a client or a generic user. The request passes through a middleware pipeline, and the controller then handles it. The controllers also perform some logic operations and populate our *model*.

The model is the representation of the state of the application. When it is associated with a view, it is called a **view model**. Once the model is populated, the controller returns a specific view, depending on the request. The purpose of the views is to present data through HTML pages.

In the case of a web API stack, which is the typical way of building web services in ASP.NET Core, the process is the same except for the view part. Instead of this, the controller serializes the model in the response.

To understand how ASP.NET Core helps developers build web services, let's go through the history of the ASP.NET framework.

The evolution of ASP.NET

The first version of ASP.NET was released in 2002 when Microsoft decided to invest in web development. They released ASP.NET Web Forms, which is a set of UI components that we can use to build web interfaces. The core idea of this approach was to provide a very high-level abstraction tool that can produce a GUI for the web. Providing this level of abstraction was a good idea because developers were not familiar with the web. However, ASP.NET Web Forms came with a lot of downsides. First of all, developers had limited control over HTML, and components had to store information in a *view state,* which was transferred and updated between the client and the server. Furthermore, the components were not correctly separated, and developers tended to mix the presentation code with the business logic code.

In order to improve the experience of developing web applications, Microsoft announced the arrival of ASP.NET MVC in 2007. This new development platform ran on the ASP.NET framework and used concepts from other development platforms that implemented MVC patterns, such as Ruby on Rails. The ASP.NET MVC framework still had some points of weakness. It was built on ASP.NET, which means it had to maintain its retro compatibility with old web forms and web services frameworks such as WCF. Furthermore, it only ran on Windows servers combined with **Internet Information Services (IIS)**.

The latest web framework to be developed by Microsoft is ASP.NET Core. It runs on .NET Core, which is cross-platform and open source. With ASP.NET Core, Microsoft made the choice to release a new lightweight framework that does not have any back-compatibility components derived from previous versions of ASP.NET.

The new .NET ecosystem

Let's look at an overview of the .NET ecosystem to understand the different frameworks that act as the foundations of ASP.NET Core. Some of the information provided here may sound obvious, but it is essential to clarify the differences between different runtimes and frameworks:

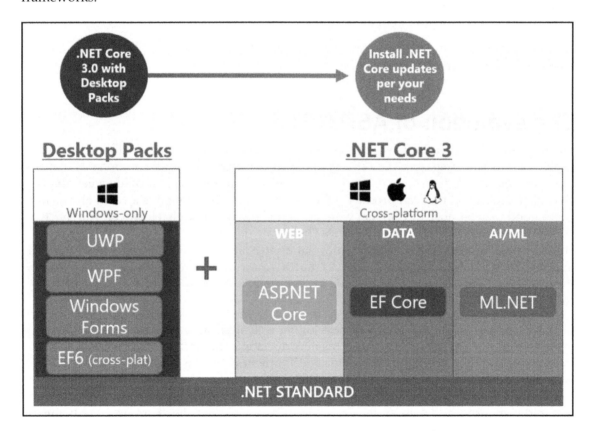

The first block is related to **Desktop Packs**, which provides the tools for the development of desktop applications starting from **.NET Core 3.0**. We will not use these tools in this book since they are strictly related to desktop development.

The second block is related to the cross-platform part of .NET Core. This set of tools allows developers to build applications on the **WEB, DATA**, and **AI/ML** domain. The **WEB** section refers to ASP.NET Core, which is a collection of libraries that comes with .NET Core. Usually, ASP.NET Core is combined with the **DATA** access part. Later in this book, we will see how we can use **EF Core** to access the database layer. Finally, the **AI/ML** section, which will not be discussed in this book, provides useful tools in the machine learning domain. At the bottom of the preceding diagram, we have a common layer, that is, **.NET STANDARD**. It allows developers to build third-party libraries that can be used by the **Desktop Packs** and by the **WEB, DATA**, and **AI/ML** parts.

In conclusion, the new .NET ecosystem can be used by any developer, including cloud developers, web developers, and desktop developers. As we mentioned previously, it also runs anywhere and on any platform. In this book, all of our examples will be based on .NET Core.

.NET STANDARD

.NET STANDARD was introduced along with .NET Core. The aim of the **.NET STANDARD** is to provide a common API surface for .NET Core and .NET Framework. It works as a unique **Base Class Library (BCL)** for our applications in both .NET Framework and .NET Core. The release of .NET Standard 2.0 has introduced 32,000 compatible APIs and supports the following framework versions:

- .NET Framework 4.6.1 +
- .NET Core 2.0 +
- Mono 5.4 +

Recently, Microsoft introduced .NET Standard 2.1. This new version provides new APIs that were introduced as part of the open-source development of .NET Core 3.0. .NET Standard 2.1 will be the common point between the new versions of .NET Core, starting from the 3.0 version, and the other versions of the upcoming frameworks, such as Mono.

You may wish to choose the .NET Standard for different reasons:

- To build third-party libraries that are compatible with both .NET Core and .NET Framework. In that case, your package will target .NET Standard 2.0. Eventually, if you want to use the newly optimized APIs that we described previously, it is possible to use multi-targeting to target both .NET Standard 2.0 and .NET Standard 2.1.
- To migrate your .NET Framework codebase gradually by isolating logic on .NET Standard projects.

For example, consider a class library project which is used by different versions of .NET. The library may run on either .NET Core or .NET Framework. To avoid maintainability pitfalls, the library package can be compiled for multiple versions of .NET Standard and it can be used by both a *.NET Core* and a *.NET Framework* solution.

Why use ASP.NET Core to build RESTful web services?

There is a massive choice of web frameworks that allow developers to build REST web services. One such framework is ASP.NET Core on .NET Core 3.1. .NET Core 3.1 provides a new, lightweight, cross-platform and opensource way to build web applications. Most importantly, it is designed to be cloud-ready: the framework is no longer part of the server, unlike in .NET Framework; instead, it is shipped with the application.

Another key point is that .NET Core maintains a *high level of modularity*, which adheres to the Unix philosophy and allows you to use only what you need in tailored applications. ASP.NET Core also introduces two new hosting solutions for web applications and web services:

- **Kestrel**: The default HTTP server for ASP.NET Core. It supports HTTPS and web sockets, and it runs on Windows, Linux, and macOS. *Kestrel* is usually combined with a *reverse-proxy,* such as NGINX, IIS, or Apache.
- **HTTP.sys**: A Windows-only HTTP server that can be used as an alternative to Kestrel on Windows.

ASP.NET Core and .NET Core are developed by Microsoft and the community, and they are *open source projects*. In the case of ASP.NET Core, open source isn't just a buzzword; all the features are community-driven, and the ASP.NET team streams a community standup video on YouTube every week, in which they discuss roadmaps, deadlines, and issues. All the .NET Core code is available on GitHub at the following links:

- **.NET Core**: The repository of .NET Core (`https://github.com/dotnet/core`)
- **ASP.NET Core**: Contains all the references to ASP.NET Core projects (`https://github.com/aspnet/AspNetCore`)

All the repositories usually come with a roadmap and some contributing guidelines. It is possible to open issues and contribute to the code base. Microsoft has also founded the .NET foundation, an independent organization that fosters open development and collaboration around the .NET ecosystem.

The ASP.NET Core team is also focused on the performance of the framework. All the benchmark results are available on GitHub: `https://github.com/aspnet/benchmarks`.

Preparing your development environment

In this section, we will show you how to set up your development environment so that you can develop web services using ASP.NET Core. As we mentioned previously, .NET Core is cross-platform, so it can run on the most common OSes. We will also look at how to interact with the .NET Core CLI, which is the starting point for building, running, developing, and testing our services.

First of all, let's start by downloading .NET Core 3.1 from `https://www.microsoft.com/net/download/`. In our case, we'll install the SDK version, which contains all the components that are required for our development environment, including ASP.NET Core.

.NET Core CLI

Unlike the .NET framework, .NET Core provides an easy to use CLI that exposes all the necessary functionalities we can use to build applications and services. Once .NET Core is installed on your machine, run the `dotnet --help` command. You will see the following result:

```
.NET Core SDK (3.1.100)
Usage: dotnet [runtime-options] [path-to-application] [arguments]
```

```
Execute a .NET Core application.

runtime-options:
  --additionalprobingpath <path> Path containing probing policy and
    assemblies to probe for.
  --additional-deps <path> Path to additional deps.json file.
  --fx-version <version> Version of the installed Shared Framework to
    use to run the application.
  --roll-forward <setting> Roll forward to framework version (LatestPatch,
    Minor, LatestMinor, Major, LatestMajor, Disable).

path-to-application:
  The path to an application .dll file to execute.

Usage: dotnet [sdk-options] [command] [command-options] [arguments]

Execute a .NET Core SDK command.

sdk-options:
  -d|--diagnostics Enable diagnostic output.
  -h|--help Show command line help.
  --info Display .NET Core information.
  --list-runtimes Display the installed runtimes.
  --list-sdks Display the installed SDKs.
  --version Display .NET Core SDK version in use.

SDK commands:
  add Add a package or reference to a .NET project.
  build Build a .NET project.
  build-server Interact with servers started by a build.
  clean Clean build outputs of a .NET project.
  help Show command line help.
  list List project references of a .NET project.
  migrate Migrate a project.json project to an MSBuild project.
  msbuild Run Microsoft Build Engine (MSBuild) commands.
  new Create a new .NET project or file.
  nuget Provides additional NuGet commands.
  pack Create a NuGet package.
  publish Publish a .NET project for deployment.
  remove Remove a package or reference from a .NET project.
  restore Restore dependencies specified in a .NET project.
  run Build and run a .NET project output.
  sln Modify Visual Studio solution files.
  store Store the specified assemblies in the runtime package store.
  test Run unit tests using the test runner specified in a .NET project.
  tool Install or manage tools that extend the .NET experience.
  vstest Run Microsoft Test Engine (VSTest) commands.
```

```
Additional commands from bundled tools:
  dev-certs Create and manage development certificates.
  fsi Start F# Interactive / execute F# scripts.
  sql-cache SQL Server cache command-line tools.
  user-secrets Manage development user secrets.
  watch Start a file watcher that runs a command when files change.

Run 'dotnet [command] --help' for more information on a command.
```

The first thing to notice is the version of .NET Core, which is the version of .NET Core, that is, `.NET Core SDK (3.1.100)`, followed by a list of **Software Development Kit (SDK)** commands. This contains the commands that are commonly executed during the development stage, such as `dotnet build`, `dotnet restore`, and `dotnet run`. These are used to build our projects, restore the NuGet dependencies, and run our project, respectively. Another relevant section is *additional tools*, which contain all the third-party CLI packages we will require, such as EF Core. In fact, the .NET Core CLI allows you to extend its functionality by adding specific tools in the form of NuGet packages.

IDEs and development tools in ASP.NET Core

.NET Core CLI is a base upon which higher-level tools such as IDEs, code editors, and **continuous integration (CI)** tools can be placed. Even though .NET Core is a cross-platform framework, there are various tools that can be used to build web applications and services on different platforms. The following table provides a recap of the different IDEs and editors that can be used to build ASP.NET Core:

Softwares	Windows	Linux	macOS X
Visual Studio 2019 (Community, Pro, and Enterprise)	Supported	-	-
Visual Studio Code and OmniSharp	Supported	Supported	Supported
Rider	Supported	Supported	Supported
Visual Studio for Mac	-	-	Supported

As you can see, it is possible to use different IDEs and code editors for different platforms. The choice you make usually depends on different factors. Let's look at an overview of the different editors:

- **Visual Studio 2019 (Community, Pro, and Enterprise)**: An editor that is well-known to anyone who has already developed on the .NET ecosystem. The community version of this product is totally free, and you can find it at `https://visualstudio.microsoft.com/it/downloads/`. Visual Studio 2019 is the most comfortable choice if you wish to start building on Windows.

- **Visual Studio Code and OmniSharp**: A popular and open source editor powered by Microsoft and the community. It is cross-platform and built on Electron. OmniSharp is a useful third-party package for Visual Studio Code and other code editors that provides some integration with .NET Core projects. It also provides an IntelliSense feature.
- **Rider**: A brand new IDE powered by JetBrains and based on the IntelliJ platform and ReSharper. It is compatible with every platform, but it is not free. I've tried it in large projects, and it works well, primarily to provide the ReSharper integration out of the box.
- **Visual Studio for Mac**: A new IDE powered by Microsoft. It is only compatible with macOS and provides a few functionalities we can use to write C# or F# code in the .NET Core ecosystem. This IDE is still at an early stage, but it has a lot of advanced features.

In conclusion, tools such as Visual Studio 2019, Rider, and Visual Studio for Mac provide a great experience when combined with .NET Core. On the other hand, Visual Studio Code is the lightest and fastest editor. In the upcoming chapters and code demonstrations, I will use the .NET Core CLI to reproduce the same steps in different operating systems.

Summary

In this chapter, we have taken an overview of the REST style by considering some concrete some concrete examples. We also learned about some of the basic concepts of the .NET ecosystem, including how it is structured and why ASP.NET Core is an excellent choice if we wish to build web services. We also looked at an overview of the .NET Core CLI and the IDEs and code editors related to the .NET ecosystem.

The topics we covered in this chapter provide a good understanding of what REST means and why is important to follow this kind of principle when we develop a web service. Furthermore, we also looked at the fundamentals for setting up .NET Core in our local environment.

The next chapter will focus on ASP.NET Core and ASP.NET Core MVC. You'll learn how to set up a project using the .NET CLI and explore some of the fundamentals concepts of ASP.NET Core.

2
Section 2: Overview of ASP.NET Core

In this section, you will learn about the ins and outs of ASP.NET Core and be provided with an overview of the key components of the ASP.NET Core application.

This section includes the following chapters:

- Chapter 2, *Overview of ASP.NET Core*
- Chapter 3, *Working with the Middleware Pipeline*
- Chapter 4, *Dependency Injection System*
- Chapter 5, *Web Service Stack in ASP.NET Core*
- Chapter 6, *Routing System*
- Chapter 7, *Filter Pipeline*

Overview of ASP.NET Core

2

In this chapter, we will explore some of the fundamental concepts of ASP.NET Core. .NET Core is cross-platform, but the IDEs and code editors that are used with it might vary depending on which OS they run on. To avoid repetition and cover all OS variants, I always use the CLI in the examples presented in this book. Furthermore, the `dotnet` instruction is the unique entry point and is also used, under the hood, by code editors and IDEs.

This chapter will cover the following topics:

- Setting up a .NET Core 3.1 and ASP.NET Core project
- The file structure of a .NET Core project template

Setting up our .NET Core project

This chapter assumes that you have already installed .NET Core version 3.1 or higher on your machine. First of all, let's start by launching the following command in our console:

```
dotnet new
```

The output will appear as follows:

```
Templates                                         Short Name          Language         Tags

Console Application                               console             [C#], F#, VB     Common/Console
Class library                                     classlib            [C#], F#, VB     Common/Library
WPF Application                                   wpf                 [C#]             Common/WPF
Windows Forms (WinForms) Application              winforms            [C#], VB         Common/WinForms
Worker Service                                    worker              [C#]             Common/Worker/Web
Unit Test Project                                 mstest              [C#], F#, VB     Test/MSTest
NUnit 3 Test Project                              nunit               [C#], F#, VB     Test/NUnit
NUnit 3 Test Item                                 nunit-test          [C#], F#, VB     Test/NUnit
xUnit Test Project                                xunit               [C#], F#, VB     Test/xUnit
Razor Component                                   razorcomponent      [C#]             Web/ASP.NET
Razor Page                                        page                [C#]             Web/ASP.NET
MVC ViewImports                                   viewimports         [C#]             Web/ASP.NET
MVC ViewStart                                     viewstart           [C#]             Web/ASP.NET
Blazor (server-side)                              blazorserverside    [C#]             Web/Blazor
ASP.NET Core Empty                                web                 [C#], F#         Web/Empty
ASP.NET Core Web App (Model-View-Controller)      mvc                 [C#], F#         Web/MVC
ASP.NET Core Web App                              webapp              [C#]             Web/MVC/Razor Pages
ASP.NET Core with Angular                         angular             [C#]             Web/MVC/SPA
ASP.NET Core with React.js                        react               [C#]             Web/MVC/SPA
ASP.NET Core with React.js and Redux              reactredux          [C#]             Web/MVC/SPA
Razor Class Library                               razorclasslib       [C#]             Web/Razor/Library/Razor Class Library
ASP.NET Core Web API                              webapi              [C#], F#         Web/WebAPI
ASP.NET Core gRPC Service                         grpc                [C#]             Web/gRPC
global.json file                                  globaljson                           Config
NuGet Config                                      nugetconfig                          Config
Dotnet local tool manifest file                   tool-manifest                        Config
Web Config                                        webconfig                            Config
Solution File                                     sln                                  Solution

Examples:
    dotnet new mvc --auth Individual
    dotnet new page
    dotnet new --help
```

The result of the *dotnet new* instruction

The preceding output shows all the .NET Core project templates available on the local machine. Each of these has a user-friendly name, a short name, and tags. They are available in **C#, F# and VB**; the default is **C#**.

To create a new template, we'll use the short name. For example, in order to create a console application, we should run the following instruction:

```
dotnet new console -n HelloWorld
```

The preceding instruction will create a new project in the current folder, with the following tree structure:

```
.
├── HelloWorld.csproj
├── Program.cs
└── obj
    ├── ...
```

The `HelloWorld.csproj` file contains all the meta-information about the project. The .NET Core version of the `.csproj` file is more lightweight compared to the `.csproj` file in previous versions of the .NET Framework. We'll discuss the new structure of this project file next in this chapter. The `Program.cs` file is the entry point of the application.

To build and execute our project, we can run the following commands inside the project folder:

```
dotnet build
dotnet run
```

As expected, we obtain the following result:

```
Hello World!
```

Unlike old .NET Framework projects, the build and run steps are lightweight processes, and they don't require any additional tools or configurations. In fact, .NET Core is not strictly chained to the development machine like the .NET Framework. Eventually, developers can write code without any other IDEs or code editors. However, for obvious reasons, it is always recommended that you use them to simplify the development process.

It is also essential to note that, once we execute the `dotnet build` command, the project files will change in the following way:

```
.
├── HelloWorld.csproj
├── Program.cs
├── bin
│   └── Debug
│       └── netcoreapp3.1
│           ├── ...
└── obj
├── Debug
│   └── netcoreapp3.1
│       ├── ...
```

The `bin/Debug/` folder contains all the app's DLLs. Below that, we can see the `netcoreapp3.1` folder, which refers to the current target framework. Therefore, if you build your project using a multi-target approach, you will find a folder for each target framework you specified. Now that we are able to run a simple console app, let's have a closer look at the *csproj* present in the project.

Overview of .csproj

As mentioned previously, in a plain console application template, there are two essential files: `ProjectName.csproj` and `Program.cs`. First of all, let's have a look at the `.csproj` file:

```
<Project Sdk="Microsoft.NET.Sdk">
    <PropertyGroup>
        <OutputType>Exe</OutputType>
        <TargetFramework>netcoreapp3.0</TargetFramework>
    </PropertyGroup>
</Project>
```

The format of the `.csproj` file is XML, just like earlier versions of the .NET Framework. The

`Sdk="Microsoft.NET.Sdk"` namespace refers to the SDK we want to use to build our project. The `PropertyGroup` node contains a set of properties, and it can be associated with some conditional behaviors. `ItemGroup` is a node that usually contains package references. In .NET Core, it is possible to specify the `TargetFramework` property to assign a target framework to our project. To set up our application as a *multi-target application*, therefore, we can change our `TargetFramework` node as follows:

```
<Project Sdk="Microsoft.NET.Sdk">
    <PropertyGroup>
        <OutputType>Exe</OutputType>
        <TargetFrameworks>netcoreapp3.1;netstandard2.0</TargetFrameworks>
    </PropertyGroup>
</Project>
```

Note that the XML node has changed from `TargetFramework` to `TargetFrameworks`, furthermore our project will be built on both .NET Core 3.1 and .NET Standard 2.0.

According to the MSBuild documentation (https://docs.microsoft.com/en-us/ visualstudio/msbuild/msbuild?view=vs-2019), it is possible to define different packages for each target framework. For example, in a double target framework project such as the previous one, we may define various dependencies for each target, as follows:

```
<Project Sdk="Microsoft.NET.Sdk">

  <PropertyGroup>
    <OutputType>Exe</OutputType>
    <TargetFrameworks>netcoreapp3.1;netstandard2.0</TargetFrameworks>
  </PropertyGroup>
  ...

  <ItemGroup Condition=" '$(TargetFramework)' == 'netstandard2.0' ">
    <PackageReference Include="Microsoft.AspNetCore.Server.Kestrel.Core"
Version="2.2.0" />
  </ItemGroup>
</Project>
```

In this case, we'll have separate references for each target: at compile-time, the framework generates two target versions, the `netstandard2.0` generated output will refer the `Microsoft.AspNetCore.Server.Kestrel.Core` package. This is an unusual type of configuration, but it comes in handy if we have a high level of customization in our project or if your project is a library consumed by different versions of .NET. The `dotnet new` command also sets a specific `OutputType` property depending on the type of project you are creating: the `OutputType` property defines whether the project is executable (`Exe`) or a library (`Library`). The significant difference is that in the first case it can be executed, whereas in the latter it does not contain any entry points from which to run the application. Therefore, we will not be able to execute the `dotnet run` command on a `<OutputType>Library</OutputType>` project type, on the other side, we do need to specify `static void Main` entry point method in case of a `<OutputType>Exe</OutputType>` project . Let's continue by discussing a bit the domain of the executable projects by walking through the *Program.cs* file of a standard console template.

The Program.cs file in detail

The `Program.cs` file is the main entry point of the application. It sets up and runs all the components we need. By default, the console application template executes a single statement:

```
using System;

namespace HelloWorld
{
    class Program
    {
        static void Main(string[] args)
```

```
        {
            Console.WriteLine("Hello World!");
        }
    }
}
```

The preceding snippet is a plain .NET Core application that runs `Console.WriteLine` to print a message in the console. In an ASP.NET Core application, the `Program.cs` file is usually utilized to initialize and run the web host.

C# version 7.1 introduced the `async void Main` method. This feature is implemented to avoid workarounds involved in running asynchronous code:

```
using System;
using System.Threading.Tasks;

namespace HelloWorld
{
    class Program
    {
        static async Task Main(string[] args)
        {
            await Task.Delay(10);
            Console.WriteLine("Hello World!");
        }
    }
}
```

In summary, the `Program.cs` file is the main execution root for applications built on .NET Core 3.1. It usually runs a set of statements in order to startup our application. In general, we should keep `Program.cs` as clean as possible to boost the reusability of our classes. In the next section, we will see how it is also possible to combine the `csproj` structure and the `Program.cs` file in order to build a simple API project.

Setting up an ASP.NET Core project

As mentioned in Chapter 1, *REST 101 and Getting Started with ASP.NET Core*, the MVC pattern is all about separating concerns. It aims to give developers some guidelines to ensure that the different components of the web application are not mixed up. The following is a refresher on the MVC pattern:

- The Model seeks to define the domain model of our application. It should also be noted that models don't contain any references to our data sources and databases. They describe the entities in our app.

- The Views part presents the data in the form of HTML pages. In web services, views are not included because the model is serialized in JSON, HTML, or other similar formats. The critical point is that views should not contain logic. They are hard to test and hard to maintain. Over the past few years, views have become increasingly more powerful. The Razor engine, the default view rendering engine provided by ASP.NET Core, has recently made several new features available. It is easy for developers to implement logic in views, but this should be avoided at all costs.
- The Controllers part of MVC handles requests from users. They take information from the request and update the model. In real business applications, controllers are usually supported by service or repository classes, which add another level to the domain model layer.

Let's have a detailed look at the default ASP.NET Core web API project template. The project uses the model and controller parts of the MVC pattern to serve a simple HTTP response with the content serialized in JSON.

First of all, let's create a new project using the following commands:

```
dotnet new webapi -n SampleAPI
```

The execution of the preceding command creates the following folder structure:

```
.
├── Controllers
│   └── WeatherForecastController.cs
├── Program.cs
├── Properties
│   └── launchSettings.json
├── SampleAPI.csproj
├── Startup.cs
├── WeatherForecast.cs
├── appsettings.Development.json
├── appsettings.json
└── obj
```

The execution of the dotnet new webapi command creates a new project file called SampleAPI inside a folder with the same name. The following is the resulting SampleAPI.csproj generated by the dotnet new webapi command:

```
<Project Sdk="Microsoft.NET.Sdk.Web">
    <PropertyGroup>
        <TargetFramework>netcoreapp3.1</TargetFramework>
    </PropertyGroup>
</Project>
```

The first thing to note is that this project uses the `Microsoft.NET.Sdk.Web` SDK, which refers to the web application SDK. Furthermore, the .NET Core framework provides different SDKs depending on the purpose of the project we are about to create. For example, in the case of a desktop application, the project will specify another SDK: `Microsoft.NET.Sdk.WindowsDesktop`. Choosing between different SDKs guarantees developers an excellent level of modularity. Secondly, the project file does not specify any particular dependency except the `netcoreapp` target framework used by the application.

The project structure

All ASP.NET Core web templates have a similar structure. The main difference lies in the `views` folder, which is not present in web API projects.

Before proceeding, let's have a more detailed look at the resulting content of the `SampleAPI` folder:

- `Program.cs` is the main entry point of the application, and it runs the default web server used by APIs.
- `Startup.cs` defines and configures our application pipeline and services.
- The `Controllers` folder contains all the controllers for our application. According to the default naming convention, ASP.NET Core searches in this folder for the controllers of our app.
- `Properties/launchSettings.json` file represents the settings for our project. This file is created when you try to change any of your project's properties, and it usually stores the application URL for our services or apps. Furthermore, if we have a quick look at the content of the file we can notice two different profiles: one with the name of the project created, and another one with the `IISExpress` name. Every project can have multiple profiles associated with it. they can be used to specify some of the launch settings, and the environment variables used by the application. Therefore, it is possible to run the application using the `dotnet run` command by specifying a profile using the `--launch-profile` flag;
- `appsettings.json` and `appsettings.{Environment}.json` contains the settings based on our environment. They are replacements for the settings section in the `web.config` file.

The Program.cs and Startup.cs files

Let's continue by examining the `Program.cs` file of a web API project:

```csharp
using System;
using System.Collections.Generic;
using System.Linq;
using System.Threading.Tasks;
using Microsoft.AspNetCore.Hosting;
using Microsoft.Extensions.Configuration;
using Microsoft.Extensions.Hosting;
using Microsoft.Extensions.Logging;

namespace SampleAPI
{
    public class Program
    {
        public static void Main(string[] args)
        {
            CreateHostBuilder(args).Build().Run();
        }

        public static IHostBuilder CreateHostBuilder(string[]
        args) =>
            Host.CreateDefaultBuilder(args)
                .ConfigureWebHostDefaults(webBuilder =>
                {
                    webBuilder.UseStartup<Startup>();
                });
    }
}
```

The preceding code imports the `Microsoft.AspNetCore.Hosting` and `Microsoft.Extensions.Hosting` namespaces. They supply the necessary references for the initialization of a new `IHostBuilder` instance created in the `CreateHostBuilder` function. The `CreateHostBuilder` function executes the `Host.CreateDefaultBuilder` method, which initializes the web host of our APIs. Furthermore, we should note that the `IHostBuilder` instance returned by the `CreateDefaultBuilder` method refers to the `Startup` class of the project. The `Main` method invokes the `CreateHostBuilder` function and executes the `Build` and `Run` methods exposed by the `IHostBuilder` interface.

Let's examine the `Startup` class (defined in the `Startup.cs` file), which is used to configure the application stack:

```csharp
using Microsoft.AspNetCore.Builder;
using Microsoft.AspNetCore.Hosting;
using Microsoft.Extensions.Configuration;
using Microsoft.Extensions.DependencyInjection;
using Microsoft.Extensions.Hosting;

namespace SampleAPI
{
    public class Startup
    {
        public Startup(IConfiguration configuration)
        {
            Configuration = configuration;
        }

        public IConfiguration Configuration { get; }

        public void ConfigureServices(IServiceCollection services)
        {
            services.AddControllers();
        }

        public void Configure(IApplicationBuilder app,
        IWebHostEnvironment env)
        {
            if (env.IsDevelopment())
            {
                app.UseDeveloperExceptionPage();
            }

            app.UseHttpsRedirection();

            app.UseRouting();

            app.UseAuthorization();

            app.UseEndpoints(endpoints =>
            {
                endpoints.MapControllers();
            });
        }
    }
}
```

The `Startup` class initializes the `IConfiguration` attribute through dependency injection. The `IConfiguration` object represents a key/value object which contains configurations for the app. By default, the `CreateDefaultBuilder` method declared in the `Program.cs` file sets `appsettings.json` as the default configuration file.

The `Startup` class has two different methods, which behave in the following ways:

- The `ConfigureServices` method configures services in our application using dependency injection. By default, it adds controllers by executing the `.AddControllers` extension method. In ASP.NET Core, the term services usually refer to any component or class that provides our application with features and functionalities. As we'll see in the next few chapters, ASP.NET Core frequently uses dependency injection to maintain a good design and loosely-coupled classes.

- The `Configure` method is used to configure the application's middleware pipeline. It accepts two arguments: `IApplicationBuilder` and `IWebHostEnvironment`. The first contains all the pipelines for our app and exposes extension methods to build our app with middleware. We'll have a look at middleware in detail in `Chapter 3`, *Working with the Middleware Pipeline*. The `IWebHostEvironment` interface gives some information about the current hosting environment of the application, such as its type and its name. In a web API project, the `Configure` method executes a list of extensions methods. The most important are the `UseRouting` and `UseEndpoints` extension methods. The execution of the `UseRouting` method defines the point in the pipeline where routing decisions are taken. The `UseEndpoints` extension method defines the actual execution of the previously selected endpoint. In the case of a web API project, the only endpoints involved are the controllers. Therefore, the `UseEndpoints` method executes the `MapControllers` extension method to initialize the default routing convention for controller classes, provided in .NET Core.

It should be noted that the ASP.NET Core `Startup` class provides a high-level, code-first way to configure the dependencies of your application through dependency injection, which means that it only initializes what you need. Furthermore, .NET Core is strongly modularity-oriented; this is one of the reasons why it performs better than the .NET Framework.

Since all pipelines and dependencies are initialized in the aforementioned class, you know exactly where they can be changed. In large applications and services with a lot of different components, it is advisable to create custom extension methods that handle the initialization of specific parts of your app.

Overview of controllers

Controllers are a fundamental part of the web API in ASP.NET Core projects. They handle incoming requests and act as the entry point of our application. We'll look at controllers in more detail in Chapter 4, *Dependency Injection*, but for now, let's examine the default WeatherForecastController provided by the web API template:

```
using System;
using System.Collections.Generic;
using System.Linq;
using Microsoft.AspNetCore.Mvc;
using Microsoft.Extensions.Logging;

namespace SampleAPI.Controllers
{
    [ApiController]
    [Route("[controller]")]
    public class WeatherForecastController : ControllerBase
    {
        private static readonly string[] Summaries = new[]
        {
            "Freezing", "Bracing", "Chilly", "Cool", "Mild", "Warm",
            "Balmy", "Hot", "Sweltering", "Scorching"
        };

        private readonly ILogger<WeatherForecastController> _logger;

        public WeatherForecastController(ILogger<WeatherForecastController>
        logger)
        {
            _logger = logger;
        }

        [HttpGet]
        public IEnumerable<WeatherForecast> Get()
        {
            var rng = new Random();
            return Enumerable.Range(1, 5).Select(index =>
            new WeatherForecast
            {
```

```
                    Date = DateTime.Now.AddDays(index),
                    TemperatureC = rng.Next(-20, 55),
                    Summary = Summaries[rng.Next(Summaries.Length)]
                })
                .ToArray();
        }
    }
}
```

`WeatherForecastController` comes with basic methods. By default, it doesn't use any data source; it simply returns some mock values. Let's proceed by having a look at the main elements of the `WeatherForecastController` class:

- The `ApiController` attribute indicates that the controller and all extended controllers serve HTTP API responses. It was introduced in ASP.NET Core version 2.1, and it is usually combined with the `ControllerBase` class.

- The `Route("api/[controller]")` attribute defines the route for our controller. For example, in this case the controller will respond to the following URI: `https://myhostname:myport/api/weatherforecast`. The `[controller]` placeholder is used to indicate the name of the controller.

- The `ControllerBase` class is usually combined with the `ApiController` attribute, and it is defined in the `Microsoft.AspNetCore.Mvc` namespace. The `ControllerBase` class indicates a controller without support for the views part. It provides a few base methods, such as `Created`, `CreatedAtAction`, and `NotFound`. It also provides some properties, for example, `HttpContext`, which contains the requests and responses of our web service.

- The `HttpGet` attribute is part of the `Microsoft.AspNetCore.Mvc` namespace. It identifies the type of HTTP method accepted by the action. It also accepts an additional parameter, such as `[HttpGet("{id}")]`, which defines the route template of the action. ASP.NET Core exposes an HTTP attribute for each HTTP verb, such as `HttpPost`, `HttpPut`, or `HttpDelete`.

Finally, we can take a brief look at the implementation of the `WeatherForecastController()` constructor method and the `Get()` method. The first initializes all dependencies of the controller class, and it is the dependency injection entry point for our class; all dependencies relating to the controllers are solved in the constructor. The `Get()` method implements the logic and returns a collection of elements that will be serialized and then passed to the HTTP response of the web API.

Summary

In this chapter, we introduced some central concepts in .NET Core. We walked through the console application and web API templates as well as the ASP.NET Core web API structure, and the structure of a controller class.

The topics covered in this chapter provide the skills necessary to start with a console application project on .NET Core, and they also provides basic knowledge regarding the arrangement of an ASP.NET Core project.

In the next chapter, we will explore a core concept of ASP.NET Core, middleware, and how it can be used to intercept requests and enhance our application stack.

Working with the Middleware Pipeline

3

The previous chapter provided an overview of ASP.NET Core projects. We looked at how to create an ASP.NET Core project and how to deal with the files and the structure involved. Also, we learned some of the basic concepts behind the MVC stack and ASP.NET Core. Now, let's explore the concept of middleware in depth. Middleware is an essential part of the ASP.NET Core platform: it helps us to deal with incoming requests and outgoing responses. Most of all, these types of components can be used to monitor performances and implement cross-cutting functionalities. The chapter starts with an introduction to the middleware concept. It goes on to show how to implement custom middleware and it ends with an overview of the built-in middleware of ASP.NET Core.

This chapter covers the following topics:

- Introducing middleware and dealing with its different aspects
- Concrete use cases for middleware in an ASP.NET Core project
- An overview of the built-in middleware of ASP.NET Core
- Implementing custom middleware

Introducing middleware

As the name suggests, middleware is a component placed between our application and incoming requests. Incoming requests hit the middleware's pipeline before they can reach the effective logic implemented in our application. As a result, middleware are considered one of the essential concepts of ASP.NET Core because it is the first layer in front of our application, and it is usually associated with cross-cutting concepts such as *logging, error handling, authentication,* and *validation.* It can also perform advanced tasks such as *conditional service initialization,* based on a request.

In general, middleware can:

- Handle, process, and modify incoming *HTTP requests*
- Handle, process, and change outgoing *HTTP responses*
- Interrupt the middleware pipeline by returning an *early response*

Furthermore, the whole ASP.NET Core stack is composed of middleware. Middleware is also compliant with some essential concepts of *clean code*:

- Each middleware focuses on a single purpose: taking a request and enhancing it. It is advisable to implement new middleware for each goal, to be compliant with the *single responsibility principle*.
- Middleware also uses the concept of *chaining*. It takes an incoming request and passes it through the next piece of middleware. Therefore, every piece of middleware enhances the request and it decides whether to interrupt or continue the middleware pipeline.

As previously mentioned, middleware can *short-circuit* the pipeline, which means that it can block our requests and skip the rest of the pipeline. This *short-circuit* concept should not be underestimated as it is an excellent way to *increase the performance* of our service. Furthermore, the request will not hit our controllers if there is something wrong or if the user is not authorized to proceed. Moreover, the middleware pipeline is usually associated with a schema that looks like this:

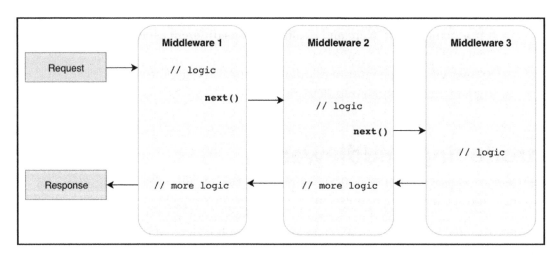

A single piece of middleware can act, and perform logic, on the *request* but also the *response*. Besides, it is essential to understand that the order of middleware counts—indeed, we declare the order when we bind it to our pipeline.

The middleware pipeline in practice

We have looked at some theory behind the middleware pipeline and how it can be useful in terms of short-circuiting and the single responsibility principle. Now let's contextualize that in ASP.NET Core. In the previous chapter, we looked at the default Web API template provided by .NET Core. Let's proceed by replacing the content of the Startup class with the following snippet of code:

```
public class Startup
{
    public Startup(IConfiguration configuration)
    {
        Configuration = configuration;
    }

    public IConfiguration Configuration { get; }

    public void ConfigureServices(IServiceCollection services)
    {
    }
    public void Configure(IApplicationBuilder app, IWebHostEnvironment env)
    {
        app.Run(async context =>
            {
                await context.Response.WriteAsync("Hello, World!");
            });
    }
}
```

We can run this project by executing the following CLI command in the SampleAPI folder:

```
dotnet run
```

The aforementioned command starts our application using the http://localhost:5000 address. We can invoke it using our browser:

As you can see, running **Hello, World!** using a middleware strategy is simple. It requires implementing the `Configure` method, which is the method whereby middleware is usually defined. `app.Run` executes a delegate method, which is the representation of our middleware. In our case, it takes the `HttpContext` of the request and writes content inside the response of the context.

It is essential to understand how the ASP.NET Core framework implements the `Run` method. Let's have a closer look at the implementation of the `Run` method by checking the code in the `Microsoft.AspNetCore.Builder` namespace:

```
using System;
using Microsoft.AspNetCore.Http;

namespace Microsoft.AspNetCore.Builder
{
    /// <summary>
    /// Extension methods for adding terminal middleware.
    /// </summary>
    public static class RunExtensions
    {
        /// <summary>
        /// Adds a terminal middleware delegate to the application's
            request pipeline.
        /// </summary>
        /// <param name="app">The <see cref="IApplicationBuilder"/>
            instance.</param>
        /// <param name="handler">A delegate that handles the
            request.</param>
        public static void Run(this IApplicationBuilder app,
        RequestDelegate handler)
        {
            if (app == null)
            {
                throw new ArgumentNullException(nameof(app));
            }

            if (handler == null)
            {
                throw new ArgumentNullException(nameof(handler));
            }

            app.Use(_ => handler);
        }
    }
}
```

The preceding code gives us more details about what we are doing. We notice that the `RequestDelegate` handler cannot be `null`, and if we go deep into the stack we can see that our delegate will be added *at the end of the pipeline* by using the `app.Use` extension method.

It is essential to understand that the order of middleware counts. The order of the middleware pipeline is implicitly defined in the `Configure` method of the `Startup` class. Furthermore, *MVC middleware* is usually the last one hit by requests; on the other hand, authorization *middleware* is generally placed before other middleware to guarantee the correct security level (putting authorization *middleware* after *MVC middleware* may damage our service and make it unsafe).

HttpContext in ASP.NET Core

In the previous example, we saw how to create middleware using the `app.Run` extension method. A key concept involved in that implementation is the `HttpContext` type, which is the unique entry point for obtaining all information about HTTP properties; it is usually related to the incoming request. The `HttpContext` attribute exposes methods and properties to get information from the request and update information in the response. The response and request information are represented by the following attributes: `HttpContext.Response` and `HttpContext.Request`. For example, in the previous case, we used the `WriteAsync` method, which wrote the `Hello World!` string in response to the current `HttpContext`.

Dependency injection is a core part of ASP.NET Core. `HttpContext` has all references to services instantiated in the current request. To be specific, it provides a `RequestServices` property, which refers to the service container. We will explore dependency injection in more detail in the next chapter. Declaring a piece of *inline* middleware using the `app.Run` method is not the only way to define new middleware. Furthermore, in the following subsection, we will see how to build middleware logic using a *class-based* approach.

Class-based middleware

Middleware can also be implemented by using a *class-based* approach. This kind of approach increases the r*eusability, testability,* and *maintainability* of middleware. A *class-based* approach involves the definition of a new type, for example. Let's have a look at class-based middleware:

```
using System.Threading.Tasks;
using Microsoft.AspNetCore.Http;

namespace Demo.WebAPI
{
    public class SampleMiddleware
    {
        private readonly RequestDelegate _next;

        public RequestCultureMiddleware(RequestDelegate next)
        {
            _next = next;
        }

        public async Task InvokeAsync(HttpContext context)
        {
            //DO STUFF
            // Call the next delegate/middleware in the pipeline
            await _next(context);
        }
    }
}
```

Let's examine some key points in this class:

- `RequestDelegate` represents the reference to the next element in the pipeline. This could be a delegate or other class-based middleware.
- `InvokeAsync` is the core part of our middleware. This contains the implementation of the middleware and calls the _next element in our pipeline. At this point, our implementation must choose between continuing the pipeline or only returning a result to the client. For example, in the case of a *not authorized* message, the middleware will interrupt the pipeline.

After defining our middleware class, we need to add it to our pipeline. An excellent way to do this is to establish a new extension method as follows:

```
public static class SampleMiddlewareExtensions
{
    public static IApplicationBuilder UseSampleMiddleware(
        this IApplicationBuilder builder)
    {
        return builder.UseMiddleware<SampleMiddleware>();
    }
}
```

After this, we can add our middleware to the pipeline in our `Startup` class by executing the extension method previously defined:

```
public class Startup
{
    // ...
    public void Configure(IApplicationBuilder app,
    IHostingEnvironment env)
    {
        app.UseSampleMiddleware();
        app.Run(async context =>
        {
            await context.Response.WriteAsync("Hello, World!");
        });
    }
}
```

The preceding implementation provides a way to encapsulate the logic of the middleware in the `SampleMiddleware` class. This approach is preferred for various reasons. First of all, the middleware class and the logic can be verified and tested using unit tests. Secondly, in an enterprise environment, it can be useful to create dedicated library projects containing common middleware used by the web services and to distribute them through the company's NuGet repository. Finally, the class-based approach provides a clear way to highlight middleware dependencies using constructor injection. We will look at this topic in more depth in `Chapter 4`, *Dependency Injection*. Now that we have seen how to declare and add middleware to the ASP.NET Core pipeline, it is necessary to cover the conditional initialization of middleware in slightly more depth.

Conditional pipeline

ASP.NET Core provides some useful operators that let us put conditional initialization logic inside the middleware pipeline. Those kinds of operators may assist in providing additional performance benefits to our services and applications. Let's have a look at some of these operators.

The IApplicationBuilder Map (this IApplicationBuilder app, PathString pathMatch, Action<IApplicationBuilder> configuration) extension method helps us to initialize our middleware by mapping a URI path; for example:

```
public static class SampleMiddlewareExtensions
{
    public static IApplicationBuilder UseSampleMiddleware(
        this IApplicationBuilder builder)
    {
        return builder.Map("/test/path", _ =>
        _.UseMiddleware<SampleMiddleware>());
    }
}
```

In this case, SampleMiddleware will only be added to our pipeline if it is called as a URI with the specified path. Notice that the Map operator can also be nested inside others: this approach provides a more advanced approach to conditional initialization.

Another useful operator is MapWhen, which only initializes the middleware provided as a parameter if the *predicate* function returns true; for example:

```
public static class SampleMiddlewareExtensions
{
    public static IApplicationBuilder UseSampleMiddleware(
        this IApplicationBuilder builder)
    {
        return  builder.MapWhen(context => context.Request.IsHttps,
        _ => _.UseMiddleware<SampleMiddleware>());
    }
}
```

In this case, if the request is HTTPS, we will initialize the SampleMiddleware class. Conditional middleware initialization can be really useful when we need to act on a specific type of request. It usually becomes necessary when we need to force the execution of some logic on HTTP request types, such as when a specific header is present in the request, or a specific protocol is used.

In conclusion, *class-based* middleware is really useful when we need to implement custom logic in the middleware pipeline, and conditional initialization provides a cleaner way to initialize our set of middleware. In ASP.NET Core, middleware is a first-class citizen of the base logic of the framework; therefore, the next section covers some use cases and some middleware that comes out of the box with ASP.NET Core.

Understanding built-in middleware

So, what are the use cases for middleware? As discussed earlier, they are usually related to cross-cutting concerns such as *logging, authentication,* and *exception handling.* ASP.NET Core itself provides some *built-in middleware* that represents a standard way to solve problems:

- `UseStaticFiles()`: Provides a way to deal with static files and assets inside your application. When the client asks for a static resource, this middleware filters the request and returns the requested file without hitting the rest of the pipeline.
- `AddResponseCaching()`: Helps developers to configure the caching system of the application. This middleware also adds all HTTP-compliant information related to the cache.
- `UseHttpsRedirection()`: This new, built-in piece of ASP.NET Core 2.1 middleware provides a way to force HTTPS redirection.
- `UseDeveloperExceptionPage()`: This shows a detailed error page (the new YSOD) in the case of exceptions. This is usually conditionally initialized, depending on the environment.

These are some built-in pieces of middleware provided by ASP.NET Core. As you can see, all middleware provides cross-cutting functionalities for your application. What's important here is that the order of middleware initialization reflects the order of our pipeline; for example:

```
public void Configure(IApplicationBuilder app, IHostingEnvironment
env)
    {
        // ...
        app.UseHttpsRedirection();
        app.UseStaticFiles();
    }
```

In this case, the `UseStaticFiles` middleware will never receive requests for static files because the MVC middleware handles them first. A general rule is to place `UseHttpsRedirection()` as the last middleware in the pipeline; otherwise, other middleware will not intercept requests.

Summary

Middleware is a useful tool for developers dealing with cross-cutting concerns. This is because it intercepts and enhances every *incoming request* and *outgoing response, and it can increase performance with early-return requests.* Concepts from logging to authentication should be handled by using middleware. The topics covered in the chapter provided you with the necessary knowledge to understand the middleware-first approach taken by the ASP.NET Core framework. Furthermore, the chapter also gave an overview of the built-in middleware of ASP.NET Core, and it described how to create custom middleware.

In the next chapter, we will explore another core topic for increasing the maintainability and testability of our code: *dependency injection.* ASP.NET Core provides out-of-the-box dependency injection, and we will also explore how to solve dependencies and how to deal with different life cycle types.

Dependency Injection System

Dependency injection is the basic building block of ASP.NET Core. This chapter shows how you can use dependency injection in order to resolve the dependencies of the classes inside an ASP.NET Core application. It also describes how you can deal with the dependency injection life cycle, and it provides some examples of how to keep the classes loosely coupled. The first part of this chapter will give you some basic theoretical ideas about dependency injection, while the second part will show you how to use it in any ASP.NET Core project.

This chapter will cover the following topics:

- What is dependency injection?
- Why implement the dependency injection pattern in real-world applications?
- Overview of the dependency injection life cycle
- How to implement dependency injections in ASP.NET Core

Dependency inversion principle

The *dependency inversion principle* is part of the SOLID principles that were established by Robert C. Martin. The purpose of the SOLID principles is to provide some guidelines to developers on how to design code in a way that is more understandable, flexible, and maintainable. The dependency inversion principle, in particular, affirms that a high-level component should not depend directly on an individual component that is concentrated on a precise procedure (low-level component); instead, they should depend on an abstraction. Therefore, abstractions should not depend on any implementation details.

A low-level component usually performs simple operations and provides simple functionalities. A high-level component, on the other hand, manages a set of individual components by orchestrating them. Real-world systems typically have more than two levels of abstractions. The concept of a high-level component is relative to the subject module; therefore, a high-level component for one component might be a low-level component for another. The concept of *abstraction* is particularly prevalent when we talk about SOLID principles. An abstract component is usually an interface or an abstract class. Therefore, it is an element that does not have any concrete implementation. In summary, the *dependency inversion principle* states that every element inside our application should only refer to *abstractions*. Let's look at a concrete example of the *dependency inversion principle* that has been applied to a system. The schema describes an add-to shopping bag e-commerce process.

It is composed of three different classes:

- The `AddToShoppingBagHandler` handles the requests from the client and sends information to `PaymentService`.
- The `PaymentService` manages information about payment methods.
- The `CurrencyConverter` component provides conversions between different currencies.

The following diagram describes the standard sequence of processing the preceding mentioned classes:

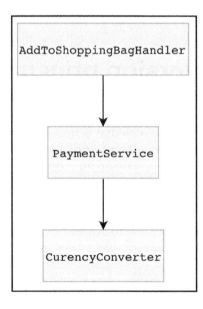

If we apply the dependency inversion principle, the direction of our dependencies will change. To be compliant with the dependency inversion principle, we should introduce some abstractions between our components, as follows:

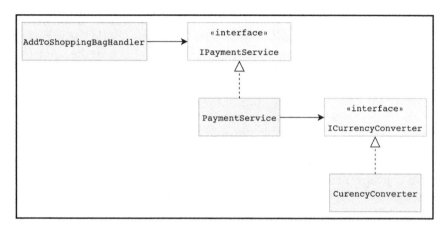

By comparing the two schemas, we deduce that the direction of the dependencies are inverted. The AddToShoppingBagHandler class now uses the IPaymentService interface, and the PaymentService type is the concrete implementation of the IPaymentService interface.

However, this schema is not yet complete. Moreover, it is not yet compliant with the second statement of the dependency inversion principle. We should make sure that our abstractions don't depend on the implementations.

Consequently, if we think in terms of architectural boundaries, our schema changes as follows:

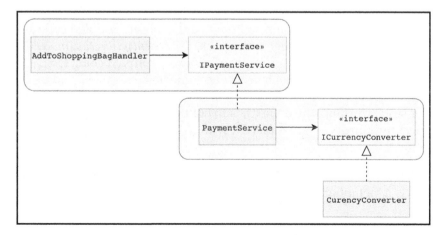

Each rounded rectangle represents a boundary. The classes and the abstractions within the same rectangle are part of the same boundary. In the .NET ecosystem, each border is a project, and our interfaces are the bridge between high-level and low-level classes.

A common inaccuracy is to place the interfaces and the implementation classes within the same boundary. In .NET, this would mean putting the `IPaymentService` interface and `PaymentService` in the same project. This approach is not necessarily wrong, but it does not respect the *dependency inversion principle*.

In conclusion, the dependency inversion principle is used to build very flexible systems, and it helps us to design a more readable, flexible, and maintainable code.

The dependency inversion principle is often confused with the idea of dependency injection because the two concepts are strongly related. If dependency inversion defines a principle to improve our systems, dependency injection is a concrete implementation of that principle.

The dependency inversion principle becomes very useful when we want to test our code, especially for the unit testing technique. Unit tests usually cover a particular function in our application, so it is necessary to isolate our classes and methods. Dependency inversion comes in handy because we can mock our abstraction and isolate our subject under testing.

Benefits of dependency injection

Dependency injection is described as follows:

> *"A set of software design patterns that enable us to develop a loosely coupled code."*

The objective of dependency injection is to implement a loosely coupled code and, as a consequence, write maintainable code. In the book, *Dependency Injection in .NET*, Mark Seemann describes a bright, real-life example of a loosely coupled code. He compares tightly coupled code with cheap hotel hairdryers: some hostels, hotels, and locker rooms bind their hairdryers directly on the wall without a plug to stop guests from stealing them. If the hairdryer stops working, the owner has to cut the power and call a technician, who has to disconnect the hairdryer and replace it with a new one. This approach is a very tedious procedure.

On the other hand, if the hairdryer is plugged into the wall, the owner has to replace it with a new one. This is a metaphor for *dependency injection.*

The first case is a *tightly coupled code*: our high-level component (the wall) uses a low-level part (the hairdryer) directly. In the second case, we have a third actor, which is the plug: the high-level element (the wall) directly uses the plug (the abstraction). The hairdryer, which is our low-level component, also uses the plug.

The second case is *more flexible and maintainable* because we can plug anything into the plug, and if the hairdryer breaks, we can replace it easily.

This is what *dependency injection* is all about. It comes with a lot of benefits for our code:

- **Late binding**: Third-party services can be plugged in and swapped with other services. This may be useful when you change one third-party dependency for another.
- **Parallel development**: Different teams can develop code at the same time by defining interaction contracts (interfaces) between components.
- **Maintainability**: The code is easy to maintain and manage.
- **Testability**: As mentioned earlier, dependency injection helps us to deal with the isolation of the dependencies of unit tests.

The more our codebase grows, the more these benefits are useful. For small codebases, dependency injection can be seen as a useless overhead, but it becomes crucial when we deal with distributed and large codebases. In the next section, we will see how to apply the concept of dependency injection to the

Dependency injection in ASP.NET Core

The dependency injection concept is a fundamental part of ASP.NET Core. A dependency injection system comes out of box with the ASP.NET Core framework, and it is the preferred way to instantiate components in our application.

ASP.NET Core usually describes types that are managed by the dependency injection container as *services*. Therefore, all the services are stored in the built-in container that is represented by the ISserviceProvider interface.

In the next part of the chapter, we will see some examples of dependency injection. As a first step, let's create a new class in the SampleAPI project inside the Controllers folder, called ValuesController.cs:

```
using System.Collections.Generic;
using Microsoft.AspNetCore.Mvc;

namespace SampleAPI.Controllers
```

```
    {
        [ApiController]
        [Route("[controller]")]
        public class ValuesController : ControllerBase
        {
            public string Get()
            {
                return string.Empty;
            }
        }
    }
```

The preceding snippet of code declares a `ValuesController` class, with a simple `Get` method. It is possible to call the route by executing the following CLI command:

dotnet run

This is also possible by calling the following endpoint:
`https://localhost:5001/values`. As a second step, we need to create a new `PaymentService.cs` file with the following code:

```
    namespace SampleAPI
    {
        public interface IPaymentService
        {
            string GetMessage();
        }

        public class PaymentService : IPaymentService
        {
            public string GetMessage() => "Pay me!";
        }

        public class ExternalPaymentService : IPaymentService
        {
            public string GetMessage() => "Pay me!, I'm an external service!";
        }
    }
```

The `PaymentService.cs` file defines the `IPaymentService` interface, which describes a `GetMessage` signature. In addition, the `IPaymentService` interface is implemented by the `PaymentService` class that returns a string. In the same way, we are defining an `ExternalPaymentService` class, which implements the `IPaymentService` interface with different behavior. The next section describes how to register the `IPaymentService` interface in order to use the `PaymentService` class.

Registering services using the dependency injection container

We can register the `IPaymentService` interface in `ConfigureServices` in the `Startup` class by adding the following code:

```
public class Startup
{
    // ...

    public void ConfigureServices(IServiceCollection services)
    {
        services
            .AddTransient<IPaymentService, PaymentService>()
            .AddControllers();
    }

    // ...
}
```

The preceding code shows a simple instantiation of a service using the ASP.NET Core container. I've omitted some parts of the `Startup` class in order to make the code more readable. The runtime executes the `services.AddTransient<IPaymentService, PaymentService>()` method in order to map the `IPaymentService` interface with the concrete implementation that was described in the `PaymentService` class. The `AddTransient` method also defines the scope of our service. We will go into detail about scopes later in this chapter.

We should also note that the dependency injection container requires the concrete class (`PaymentService`) in order to implement the abstraction (`IPaymentService`) and add the instance to the container.

Registering services conditionally

In a real-world application, it is common practice to conditionally register some services depending on their environment variables. This practice is useful when we want to initialize third-party dependencies differently, such as a data source. The following code shows how to register services conditionally, based on the environment:

```
using Microsoft.AspNetCore.Hosting;
using Microsoft.Extensions.Configuration;
using Microsoft.Extensions.DependencyInjection;
using Microsoft.Extensions.Hosting;
```

```
namespace SampleAPI
{
    public class Startup
    {

        public Startup(IConfiguration configuration,
        IWebHostEnvironment env)
        {
            Configuration = configuration;
            Environment = env;
        }

        public IConfiguration Configuration { get; }

        public IWebHostEnvironment Environment { get; }

        public void ConfigureServices(IServiceCollection services)
        {
            if (Environment.IsDevelopment())
            {
                services.AddTransient<IPaymentService, PaymentService>();
            }
            else
            {
                services.AddTransient<IPaymentService,
                ExternalPaymentService>();
            }
        }

        // ...
    }
}
```

The example uses the IWebHostEnvironment interface to detect the IsDevelopment() environment. In this case, it initializes PaymentService. Otherwise, it initializes the ExternalPaymentService implementation. This practice is widespread in testing environments, especially when initializing testing services or a data source. It is common in broad business applications to register services conditionally for testing and development purposes. In Chapter 10, *Implementing the RESTful HTTP Layer*, we will see some concrete examples that have been applied to integration testing. It is essential to keep testing environments isolated in order to avoid false-positive results. Furthermore, registering services conditionally also helps us to improve the flexibility of our code. In the next subsections, we will see how to use constructor injection and action injection in order to resolve the dependencies of the controller classes.

Constructor injection

We have just seen how we can initialize services in our `Startup` class, but how can we consume these services? By default, the built-in dependency injection container of ASP.NET Core uses the constructor injection pattern to retrieve services. We can modify `ValueController` to use `IPaymentServices` by adding the interface as a parameter of the controller constructor:

```
using Microsoft.AspNetCore.Mvc;

namespace SampleAPI.Controllers
{
    [ApiController]
    [Route("[controller]")]
    public class ValuesController : ControllerBase
    {
        private IPaymentService paymentService { get; set; }

        public ValuesController(IPaymentService paymentService)
        {
            this.paymentService = paymentService;
        }
        public string Get()
        {
            return paymentService.GetMessage();
        }
    }
}
```

As you can see, we can inject the `IPaymentService` interface into the constructor of our class. It should be noted that to be compliant with constructor injection, the constructor has to abide by the following rules:

- **The constructor should be public**: If our constructor is not public, the reflection process cannot access the constructor.
- **There should be only one applicable constructor**: For example, if we declare multiple constructors in our `ValuesController` class, such as `public ValuesController(IPaymentService paymentService)` or `public ValuesController(IPaymentService paymentService, string[] paymentTypes = new string[] { 1, 2, 3 })`, the runtime would throw `InvalidOperationException`. There should be only one constructor that is suitable for dependency injection.

- You can only pass arguments that *are not provided* by dependency injection if they have a *default value*. For example, the following constructor is suitable for constructor injection: `public ValuesController(IPaymentService paymentService, string[] paymentTypes = new string[] { 1, 2, 3 })`.

The resolution of the dependencies happens during the runtime execution; therefore, we need to adhere to these rules in order to avoid pitfalls when we alter the dependencies of a controller class.

In conclusion, dependency injection provides a smart way to resolve the dependencies of classes. You should also try to be compliant with the **Single Responsibility Principle (SRP)**. The SRP states that a class should have responsibility for a single part of the functionality. Classes with a lot of injected dependencies are probably not compliant with the SRP. Avoiding these kinds of bad design practices improves the maintainability of our code, and avoids our classes being tightly coupled with static functionalities, which prevent them from being testable. Let's proceed with the next section that covers the action method injection technique.

Action method injection

A valid alternative to constructor injection is the action method injection. Sometimes, controllers use some dependencies in only one action method. In those cases, it may be useful to inject our dependency just in this action method, in order to improve the performance of our code. To perform an action method injection, we should use the `[FromServices]` attribute. For example, look at the following snippet of code:

```
using Microsoft.AspNetCore.Mvc;

namespace SampleAPI.Controllers
{
    [ApiController]
    [Route("[controller]")]
    public class ValuesController : ControllerBase
    {
        [HttpGet]
        public ActionResult<string> Get(
            [FromServices]IPaymentService paymentService)
        {
            return paymentService.GetMessage();
        }
    }
}
```

The example, as aforementioned, uses the action method injection. We are injecting our service into the `Get` action method which is the only consumer of the dependency. Although constructor injection is widely adopted, the action method injection technique becomes useful when you don't use the dependency on the whole controller. This only guarantees a lazy resolution of the dependencies when the action method is invoked. We should also note that this approach is strictly dependent on the MVC stack, because the resolution of the service is performed in the model-binding phase of the execution; therefore, it is only supported in the action method and in the filter classes. The next section will be focused on the services life cycle types that are provided by ASP.NET Core.

Services life cycle

A key point to master when we deal with dependency injection is the services life cycle. The services life cycle is an essential concept about performance, because a wrong service life cycle may cause complicated performance degradation.

The object lifetime in .NET is simple: the object is *instantiated*, *used*, and finally *disposed of* by the garbage collector. The *dispose* phase is the most relevant in terms of performance. In a dependency injection process, the consumer of a specific dependency does not control its lifetime. Indeed, dependencies are usually initialized by the dependency injection container, and they continue to exist until all their consumers hold them.

 A typical performance issue that engineers face in large applications is the *memory leak*. The garbage collector fails to clean objects because they are still referred to as consumers. Consequently, the memory of the server increases until it reaches saturation. It is not easy to find and solve these kinds of performance issues. In a .NET ecosystem, tools such as dotMemory can help you to analyze the instances of the objects that are created by your application, and eventually detect performance issues of this type.

Speaking of dependency injection, the default life cycle types in ASP.NET Core are *transient*, *scoped*, and *singleton*. Let's discuss them more in detail.

Transient life cycle

The services define the transient life cycle using the `.AddTransient()` method. Every time the consumer requires the initialization of a transient service, the dependency injection container returns a new instance. The transient life cycle is the safest life cycle, because it returns a new instance each time, and instances are not shared between consumers. It is also, however, the least efficient, because it can create a huge number of instances, especially in the web environment.

Scoped life cycle

The services define the scoped life cycle `.AddScoped()` method. Scoped instances are created once per request. The scoped life cycle is preferable compared to the transient life cycle regarding performance, but it is less efficient than the singleton life cycle. A scoped approach is usually applied to repository classes and services, and each request to the server will cause the creation of a new instance.

Singleton life cycle

In the singleton life cycle, each time a consumer asks for a new instance, the same instance is provided. This is the most efficient life cycle because there is only a single instance, so the amount of consumed memory is minimal. However, it is recommended that you only use the singleton life cycle for thread-safe components.

Life cycle madness

The term *life cycle madness* is a quote from Jeffrey Richter's *CLR via C#*, and its chapter about threading. Understanding the life cycle of dependencies is important in order to avoid performance issues in our application. Above all, we should avoid the following cases:

- **Consuming scoped dependencies in a singleton consumer**: As previously mentioned, a scoped life cycle means that a new instance is created for each request. When we try to consume a scoped instance in a singleton life cycle, the runtime will throw an exception as follows: `InvalidOperationException: Cannot consume scoped service 'Services.MyScopedService' from singleton 'Services.MySingletonService'`. This is because the runtime cannot create a scoped service for each request when it is referred to by a singleton instance.

- **Consuming transient dependencies in a singleton consumer**: Similarly, if we use a transient dependency inside a singleton instance, the runtime will not create a new instance of the transient service each time. Furthermore, the transient service will be initialized only once because it is declared in a singleton. Also, the runtime *will not throw an exception*, because a new instance of the transient service is not requested, as the singleton always uses the same one.

In order to prevent possible bugs and runtime errors, it is important to avoid the situation in which a singleton refers to a scoped or transient service. In the first case, the runtime will throw an exception, while in the second case, the singleton consumer will always use the same instance. These behaviors must be avoided in order to prevent any memory issues and performance degradation inside our APIs. The following subsection explains how to use dependency injection in the middleware classes.

Injecting services into middleware

As discussed earlier, middleware can instantiate dependencies through a dependency injection container. We should take the life cycle of the middleware into consideration: they are initialized once per application lifetime. As a consequence, if we try to consume a *scoped* or *transient instance* into our middleware we shouldn't inject them through the constructor of the middleware, because this will cause some dependency resolution issues. A good way to avoid this is to use the parameter injection in the Invoke or InvokeAsync methods:

```
namespace Middleware
{
    public class MyMiddleware
    {
        readonly RequestDelegate _next;

        public MyMiddleware(RequestDelegate next)
        {
            _next = next;
        }

        public async Task InvokeAsync(HttpContext context,
                                IPaymentService paymentService)
        {
            Console.WriteLine(paymentService.GetMessage());

            await _next(context);
        }
    }
}
```

The other middleware implementation injects `IPaymentService` in the `InvokeAsync` method. Unlike the middleware constructor, the `InvokeAsync` method is called for each request. Consequently, it is suitable for both a *scoped life cycle* and a *transient life cycle*.

When you want to inject a transient service or a scoped service into middleware, you should inject them in the `Invoke` or `InvokeAsync` methods in order to avoid life cycle problems. Furthermore, middleware is a cross-cutting component, which means that the application runs them at every request. Therefore, you must pay extra attention when you implement middleware, in order to avoid spreading performance issues across all of the applications.

Summary

This chapter has shown us how to deal with the ASP.NET Core default dependency injection engine. The chapter provides various examples that are related to dependency injection, how to use dependency injection in controllers and middleware, and describes the life cycle concepts of the registered services. The next chapter will discuss the controllers and the action methods in detail. It will show you how to use these in order to serialize data and expose it as a web service.

Web Service Stack in ASP.NET Core

5

This chapter describes how to deal with controllers and actions in a web service stack. Controllers are a fundamental part of ASP.NET Core; they are the entry point of the HTTP requests. In this chapter, we will look closely at the mechanics of the controller classes and how they can transfer information to the client using the HTTP protocol.

This chapter covers the following topics:

- What is a controller?
- Handling requests using controllers and actions
- How to deal with DTO objects
- Implementing validation

By the end of the chapter, the reader will have a general overview of the web stack provided by ASP.NET Core and will know how to deal with incoming HTTP requests using controllers and actions.

What is a controller?

Controllers are the C part of the MVC pattern. They are a set of actions that usually handle requests from a client. You should bear in mind that what we are discussing in this chapter refers to the MVC stack that's defined by ASP.NET Core. Furthermore, if we take as reference the incoming requests, remember that they have already passed through the others middleware in the middleware pipeline and that they have already hit the *MVC middleware*.

The following diagram shows how a request is typically handled:

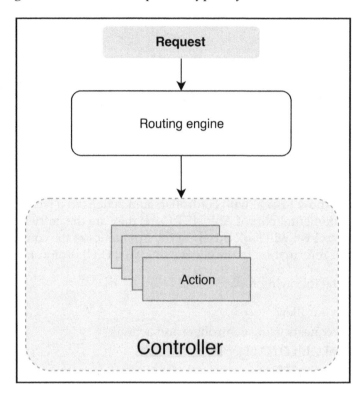

As we discussed in Chapter 1, *REST 101 and Getting Started with ASP.NET Core*, the incoming request is usually generated by a client: the browser, another API, or an external system. The request is composed of an *HTTP verb,* a *URI, body payload*, and other additional information. The **Routing engine** handles the request and passes it to an *action method* inside one of our *controllers*. The **Action** methods usually proceed by providing a response. Furthermore, controllers usually interact with third-party systems through other classes, such as databases or other services. Finally, they serve the result in a specific format. In the case of MVC applications, they usually return a view, while in the case of the web API, they return the result in a format such as **JSON/XML**:

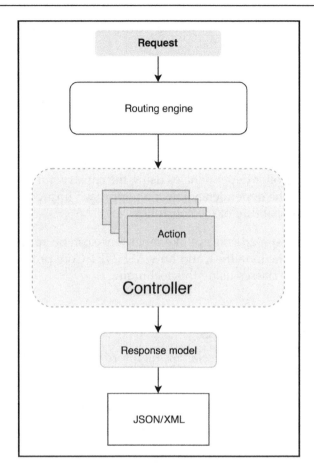

The preceding diagram shows the flow of an incoming request through the model-controller stack. As you can see, the flow is omitting the views part of the MVC stack since it is not useful for the purpose of building web services. The next part focuses on controllers and explains how to identify a controller.

Identifying controllers

Controllers and actions are usually decorated with attributes and filters in a sort of meta-programming style, which allows developers to understand the purpose of the implemented code. ASP.NET Core follows a set of criteria to find the controllers in our project, usually by using a filesystem convention. Controllers are generally stored in the Controllers folder.

In order to be identified by the routing system, a controller class needs to be compliant with one of the following rules:

- The class is suffixed with `Controller`, or it inherits from a class that has the `Controller` suffix
- The class is decorated with the `[Controller]` or the `[ApiController]` attribute, which identifies it as a controller class

 As we mentioned in Chapter 4, *Dependency Injection*, it is recommended to define controller dependencies using the constructor or action injection explicitly. The dependency injection approach improves the testability and maintainability of the controller.

Now, let's see how a widespread concept like inheritance can be applied to the controllers in order to extend their functionalities, and how ASP.NET Core provides some of the bases attributes to the controller classes using this technique.

Extending controllers

As already mentioned, controllers are classes, therefore they can extend other types, including other controllers. This technique can be applied so that we can reuse a particular implementation or feature. In general, the controllers extend the `Controller` or `ControllerBase` classes, which are part of the ASP.NET Core framework. These base classes provide some utilities to manage requests and responses on behalf of the controller. First of all, let's analyze the difference between the `Controller` and `ControllerBase` classes:

- `ControllerBase` represents a base class for an MVC controller without view support. It provides some essential attributes to child classes, such as the `HttpContext`, `Request`, and `Response` attributes.
- The `Controller` class extends the `ControllerBase` class, but it also adds some properties and methods for managing views, such as the `ViewData` attribute and the `View()` and `PartialView()` methods.

When we deal with RESTful APIs and with web services in general, the `ControllerBase` class provides sufficient utilities. If we are dealing with views, however, we should extend the `Controller` class.

The ApiController attribute

From version 2.1, ASP.NET Core introduced a new attribute, that is, the `ApiController` attribute:

```
using Microsoft.AspNetCore.Mvc;

namespace SampleAPI.API.Controllers
{
    [Route("api/[controller]")]
    [ApiController]
    public class ValuesController : ControllerBase
    {
      // ...
    }
{
```

The `ApiController` attribute is commonly coupled with the `ControllerBase` class to enable REST-specific behavior for controllers, and it allows us to build HTTP APIs. First of all, it provides *implicit model state validation*, which means that we do not need to explicitly check the `ModelState.IsValid` attribute in each action. Secondly, it also implicitly defines the model binding attributes, which means that we do not need to specify the `[FromBody]`, `[FromForm]`, `[FromHeader]`, `[FromQuery]`, or `[FromRoute]` attributes for each parameter. ASP.NET Core will define these for us using the following criteria:

- `[FromBody]` is used for complex type parameters, such as custom classes or built-in objects.
- `[FromForm]` is inferred for action parameters of the `IFormFile` or `IFormFileCollection` type.
- `[FromRoute]` is inferred for any action parameter whose name matches a setting in the route template.
- `[FromQuery]` is inferred for any other action parameters.

Let's examine the following generic action method:

```
[Route("api/[controller]")]
public class ValuesController : ControllerBase
{
    // ...

    [HttpPost]
    public IActionResult Post([FromBody]ValueRequest request)
    {
        if (ModelState.IsValid)
        {
```

```
            return BadRequest(ModelState);
        }

        return Ok();
    }

    // ..
}
```

After the application of the `ApiController` attribute, the action method can be minimized, as shown here:

```
[Route("api/[controller]")]
[ApiController]
public class ValuesController : ControllerBase
{
    // ...

    [HttpPost]
    public IActionResult Post(ValueRequest request)
    {
        return Ok();
    }

    // ..
}
```

The `[FromBody]` attribute is implicitly specified because of the `ValueRequest` complex type. In the same way, the `ModelState.IsValid` check is also implicit: if the client passes a model that is not valid for the action, it will return `400 bad requests`. In the next section, we will look into the implementation of a simple controller that can handle and perform some logic using a repository class.

Handling requests using controllers and actions

The purpose of action methods is to handle and respond to incoming requests. The example described in this section will show you how to deal with HTTP requests using controllers. We will apply some of the concepts we have looked at in previous chapters, such as dependency injection. The following example will use the same project structure we created in *Setting up an ASP.NET Core project* section of `Chapter 2`, *Overview of ASP.NET Core*.

The source code for this section is available on GitHub at `https://github.com/PacktPublishing/Hands-On-RESTful-Web-Services-with-ASP.NET-Core-3`.

The next subsection introduces a plain in-memory repository that will be used to store some data and retrieve it through our controller stack. The purpose of this type of repository is to set up a quick storage system without introducing any additional application complexity.

Creating an in-memory repository

The simplest way to create an *in-memory* repository is to define a singleton class with a private attribute, which represents a collection of elements. The repository will be initialized as a *singleton type*; therefore, this specific life cycle guarantees that data will be persistent until the application is restarted.

At this stage, we don't need to use a repository with a real data source because we only need to focus on the HTTP part of our example and not how the data is stored. Later on in this book, we will take a look closer at the data access part.

First of all, we need a model that represents the data we want to store using our repository. Let's create a new folder, called `Models`, and create a new class named `Order.cs`:

```
using System;
using System.Collections.Generic;

namespace SampleAPI.Models
  {
   public class Order
      {
          public Guid Id { get; set; }
          public IEnumerable<string> ItemsIds { get; set; }
      }
  }
```

Now, we need to define a new interface called `IOrderRepository`. The interface represents our order repository, and it will be located in a new folder called `Repositories`:

```
using System;
using System.Collections.Generic;
using SampleAPI.Models;

namespace SampleAPI.Repositories
{
    public interface IOrderRepository
    {
        IEnumerable<Order> Get();
        Order Get(Guid orderId);
        void Add(Order order);
        void Update(Guid orderId, Order order);
        Order Delete(Guid orderId);
    }
}
```

Our interface is implemented by the `MemoryOrderRepository` class, which provides the concrete logic of our interface:

```
using System;
using System.Collections.Generic;
using System.Linq;
using SampleAPI.Models;

namespace SampleAPI.Repositories
{
    public class MemoryOrderRepository : IOrderRepository
    {
        private IList<Order> _orders { get; set; }
        public MemoryOrderRepository()
        {
            _orders = new List<Order>();
        }
        public IEnumerable<Order> Get() => _orders;

        public Order Get(Guid orderId)
        {
            return _orders.FirstOrDefault(o => o.Id == orderId);
        }
        public void Add(Order order)
        {
            _orders.Add(order);
        }
```

```
public void Update(Guid orderId, Order order)
{
    var result = _orders.FirstOrDefault(o => o.Id == orderId);

    if (result != null) result.ItemsIds = order.ItemsIds;
}
public Order Delete(Guid orderId)
{
    var target = _orders.FirstOrDefault(o => o.Id == orderId);
    _orders.Remove(target);

    return target;
}
    }
}
```

The `MemoryOrderRepository` class initializes a private list of the `Order` type. Furthermore, it also defines some operations that we can use to manipulate the list of orders, that are, the `Get`, `Add`, `Update`, and `Delete` methods. These methods use the LINQ syntax to act on the list elements. Furthermore, the main collection that's represented by the `_orders` attribute is declared as private in order to prevent any external access.

 Note that each namespace path reflects the structure of the filesystem. For example, the `SampleAPI.Repositories` namespace reflects the `Sample.API/Repositories` filesystem path.

Finally, we can proceed by initializing the `MemoryOrderRepository` implementation as *a singleton*. To do that, we need to modify the `Startup` class and add our service to the *services collection* using the `AddSingleton` method:

```
using Microsoft.AspNetCore.Builder;
using Microsoft.AspNetCore.Hosting;
using Microsoft.Extensions.Configuration;
using Microsoft.Extensions.DependencyInjection;
using Microsoft.Extensions.Hosting;
using SampleAPI.Repositories;

namespace SampleAPI
{
    public class Startup
    {

        public IConfiguration Configuration { get; }
        // ..
```

```
public void ConfigureServices(IServiceCollection services)
{
    services
        .AddSingleton<IOrderRepository, MemoryOrderRepository>()
        .AddControllers();
}
// ...
    }
}
```

 The following example uses the `IOrderRepository` interface for demonstration and learning purposes. I strongly suggest that you avoid using singleton instances to store data in memory since singleton instances are not persistent storage, and this also causes performance degradation in our application.

In summary, we now have an `Order` class that describes a single order. The `IOrderRepository` interface allows us to store and read the data, and it has an in-memory implementation provided by the `MemoryOrderRepository` type, which uses the memory as a data store. Now, we have all the necessary components so that we can deal with the data and we can proceed by handling the client request through our controller.

Handling client requests

Every time we implement a class, we should always bear the *single responsibility principle* in mind. Therefore, the action methods inside our controllers should be simple handlers that call methods that act as data. The controllers in an ASP.NET Core service usually behave as follows:

- They make calls other classes in order to obtain or update data held in, for example, a repository class.
- They handle exceptions. The action methods typically wrap the calls of other objects to catch exceptions. These are then presented to the client.
- They enhance the returned data using the required HTTP conventions.

Let's proceed and build our controller class by creating a new `OrderController` type inside the `Controllers` folder. This bit of code includes the `ApiController` attribute and the extension to the `ControllerBase` class:

```
. . .
[Route("api/order")]
[ApiController]
public class OrderController : ControllerBase {}
. . .
```

ASP.NET Core provides two ways to deal with routing:

- Decorating controllers with attributes
- Extending the default routing system (for example, using the `MapRoute` method)

Defining routes using attributes covers a lot of cases and is suitable for a range of business requirements. It is also more straightforward in regard to the maintainability and readability of our code. The `[Route("api/order")]` attribute maps a specific controller to one particular route. In this case, the `OrderController` will respond at the `//hostname/api/order` URI. In addition, the ASP.NET Core framework also provides two placeholders: `[controller]` and `[action]`. They can be used to refer to the current controller or to the immediate action. For example, the previous snippet can also be written as follows:

```
. . .
[Route("api/[controller]")]
[ApiController]
public class OrderController : ControllerBase
. . .
```

I strongly suggest avoiding the use of the `[controller]` and `[action]` placeholders. If you refactor the name of your controllers or actions, you also change the routing of your service without throwing any errors. Therefore, it can cause problems in systems with interdependent services.

Let's proceed by initializing and resolving the dependencies of the `OrderController` class. Furthermore, we will see how we can inject and initialize the `IOrderRepository` interface into the controller.

Handling HTTP methods using actions

Now that we have the `OrderController` definition and the `IOrderRepository` interface has been registered through the dependency injection engine, we can proceed by defining the explicit dependencies using *constructor injection*:

```
using System;
using Microsoft.AspNetCore.Mvc;
using SampleAPI.Models;

namespace SampleAPI.Controllers
  {
      [Route("api/order")]
      [ApiController]
      public class OrderController : ControllerBase
      {
          private readonly IOrderRepository _orderRepository;

          public OrderController(IOrderRepository orderRepository)
          {
              _orderRepository = orderRepository;
          }

          ...

      }
  }
```

The `OrderController` class depends on the `IOrderRepository` class, and it uses constructor injection to resolve the dependency. This dependency is clearly visible if we check the constructor signature of the controller. In most cases, you can get an idea of the level of complexity of a class by counting the number of dependencies that have been injected into the *constructor*. Therefore, as a general rule, when you see a class with a lot of dependencies injected into it, it is probably not compliant with the *single responsibility principle*.

The controller classes usually group a set of action methods. As we discussed in Chapter 1, *REST 101 and Getting Started with ASP.NET Core*, HTTP verbs are essential in web APIs and REST services. They are used to indicate a specific operation on our data. For example, an HTTP GET corresponds to a read operation, while an HTTP POST corresponds to a creation action. Let's continue with the implementation of the HTTP GET actions:

```
[Route("api/order")]
[ApiController]
public class OrderController : ControllerBase
    {
  private readonly IOrderRepository _orderRepository;
```

```
public OrderController(IOrderRepository orderRepository)
{
    _orderRepository = orderRepository;
}

[HttpGet]
public IActionResult Get()
{
  return  Ok(_orderRepository.Get());
}

[HttpGet("{id:guid}")]
public IActionResult GetById(Guid id)
{
  return Ok(_orderRepository.Get(id));
}
...
```

The implementation describes two actions, which means there are two different routes:

Http verb	URI	Action
GET	hostname/api/order	[HttpGet] IActionResult Get()
GET	hostname/api/order/<guid>	[HttpGet("{id:guid}")] IActionResult GetById(Guid id)

As we mentioned previously, ASP.NET Core handles incoming requests and maps them to actions using the routing middleware. Routes are defined both in the startup code and in the attributes. Each HTTP verb has its corresponding attribute: HttpGet corresponds to the GET method, HttpPost corresponds to the POST method, and so on.

In general, HTTP verb attributes have a signature that looks as follows:

```
[HttpVerbAttribute(string template, [Name = string], [Order = string]]
```

The *template* is a string parameter that represents the URL of a specific action. It may also accept some *routing constraints*. For example, [HttpGet("{id:guid}")] will receive a GUID identifier in the form of a string:

```
https://localhost:5001/api/order/7719c8d3-79f4-4fbd-b99a-2ff54c5783d2
```

We will look at routing constraints in more detail in Chapter 6, *Routing System*.

 It is essential to bear in mind that routing constraints are not meant to be a validation system. If we have an invalid route, our service will return 404 Not Found and not 400 Bad Request.

The `Name` parameter of the attribute indicates the route name that identifies that action method. In general, it doesn't have any impact on the routing system. Besides, it is used to refer to the routing rule during the generation of the URL, and it must be unique in the entire code base. By following the preceding specifications, it is easy to implement the other CRUD operations in our controller. The result looks as follows:

```
using System;
using System.Collections.Generic;
using Microsoft.AspNetCore.Mvc;
using SampleAPI.Models;
using SampleAPI.Repositories;

namespace SampleAPI.Controllers
{
    [Route("api/order")]
    [ApiController]
    public class OrderController : ControllerBase
    {
        private readonly IOrderRepository _orderRepository;

        public OrderController(IOrderRepository ordersRepository)
        {
            _orderRepository = ordersRepository;
        }

        [HttpGet]
        public IActionResult Get()
        {
            return Ok(_orderRepository.Get());
        }

        [HttpGet("{id:guid}")]
        public IActionResult GetById(Guid id)
        {
            return Ok(_orderRepository.Get(id));
        }

        [HttpPost]
        public IActionResult Post(Order request)
        {
            var order = new Order()
            {
                Id = Guid.NewGuid(),
                ItemsIds = request.ItemsIds
            };

            _orderRepository.Add(order);
```

```
            return Ok();
        }

        [HttpPut("{id:guid}")]
        public IActionResult Put(Guid id, Order request)
        {
            var order = new Order
            {
                Id = id,
                ItemsIds = request.ItemsIds
            };

            _orderRepository.Update(id, order);
            return Ok();
        }

        [HttpDelete("{id:guid}")]
        public IActionResult Delete(Guid id)
        {
            _orderRepository.Delete(id);
            return Ok();
        }
    }
}
```

Now that we've had a quick look at the implementation controller, let's have a closer look at the actions that are defined by it:

HTTP verb	URI	Action
GET	hostname/api/order	[HttpGet] IActionResult Get()
GET	hostname/api/order/<guid>	[HttpGet("{id:guid}")] IActionResult GetById(Guid id)
POST	hostname/api/order	[HttpPost] IActionResult Post(Order request)
PUT	hostname/api/order/<guid>	[HttpPut("{id:guid}")] IActionResult Put(Guid id, Order request)
DELETE	hostname/api/order/<guid>	[HttpDelete("{id:guid}")] IActionResult Delete(Guid id)

We should also notice that the controller does not implement any validation on the input data. Furthermore, the [ApiController] attribute, when applied on top of a class, provides the *out-of-the-box validation* and model binding of ASP.NET Core. Therefore, all the associated objects, such as the Order request parameter, must be passed from the body of the request in case they are required.

To run the ASP.NET Core api, we should run our application by executing `dotnet run` inside the project folder and perform an HTTP request using `curl` or whatever client, as follows:

```
curl -X GET  https://localhost:5001/api/order  -H 'Content-Type:
application/json' -k
```

The preceding command executes a GET request on the `/api/order` URL, using the `Content-Type: application/json`. Since ASP.NET Core provides HTTPS out-of-box we can ignore the certificate validation using the `-k` flag. Later in the book, we will see how to install the certificate locally.

The output will look as follows:

```
[]
```

For Windows users, starting from Windows 10, build 17063 (https://devblogs.microsoft.com/commandline/tar-and-curl-come-to-windows/), the OS ships with a copy of `curl` already set up and ready to use. However, it is possible to download and install `curl` from https://curl.haxx.se/. Another option is to install `curl` using the Chocolatey package manager by executing `choco install curl` on your command line.

Futhermore, if we try to perform a `curl` command with an empty payload as follow:

```
curl -X POST   https://localhost:5001/api/order -H 'Content-Type:
application/json' -d '' -k
```

The output will look as follows:

```
{
  "type": "https://tools.ietf.org/html/rfc7231#section-6.5.1",
  "title": "One or more validation errors occurred.",
  "status": 400,
  "traceId": "|7c58576e-47baf080f74cf2ab.",
  "errors": {
    "": [
      "A non-empty request body is required."
    ]
  }
}
```

In this case, we have passed an empty body payload using the $-d$ empty flag. Therefore, the out-of-the-box model validation returns the error message in the request's response, and it returns an HTTP 400 Bad request message.

 In real-world applications, this kind of validation is not enough. It is usually replaced by some custom validations, such as *data annotation* or *fluent validation*. We will look at these techniques in more detail later in this chapter.

Responding to requests

Now that we have a controller that is able to handle our requests, we should focus on the response part. Looking at the OrderController from the response point of view, we may notice that it is not compliant with REST specifications. None of the action methods considers any failure states. What should happen if our data source is down? What should happen if the requested order is not present in our repository?

Let's start by checking what happens when we ask for an order that doesn't exist. To proceed with this check, all we need to do is make a curl request with a GUID that doesn't exist:

```
curl -X GET
https://localhost:5001/api/order/a54f58bc-216d-4a40-8040-bafaec68f2de -H
'Content-Type: application/json' -i -k
```

The preceding command-line instruction will produce the following output:

```
HTTP/1.1 204 No Content
Date: Fri, 17 Aug 2018 14:37:58 GMT
Server: Kestrel
Content-Length: 0
```

As we can see from the response, ASP.NET Core automatically handles the empty result, and it returns the HTTP status 204 No Content. It is important to note that all these behaviors came out of the box. Besides, it is also possible to override the default components and add our own custom validation implementation and response handling.

CreateAt response

The Post action method is responsible for creating resources. Another principal responsibility of the Post action method is to tell the client where the resource is created and how to access it. This responsibility is usually implemented within the action method. ASP.NET Core provides two methods that can give this information to the client, which are CreatedAtAction and CreatedAtRoute. The following example shows how to use the CreatedAtAction method in our Post action:

```
...
        [HttpPost]
        public IActionResult Post(Order request)
        {
            var order = new Order()
            {
                Id = Guid.NewGuid(),
                ItemsIds = request.ItemsIds
            };

            _orderRepository.Add(order);
            return CreatedAtAction(nameof(GetById), new { id = order.Id },
null);
        }
...
```

After that, the response to the below POST request will appear as follows:

```
curl -X POST https://localhost:5001/api/order/ -H 'Content-Type:
application/json' -d '{"itemsIds": ["1","4"]}' -i -k


HTTP/1.1 201 Created
Date: Mon, 20 Aug 2018 11:19:49 GMT
Server: Kestrel
Content-Length: 0
Location:
https://localhost:5001/api/orders/372459c7-6e16-4276-b286-f341d7009c43
```

As you can see, the response contains the 201 Created header. It also provides the Location of the resource. This kind of information is useful for the client so that we can get more information about the resource.

The `CreateAtAction` method accepts three parameters:

- `actionName` represents the name of the action that's used for generating the URL.
- `routeValues` is an object that contains all the parameters of the action.
- `value` is an object that represents the content of the response.

An alternative to `CreateAtAction` is `CreateAtRoute`, which takes the `routeName` and generates the same result as `CreateAtAction`.

Updating resources

The `Put` action handles how resources are updated. We should bear in mind that the `PUT` verb is intended as a total replacement of the specific resource. Therefore, when we call an API using a `PUT` verb, all the resource fields will be replaced with the *body payload*. As we will see later in this chapter, for a more precise update for some of the specific fields of our entity, it is better to use the `PATCH` verb.

Another critical thing to keep in mind when we implement a `Put` action is that we need to handle Ids that don't exist. APIs usually manage non-existent IDs in `Put` actions using two different approaches:

- When the client makes an update request on a non-existent ID, the API creates a new record with that resource.
- When the client makes an update request on a non-existent ID, the API informs the client that the resource doesn't exist with a `404 Not Found` error.

 I'm not a massive supporter of `CreateOrUpdate` methods. I prefer to keep the `Put` action compliant with the *single responsibility principle*. Therefore, separate the *create* and *update* operations into two different action methods.

Let's see how we can implement our `Put` action:

```
. . .
            [HttpPut("{id:guid}")]
            public IActionResult Put(Guid id, Order request)
            {
                var order = _orderRepository.Get(id);
                if (order == null)
                    return NotFound(new { Message = $"Item with id {id} not
    exist." });
```

```
order.ItemsIds = request.ItemsIds;

_orderRepository.Update(id, order);
return Ok();
}
...
```

The first step is to check whether the order with the corresponding id exists. If it doesn't exist, the application returns a 404 Not Found error. Otherwise, it performs the update operation and returns 200 Ok.

 Note that the NotFound result also contains a message. In real-world applications, this message is usually associated with a piece of code, that is, a custom error, and it is serialized into JSON or XML format.

It is also significant to consider what should happen when the request contains null in itemsIds. It is essential to understand the difference between a null request object and an empty request object. In the first case, the client may accidentally call our APIs without passing any value. In the second case, the client explicitly requests our resource to be replaced with an empty value. Let's modify our code to avoid null request values by adding the following guard as the first statement of our Put method:

```
...
[HttpPut("{id:guid}")]
public IActionResult Put(Guid id, Order request)
    {
        if (request.ItemsIds == null)
            return BadRequest();
...
```

The preceding if statement returns a BadRequest message if the ItemsIds field is null. Therefore, the client that sent the request will now the source of the issue. In the next section, we will discover another widespread update technique implemented in RESTful web services.

Partial updating

Put actions are used to replace a resource with another one. Therefore, the client must add the whole entity in the *body payload* of the request. If our entity is a complex object, keeping the entire entity in memory may cause performance issues. It is possible to avoid these problems by implementing a Patch action instead. The Patch action usually modifies an existing resource without replacing it, therefore you are able to specify only one the field you want to update. Let's see how we can perform this kind of action in ASP.NET Core.

First of all, let's add a new field to our Order.cs class:

```
using System;
using System.Collections.Generic;

namespace SampleAPI.Models
 {
  public class Order
     {
         public Guid Id { get; set; }
         public IEnumerable<string> ItemsIds { get; set; }
         public string Currency { get; set; }
     }
 }
```

Now, the Order class contains an additional field that represents the currency of our orders. Let's create a Patch action in our OrderController. The code we are going to implement uses two NuGet packages that provide the support for the PATCH method and all the types that help us to perform the operations related to that type of HTTP verb. We can add the package to our project by running the following instructions in the SampleAPI project folder:

```
dotnet add package Microsoft.AspNetCore.JsonPatch
dotnet add package Microsoft.AspNetCore.Mvc.NewtonsoftJson
```

The first NuGet package provides the JsonPatchDocument class type, the second package enables the NewtonsoftJson serializer needed by the PATCH operation support. In addition, we should also enable the NewtonsoftJson serializer into the application by adding the following extension method in the Startup class:

```
public class Startup
{
    ...

    public void ConfigureServices(IServiceCollection services)
    {
        services
```

```
                            .AddSingleton<IOrderRepository, MemoryOrderRepository>()
                            .AddControllers()
                            .AddNewtonsoftJson();
            }
```

Furthermore, it is possible to implement the `Patch` action method in the following way:

```
[HttpPatch("{id:guid}")]
public IActionResult Patch(Guid id, JsonPatchDocument<Order> requestOp)
{
    var order = _orderRepository.Get(id);
    if (order == null)
    {
        return NotFound(new { Message = $"Item with id {id} not exist." });
    }

    requestOp.ApplyTo(order);
    _orderRepository.Update(id, order);

    return Ok();
}
```

The aforementioned code has three key points:

- The action method reacts to the `HttpPatch` verb requests. Just like the `Put` action, it accepts a `Guid` as the input parameter, which identifies the target resource.
- The action method also accepts a `JsonPatchDocument` as the payload of the body. The `JsonPatchDocument` class is a generic class that is part of the ASP.NET Core Framework. More specifically, our action uses the `JsonPatchDocument<Order>` type to implement operations on our `Order` class.
- The action method applies the `JsonPatchDocument` class using the `ApplyTo` method, which merges the changes in the request to our target resource. Finally, it updates the repository.

The `JsonPatchDocument` class accepts a specific request schema. For example, the following `curl` operation performs a partial update through the `PATCH` verb:

```
curl -X PATCH \
  https://localhost:5001/api/order/5749c944-239c-4c0c-8549-2232cf585473 \
  -H 'Content-Type: application/json' \
  -d '[
  {
    "op": "replace", "path": "/itemsIds", "value" : [1,2]
  }
]' -k
```

In this case, the body payload is a JSON array of objects: every object is composed of an `op` field, a `path`, and a `value`.

The `op` field describes the operation to perform on our target, `path` refers to the name of our field, and `value` is the replacement for our target. In this case, the request will replace the `itemsIds` field with the value `[1,2]`. Furthermore, the `op` field accepts a bunch of operations on data, including `add` and `remove`. As we saw previously, the syntax is almost the same as it was in the previous example:

```
[{
    "op": "add", "path": "/itemsIds", "value" : [3]
},
{
    "op": "remove", "path": "/itemsIds"
}]
```

`JsonPatchDocument` is compliant with the specification of the **Internet Engineering Task Force (IETF)**, an organization that promotes internet standards. You can find out more information about the `Patch` document syntax in the declaration of the standard at the following link: `https://tools.ietf.org/html/rfc5789`. All the other specifications about the HTTP method that we've discussed in this chapter can also be found here. You should pay attention when using the `JsonPatchDocument` object. The client may request to update a read-only field or a non-existent field. Furthermore, the `JsonPatchDocument` type requires a **validation step**. This problem is usually solved by creating a custom **data transfer object (DTO)** model for this kind of request.

Let's move on to the next subsection, which describes the deleting process for the resources and how to implement the resulting action method in the controller class.

Deleting resources

The Delete action method is marked with the HttpDelete attribute. It usually accepts the identifier of the resource to remove.

 In real-world applications, Delete action methods do not perform physical delete operation on the database. They actually carry out update operations. Real-world applications and web services typically perform soft deletes instead of physical deletes because it is essential to keep track of historical data and information that's stored by our services. If we think about an e-commerce application, for example, it would be crucial to keep track of orders that have been dispatched by our system. *Soft deletes* are usually implemented using an isDeleted flag or an object that represents the status of our resource. All the other routes that are implemented in our APIs should implement logic to filter out all the resources in a deleted state. For example, a Get route should exclude all the deleted resources before presenting them to the client.

In our case, we are going to implement a real delete operation on our IOrderRepository. The Delete action methods usually return a 204 No Content error to confirm the deletion or a 404 Not Found error if the client passes a non-existent identifier:

```
[HttpDelete("{id:guid}")]
public IActionResult Delete(Guid id)
{
    var order = _orderRepository.Get(id);

    if (order == null)
    {
        return NotFound(new { Message = $"Item with id {id} not exist." });
    }

    _orderRepository.Delete(id);
    return NoContent();
}
```

The implementation fetches the resource with the corresponding id from the IOrderRepository interface. It proceeds by checking whether the resource is null, and in this case, it will produce a not found error. If the order entity is present in the data source, it continues with the deletion process, and it returns a no content result. Now, let's proceed by having a look at the asynchronous process using a web service.

Asynchronous processing and acceptance status

Sometimes, the operations on our resources are not applied immediately. Consider an order on an e-commerce website: it takes time to be dispatched and sent to our storage system. Therefore, data placed into a queue or something similar and handled as soon as possible.

These kinds of asynchronous processing structures may also be present in a web service. We also need to represent them and communicate with the client when these kinds of processes start.

In general, these kinds of processes have the following workflow:

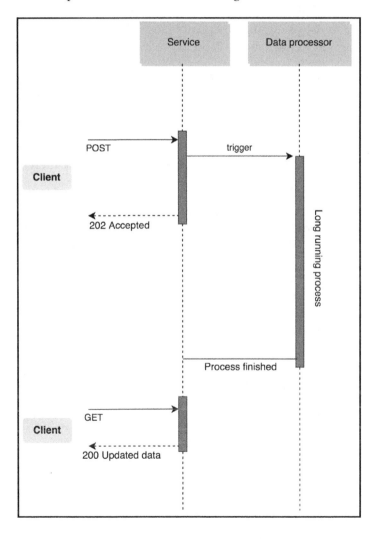

The previous schema shows how the client interacts with an asynchronous process:

1. The client sends a POST request to our services. The POST request triggers an asynchronous operation, which updates and adds the order to our storage.

2. The action method receives the request from the client and, if the request structure is as expected, triggers the asynchronous process and returns 202 Accepted to the client. Otherwise, it returns 403 Bad Request. The 202 Accept code indicates that the asynchronous operation is running, but that it hasn't finished yet.

3. The client doesn't know precisely when the asynchronous process will end, but it is up to it to recall our service once the information has been updated. The 202 Accepted message it is usually combined with a JSON message that contains some information, such as the estimated time, or the code of the process.

 Note that all the example URIs present in this book doesn't contain *verbs*. For example, the previous implementation describes a process for generating new order. As you can see, the URI is <hostname>/api/orderrequest, and the only element that contains a verb is the HTTP method, which is POST. We shouldn't use *verbs* in URIs because they are used to identify resources and must, therefore, be nouns.

The next step in our web service stack journey is to see how we can decouple the requests and the response object from the core entities that are used by our application. This approach becomes really useful when a web service's complexity increases.

Data transfer objects

In the previous section, we looked at how to manage HTTP requests and responses using controllers. In this section, we will look at how to manage complex objects in our requests and responses. This section is more focused on the *M* part of the MVC pattern. First of all, let's distinguish between three different types of model that are usually present in web services:

- The **Domain model** describes the entities and the resources in our web services. It often reflects the schema of our data source, and it is very close to the lower level and the business logic of the application.

- The **Request model** is the representation of the model of the request. Each action method in our controller usually has its own **Request model**. As we will see later in this chapter, this is also the model that's associated with the validation of the request.
- The **Response model** is the view model, or the presentation model, of the web service. It represents the response of the request, and there is usually one **Response model** per action method.

The following workflow schema shows how the models in our application are laid out:

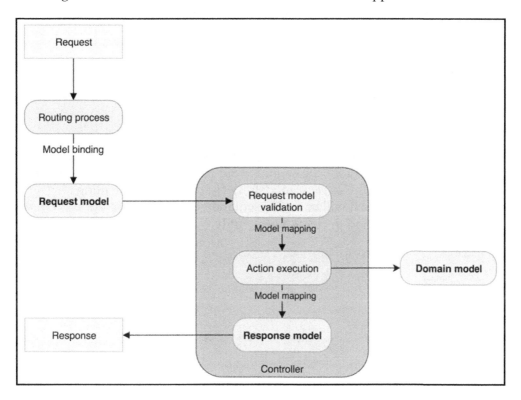

As you can see, the **Request model** is the front part of our service; it represents the request. The **Domain model** is used to describe our stored data. Finally, the *response model* presents the data to the client. The request and response model are also defined as **data transfer objects (DTOs)**. These are not model classes at all; they transport information between the client and the server.

Implementing request models

Now, let's look at the implementation of some DTOs in practice. The `Order` entity describes some actions that accept `List<string>` as input. Let's suppose that the implementation is getting more complex and our service needs to store additional information about our orders:

```
using System;
using System.Collections.Generic;

namespace SampleAPI.Models
 {
  public class Order
     {
         public Guid Id { get; set; }
         public IEnumerable<string> ItemsIds { get; set; }
         public string Currency { get; set; }
     }
 }
```

The *domain model* is a critical part of our application. It is essential to keep it separated from the *request/response model*. Therefore, we should avoid having the *domain model* tightly coupled with the *request* and the *response* models. Let's start by implementing the `OrderRequest` class, which will be a representation of the *create request model*. It will be used by the `Post` action method to create a new entity:

```
using System.Collections.Generic;

namespace SampleAPI.Requests
{
    public class OrderRequest
    {
        public IEnumerable<string> ItemsIds { get; set; }

        public string Currency { get; set; }
    }
}
```

The `OrderRequest` class contains the same fields as the `Order` *domain model*, apart from the `Id` field. This is because the client of the API should not insert the `Id` information. The request model makes our filesystem in a separate folder. In this case, as you can see from the namespace, `OrderRequest` is stored in the `Requests` folder. Our `OrderController` can use `OrderRequest` as follows:

```
[Route("api/order")]
[ApiController]
public class OrderController : ControllerBase
{
    ...

    [HttpPost]
    public IActionResult Post(OrderRequest request)
    {
        var order = Map(request);
        _orderRepository.Add(order);

        return CreatedAtAction(nameof(GetById), new { id = order.Id },
        null);
    }

    ...

    private Order Map(OrderRequest request)
    {

        return new Order
        {
            Id = Guid.NewGuid(),
            ItemsIds = request.ItemsIds,
            Currency = request.Currency
        };
    }
    ...
```

The `Post` action method accepts a parameter of the `OrderRequest` type, which is the representation of the order request that we want to create. To link incoming data with the domain model, we should create a `Map` method that initializes a new domain model that's populated with the request model. Furthermore, we should also create a new instance of the `Order` object with the requested data and combine it with `IOrderRepository`. The same concept can be applied to the `Put` action method of our controller:

```
    ...

    [HttpPut("{id:guid}")]
```

```
        public IActionResult Put(Guid id, OrderRequest request)
        {
            var order = _orderRepository.Get(id);

            if (order == null)
            {
                return NotFound(new { Message = $"Item with id {id} not
exist." });
            }

            order = Map(request, order);

            _orderRepository.Update(id, order);

            return Ok();
        }
        private Order Map(OrderRequest request, Order order)
        {
            order.ItemsIds = request.ItemsIds;
            order.Currency = request.Currency;

            return order;
        }
        ...
```

In this case, we create a new Map method, which takes two parameters as input: the OrderRequest and the Order, and we can proceed by assigning each property of the request object to the order.

Implementing response models

As we mentioned previously, another critical part of our APIs is the response model. The response model classes act as filters between the *domain model* and the *client*. For example, let's think about a particular field in our domain model that, for whatever reason, must not be part of our response. Response models help us deal with cases such as these.

Let's suppose that we need to implement a *soft-delete* in our APIs. As we mentioned earlier, a *soft-delete* is a way to mark a record for the deletion or to temporarily prevent it from being selected. To perform a soft-delete on MemoryOrderRepository, we should add an IsInactive flag, which marks the target record as deleted:

```
public class Order
{
    public Guid Id { get; set; }
```

```
        public IEnumerable<string> ItemsIds { get; set; }

        public string Currency;

        public bool IsInactive { get; set; }
    }
```

The `IsInactive` flag indicates whether `Order` is inactive or not. To complete the *soft-delete* implementation, we should change the `MemoryOrderRepository`. It should now cancel orders using the `IsInactive` flag.

Furthermore, the `Get` method inside the repository should filter all the records by excluding inactive orders:

```
    . . .
    public class MemoryOrderRepository : IOrderRepository
      {

            public IEnumerable<Order> Get() => _orders.Where(o =>
    !o.IsInactive).ToList();
            public Order Get(Guid orderId)
            {
                return _orders
                    .Where(o => !o.IsInactive)
                    .FirstOrDefault(o => o.Id == orderId);
            }
            public Order Delete(Guid orderId)
            {
                var target = _orders.FirstOrDefault(o => o.Id == orderId);

                target.IsInactive = true;
                Update(orderId, target);
                return target;
            }
    . . .
```

These changes eliminate inactive orders from the responses of our APIs. Since the `IsInactive` flag is implicit in the response of our APIs, we don't need to serialize the `IsInactive` flag in the response JSON. Consequently, we can decouple the response of the `Get` action method from our domain model by adding a new response class called `OrderResponse`. It can be defined in the following way:

```
    using System;
    using System.Collections.Generic;

    namespace SampleAPI
```

```
    {
    public class OrderResponse
    {
        public Guid Id { get; set; }
        public IEnumerable<string> ItemsIds { get; set; }
        public string Currency { get; set; }
    }
}
```

As you can see, the OrderResponse class model exposes all the fields except for the IsInactive flag. At this point, we can proceed by editing the OrderController class so that it maps the Order entity with the OrderResponse model in the following way:

```
    . . .

    public class OrderController : ControllerBase
    {

        . . .

        [HttpGet]
        public IActionResult Get()
        {

            return Ok(Map(_orderRepository.Get()));
        }

        [HttpGet("{id:guid}")]
        public IActionResult GetById(Guid id)
        {
            return Ok(Map(_orderRepository.Get(id)));
        }

    . . .

        private IEnumerable<OrderResponse> Map(IEnumerbale<Order> orders)
        {
            return orders.Select(Map).ToList();
        }

        private OrderResponse Map(Order order)
        {
            return new OrderResponse
            {
                Id = order.Id,
                ItemsIds = order.ItemsIds,
                Currency = order.Currency
            };
```

```
        }
    }
```

This approach allows us to decouple the domain model from the response of our API. The `Map` method is the point at which we can decide which fields we should show.

Implementing validation of requests

We can now create dedicated types to represent our requests, but we should also consider adding validation. Validation is important if we wish to prevent messy data and possible exceptions in our web service. ASP.NET Core provides an out of the box way for us to implement validation in our controllers and services: `System.ComponentModel.DataAnnotations`. The namespace provides a set of attributes that can be used to describe the validation of model fields. For example, consider the following code snippet:

```
using System.Collections.Generic;

namespace SampleAPI.Requests
{
    public class OrderRequest
    {
        public IEnumerable<string> ItemsIds { get; set; }
        public string Currency { get; set; }
    }
}
```

In this case, the `[Required]` attribute specifies that both the `ItemsIds` and `Currency` attributes should not be `null` or empty; otherwise, the APIs will return the following validation message:

```
{
    "ItemsIds": [
        "The ItemsIds field is required."
    ]
}
```

Simply reading through the model allows us to understand the constraints that were defined for the model, so this approach improves the readability and maintainability of our code. Furthermore, ASP.NET Core provides several popular built-in validation attributes: `[EmailAddress]`, `[StringLength]`, `[Url]`, `[CreditCard]`, and `[RegularExpression]`.

In the `Currency` field, we may add a constraint as follows:

```
public class OrderRequest
  {
      [Required]
      public IEnumerbale<string> ItemsIds { get; set; }
      [Required]
      [StringLength(3)]
      public string Currency {get; set;}
  }
```

In this case, the `Currency` attribute will contain a currency code, such as EUR or USD. We can add a restriction on the maximum length of the field so that it is limited to three characters.

Custom validation attributes

ASP.NET Core provides a way for us to create custom validations for our requests by extending `ValidationAttribute`, which means we can create custom validators for our types. Let's create a more appropriate validation for our `Currency` attribute:

```
using System.Collections.Generic;
using System.ComponentModel.DataAnnotations;
using System.Linq;

namespace SampleAPI.Requests
{
    public class CurrencyAttribute : ValidationAttribute
    {
        private readonly IList<string> _acceptedCurrencyCodes =
        new List<string>{
            "EUR",
            "USD",
            "GBP"
        };

        protected override ValidationResult IsValid(object value,
        ValidationContext validationContext)
        {
            return _acceptedCurrencyCodes.Any(c => c == value.ToString()) ?
                ValidationResult.Success
                : new ValidationResult($"{validationContext.MemberName} is
                not an accepted currency");
        }
    }
}
```

The preceding implementation matches the request model currency with the list of `_acceptedCurrencyCodes`. If the match is successful, it returns `ValidationResult.Success`; otherwise, it returns a new validation result with a validation message. The `MemberName` attribute provides the name of the property that is associated with the custom validation attribute. Creating a custom validation attribute can be useful when we implement a more complex validation that involves third-party services or aggregate operations on the subject of the validation.

Summary

In this chapter, we have seen how we can build a web service stack using ASP.NET Core. We also looked at how to implement CRUD operations on a repository and how to deal with data transfer objects and validation. This chapter has provided a starting point and the knowledge we need to build a very simple web service using ASP.NET Core, including how to handle requests, how to use model binding, and how to validate requests.

In the next chapter, we will cover the routing system of ASP.NET Core in more detail by exploring how it can be extended and customized.

6
Routing System

This chapter describes the routing functionalities of ASP.NET Core. The routing part of the framework is designed to provide a dynamic routing system that's fully customizable and overridable to cover most of the use cases of a web service. Here, we will discover how to use *conventional* and *attribute routing* approaches, and then we will dig into the use of routing constraints in order to match complex rules and provide higher customization.

In this chapter, we will cover the following topics:

- A brief overview of the routing system
- Conventional routing versus attribute routing
- Binding routing parameters
- Routing constraints
- Custom attribute routing and custom routing constraints

The topics covered in this chapter provide some basic knowledge around the routing system of ASP.NET Core and how to use the routing engine of ASP.NET Core to cover all the use cases that are needed by our web service.

Overview of the routing system

The routing system of ASP.NET Core maps an incoming request to a *route handler*. In ASP.NET Core, the Startup class is responsible for configuring the routes that are needed by the application. Furthermore, the routing functionalities of ASP.NET Core are implemented using a middleware approach. Let's take a closer look at the Startup class and how it initializes the routing system:

```
public class Startup
{
    ...
    public void Configure(IApplicationBuilder app, IWebHostEnvironment env)
    {
```

```
        app.UseRouting();
        ...
        app.UseEndpoints(endpoints =>
        {
            endpoints.MapControllers();
        });
    }
}
```

The preceding code uses two extension methods: UseRouting and UseEndpoints. These methods were introduced in the latest release of ASP.NET Core. In the previous version of the framework, the routing system was initialized with the UseMvc extension method, which is now deprecated. The UseRouting extension method is used to define where, in the middleware pipeline, the routing decisions are made. On the other side, the UseEndpoints extension method declares the mapping of effective routes. For example, in the preceding code snippet, the Startup class uses the MapControllers() extension method to map the controller routes and declares the default routing convention that's implemented by ASP.NET Core.

To summarize, when the Startup class executes the UseRouting and UseEndpoints extension methods, ASP.NET Core adds a new EndpointRoutingMiddleware class to mark the routing point and EndpointMiddleware in the pipeline, which describes our routes. The preceding calls can be summarized as follows:

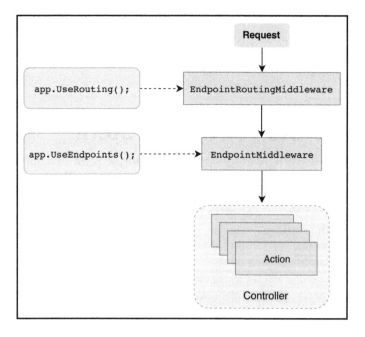

Furthermore, it is possible to define new *route templates* inside our `Startup` class using the following syntax:

```
...
public void Configure(IApplicationBuilder app, IWebHostEnvironment env)
{
    ...
    app.UseEndpoints(endpoints =>
    {
        endpoints.MapControllerRoute("default",
"{controller}/{action}/{id?}");
    });
}
...
```

This implementation creates a new *route template* that maps a generic route such as `https://myhostname/mycontroller/myaction` with a controller named `MyController` and an action named `MyAction`. This way of defining routing is called **conventional routing**, in the sense that it establishes a convention between our handlers (the controllers) and the URI system. We will discuss conventional routing in more detail in the next section.

Conventional routing

The *conventional routing* is the default routing approach in ASP.NET Core. As we have already seen, this approach uses the `app.UseEndpoints` extension method in the `Startup` class to declare routing templates:

```
    app.UseEndpoints(endpoints =>
    {
        endpoints.MapControllerRoute("default",
"{controller}/{action}/{id?}");
    });
```

By default, ASP.NET Core applies the `default` *route template* to the routing engine, which maps each segment of our URL with the `controller` name, the `action` name, and the `id` name, respectively. Furthermore, it is possible to define multiple routes in our application by adding them to the routing builder in the `Startup` class:

```
app.UseEndpoints(endpoints =>
{
    endpoints.MapControllerRoute("default", "{controller}/{action}/{id?}");

    endpoints.MapControllerRoute("order", "order/givemeorders", new {
```

```
controller = "Order", action = "Get" });
});
```

In this case, the `https://myhostname/order/givemeorders` route will be mapped to the `Get` action of `OrderController`. We should notice that the routing template example we defined in the preceding code is not compliant with the REST architectural style. Accordingly, it doesn't respect the 2nd level of the Richardson Maturity Model, as mentioned in Chapter 1, *REST 101 and Getting Started with ASP.NET Core*. Furthermore, if we apply the `default` routing template to `OrderController` we discussed in previous chapters, the `Get` action method will respond to the following URI: `https://localhost/order/get`.

To make our routing template compliant with the Richardson Maturity Model, let's introduce the `Map` method that's provided by ASP.NET Core. It is possible to map different HTTP verbs using *routing templates*, as follows:

```
app.UseEndpoints(endpoints =>
{
    endpoints.MapGet("order", context => context.Response.WriteAsync("Hi,
from GET verb!"));
    endpoints.MapPost("order", context => context.Response.WriteAsync("Hi,
from POST verb!"));
});
```

The `MapGet`, `MapPost`, `MapPut`, and `MapDelete` methods accept the *route template* as the first parameter and a `RequestDelegate` method, which provides a way to handle `HttpContext` of the current request. However, it is not possible to call the `OrderController` logic in `RequestDelegate` because there isn't an effortless way to access the controllers' instances from the context. Therefore, there isn't an easy way to implement a REST-compliant routing system using *conventional routing*. In general, conventional routing is mainly designed for web applications that serve views and HTML. An alternative solution is to use the *attribute routing* technique, which is the most solid way to implement controllers' routing in a web services context.

Attribute routing

The *attribute routing* technique is a different way to implement routing in ASP.NET Core. It moves the declaration of routing within the controllers' implementation using attributes to describe the routes in a metaprogramming way:

```
[Route("api/order")]
[ApiController]
public class OrderController : ControllerBase
{
    private readonly IOrderRepository _orderRepository;

    public OrderController(IOrderRepository orderRepository)
    {
        _orderRepository = orderRepository;
    }
...
```

The Route attribute declares the routing template within the controller or the action. The routing attribute is the default approach of the web API template in ASP.NET Core. Another critical thing to notice is that this practice doesn't need any route definition in the Startup class; therefore, app.MapControllers() is invoked without route parameters.

Furthermore, this kind of approach also provides more flexibility when it comes to binding each action method with a specific route:

```
[Route("api/order")]
[ApiController]
public class OrderController : ControllerBase
{
    [HttpGet]
    public IActionResult Get() {
        ...
    }

    [HttpGet("{id:guid}")]
    public IActionResult GetById(Guid id) {
        ...
    }

    [HttpPost]
    public IActionResult Post(OrderRequest request) {
        ...
    }
```

```
[HttpPut("{id:guid}")]
public IActionResult Put(Guid id, OrderRequest request) {
    ...
}

[HttpPatch("{id:guid}")]
public IActionResult Patch(Guid id, JsonPatchDocument<Order>
requestOp) {
    ...
}

[HttpDelete("{id:guid}")]
public IActionResult Delete(Guid id) {
    ...
}
}
```

The preceding controller uses HttpVerb to map each action method to one particular HTTP verb. Furthermore, it also uses the HttpVerb attribute to define the last segment of the URI, which usually contains the parameters of our target resource.

 The Route("api/order") attribute defines a static route segment. ASP.NET Core provides some reserved placeholders, that is, [controller], [action], and [area], which are replaced at runtime with the corresponding controller, action, or area. For example, we can achieve the same result by using Route("api/[controller]") because the OrderController name will replace the [controller] placeholder. As I mentioned in the previous chapter, I strongly suggest that you avoid this kind of approach because, in a real-world application, you may accidentally change the route of your API by merely refactoring a controller's name.

Moving forward, let's have a look at custom attribute routing.

Custom attribute routing

The routing engine of ASP.NET Core also provides a way for us to create our routing attributes. This technique is useful in complex routing systems where it is essential to keep a conceptual order between different routes. An example of a custom routing definition is as follows:

```
using System;
using Microsoft.AspNetCore.Mvc.Routing;
```

```
namespace SampleAPI.CustomRouting
{
    public class CustomOrdersRoute : Attribute, IRouteTemplateProvider
    {
        public string Template => "api/orders";

        public int? Order { get; set; }

        public string Name => "Orders_route";
    }
}
```

The class extends the `Attribute` abstract class, which is to be applied as an attribute. It implements `IRouteTemplateProvider` to get the attributes of the *routing template workflow*. As a result, the application of the attribute looks as follows:

```
[CustomOrdersRoute]
[ApiController]
public class OrderController : ControllerBase
{
    ...
```

This approach is really useful when we want to implement a more complex routing system. Therefore, it is possible to apply concepts such as inheritance to improve the reusability of the implemented routing rules.

This section provided an understanding of different routing approaches of ASP.NET Core: *conventional routing* and *attribute routing*. In the next section, we will discover how to use the *routing constraints* rules provided by the framework.

Routing constraints

Routing constraints are part of the templating routing system of ASP.NET Core. They provide a way for us to match a route with a parameter type or a set of values, like so:

```
app.UseEndpoints(endpoints =>
{
    endpoints.MapControllerRoute("default",
"{controller}/{action}/{id:guid?}");
});
```

In this case, our route template will match all
the `https://myhostname/mycontroller/myaction` calls and all the calls that present a
valid `Guid` as an `id` parameter, for
example, `https://myhostname/mycontroller/myaction/4e10de48-9590-4531-980`
`5-799167d58a44`. The `{id:guid?}` expression gives us two pieces of information about
constraints: first, the parameter must have the `guid` type, and secondly, it is specified as
optional using the `?` character. ASP.NET Core provides a rich set of built-in *routing
constraints* such as *min* and *max values*, *regular expressions,* and *range*. It is also possible to
combine them using the colon operator (`:`), like so:

```
app.UseEndpoints(endpoints =>
{
    endpoints.MapControllerRoute("default",
"{controller}/{action}/{id:int:min(1)}");
});
```

In this case, we are combining the `int` constraint with the `min(1)` constraint. Therefore, we
can cover a large number of use cases and business rules. In addition, we can improve our
routing matching logic by providing different action methods for the same URI that is
receiving a different type of data. It is also important to note that the same *routing
constraints* can also be applied to the attribute routing part:

```
[Route("api/mycontroller")]
[ApiController]
public class MyControllerController : ControllerBase
{
    [HttpGet({id:int:min(1)})]
    public IActionResult Get() {
        ...
    }
}
```

ASP.NET Core provides a rich set of default routing constraints that can be used out of the
box. The following link lists all the additional default routing constraints of ASP.NET
Core: `https://docs.microsoft.com/en-us/aspnet/core/fundamentals/routing?view=`
`aspnetcore-3.0#route-constraint-reference`.

Custom constraints

If default constraints don't cover all the business rules of your application, ASP.NET Core exposes all the necessary components to extend the behavior of route constraints so that you can define your own rules. It is possible to extend routing constraints by implementing the IRouteConstraint interface provided by Microsoft.AspNetCore.Routing, like so:

```
using System.Collections.Generic;
using Microsoft.AspNetCore.Http;
using Microsoft.AspNetCore.Routing;

namespace SampleAPI.CustomRouting
{
    public class CurrencyConstraint : IRouteConstraint
    {
        private static readonly IList<string> _currencies =
            new List<string> { "EUR", "USD", "GBP" };
        public bool Match(HttpContext httpContext, IRouter route,
            string routeKey, RouteValueDictionary values,
            RouteDirection routeDirection)
        {
            return
_currencies.Contains(values[routeKey]?.ToString().ToLowerInvariant());
        }
    }
}
```

The preceding code shows an example of the implementation of IRouteConstraint. The interface exposes the Match method, which allows us to match the incoming route values with a custom set of values. In this case, the constraint matches a set of currencies. In order to use CurrencyConstraint, it is necessary to configure it in the ConfigureServices method:

```
public void ConfigureServices(IServiceCollection services)
{
    ...
    services.Configure<RouteOptions>(options => {
        options.ConstraintMap.Add("currency", typeof(CurrencyConstraint));
    });
    ...
}
```

It is possible to use the custom `CurrencyConstraint` routing constraint using the regular syntax:

```
endpoints.MapControllerRoute("default",
"{controller}/{action}/{currency}");
```

In this case, the `default` route will match only the parameter that's using the logic that's implemented in the `CurrencyConstraint` class. Therefore, it will match the `https://localhost/controller/action/eur`, `https://localhost/controller/action/usd`, and `https://localhost/controller/action/gbp` URIs.

Summary

The ASP.NET Core routing system can be extended and used to cover a lot of use cases. In general, it provides all the necessary functionalities out of the box. It is essential to understand that *conventional routing* is generally used by web applications, while web services routing is usually achieved by applying the *attribute routing*. This chapter described how to deal with these two approaches, how to use the out-of-box constraints provided by ASP.NET Core and how to implement our custom routing constraints. In the next chapter, we will look at how to deal with the filter pipeline of ASP.NET Core and in which way they differ from the implementation of the middleware classes.

7
Filter Pipeline

In this chapter, we will cover another essential topic in ASP.NET Core: the filter pipeline. Filters are a vital component that we can use to achieve cross-cutting implementation in our services. Although we have already seen how to implement cross-functionalities using the middleware pipeline, filters are more specialized components that are linked to the MVC pipeline. Therefore, filters can be used to implement more specific logic, related to the controller's execution. This chapter will show you how to implement these filters and will describe some concrete use cases.

We will cover the following topics in this chapter:

- An introduction to filters in ASP.NET Core
- How to implement and apply filters to the filter pipeline
- Some concrete use cases for filters
- How to use resolve dependencies in the filter pipeline

This chapter provides information about the filter stack in .NET Core and how to use filters to enhance the features of our web services.

Introduction to filters

Filters come in handy when we wish to build *cross-cutting concepts* in the MVC stack of ASP.NET Core. They are useful when we wish to implement features such as authorization or caching. ASP.NET Core provides some out-of-the-box filter types. Each of these can be used for a specific purpose in our service:

Filter type	Type description
Authorization	This kind of filter is related to the authorization of users. It is the first filter that's executed in the filter pipeline and can short-circuit the pipeline of requests.
Resource	Resource filters run immediately after authorization filters and after the rest of the pipeline has completed. They're useful when we wish to implement caching or for performance implementations.
Action	Action filters are focused on the life cycle of action methods. They intercept and change the arguments and the returning results of action methods.
Exception	Exception filters are used to intercept and apply cross-cutting policies to unhandled exceptions.
Result	Result filters are executed immediately before and after the execution of an action result. They are usually implemented to change the formatting of the outcome. It is essential to note that they are executed only when the action method is completed successfully.

 It is crucial to note that filters act in the domain of the MVC middleware, which implies that action filters are unable to operate outside the MVC context. Therefore, filters are more specific than middleware; they can be applied to a subset of requests, and they have access to some MVC components, for example, `ModelState`.

The following diagram shows the workflow of different types of action filters in a request-response workflow:

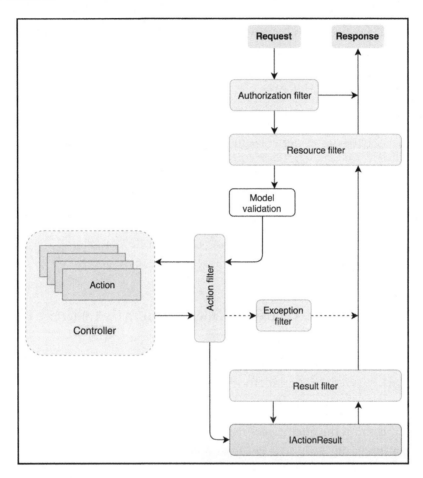

As you can see, in a request-response pipeline, different types of filters act at various stages. *Authorization filters* act before everything else and block the requests in the event any of the privileges are wrong. *Resource filters* operate before model validation and model binding of the request and also when the results of our request come back from the server. The *action filter* type acts before and after an action's invocation. Furthermore, if an action throws an exception, the *exception filter* is triggered. At the end of the pipeline, the *result filter* operates on the IActionResult final object instance. Now that we know about the different filter types that are provided by ASP.NET Core, we will look at some concrete implementation examples.

Concrete filter implementations

In general, filters can be implemented by extending the built-in types provided by ASP.NET Core. Let's walk through a simple declaration of a custom action filter:

```
using Microsoft.AspNetCore.Mvc.Filters;

namespace SampleAPI.Filters
{
        public class CustomActionFilter : IActionFilter
        {
            public void OnActionExecuting(ActionExecutingContext context)
            {
                // do something before the action executes
            }

            public void OnActionExecuted(ActionExecutedContext context)
            {
                // do something after the action executes
            }
        }
}
```

The CustomActionFilter class implements the IActionFilter interface type, which offers two different methods:

- The OnActionExecuting method is triggered before the execution of the action.
- The OnActionExecuted method is executed after the action.

Both methods receive the execution context as a callback parameter, which provides some useful information about the *filter's stack metadata*, the *controllers*, the *action arguments*, and *route data*. Furthermore, the context parameter also provides access to the HttpContext attribute we looked at in previous chapters. The HttpContext provides all the necessary properties so that we can access dependency injection services and the request/response data. ASP.NET Core heavily uses the asynchronous stack. This means it also provides an interface that we can use to implement asynchronous filters.

Asynchronous filters

Filters support both asynchronous and synchronous behaviors. As we saw in the previous example, `CustomActionFilter` implements two synchronous methods: `OnActionExecuting` and `OnActionExecuted`. In the case of an asynchronous filter, the implementation is different:

```
using System.Threading.Tasks;
using Microsoft.AspNetCore.Mvc.Filters;

namespace SampleAPI.Filters
{
    public class CustomActionFilterAsync : IAsyncActionFilter
    {
        public async Task OnActionExecutionAsync(ActionExecutingContext
         context, ActionExecutionDelegate next)
        {
            //Before

            var resultContext = await next();

            //After
        }
    }
}
```

`CustomActionFilterAsync` implements the `async` version of the action filter class, that is, `IAsyncActionFilter`, and implements only one method, that is, `OnActionExecutionAsync`. This template is similar to a middleware implementation; the `next()` method triggers the execution of the rest of the pipeline. Therefore, everything before the `await next()` statement is executed before the execution of the action filter, while everything after the `await next()` statement is performed after the action's execution. It is essential to note that the framework searches for the `async` implementation first and then for the *synchronous* implementation.

The scope of filters

Filters inherit a different scope based on their initialization in our codebase. In practice, a filter may have three different scopes:

- **Global scope**: This means that the filter covers the whole MVC pipeline. Every call to a specific MVC route will pass through that filter.
- **Controller scope**: In this case, the filter is initialized as an attribute in one or multiple controller classes. It will act only on requests that have been directed to the target controllers.
- **Action scope:** The filter is initialized as an attribute in one or multiple action methods. It will act only on requests that have been directed to the target methods.

It is also essential to understand that filters are executed, depending on the scope, in a specific order: first of all, all *global scope filters* run, followed by *controller scope filters*, and finally *action scope filters*. In the next subsection, we will look at the implementation of the different scopes in more detail.

The use of filters

As we mentioned previously, filters can have three different scopes: *global*, *controller*, and *action*. In the first case, the filter is applied globally in the Startup class. In the other two cases, the filter is used in the form of an attribute and is usually applied to the controller class definition or the action method definition. Let's take a closer look at these different approaches. The application of a filter in the Startup class means that the filter covers all the routes in the MVC pipeline, as follows:

```
public class Startup
{
    ...
    public void ConfigureServices(IServiceCollection services)
    {
        services
            .AddControllers(config => config.Filters.Add(new
            CustomFilter()));
    }

    ...
}
```

In this case, `CustomFilter` has a *global scope*. The `config.Filters` attribute is a collection of `IFilterMetadata` interfaces. This interface is used to describe the filters that are present in our MVC pipeline. It should be noted that the collection doesn't check duplicates, which means that we may potentially add two filters of the same type.

Since `FilterCollection` doesn't consider duplicates, it is possible that, in a large codebase, a filter type is accidentally initialized more than once, which may affect the performance of our service. It is vital to pay attention to code merges, especially in a distributed team. By using pull requests and holding code review meetings, this kind of silent issue can be avoided.

On the other hand, the *controller scope* and the *action scope* are restricted to a specific controller or action. The best way to use a filter on a particular controller or action is by extending a filter attribute. ASP.NET Core provides some built-in filter attributes. For each filter type, the framework provides a corresponding class that provides methods for overriding. For example, this is the case for the `ActionFilterAttribute` type:

```
using Microsoft.AspNetCore.Mvc.Filters;

namespace SampleAPI.Filters
{
        public class CustomControllerFilter : ActionFilterAttribute
        {
            public override void OnActionExecuting(ActionExecutingContext
             context)
            {
                // do something before the action executes
            }

            public override void OnActionExecuted(ActionExecutedContext
             context)
            {
                // do something after the action executes
            }
        }
}
```

The `CustomControllerFilter` extends the `ActionFilterAttribute` type, which contains the `OnActionExecuting` and `OnActionExecuted` methods. The filter can be applied to a specific controller class or action method using the syntax of the attributes:

```
. . .
    [Route("api/order")]
    [CustomControllerFilter]
```

```
public class OrderController : ControllerBase
{
...
```

Under the hood, `ActionFilterAttribute` is an abstract class and implements the `IActionFilter` interface type, which we looked at previously. Therefore, by taking a quick look at the `ActionFilterAttribute` class, we can assume that this abstract class also provides the `IAsyncActionFilter`, `IResultFilter`, and `IAsyncResultFilter` methods:

```
[AttributeUsage(AttributeTargets.Class | AttributeTargets.Method,
AllowMultiple = true, Inherited = true)]
public abstract class ActionFilterAttribute :
Attribute, IActionFilter, IFilterMetadata, IAsyncActionFilter,
IResultFilter, IAsyncResultFilter, IOrderedFilter
{
    ...
}
```

The preceding code snippet describes how ASP.NET Core always provides an easy way for us to customize and extend the behavior of our frameworks. Furthermore, the user has full control over the code and the interfaces provided by the framework. Eventually, we can easily create a custom abstract type that implements a custom behavior for the filter and can be extended by other concrete filter classes.

Life cycle and dependency injection

As we already said, Dependency injection is a core technique in ASP.NET Core. Filters usually rely on other components to provide the filter logic. Before discussing injecting dependencies in filters, we need to understand the life cycle process. In general, when we apply a filter as an attribute, the life cycle of the filter is restricted to the request, which means that it is reinitialized for each request. The `ServiceFilter` attribute provides a valid alternative to overriding this kind of behavior. Therefore, the `ServiceFilter` attribute uses the *service provider* to create filter objects, which means that our filter is managed just like any other service declared through the dependency injection system of ASP.NET Core.

For example, let's consider the implementation of the `CustomActionFilter` class we defined previously:

```
using Microsoft.AspNetCore.Mvc.Filters;

namespace SampleAPI.Filters
```

```
{
    public class CustomActionFilter : IActionFilter
    {
        public void OnActionExecuting(ActionExecutingContext context)
        {
            // do something before the action executes
        }

        public void OnActionExecuted(ActionExecutedContext context)
        {
            // do something after the action executes
        }
    }
}
```

It is possible to initialize the `CustomActionFilter` type using the `AddSingleton` extension method in the `Startup` class:

```
...
public void ConfigureServices(IServiceCollection services)
{
    services
        .AddSingleton<IOrderRepository, MemoryOrderRepository>()
        .AddSingleton<CustomActionFilter>()
    ...
}
...
```

We can then use it in our controllers or action methods, as follows:

```
...
[ServiceFilter(typeof(CustomActionFilter))]
public class OrderController : ControllerBase
{
    ...
```

This approach guarantees that we override the life cycle of the filters by explicitly defining the life cycle type in the *service provider*. Therefore, the filter pipeline is integrated and initialized using the dependency injection engine of ASP.NET Core. Moreover, it is also possible to resolve filter dependencies using the dependency injection engine. There are two injection techniques related to filters:

- Using the `ServiceFilter` technique
- Using the `TypeFilterAttribute` technique

As we saw previously, the `ServiceFilter` type adds the instance of filters in the service provider. It is possible to inject the dependency into a filter by adding it to the constructor. We can do this using *constructor injection*:

```
using Microsoft.AspNetCore.Mvc.Filters;
using Microsoft.Extensions.Logging;

namespace SampleAPI.Filters
{
    public class CustomActionFilter: IActionFilter
    {
        private readonly ILogger _logger;
        public CustomActionFilter(ILogger logger)
        {
            _logger = logger;
        }
        public void OnActionExecuting(ActionExecutingContext context)
        {
            _logger.LogInformation("Logging OnActionExecuting");
        }

        public void OnActionExecuted(ActionExecutedContext context)
        {
            _logger.LogInformation("Logging OnActionExecuted");
        }
    }
}
```

The preceding code injects the `ILogger` interface into the constructor and uses the exposed `LogInformation` extension method. It is also possible to not pass through the *service provider* using `TypeFilterAttribute` by referring to our filter using the type and not the instance. We do this by declaring another class that extends `TypeFilterAttribute`, which passes the type of our filter to the base class:

```
public class CustomActionFilterAttribute : TypeFilterAttribute
{
    public CustomActionFilterAttribute() : base(typeof(CustomActionFilter))
    {
    }
}
```

Then it applies the attribute to the target controller:

```
...
[CustomActionFilterAttribute]
public class OrderController : ControllerBase
{
...
```

The `CustomActionFilterAttribute` class extends the `TypeFilterAttribute` base class and calls the base constructor by referring to the `CustomActionFilter` type. This approach enhances the usability of filter attributes that depend on other classes. Now that we have a complete understanding of filters and know how to apply them to the filter pipeline, we can take a look at some concrete use cases.

Filter use cases

This section will show some concrete use cases for filters. In general, each time you have to replicate the behavior in an action or a controller, you can use filters to centralize the logic. Filters also provide a declarative approach, which helps us keep your code clean and readable.

Existing entity constraints

Action methods of controllers usually perform constraints on incoming data. A common practice is to centralize that kind of logic in filters. Let's take, for example, `OrderController`, which we discussed in the previous chapter:

```
using System;
using System.Collections.Generic;
using System.Linq;
using Microsoft.AspNetCore.JsonPatch;
using Microsoft.AspNetCore.Mvc;
using SampleAPI.Filters;
using SampleAPI.Models;
using SampleAPI.Repositories;
using SampleAPI.Requests;

namespace SampleAPI.Controllers
{
    [Route("api/order")]
    [ApiController]
    public class OrderController : ControllerBase
    {
        private readonly IOrderRepository _orderRepository;

        public OrderController(IOrderRepository ordersRepository)
        {
            _orderRepository = ordersRepository;
        }
```

```
...

[HttpPut("{id:guid}")]
[OrderExists]
public IActionResult Put(Guid id, OrderRequest request)
{
    if (request.ItemsIds == null)
    {
        return BadRequest();
    }

    var order = _orderRepository.Get(id);

    if (order == null)
    {
        return NotFound(new { Message = $"Item with id {id}
         not exist." });
    }

    order = Map(request, order);

    _orderRepository.Update(id, order);
    return Ok();
}

[HttpPatch("{id:guid}")]
[OrderExists]
public IActionResult Patch(Guid id, JsonPatchDocument<Order>
 requestOp)
{
    var order = _orderRepository.Get(id);
    if (order == null)
    {
        return NotFound(new { Message = $"Item with id {id} not
         exist." });
    }

    requestOp.ApplyTo(order);
    _orderRepository.Update(id, order);

    return Ok();
}

[HttpDelete("{id:guid}")]
[OrderExists]
public IActionResult Delete(Guid id)
{
    var order = _orderRepository.Get(id);
```

```
            if (order == null)
            {
                return NotFound(new { Message = $"Item with id {id} not
                exist." });
            }

            _orderRepository.Delete(id);
            return NoContent();
        }


        ...

    }
}
```

Three out of five action methods perform the same *existing check* by calling
_orderRepository:

```
var order = _orderRepository.Get(id);

if (order == null)
{
    return NotFound(new { Message = $"Item with id {id} not exist." });
}
```

A recommended practice is to extract this logic and put it somewhere else, possibly an
action filter, so that it can be used across action methods. It is specific enough to be used
only when necessary. Let's start by setting up our filter and adding the dependency with
IOrderRepository:

```
using System.Threading.Tasks;
using Microsoft.AspNetCore.Mvc;
using Microsoft.AspNetCore.Mvc.Filters;
using SampleAPI.Repositories;

namespace SampleAPI.Filters
{
    public class OrderExistsAttribute : TypeFilterAttribute
    {
        public OrderExistsAttribute() : base(typeof
            (OrderExistsFilterImpl)) { }

        private class OrderExistsFilterImpl : IAsyncActionFilter
        {
            private readonly IOrderRepository _orderRepository;

            public OrderExistsFilterImpl(IOrderRepository orderRepository)
            {
                _orderRepository = orderRepository;
```

```
            }

            public async Task OnActionExecutionAsync(ActionExecutingContext
            context, ActionExecutionDelegate next)
            {
                ...
            }
        }
    }
}
```

The `OrderExistsFilterImpl` class provides the basic setup for an action filter. It accepts `IOrderRepository` as a dependency and implements `OnActionExecutionAsync`. This implementation class is contained in an attribute class that implements `TypeFilterAttribute`.

After declaring the attribute class, we can proceed by implementing the logic. `OrderExistsAttribute` has three purposes:

- To check whether the incoming request contains an `id`
- To check whether the requested `id` is a `Guid`
- To query `IOrderRepository` to check whether the entity exists

Let's proceed by describing a possible implementation of the previous logic:

```
using System;
using System.Threading.Tasks;
using Microsoft.AspNetCore.Mvc;
using Microsoft.AspNetCore.Mvc.Filters;
using SampleAPI.Repositories;

namespace SampleAPI.Filters
{
    public class OrderExistsAttribute : TypeFilterAttribute
    {
        public OrderExistsAttribute() : base(typeof(OrderExistsFilterImpl))
        {
        }

        private class OrderExistsFilterImpl : IAsyncActionFilter
        {
            private readonly IOrderRepository _orderRepository;

            public OrderExistsFilterImpl(IOrderRepository orderRepository)
            {
                _orderRepository = orderRepository;
```

```
}

public async Task OnActionExecutionAsync(ActionExecutingContext
context, ActionExecutionDelegate next)
{
    if (!context.ActionArguments.ContainsKey("id"))
    {
        context.Result = new BadRequestResult();
        return;
    }

    if (!(context.ActionArguments["id"] is Guid id))
    {
        context.Result = new BadRequestResult();
        return;
    }

    var result = _orderRepository.Get(id);

    if (result == null)
    {
        context.Result =
         new NotFoundObjectResult(
         new {Message = $"Item with id {id} not exist."});
        return;
    }

    await next();
}
}
}
}
```

First of all, the code checks whether our action arguments, which are populated by the model binder, contain any key by using the `!context.ActionArguments.ContainsKey("id")` statement. If the check is not true, the action filters interrupt the pipeline by adding a `BadRequestResult` to the response and exiting from the method. Secondly, the code checks whether the requested `id` is a `Guid` using `!(context.ActionArguments["id"] is Guid id)`. In this case, if the condition fails, it returns a `BadRequestResult` and interrupts the pipeline. Finally, the action filter calls `IOrderRepository` and checks whether the requested entity exists. If the test is positive, it continues the pipeline by calling the `await next();` method; otherwise, it returns a `BadRequestResult`.

In conclusion, we can add our attribute on top of methods that perform the actual checks and remove the previously replicated code that's inside each action method:

```
[Route("api/order")]
[ApiController]
public class OrderController : ControllerBase
{
    ...

    [HttpGet("{id:guid}")]
    [OrderExists]
    public IActionResult GetById(Guid id) { ... }

    [HttpPut("{id:guid}")]
    [OrderExists]
    public IActionResult Put(Guid id, UpdateOrderRequest request) { ... }

    [HttpPatch("{id:guid}")]
    [OrderExists]
    public IActionResult Patch(Guid id, JsonPatchDocument<Order> requestOp)
    { ... }

    [HttpDelete("{id:guid}")]
    [OrderExists]
    public IActionResult Delete(Guid id) { ... }
    ...
}
```

This kind of approach is compliant with the *DRY principle*. Furthermore, we can reuse the filter and handle the logic in a unique entry point.

 Before ASP.NET Core 2.1, the same approach was used to check whether a model was valid. Instead of replicating the Model.IsValid *check-in* in each action, the logic was centralized in an action filter. With the introduction of the built-in ApiController attribute, the constraint has now become implicit.

Next, let's have a look at altering exceptions.

Altering exceptions

Another common use for filters is changing the response of a specific request. Filters are handy in these cases because they can only be applied to particular action methods. Some services need to return a custom format to the client, for example, when they are used by a legacy system that only accepts a specific format or when they need to provide a response that's been wrapped by a particular envelope. ASP.NET Core provides the IExceptionFilter interface for this, which allows us to overload the exceptions and send a custom response to the client.

Furthermore, if an exception is thrown, it follows two different behaviors, depending on the environment. If the API triggers an exception and it is running in a development environment, it returns a current detailed exception page, which looks as follows:

If we are in a *production environment,* it merely returns a generic 500 Internal Server Error. These two behaviors are defined by default in the out of the box Web API template of ASP.NET Core:

```
public class Startup
{
    ....
    public void Configure(IApplicationBuilder app, IWebHostEnvironment env)
    {
        if (env.IsDevelopment())
```

```
            app.UseDeveloperExceptionPage();
        else
            app.UseHsts();


    ...
    }
```

In a real-world application, it is usually necessary to provide detailed information to the client, thereby guaranteeing reliable communication between the server and the client.

 In real-world applications, errors are an essential part of services. In some cases, companies institute an internal error code definition so that they can build more flexible APIs that can handle errors in a better way and establish resilient communication between themselves.

To implement custom exceptions, we should extend the `IExceptionFilter` interface. The following code is a possible implementation of this:

```csharp
using System.Net;
using Microsoft.AspNetCore.Hosting;
using Microsoft.AspNetCore.Mvc;
using Microsoft.AspNetCore.Mvc.Filters;
using Microsoft.Extensions.Hosting;
using Microsoft.Extensions.Logging;

namespace SampleAPI.Filters
{
    public class CustomExceptionAttribute : TypeFilterAttribute
    {
        public CustomExceptionAttribute() : base(typeof
            (HttpCustomExceptionFilterImpl))
        {
        }

        private class HttpCustomExceptionFilterImpl : IExceptionFilter
        {
            private readonly IWebHostEnvironment _env;
            private readonly ILogger<HttpCustomExceptionFilterImpl>
             _logger;
            public HttpCustomExceptionFilterImpl(IWebHostEnvironment env,
              ILogger<HttpCustomExceptionFilterImpl> logger)
            {
                _env = env;
                _logger = logger;
            }
```

```
            public void OnException(ExceptionContext context)
            {
                _logger.LogError(new EventId(context.Exception.HResult),
                    context.Exception,
                    context.Exception.Message);

                var json = new JsonErrorPayload
                {
                    Messages = new[] {"An error occurred. Try it again."}
                };

                if (_env.IsDevelopment())
                {
                    json.DetailedMessage = context.Exception;
                }

                var exceptionObject = new ObjectResult(json)
                {StatusCode = 500};

                context.Result = exceptionObject;
                context.HttpContext.Response.StatusCode =
                  (int) HttpStatusCode.InternalServerError;
            }
        }
    }
    public class JsonErrorPayload
    {
        public string[] Messages { get; set; }

        public object DetailedMessage { get; set; }
    }
}
```

The framework invokes the `HttpCustomExceptionFilterImpl` class each time an exception is thrown. The class has two dependencies: `ILogger` and `IWebHostEnvironment`. The `OnException` method logs the exception using the `ILogger` class and creates a new instance of `JsonErrorPayload`, which contains a generic message and some details about the exception. Finally, the `OnException` method returns the 500 Internal server error status code, as well as the `exceptionObject` that was just created.

The detailed exception message may have some value, depending on `IWebHostEvinronment`. This kind of approach is useful in a production context to avoid revealing sensitive information about the service.

In conclusion, if our service throws an exception, our `IExceptionFilter` transforms it into a new JSON response:

```
{
    "messages": [
        "An error occurred. Try it again."
    ],
    "detailedMessage": {
        "ClassName": "System.Exception",
        "Message": "My custom exception",
        "Data": null,
        "InnerException": null,
        "HelpURL": null,
        "StackTraceString": " at
         Sample.API.Filters.Controllers.OrderController.Get() in
         /Projects/Sample.API.Filters/
         Controllers/OrderController.cs:line 30\n at
         lambda_method(Closure , Object , Object[] )\n ",
        "RemoteStackTraceString": null,
        "RemoteStackIndex": 0,
        "ExceptionMethod": null,
        "HResult": -2146233088,
        "Source": "HandsOn.API.Filters",
        "WatsonBuckets": null
    }
}
```

Summary

In this chapter, we looked at some filter concepts in ASP.NET Core. We introduced different types of filters, how they work, and the specific purpose of each kind in the MVC pipeline. We have also seen how to implement filters and explored some concrete use cases to understand and discover the power of filters so that we can achieve cross-cutting concerns.

The next chapter is dedicated to the data access layer methodologies in ASP.NET Core. You will be introduced to the repository pattern, which will describe the implementation of the data access layer using EF Core and Dapper. Furthermore, we will also describe some testing techniques that verify the data access layer part of an ASP.NET Core application.

3
Section 3: Building a Real-World RESTful API

In this section, we will walk through the implementation of some concrete implementations of a RESTful web service. The section provides concrete approaches in the implementation and testing of a web service. In the first phase, we will focus on the implementation of the web service by differentiating it into three layers: data access, domain, and HTTP layer. Furthermore, we will see how to run the service locally by using some containerization technologies, and we will discover some concrete patterns for communication between multiple web services. Finally, we will have an overview on how to secure the service through the implementation of the token-authentication.

As we mentioned in Chapter 1, *REST 101 and Getting Started with ASP.NET Core*, the following examples require you to have .NET Core 3.1 installed on your OS. It is also suggested that you install an IDE that supports .NET Core, such as Visual Studio 2019, Visual Studio for Mac, or the Rider IDE. You can use the Visual Studio Code as an alternative, but keep in mind that you will not have the IntelliSense and code analysis comfort provided by the other editors.

 All the code described in this section is available on GitHub at https://github.com/PacktPublishing/Hands-On-RESTful-Web-Services-with-ASP.NET-Core-3.

This section includes the following chapters:

8
Building the Data Access Layer

Starting from this chapter, we are going to walk through the concrete implementation of the web service part using .NET Core. We will cover some key aspects of developing real web services—from the design of the data access layer to the implementation of the HTTP routes.

In this chapter, we will start by defining the data access part. The data access part is necessary to store information in a database or data source, and it is usually one of the most delicate parts of an application. We will be focusing on the implementation of a catalog web service. Additionally, we will explore different third-party tools for accessing our data and explain how to set up a project and implement a data domain.

This chapter will cover the following topics:

- Designing project entities
- Choosing the right tool
- Implementing a data access layer using EF Core
- Implementing a data access layer using Dapper
- Testing a data layer using the in-memory database

 The code in this chapter is available from the following GitHub repository: https://github.com/PacktPublishing/Hands-On-RESTful-Web-Services-with-ASP.NET-Core-3.

Setting up the project

Just like previous chapters, we can start by creating a new project using the web API template. Let's open the terminal and execute the following commands:

```
mkdir Catalog.API
cd Catalog.API
dotnet new sln -n Catalog.API
mkdir src
cd src
dotnet new webapi -n Catalog.API
dotnet sln ../Catalog.API.sln add Catalog.API
```

The first dotnet new command creates a new solution file named Catalog.API. The second dotnet new instruction creates a new web API project in the src folder. Finally, the last dotnet sln command adds the project to our solution.

The resulting filesystem structure looks like the following:

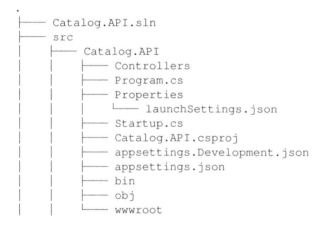

The src folder will contain all our code and the additional projects we will add in the book. Later on in this chapter, we will also add a tests folder that will contain all the tests for our projects.

Implementing the domain model

As discussed in the *Data transfer* section in Chapter 5, *Web Service Stack in ASP.NET Core*, the *domain model* is the representation of the data handled by our service. Thinking about a *catalog web service* for a music store, the primary data we need to process includes the *entities* used by the API.

To guarantee reusability and loose coupling, we are going to define the domain model of the service in a separate project. First of all, let's create a new Catalog.Domain project inside the src folder by executing the following command:

```
dotnet new classlib -n Catalog.Domain -f netstandard2.1
```

The above command also specifies the netstandard2.1 version as target framework. Furthermore, after creating the Catalog.Domain project, we need to add it to our solution:

```
dotnet sln ../Catalog.API.sln add Catalog.Domain
```

The preceding instruction adds a reference to the Catalog.Domain project to the Catalog.API.sln file. Therefore, we are now ready to design and implement the entities of our web service.

Designing entities

We can now proceed with the design phase of the entities we need for this implementation. Let's start with the Item class, which will be the central entity in our domain model. It is a representation of a music album, and it contains all the attributes and characteristics related to albums, including the *description, name, release date,* and *format.* The entity will also provide some additional information that is usually present in a catalog, such as available stock, a picture, and the price.

Let's start by designing a diagram to describe our code:

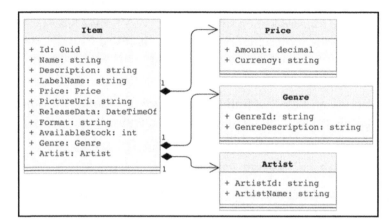

This diagram defines the entities involved in the service:

- `Item` is the primary entity in our claim. It contains all the information about the album and the references to the *artist* and the *genre*.
- The `Artist` entity represents the artist associated with the album.
- The `Genre` entity represents the music genre associated with the album.
- The `Money` entity represents the price of the album. This is a complex type that contains the amount of *money* and the *currency* it is in.

Implement entities

Now we have defined which properties and objects are included in the catalog service, let's start by implementing the entities as concrete types. All domain models are conventionally stored in the `Entities` folder in the `Catalog.Domain` project. The first type we are creating is the `Item` class:

```
using System;

namespace Catalog.Domain.Entities
{
    public class Item
    {
        public Guid Id { get; set; }
        public string Name { get; set; }
        public string Description { get; set; }
        public string LabelName { get; set; }
```

```
        public Price Price { get; set; }
        public string PictureUri { get; set; }
        public DateTimeOffset ReleaseDate { get; set; }
        public string Format { get; set; }
        public int AvailableStock { get; set; }
        public Genre Genre { get; set; }
        public Artist Artist { get; set; }
    }
}
```

First, we can see that the definition of the Item class contains some references to the other types. It is crucial to note that the implementation uses the Guid type to specify Id. The primary purpose of that approach is to avoid conflicts in the event of a merger between two different data sources or catalogs.

Let's proceed by defining the related entities of our domain model:

```
using System;

namespace Catalog.Domain.Entities
{
    //Artist.cs file
    public class Artist
    {
        public Guid ArtistId { get; set; }
        public string ArtistName { get; set; }
    }
    //Genre.cs file
    public class Genre
    {
        public Guid GenreId { get; set; }
        public string GenreDescription { get; set; }
    }
    //Price.cs file
    public class Price
    {
        public decimal Amount { get; set; }
        public string Currency { get; set; }
    }
}
```

For representational purposes, the following classes are implemented in the same fragment of code. Note that they are defined in different files: Artist.cs, Genre.cs, and Price.cs.

The preceding code defines the related entities contained in our domain model. The `Artist` class represents an artist related to an album. It includes `Guid id` and `ArtistName`. In the same way, the `Genre` class is another category type that represents the genre of a specific album. Finally, the `Price` class represents the price (and the currency) of the product.

Data access using ORMs

Data access is the part of our service that helps us to perform reading or writing operations on the data source. The data access section is usually combined with an ORM. In general, we can define an ORM as an object-relational mapping tool for converting relational data between incompatible type systems using an object-oriented programming approach.

ORM tools or packages are a bridge between a data source and a web application. They map the information represented in relational tables into classes and, consequently, objects.

In the .NET ecosystem, we can choose between a vast number of different ORMs. The one that is officially maintained by Microsoft is EF Core.

EF Core is an open source ORM powered by Microsoft and the community. It is the default ORM used in .NET Core applications and web services. In this chapter, we will also have an overview of **Dapper**, an open source micro-ORM powered by Stack Exchange and the community. Both EF Core and Dapper are distributed as NuGet packages, and, in general, they are very well integrated with the .NET Core framework.

Finding the right tool for the job

EF Core and Dapper provide an abstraction level over our data source. Nevertheless, both of them have some pros and cons. It is essential to bear in mind that, for every project we are working on, we should seek to find the right tool for the job.

Let's analyze some pros and cons for these two libraries. Before that, we should take a quick look at some demo queries in order to understand the differences between the two. The following snippet describes a sample query using EF Core:

```
using (var context = new CatalogContext()) {
    var items = context.Items
                        .Where(b => b.Description.Contains("various
                        artists"))
                        .ToList();
}
```

In the preceding code, we search for every Item entity with a corresponding description. Let's proceed by taking a Dapper query as an example:

```
connection.Query<Item>("select * from (select Id from dbo.Catalog where
Description like '%@searchTerm%', new { searchTerm = "various artists" });
```

As you can see, EF Core provides a high level of abstraction over our data source.

Moreover, EF Core, by default, allows developers to query data using collections (integrated with LINQ). This type of approach is quick and easy, but it comes at a cost: EF Core translates queries into the SQL language, and, sometimes, it produces SQL queries that are not optimized. EF Core also encourages a code-first approach over the database, which means that all the entities that are present on the database side are generated using C# code. This may seem easy when you have a single object, but it can present maintainability problems when you have complex entities.

 In complex entities, or applications that use the code-first approach, the code that generates database entities is usually implemented in a separate project and repository to avoid tight coupling between the database and the entire solution.

A common problem with EF Core, though, is the early fetching of resources. For example, consider a query such as this:

```
List<Item> items = db.Items.ToList();
List<Item> variousArtistItems = items
                .Where(s => s.Description.Contains("various
                    artist") == city).ToList();
```

It produces a SQL query similar to the following:

```
SELECT [i].[Id],
       [i].[Description],
       [i].[ArtistId],
       [i].[GenreId],
FROM   [dbo].[Items] as [i]
```

As you can see, despite the fact we use the `Where` clause, earlier the `ToList` method evaluated the query without considering the `Where` clause. To get a better result, we should execute the `Where` statement before the evaluation:

```
List<Item> variousArtistItems = db.Items
                    .Where(s => s.Description.Contains("various
                        artist") == city).ToList();
```

This kind of procedure is better both for performance and network reasons. It may seem simple enough, but it is quite common that these kinds of error are introduced in the codebase in distributed teams, and they can be quite tricky to spot in the code review process.

In terms of Dapper, which is a micro-ORM, the abstraction level changes. Dapper provides more *transparent* access to the data source. It guarantees, by default, a clear way to query your data by using plain SQL or stored procedures. Consequently, it also ensures better performance. On the other hand, it is tightly coupled with the data source, because it executes queries using the data source query language.

In summary, this chapter will cover both EF Core and Dapper libraries. To choose between them, you should consider the skills already present in your team and how the service can be performance-optimized. If your team has a strong knowledge of SQL, you may proceed by implementing stored procedures instead of using EF Core. On the other hand, if your team doesn't already have SQL skills, you should consider using EF Core.

Implementing a data access layer using EF Core

In this section, we will explore how to build a data access layer using the repository pattern and EF Core. The **repository pattern** is an additional abstraction over our data source. It provides reading and writing operations on data.

Defining the repository pattern and unit of work

Before we start, we need to define some interfaces in the `Catalog.Domain` project. Let's proceed by setting a generic interface to determine the unit of work of our repository:

```
using System;
using System.Threading;
using System.Threading.Tasks;

namespace Catalog.Domain.Repositories
{
    public interface IUnitOfWork : IDisposable
    {
        Task<int> SaveChangesAsync(CancellationToken cancellationToken =
        default(CancellationToken));
        Task<bool> SaveEntitiesAsync(CancellationToken cancellationToken =
        default(CancellationToken));
    }
}
```

`IUnitOfWork` defines two methods: `SaveChangesAsync` and `SaveEntitiesAsync`. These two methods are used to save changes in our collection to the database effectively. These methods are both asynchronous: they return a `Task` type and they accept a `CancellationToken` type as a parameter. The `CancellationToken` parameter provides a way to stop pending asynchronous operations.

In some cases, the repository pattern is implemented in such a way that, when you update or create new elements in a collection, those changes are automatically saved to the database. I prefer to keep the effective saving operation separate from the reading and writing part. This can be achieved using the unit of work approach. Therefore, the repository allows the higher layers to perform get, create, and update operations on the memory collection, while the *unit of work* implements a way to transfer those changes to the database.

Let's proceed by defining an `IRepository` interface at the same folder level as the `IUnitOfWork` interface defined previously:

```
namespace Catalog.Domain.Repositories
{
    public interface IRepository
    {
        IUnitOfWork UnitOfWork { get; }
    }
}
```

As you can see, `IRepository` does not implicitly use the `IUnitOfWork` interface. Additionally, it exposes the `UnitOfWork` instance as a property of the class. This approach guarantees that all the consumers of the `IRepository` interface must explicitly update the database by calling the `SaveChangesAsync` or `SaveEntitiesAsync` methods.

The final step is to define the `IItemRepository` interface, as follows:

```
using System;
using System.Collections.Generic;
using System.Threading.Tasks;
using Catalog.Domain.Entities;

namespace Catalog.Domain.Repositories
{
    public interface IItemRepository : IRepository
    {
        Task<IEnumerable<Item>> GetAsync();
        Task<Item> GetAsync(Guid id);
        Item Add(Item item);
        Item Update(Item item);
    }
}
```

The interface extends the `IRepository` class and refers to the `Item` entity that was defined previously. `IItemRepository` defines reading and writing operations over our data source. You may notice that the `Add`, `Update`. This is because they only act on the collection stored in the memory of the application, and the effective saving operation is performed by the unit of work.

Connecting our repository to the database

Once we have defined the `IItemRepository` interfaces and all the abstractions in the domain project, we should continue by creating the classes that will represent the concrete implementation of the previously defined abstractions. We will also create a new `Catalog.Infrastructure` project containing all the implementations of our repositories and the classes that represent the layer between our service and the database. Let's create the `Catalog.Infrastructure` project by executing the following commands in the `src` folder:

```
dotnet new classlib -n Catalog.Infrastructure -f netstandard2.1

dotnet sln ../Catalog.API.sln add Catalog.Infrastructure
```

Once finished, the folder structure for our solution looks as follows:

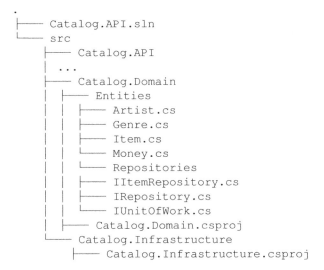

```
.
├── Catalog.API.sln
└── src
    ├── Catalog.API
    │   ...
    ├── Catalog.Domain
    │   ├── Entities
    │   │   ├── Artist.cs
    │   │   ├── Genre.cs
    │   │   ├── Item.cs
    │   │   └── Money.cs
    │   │   └── Repositories
    │   │   ├── IItemRepository.cs
    │   │   ├── IRepository.cs
    │   │   └── IUnitOfWork.cs
    │   ├── Catalog.Domain.csproj
    └── Catalog.Infrastructure
        ├── Catalog.Infrastructure.csproj
```

Before proceeding with the implementation of `IItemRepository`, we need to add the `Microsoft.EntityFrameworkCore` NuGet package to the `Catalog.Infrastructure` project by executing the following command inside the project folder:

```
dotnet add package Microsoft.EntityFrameworkCore
```

After that, we can proceed by adding the reference to the `Catalog.Domain` project into the infrastructure project, using the following command:

```
dotnet add reference ../Catalog.Domain
```

DbContext definition

`DbContext` is one of the abstractions between our application and the database. It enables us to interact with, and perform operations over, data. A `DbContext` implementation is also the representation of a session between our application and the database, and it can be used to query and save the instances of the application entities into our data source. Let's take a quick look at the `DbContext` implementation in the `Catalog.Infrastructure` project:

```
using System.Threading;
using System.Threading.Tasks;
using Catalog.Domain.Entities;
using Catalog.Domain.Repositories;
using Microsoft.EntityFrameworkCore;
```

```
namespace Catalog.Infrastructure
{
    public class CatalogContext : DbContext, IUnitOfWork
    {
        public const string DEFAULT_SCHEMA = "catalog";
        public DbSet<Item> Items { get; set; }

        public CatalogContext(DbContextOptions<CatalogContext> options) :
         base(options)
        {
        }

        protected override void OnModelCreating(ModelBuilder modelBuilder)
        {
        }

        public async Task<bool> SaveEntitiesAsync(CancellationToken
         cancellationToken = default(CancellationToken))
        {
            await SaveChangesAsync(cancellationToken);
            return true;
        }
    }
}
```

After taking a quick look at the code, we should mention the following:

- The CatalogContext class represents our unit of work; therefore, it implements the IUnitOfWork interface.
- It uses the DbSet<Item> type to represent the collection of Item instances.
- The constructor of the CatalogContext class accepts a mandatory argument, which represents DbContextOptions. These options are used to specify some key information about the connection with the database. This includes the database provider to be used, the connection string to that database, and all the tracking policies used by the ORM.
- The CatalogContext class also implements SaveEntitiesAsync, which calls the SaveChangesAsync method derived by the DbContext class.

Once we have CatalogContext, we can continue by implementing the IItemRepository interface.

Implementing the repository

The following subsection focuses on building the concrete implementation of the IItemRepository interface. It is vital to note that the IItemRepository interface is located in the Catalog.Domain project and the implementation of ItemRepository is in the Catalog.Infrastructure project.

Once we have built the DbContext class, we can proceed by implementing the concrete ItemRepository class:

```
using System;
using System.Collections.Generic;
using System.Linq;
using System.Threading.Tasks;
using Catalog.Domain.Entities;
using Catalog.Domain.Repositories;
using Microsoft.EntityFrameworkCore;

namespace Catalog.Infrastructure.Repositories
{
    public class ItemRepository
        : IItemRepository
    {
        private readonly CatalogContext _context;

        public IUnitOfWork UnitOfWork => _context;

        public ItemRepository(CatalogContext context)
        {
            _context = context ?? throw new
              ArgumentNullException(nameof(context));
        }

        public async Task<IEnumerable<Item>> GetAsync()
        {
            return await _context
                .Items
                .AsNoTracking()
                .ToListAsync();
        }

        public async Task<Item> GetAsync(Guid id)
        {
            var item = await _context.Items
                .AsNoTracking()
                .Where(x => x.Id == id)
                .Include(x => x.Genre)
```

```
                        .Include(x => x.Artist).FirstOrDefaultAsync();

            return item;
        }

        public Item Add(Item order)
        {
            return _context.Items
                .Add(order).Entity;
        }

        public Item Update(Item item)
        {
            _context.Entry(item).State = EntityState.Modified;
            return item;
        }
    }
}
```

The preceding code implements the CRUD operations previously defined in the
IItemRepository interface. It also exposes CategoryContext using the IUnitOfWork
interface. This kind of approach guarantees that the consumer of IItemRepository can
modify and query our collections and also update the data source with the corresponding
changes. Let's walk-through the methods implemented in the preceding code:

- The GetAsync() method uses the context to retrieve the collection of Items
  entities. The method uses the AsNoTracking() method explicitly in order to
  prevent the tracking of entities. This extension method can be used every time
  you don't need to perform writing operations on entities, and it is meant for
  read-only data.
- GetAsync(Guid id) overloads the previously mentioned method, and it
  uses AsNoTracking() for the same purpose described previously. This method
  also gets details of the related entities (Genre and Artist) by using the
  Include() extension method provided by EF Core.

- The Add(Item entity) method uses the context to add the entity passed as a
  parameter and it returns the added entity to the caller.
- The Edit method updates the target entity from the context and
  sets EntityState.Modified. This approach guarantees that, once the entity is
  in a modified state, it will be updated at the saving step.

The preceding code doesn't implement the `Delete` method. This is because the delete process will be implemented later on in the book. We will essentially perform a soft deletion of our data.

Transforming entities into a SQL schema

EF Core encourages the code-first approach in our services. The **code-first** technique consists of defining some entity classes in C# and using them to generate tables on the database side. The same approach is applied to all the relationships and constraints that are usually present in a SQL ecosystem, such as the index, the primary keys, and the foreign keys. This section demonstrates how to use this kind of approach to generate the database schema.

First of all, let's start by taking back our `Item.cs` entity and adding an ID that represents the relationship with the other entities:

```csharp
using System;

namespace Catalog.Domain.Entities
{
    //Item.cs file
    public class Item
    {
        public Guid Id { get; set; }
        public string Name { get; set; }
        public string Description { get; set; }
        public string LabelName { get; set; }
        public Price Price { get; set; }
        public string PictureUri { get; set; }
        public DateTimeOffset ReleaseDate { get; set; }
        public string Format { get;set; }
        public int AvailableStock { get; set; }
        public Guid GenreId { get; set; }
        public Genre Genre { get; set; }
        public Guid ArtistId { get; set; }
        public Artist Artist { get; set; }
    }
    //Artist.cs file
    public class Artist
    {
        public Guid ArtistId { get; set; }
        public string ArtistName { get; set; }
        public ICollection<Item> Items {get; set;}
    }
```

```
//Genre.cs file
public class Genre
{
    public Guid GenreId { get; set; }
    public string GenreDescription { get; set; }
    public ICollection<Item> Items {get; set;}
}
}
```

The preceding code describes the *many-to-one* relationship between the Item class and the Artist class and between the Item class and the Genre class. Additionally, both the Artist and Genre entities have a collection that refers to a collection of Item entities.

Let's continue by implementing the constraints of our Item entity using the Fluent API approach. In general, EF Core ORM implements the Fluent API's technique to help us to deal with the constraint's definitions.

In general, the Fluent API, also called the **Fluent interface**, is a method for composing object-oriented APIs that are essentially based on method chaining. The chain between methods produces source code that is very close to written prose; for example, myList.First().Items.Count().ShouldBe(2). You can see how readable this example is; it can be understood by anyone. Most EF Core constraints are usually built using this kind of approach.

Let's proceed by adding a new folder called SchemaDefinitions inside our Catalog.Infrastructure project. The folder will contain all the schema definitions implemented for the application and all the definitions of the constraints between the entities. For example, in the case of the Item entity, we need to create a new ItemEntitySchemaDefinition class:

```
using System;
using Catalog.Domain.Entities;
using Microsoft.EntityFrameworkCore;
using Microsoft.EntityFrameworkCore.Metadata.Builders;
namespace Catalog.Infrastructure.SchemaDefinitions
{
    public class ItemEntitySchemaDefinition :
        IEntityTypeConfiguration<Item>
    {
        public void Configure(EntityTypeBuilder<Item> builder)
        {
            builder.ToTable("Items", CatalogContext.DEFAULT_SCHEMA);
            builder.HasKey(k => k.Id);
```

```
builder.Property(p => p.Name)
    .IsRequired();

builder.Property(p => p.Description)
    .IsRequired()
    .HasMaxLength(1000);

builder
    .HasOne(e => e.Genre)
    .WithMany(c => c.Items)
    .HasForeignKey(k => k.GenreId);

builder
    .HasOne(e => e.Artist)
    .WithMany(c => c.Items)
    .HasForeignKey(k => k.ArtistId);

builder.Property(p => p.Price).HasConversion(
    p => $"{p.Amount}:{p.Currency}",
    p => new Price
    {
        Amount = Convert.ToDecimal(
         p.Split(':', StringSplitOptions.None)[0]),
        Currency = p.Split(':', StringSplitOptions.None)[1]
    });
        }
    }
}
```

This is the schema definition of the `Item` entity constraints. The class implements the `IEntityTypeConfiguration<T>` interface exposed by the `Microsoft.EntityFrameworkCore.SqlServer` package. It is necessary to add a new reference to the `Catalog.Infrastructure` project by using the following command:

`dotnet add package Microsoft.EntityFrameworkCore.SqlServer`

The package provides an extension method to interact with a SQL server database: the `Configure` method implementation defines rules, which will be applied to the `Item` entity. Because of the Fluent API approach, it is easy to understand these rules:

- The `ToTable` method is used to define the name of the SQL table explicitly
- The `HasKey` method sets the property as the primary key for this entity type
- The `IsRequired` method is used to mark all the required features

EF Core provides different *out-of-box* configurations for our properties; a complete list is available at `https://docs.microsoft.com/en-us/ef/core/modeling/`. These properties can be combined to obtain a better result regarding the correct representation of our domain model.

The `Configure` method also adds some additional constraints to the *one-to-many* relationship between the `Item` entity and the `Artist` and `Genre` entities:

```
...
        builder
            .HasOne(e => e.Genre)
            .WithMany(c => c.Items)
            .HasForeignKey(k => k.GenreId);
        builder
            .HasOne(e => e.Artist)
            .WithMany(c => c.Items)
            .HasForeignKey(k => k.ArtistId);
    ...
```

This snippet specifies the relationships of the `Item` entity. Note that we follow a fluent approach. In this specific case, we are defining a 1-N relationship between the `Item` class and the `Artist` and `Genre` classes, by specifying `GenreId` and `ArtistId` as the foreign keys.

Custom conversions using the Fluent API

EF Core also provides a way to add custom conversions. This approach may be useful for providing a custom representation of complex entities. As an example, let's take the following snippet of code declared in `ItemEntitySchemaDefinition`:

```
builder.Property(p => p.Price).HasConversion(
    p => $"{p.Amount}:{p.Currency}",
    p => new Price
    {
        Amount = Convert.ToDecimal(p.Split(':',
          StringSplitOptions.None)[0]),
        Currency = p.Split(':', StringSplitOptions.None)[1]
    });
```

The `HasConversion` method offers a way to customize data inserted into the database. This method serializes the `Price` field, which is of the `Price` type, into a string by using the following format: `34.05:EUR`. On the other hand, when the `Price` data is read from the database, the string is deserialized into the `Price` type.

Applying the schema definition on the current data context

To utilize the schema implemented in the ItemEntitySchemaDefinition class, we should apply it in the OnModelCreating method contained in the CatalogContext class:

```csharp
using System.Threading;
using System.Threading.Tasks;
using Microsoft.EntityFrameworkCore;
using Catalog.Domain.Entities;
using Catalog.Domain.Repositories;
using Catalog.Infrastructure.SchemaDefinitions;


namespace Catalog.Infrastructure
{
    public class CatalogContext : DbContext, IUnitOfWork
    {
        public const string DEFAULT_SCHEMA = "catalog";
        public DbSet<Item> Items { get; set; }


        public CatalogContext(DbContextOptions<CatalogContext> options)
            : base (options) { }


        protected override void OnModelCreating(ModelBuilder modelBuilder)
        {
            modelBuilder.ApplyConfiguration(new
ItemEntitySchemaDefinition());
            base.OnModelCreating(modelBuilder);
        }

        public async Task<bool> SaveEntitiesAsync(CancellationToken
            cancellationToken = default(CancellationToken))
        {
            await SaveChangesAsync(cancellationToken);
            return true;
        }
    }
}
```

The preceding code uses the `ApplyConfiguration` extension method to apply configurations to the SQL schema during the runtime execution. It is important to note that the `OnModelCreating` method implemented in the class always calls the `base.OnModelCreating` method of the parent class, in order to preserve the behavior of the extended class.

Generating a schema for the Artist and Genre entities

The preceding process can also be applied to the `Artist` and `Genre` entities. The following code shows the definitions of the two entities in the `Catalog.Domain.Entities` namespace:

```
using System.Collections.Generic;

namespace Catalog.Domain.Entities
{
    //Artist.cs
    public class Artist
    {
        public Guid ArtistId { get; set; }
        public string ArtistName { get; set; }
        public ICollection<Item> Items { get; set; }
    }

    //Genre.cs
    public class Genre
    {
        public Guid GenreId { get; set; }
        public string GenreDescription { get; set; }
        public ICollection<Item> Items { get; set; }
    }
}
```

Consequently, we can add two files to the `Catalog.Infrastructure` project as follows:

```
//SchemaDefinitions/ArtistEntitySchemaConfiguration.cs
using Microsoft.EntityFrameworkCore;
using Microsoft.EntityFrameworkCore.Metadata.Builders;
using Catalog.Domain.Entities;

namespace Catalog.Infrastructure.SchemaDefinitions
{
    public class ArtistEntitySchemaConfiguration :
        IEntityTypeConfiguration<Artist>
    {
        public void Configure(EntityTypeBuilder<Artist> builder)
```

```
        {
            builder.ToTable("Artists", CatalogContext.DEFAULT_SCHEMA);
            builder.HasKey(k => k.ArtistId);
            builder.Property(p => p.ArtistId);

            builder.Property(p => p.ArtistName)
                .IsRequired()
                .HasMaxLength(200);
        }
    }
}
```

The `GenreEntitySchemaConfiguration.cs` file looks as follows:

```
//SchemaDefinitions/GenreEntitySchemaConfiguration.cs
using Catalog.Domain.Entities;
using Microsoft.EntityFrameworkCore;
using Microsoft.EntityFrameworkCore.Metadata.Builders;

namespace Catalog.Infrastructure.SchemaDefinitions
{
    public class GenreEntitySchemaConfiguration :
        IEntityTypeConfiguration<Genre>
    {
        public void Configure(EntityTypeBuilder<Genre> builder)
        {
            builder.ToTable("Genres", CatalogContext.DEFAULT_SCHEMA);
            builder.HasKey(k => k.GenreId);
            builder.Property(p => p.GenreId);
            builder.Property(p => p.GenreDescription)
                .IsRequired()
                .HasMaxLength(1000);
        }
    }
}
```

Both `GenreEntitySchemaConfiguration` and `ArtistEntitySchemaConfiguration` define the keys for our tables using the `HasKey` method. As we have already discussed, they use the same fluent approach applied to the `ItemEntitySchemaConfiguration` class defined previously. Also, we need to include `GenreEntitySchemaConfiguration` and `ArtistEntitySchemaConfiguration` in the `OnModelCreating` method of the `CatalogContext` class:

```
    public class CatalogContext : DbContext, IUnitOfWork
    {
...
        protected override void OnModelCreating(ModelBuilder modelBuilder)
```

```
    {
            modelBuilder.ApplyConfiguration(new
ItemEntitySchemaDefinition());
            modelBuilder.ApplyConfiguration(new
GenreEntitySchemaConfiguration());
            modelBuilder.ApplyConfiguration(new
ArtistEntitySchemaConfiguration());

            base.OnModelCreating(modelBuilder);
    }
...
    }
```

I've omitted the full definition of the `CatalogContext` class for brevity. The significant change is the extension of the `OnModelCreating` method by applying the configuration for the `GenreEntitySchemaConfiguration` and `ArtistEntitySchemaConfiguration` classes.

Executing migrations

The last step in implementing data access using EF Core is to connect a `DbContext` instance to the database and run the migrations using the command exposed by the .NET CLI. Before doing that, we need to have a working database in our local environment. To keep our local development environment as lightweight as possible, this example will use a Docker image of Microsoft SQL Server on Linux. It is possible to get the Docker image here: `https://hub.docker.com/r/microsoft/mssql-server-linux/`. If you don't have any previous experience with Docker, you can follow this guide to install and set it up on your local machine: `https://docs.microsoft.com/en-us/sql/linux/quickstart-install-connect-docker?view=sql-server-2017`.

 Containers are an excellent way to quickly set up your local environment without the need to configure a lot of different tools and systems. Nowadays, Microsoft is investing a lot in simplifying their systems and processes, both for developers and cloud systems.

After running our SQL instance, let's create a new database called `Store`, by running the following commands:

```
docker exec -it sql1 "bash"

/opt/mssql-tools/bin/sqlcmd -S localhost -U SA -P '<YOUR_PASSWORD>'

1> CREATE LOGIN catalog_srv WITH PASSWORD = 'P@ssw0rd';
2> CREATE DATABASE Store;
```

```
3> GO
1> USE Store;
2> CREATE USER catalog_srv;
3> GO
1> EXEC sp_addrolemember N'db_owner', N'catalog_srv';
2> GO
```

A valid alternative to the CLI is to use a SQL editor. One recommended tool is the `mssql` extension for VS Code: `https://docs.microsoft.com/en-us/sql/linux/sql-server-linux-develop-use-vscode?view=sql-server-2017`. Otherwise, you can download this cross-platform SQL editor based on VS Code: `https://docs.microsoft.com/en-us/sql/azure-data-studio/download?view=sql-server-2017`.

Once we get Microsoft SQL Server working in our local environment, we can proceed by connecting our service with the database. The `Startup` class already present in the `Catalog.API` project will define the connection string and the provider used by our service. As we will see, all the migration classes will also be stored in the same project. This kind of approach guarantees a unique entry point, `Catalog.API`, for our .NET CLI instructions, without being tightly coupled with the database logic (`Catalog.Infrastructure`).

Before proceeding further, we need to add the `Catalog.Infrastructure` project as a reference for the API project by using the following command in the API project folder:

```
dotnet add reference ../Catalog.Infrastructure
```

The API project also requires you to refer to the `Microsoft.EntityFrameworkCore.Design` NuGet package, which shares design-time components for EF Core tools. We can add the latest version of the package by executing the following CLI instruction into the `Catalog.API` project folder:

```
dotnet add package Microsoft.EntityFrameworkCore.Design
```

After that, we can proceed by adding the database connection in the `Startup` class:

```
using System;
using System.Reflection;
using Microsoft.AspNetCore.Builder;
using Microsoft.AspNetCore.Hosting;
using Microsoft.AspNetCore.Mvc;
using Microsoft.Extensions.Configuration;
using Microsoft.Extensions.DependencyInjection;
using Microsoft.EntityFrameworkCore;
using Catalog.Infrastructure;
```

```
namespace Catalog.API
{
    public class Startup
    {
        public Startup(IConfiguration configuration)
        {
            ...
        }

        ...
        public void ConfigureServices(IServiceCollection services)
        {
            services
              .AddEntityFrameworkSqlServer()
              .AddDbContext<CatalogContext>(contextOptions =>
              {
                  contextOptions.UseSqlServer(
  "Server=localhost,1433;Initial Catalog=Store;User
Id=<SA_USER>;Password=<PASSWORD>",
                        serverOptions => {
                            serverOptions.MigrationsAssembly
                            (typeof(Startup).Assembly.FullName); });
              });
            ...
        }

        public void Configure(IApplicationBuilder app,
            IHostingEnvironment env)
        {
            ...
        }
    }
}
```

The `ConfigureServices` method contains the initialization of the SQL connection. First of all, it adds the services required by the SQL provider using `AddEntityFameworkSqlServer`. Following that, it adds `CatalogContext`, utilizing the `AddContext<T>` generic method by passing an action method of the `Action<DbContextOptionsBuilder>` type.

Finally, the action method configures the SQL Server provider by using the `UseSqlServer` extension method and passing the connection string for our database. The `MigrationsAssembly` method defines where the assemblies should be stored. In this case, it specifies that all migrations will be stored in our `Catalog.API` project.

To keep our `Startup` class clean and readable, we may create a custom extension method to initialize the connection to the `Catalog` database. Let's create a new folder called `Extensions` in our `Catalog.API` project, add a new `DatabaseExtension` class, and move our code into a new `AddCatalogContext` method:

```
using Catalog.Infrastructure;
using Microsoft.EntityFrameworkCore;
using Microsoft.Extensions.DependencyInjection;

namespace Catalog.API.Extensions
{
        public static class DatabaseExtensions
        {
            public static IServiceCollection AddCatalogContext(this
                IServiceCollection services)
            {
                return services
                    .AddEntityFrameworkSqlServer()
                    .AddDbContext<CatalogContext>(contextOptions =>
                    {
                        contextOptions.UseSqlServer(
                            "Server=localhost,1433;Initial
Catalog=Store;User Id=<SA_USER>;Password=<PASSWORD>",
                            serverOptions => {
                                serverOptions.MigrationsAssembly
  (typeof(Startup).Assembly.FullName); });
                    });
            }
        }
}
```

We can simplify the `Startup` class as follows:

```
public class Startup
  {
      ...

      public void ConfigureServices(IServiceCollection services)
      {
          services.AddCatalogContext();
          ...
      }
  }
```

Now that the `Startup` class is ready, execute `migrations` in the `Catalog.API` project folder using the following commands:

```
dotnet ef migrations add InitMigration
dotnet ef database update
```

The first command generates the `Migration` folder and two different files inside it:

- `{timestamp}_InitMigration.cs`: This class creates the tables, constraints, and indexes present in the database.
- `CatalogContextModelSnapshot.cs`: This is formed only on the first migration command and represents the current state of the entities of the service.

Every migration class, including the one we just generated, has the following structure:

```
using Microsoft.EntityFrameworkCore.Migrations;

namespace Catalog.API.Migrations
{
    public partial class InitMigration : Migration
    {
        protected override void Up(MigrationBuilder migrationBuilder)
        {
            ...
        }

        protected override void Down(MigrationBuilder migrationBuilder)
        {
            ...
        }
    }
}
```

The class contains two methods: `Up` and `Down`. The `Up` method is called during the generation of the database schema. The `Down` method is called during the deletion of the schema.

The generated tables and SQL entities are created under the `catalog` schema. The `dotnet ef` CLI tool will create a new migration class each time we execute the following command:

```
dotnet ef migrations add <migration_name>
```

The schema of the database will be refreshed every time we run the EF Core update process Core inside our project folder. Therefore, we can proceed by executing the following CLI command in the `Catalog.API` project folder:

```
dotnet ef database update
```

The preceding command creates the SQL schema using the migrations stored in the `Migration` folder of the project: it will connect to the database specified in the connection string, which is stored in the `AddCatalogContext()` extension method. In the next section, we will examine how to move the specified connection string into the `appsettings.json` file.

Defining the configuration part

As discussed in `Chapter 2`, *Overview of ASP.NET Core*, the `appsettings.json` file usually contains the application settings. The connection strings are typically stored in that file. Therefore, that kind of approach makes our service more reusable and configurable, especially when it is already running in a staging or production environment. Let's move the connection string from the `AddCatalogContext` method to the `appsettings.json` file in the following way:

```
{
...
   "DataSource": {
     "ConnectionString": "Server=localhost,1433;Initial Catalog=Store;User
Id=catalog_srv;Password=P@ssw0rd"
   }
}
```

In this way, we can read the connection string and pass it to `AddCatalogContext` as a parameter using the following syntax:

```
..
public void ConfigureServices(IServiceCollection services)
{
..
services.AddCatalogContext(Configuration.GetSection("DataSource:ConnectionS
tring").Value);
   ...
}
..
```

Therefore, we need to change the signature of the `AddCatalogContext` extension method by adding a `connectionString` parameter as follows:

```
public static IServiceCollection AddCatalogContext(this IServiceCollection
services, string connectionString)
```

We can pass the newly defined `connectionString` parameter to the `UseSqlServer` extension method. In the next section, we will go on to test the repository logic implemented in this section.

Testing the EF Core repository

This section covers some common testing practices used to test .NET Core applications. More specifically, it focuses on testing the repository part of the application. First of all, let's create a new test project by executing the following commands in the root folder of the project (the same folder as the `.sln` file):

```
mkdir tests
cd tests

dotnet new xunit -n Catalog.Infrastructure.Tests
dotnet sln ../Catalog.API.sln add Catalog.Infrastructure.Tests
```

As a result, we have created a new `tests` directory, which will contain all the test projects of the service. We also created a new `Catalog.Infrastructure.Tests` project using the `xunit` template.

`xunit` is a very popular test framework in the .NET ecosystem, and it is the default choice for testing in .NET Core framework templates. Because we created our project using the `xunit` template, the `Catalog.Infrastructure.Tests.csproj` file will contain references to the `xunit` packages:

```
<ItemGroup>
  <PackageReference Include="Microsoft.NET.Test.Sdk" Version=".." />
  <PackageReference Include="xunit" Version=".." />
  <PackageReference Include="xunit.runner.visualstudio" Version=".." />
  <DotNetCliToolReference Include="dotnet-xunit" Version=".." />
</ItemGroup>
```

These packages allow us to run unit tests by using the `dotnet test` CLI instruction in the test project folder at the solution level, or by using test runner tools integrated into our preferred IDE, such as Visual Studio or Rider.

Seeding data using DbContext

Let's continue by looking at another EF Core feature, which allows us to seed data. The seeding data technique facilitates testing environments to get a **default** snapshot of our integration test database.

Let's walk through an example of database seeding using .NET Core. First of all, let's create a new `Data` folder and add the JSON files that contain the test records. For brevity, I've included both the `artist.json` file and the `genre.json` file in the same snippet of code:

```
// Data/artist.json
[
    {
        "ArtistId": "3eb00b42-a9f0-4012-841d-70ebf3ab7474",
        "ArtistName": "Kendrick Lamar",
        "Items": null
    },
    {
        "ArtistId": "f08a333d-30db-4dd1-b8ba-3b0473c7cdab",
        "ArtistName": "Anderson Paak.",
        "Items": null
    }
]

// Data/genre.json
[
    {
        "GenreId": "c04f05c0-f6ad-44d1-a400-3375bfb5dfd6",
        "GenreDescription": "Hip-Hop",
        "Items": null
    }
]
```

The aforementioned files contain data related to the `Genre` and `Artist` entities. In the same way, we can proceed by creating a new `item.json` file containing information about the `Item` entity:

```
//item.json
[
    {
        "Id": "86bff4f7-05a7-46b6-ba73-d43e2c45840f",
        "Name": "DAMN.",
        "Description": "DAMN. by Kendrick Lamar",
        "LabelName": "TDE, Top Dawg Entertainment",
        "Price": {
            "Amount": 34.5,
            "Currency": "EUR"
```

```
        },
        "PictureUri": "https://mycdn.com/pictures/45345345",
        "ReleaseDate": "2017-01-01T00:00:00+00:00",
        "Format": "Vinyl 33g",
        "AvailableStock": 5,
        "GenreId": "c04f05c0-f6ad-44d1-a400-3375bfb5dfd6",
        "Genre": null,
        "ArtistId": "3eb00b42-a9f0-4012-841d-70ebf3ab7474",
        "Artist": null
    },
    {
        "Id": "b5b05534-9263-448c-a69e-0bbd8b3eb90e",
        "Name": "GOOD KID, m.A.A.d CITY",
        "Description": "GOOD KID, m.A.A.d CITY. by Kendrick Lamar",
        "LabelName": "TDE, Top Dawg Entertainment",
        "Price": {
            "Amount": 23.5,
            "Currency": "EUR"
        },
        "PictureUri": "https://mycdn.com/pictures/32423423",
        "ReleaseDate": "2016-01-01T00:00:00+00:00",
        "Format": "Vinyl 33g",
        "AvailableStock": 6,
        "GenreId": "c04f05c0-f6ad-44d1-a400-3375bfb5dfd6",
        "Genre": null,
        "ArtistId": "3eb00b42-a9f0-4012-841d-70ebf3ab7474",
        "Artist": null
    },
    {
        "Id": "be05537d-5e80-45c1-bd8c-aa21c0f1251e",
        "Name": "Malibu",
        "Description": "Malibu. by Anderson Paak",
        "LabelName": "Steel Wool/OBE/Art Club",
        "Price": {
            "Amount": 23.5,
            "Currency": "EUR"
        },
        "PictureUri": "https://mycdn.com/pictures/32423423",
        "ReleaseDate": "2016-01-01T00:00:00+00:00",
        "Format": "Vinyl 43",
        "AvailableStock": 3,
        "GenreId": "c04f05c0-f6ad-44d1-a400-3375bfb5dfd6",
        "Genre": null,
        "ArtistId": "f08a333d-30db-4dd1-b8ba-3b0473c7cdab",
        "Artist": null
    }
]
```

These files hold some seed data to add to our database before each test. To read them, we need to include the `Newtonsoft.Json` package in the `Catalog.Infrastructure.Tests` project using the following command in the project folder:

```
dotnet add package Newtonsoft.Json
```

We should also ensure that the JSON files are copied to the `bin` folder during the compilation step by adding the following code to `Catalog.Infrastructure.Tests.csproj`:

```
...
<ItemGroup>
  <None Update="Data\artist.json">
    <CopyToOutputDirectory>PreserveNewest</CopyToOutputDirectory>
  </None>
  <None Update="Data\genre.json">
    <CopyToOutputDirectory>PreserveNewest</CopyToOutputDirectory>
  </None>
  <None Update="Data\item.json">
    <CopyToOutputDirectory>PreserveNewest</CopyToOutputDirectory>
  </None>
</ItemGroup>
..
```

The next step is to implement a method to read data from JSON and serialize it in our database context. Also, we should add the `Microsoft.EntityFrameworkCore` NuGet package to the test project using the following CLI command:

```
dotnet add package Microsoft.EntityFrameworkCore
```

The aforementioned package will provide the EF Core `ModelBuilder` type, which is used to generate the mock data used by our tests. Since we will use some of the code implemented in the `Catalog.Infrastructure` project, we should also add a reference to the test project using the following command in the root of the solution:

```
dotnet add ./tests/Catalog.Infrastructure.Tests reference
./src/Catalog.Infrastructure
```

After that, we can create a new extension method, named `Seed<T>`, inside a new `Extensions` folder in the `Catalog.Infrastructure.Tests` project:

```
using System.IO;
using Microsoft.EntityFrameworkCore;
using Newtonsoft.Json;

namespace Catalog.Infrastructure.Tests.Extensions
{
    public static class ModelBuilderExtensions
    {
        public static ModelBuilder Seed<T>(this ModelBuilder
            modelBuilder, string file) where T : class
        {
        using (var reader = new StreamReader(file))
        {
            var json = reader.ReadToEnd();
            var data = JsonConvert.DeserializeObject<T[]>(json);
            modelBuilder.Entity<T>().HasData(data);
        }

        return modelBuilder;
        }
    }
}
```

EF Core 2.1 has introduced a new way to perform data seeding in our database by exposing the `HasData<T>` method. The preceding code allows us to read a JSON file and serialize it into entities referred by `modelBuilder`. This approach provides a way to seed our mock database using the data written in the JSON files.

Finally, we can proceed by creating a new context in the `Catalog.Infrastructure.Tests` project named `TestCatalogContext`:

```
using Microsoft.EntityFrameworkCore;
using Catalog.Domain.Entities;
using Catalog.Infrastructure.Tests.Extensions;

namespace Catalog.Infrastructure.Tests
{
    public class TestCatalogContext : CatalogContext
    {
        public TestCatalogContext(DbContextOptions<CatalogContext> options)
    : base(options)
        {
        }
```

```
protected override void OnModelCreating(ModelBuilder
    modelBuilder)
{
    base.OnModelCreating(modelBuilder);
    modelBuilder.Seed<Artist>("./Data/artist.json");
    modelBuilder.Seed<Genre>("./Data/genre.json");
    modelBuilder.Seed<Item>("./Data/item.json");
}
    }
}
```

Here, `TestCatalogContext` class extends the `CatalogContext` class present in the `Catalog.Infrastructure` project, and overrides the `OnModelCreating` method to call the `Seed<T>` extension method on our entities. Consequently, when a consumer initializes the database using `TestCatalogContext`, it will have all the prepopulated data written in the JSON.

Note here that the `TestCatalogContext` extends the `DbContextOptions<CatalogContext>` option in the constructor in order to initialize the `CatalogContext` base class.

Initializing the testing class

Let's proceed by creating a new testing class in our `Catalog.Infrastructure.Tests` project called `ItemRepositoryTests`:

```
using Xunit;

namespace Catalog.Infrastructure.Tests
{
    public class ItemRepositoryTests
    {
        [Fact]
        public void should_get_data()
        {
            Assert.True(true);
        }
    }
}
```

The Xunit framework identifies test classes using the Fact attribute. Every class that contains a method that has the Fact attribute or, as we'll see later in this section, the Theory attribute, will be considered as a test by the unit test runner.

Let's continue by adding our first test method. This checks the GetAsync method of the ItemRepository class:

```
using System.Threading.Tasks;
using Microsoft.EntityFrameworkCore;
using Shouldly;
using Catalog.Infrastructure.Repositories;
using Xunit;

namespace Catalog.Infrastructure.Tests
{
    public class ItemRepositoryTests
    {
        [Fact]
        public async Task should_get_data()
        {
            var options = new DbContextOptionsBuilder<CatalogContext>()
                .UseInMemoryDatabase(databaseName: "should_get_data")
                .Options;

            await using var context = new TestCatalogContext(options);
            context.Database.EnsureCreated();
            var sut = new ItemRepository(context);
            var result = await sut.GetAsync();

            result.ShouldNotBeNull();
        }
    }
}
```

This code initializes a new Options object using DbContextOptionsBuilder<T>, which is of the CatalogContext type. It also uses the UseInMemoryDatabase extension method to create a new in-memory database instance with a given name. Since DbContext is extended by the CatalogContext class, which implements the IAsyncDisposable type, it is possible to use the await using var keywords. This approach avoids any type of nesting and provides a cleaner way of reading code, by avoiding the any use of nesting:

```
...
    using (var context = new TestCatalogContext(options))
    {
        context.Database.EnsureCreated();
        var sut = new ItemRepository(context);
```

```
        var result = await sut.GetAsync();

        result.ShouldNotBeNull();
    }
...
```

To build the code, it is necessary to add the following package to the `Catalog.Infrastructure.Tests` project:

dotnet add package Microsoft.EntityFrameworkCore.InMemory

 The `UseInMemoryDatabase` extension method is useful for configuring a new in-memory database instance. It is important to note that it is not designed to be a relational database. Furthermore, it doesn't perform any database integrity checks or constraint checks. For more appropriate testing, we should use the in-memory version of SQLite. You can find more information about the SQLite provider in the following documentation: https://docs.microsoft.com/en-us/ef/core/miscellaneous/testing/sqlite.

After the creation of a new `Options` object, the `should_get_data` method creates a new instance of `TestCatalogContext`, and calls the `EnsureCreated()` method, which ensures that the context exists in the in-memory database. The `EnsureCreate` method also implicitly calls the `OnModelCreating` method. After that, the test initializes a new `ItemRepository` by using the context and executes the `GetAsync` method. Finally, it checks the result using `result.ShouldNotBeNull()`.

 Note that all test examples in this book use `Shouldly` as an assertion framework. `Shouldly` focuses on giving error messages that are concise and straightforward when an assertion fails. It is possible to avoid the use of `Shouldly` by using the default assertion framework built-in to .NET Core. You can find more information about `Shouldly` from the following link: https://github.com/shouldly/shouldly. It is possible to add the `Shouldly` package executing the following CLI instruction in the `Catalog.Infrastructure.Tests` project: `dotnet add package Shouldly`.

Let's continue by implementing tests for all the methods implemented in the `ItemRepository` class:

```
using System;
using System.Threading.Tasks;
using Microsoft.EntityFrameworkCore;
using Shouldly;
```

```
using Catalog.Infrastructure.Repositories;
using Xunit;

namespace Catalog.Infrastructure.Tests
{
    public class ItemRepositoryTests
    {
        [Fact]
        public async Task should_get_data()
        {
            var options = new DbContextOptionsBuilder<CatalogContext>()
                .UseInMemoryDatabase("should_get_data")
                .Options;

            await using var context = new TestCatalogContext(options);
            context.Database.EnsureCreated();

            var sut = new ItemRepository(context);
            var result = await sut.GetAsync();

            result.ShouldNotBeNull();
        }

        [Fact]
        public async Task should_returns_null_with_id_not_present()
        {
            var options = new DbContextOptionsBuilder<CatalogContext>()
                .UseInMemoryDatabase(databaseName:
                    "should_returns_null_with_id_not_present")
                .Options;

            await using var context = new TestCatalogContext(options);
            context.Database.EnsureCreated();

            var sut = new ItemRepository(context);
            var result = await sut.GetAsync(Guid.NewGuid());

            result.ShouldBeNull();
        }

        [Theory]
        [InlineData("b5b05534-9263-448c-a69e-0bbd8b3eb90e")]
        public async Task should_return_record_by_id(string guid)
        {
            var options = new DbContextOptionsBuilder<CatalogContext>()
                .UseInMemoryDatabase(databaseName:
                    "should_return_record_by_id")
                .Options;
```

```
        await using var context = new TestCatalogContext(options);
        context.Database.EnsureCreated();

        var sut = new ItemRepository(context);
        var result = await sut.GetAsync(new Guid(guid));

        result.Id.ShouldBe(new Guid(guid));
    }
...
```

The preceding snippet defines tests that cover the `GetAsync` methods. The first method, `should_get_data`, tests the `GetAsync()` overload with no parameters, while the second method tests the `GetAsync(guid id)` overload. In both cases, we use `InMemoryDatabase` to emulate the underlying data source. In the same `ItemRepositoryTests` class, it is also possible to define test cases related to create/update actions:

```
...
        [Fact]
        public async Task should_add_new_item()
        {
            var testItem = new Item
            {
                Name = "Test album",
                Description = "Description",
                LabelName = "Label name",
                Price = new Price { Amount = 13, Currency = "EUR" },
                PictureUri = "https://mycdn.com/pictures/32423423",
                ReleaseDate = DateTimeOffset.Now,
                AvailableStock = 6,
                GenreId = new Guid("c04f05c0-f6ad-44d1-a400-3375bfb5dfd6"),
                ArtistId = new Guid("f08a333d-30db-4dd1-b8ba-3b0473c7cdab")
            };
            var options = new DbContextOptionsBuilder<CatalogContext>()
                .UseInMemoryDatabase("should_add_new_items")
                .Options;

            await using var context = new TestCatalogContext(options);
            context.Database.EnsureCreated();

            var sut = new ItemRepository(context);

            sut.Add(testItem);
            await sut.UnitOfWork.SaveEntitiesAsync();

            context.Items
                .FirstOrDefault(_ => _.Id == testItem.Id)
```

```
                    .ShouldNotBeNull();
    }

    [Fact]
    public async Task should_update_item()
    {
        var testItem = new Item
        {
            Id = new Guid("b5b05534-9263-448c-a69e-0bbd8b3eb90e"),
            Name = "Test album",
            Description = "Description updated",
            LabelName = "Label name",
            Price = new Price { Amount = 50, Currency = "EUR" },
            PictureUri = "https://mycdn.com/pictures/32423423",
            ReleaseDate = DateTimeOffset.Now,
            AvailableStock = 6,
            GenreId = new Guid("c04f05c0-f6ad-44d1-a400-3375bfb5dfd6"),
            ArtistId = new Guid("f08a333d-30db-4dd1-b8ba-3b0473c7cdab")
        };

        var options = new DbContextOptionsBuilder<CatalogContext>()
            .UseInMemoryDatabase("should_update_item")
            .Options;

        await using var context = new TestCatalogContext(options);
        context.Database.EnsureCreated();

        var sut = new ItemRepository(context);
        sut.Update(testItem);

        await sut.UnitOfWork.SaveEntitiesAsync();

        context.Items
            .FirstOrDefault(x => x.Id == testItem.Id)
            ?.Description.ShouldBe("Description updated");
    }
...
}
```

Finally, the `ItemRepositoryTests` class provides test coverage for all CRUD methods implemented by the `ItemRepository` class. The `should_get_data`, `should_returns_null_with_id_not_present`, and `should_return_record_by_id` methods execute the `GetAsync` method and check whether the result is what we expect. The `should_add_new_item` and `should_update_item` test cases provide test coverage for the `ItemRepository.Add` and `ItemRepository.Update` methods. Both the tests initialize a new record of type `Item` and they update the database through the methods exposed by the `ItemRepository` type.

As a result, we can run our tests by executing the following command in the `Catalog.Infrastructure.Tests` folder:

```
dotnet test
```

The preceding command executes tests implemented in the project. Therefore, the result will be a report with a list of tests that have succeeded. As an alternative, we can also choose to run tests using the tests runner provided by the IDE. Now that we have completed the data access part using EF Core combined with the code-first approach, we can also take a quick look at Dapper, and how it can be useful by providing a more lighter way to access data.

Implementing a data access layer using Dapper

Another standard tool that provides a way to implement a data access layer is Dapper. We have already taken an overview of Dapper, but this section will cover in more detail how to deal with this package and how to use it to implement a data access layer. The following process will be more SQL-heavy. We will also demonstrate how you can deal with some stored CRUD procedures.

 Note that EF Core also provides a way to query data sources by using stored procedures. Moreover, it exposes methods such as `DbSet<TEntity>.FromSql()` or `DbContext.Database.ExecuteSqlCommand()`. So, why use Dapper? As mentioned previously, Dapper is a micro-ORM that is simple and faster than EF Core. EF is more of a multipurpose ORM, and it adds a discrete overhead on each operation performed.

Before starting, let's create another project inside the `src` folder called
`Catalog.InfrastructureSP`, by launching the following command inside the `src` folder:

```
dotnet new classlib -n Catalog.InfrastructureSP
```

After creating the `Catalog.InfrastructureSP` project, we need to add it to our solution:

```
dotnet sln ../Catalog.API.sln add Catalog.InfrastructureSP
```

The preceding command includes the `Catalog.InfrastructureSP` project in the
solution. Once we have set up our new project containing all the alternative
implementation of the data access layer, we can proceed by implementing the core part of
the project using a SQL-first approach.

Creating stored CRUD procedures

In the current example, we use some stored procedures that implement create, read, and
update operations. In this book, we will not go into much detail about the SQL server
programming model, but it is essential to understand that the code-first approach is not the
only way to proceed. Stored procedures are an excellent way to implement interactions
between services and a database.

 Stored procedures are the best way to interact with databases.
Developers can proceed by executing complex queries and calling the
procedure name. This modular approach provides some benefits in terms
of permission configuration, faster network traffic, and faster execution.

First of all, let's create stored procedures to read data:

```
create procedure [catalog].[GetAllItems]
as
begin
    select [Id]
        [Name]
        , [Description]
        , [LabelName]
        , [Price]
        , [PictureUri]
        , [ReleaseDate]
        , [Format]
        , [AvailableStock]
        , [GenreId]
        , [ArtistId]
    from [catalog].[Items]
end
```

The first snippet of code defines the `GetAllItems` stored procedure. It returns the whole collection of items. For demonstration purposes, the procedure doesn't include any performance optimization. When we perform a `select` query on a large table, with a lot of records, it is necessary, at least, to insert a top statement to avoid long-running queries and timeout problems. Moreover, in a real-world application, it is uncommon to see a query without a specific filter. Let's continue by creating the `GetItemById` procedure:

```
create procedure [catalog].[GetItemById]
    @Id uniqueidentifier
as
begin
    select [Id]
        [Name]
      ,[Description]
      ,[LabelName]
      ,[Price]
      ,[PictureUri]
      ,[ReleaseDate]
      ,[Format]
      ,[AvailableStock]
      ,[GenreId]
      ,[ArtistId]
    from [catalog].[Items]
    where Id = @Id
end
```

These two procedures are quite simple. The first one selects all the records from the `catalog. Item` table. The second one accepts an `Id` as the parameter and allows us to retrieve just the corresponding record.

The next step is to implement operations to do with creating and updating a record. Both implementations are quite simple – the `InsertItem` and `UpdateItem` stored procedures wrap `insert` and `update` SQL statements:

```
create procedure [catalog].[InsertItem] (
 @Id uniqueidentifier,
 @Name nvarchar(max),
 @Description nvarchar(1000),
 @LabelName nvarchar(max) NULL,
 @Price nvarchar(max) NULL,
 @PictureUri nvarchar(max) NULL,
 @ReleaseDate datetimeoffset(7),
 @Format nvarchar(max) ,
 @AvailableStock int,
 @GenreId uniqueidentifier,
 @ArtistId uniqueidentifier
```

```
)
as
begin
  insert into  [catalog].[Items]  (Id, Name,
Description,LabelName,Price,PictureUri, ReleaseDate,
  Format,AvailableStock, GenreId,ArtistId)
  output inserted.*
  values    (@Id,
            @Name,
            @Description,
            @LabelName,
            @Price,
            @PictureUri,
            @ReleaseDate,
            @Format,
            @AvailableStock,
            @GenreId,
            @ArtistId)
end
```

The InsertItem stored procedure executes a simple insert statement on the database by accepting data as parameters of the stored procedure. Let's proceed by defining the UpdateItem stored procedure:

```
create procedure [catalog].[UpdateItem] (
@Id uniqueidentifier,
@Name nvarchar(max),
@Description nvarchar(1000),
@LabelName nvarchar(max) NULL,
@Price nvarchar(max),
@PictureUri nvarchar(max) NULL,
@ReleaseDate datetimeoffset(7) NULL,
@Format nvarchar(max) ,
@AvailableStock int,
@GenreId uniqueidentifier,
@ArtistId uniqueidentifier
)
as
begin
  update [catalog].[Items]
  set Name = @Name,
      Description = @Description,
      LabelName = @LabelName,
      Price = @Price,
      PictureUri = @PictureUri,
      ReleaseDate = @ReleaseDate,
      Format = @Format,
      AvailableStock = @AvailableStock,
```

```
        GenreId = @GenreId,
        ArtistId = @ArtistId
    output inserted.*
    where Id = @Id
end
```

Note that both operations use the `output` statement to retrieve the inserted, or updated, record as a result of the execution. In that way, we can retrieve the updated record from our repository pattern without extra effort.

> Microsoft SQL Server provides a way to return inserted or deleted data using the *output* operator. It returns information from, or expressions based on, each row affected by an INSERT, UPDATE, DELETE, or MERGE statement.

Finally, to get these scripts working, it is necessary to execute them in our database. I suggest using the previously mentioned SQL Operations Studio tool or another SQL client to run these scripts in the `Catalog` database.

Implementing the IItemRepository interface

In *Implementing the data access layer using EF Core* section, we used two different interfaces to get the jobs done: `IItemRepository`, which contains all the CRUD operations, and `IUnitOfWork`, which covers the unit of work pattern. For each CRUD operation, we need to call the `IUnitOfWork` interface to save our changes in the database. On the other hand, the application of Dapper as a micro-ORM doesn't need to provide a unit of work interface because ORM executes queries directly on the database using the stored procedures. For that reason, we don't need to implement the `IRepository` interface anymore and, consequently, we will not implement the `IUnitOfWork` interface either.

So, as a first step, we should remove the `IRepository` interface implementation from our `IItemRepository` interface. Also, in this case, we can see the real power of dependency inversion: `Catalog.Domain` does not depend on `Catalog.Infrastructure`. It can also change the contract and requirements, and it forces `Catalog.Infrastructure` to alter its behavior:

```
using System;
using System.Collections.Generic;
using System.Threading.Tasks;
using Catalog.Domain.Infrastructure.Entities;

namespace Catalog.Domain.Infrastructure.Repositories
{
```

```
public interface IItemsRepository
{
    Task<IEnumerable<Item>> GetAsync();
    Task<Item> GetAsync(Guid id);
    Item Add(Item order);
    Item Update(Item item);
    Item Delete(Item item);
}
}
```

The next step is to add Dapper to our `Catalog.InfrastructureSP` project by executing the following command:

dotnet add package Dapper

Let's proceed by implementing the `IItemRepository` interface using the `ItemRepository` class in the `Catalog.InfrastructureSP` project:

```
using System;
using System.Collections.Generic;
using System.Data;
using System.Data.SqlClient;
using System.Threading.Tasks;
using Dapper;
using Catalog.Domain.Entities;
using Catalog.Domain.Infrastructure.Repositories;

namespace Catalog.InfrastructureSP
{
    public class ItemRepository : IItemRepository
    {
        private readonly SqlConnection _sqlConnection;

        public ItemRepository(string connectionString)
        {

            _sqlConnection = new SqlConnection(connectionString);
        }

        public async Task<IEnumerable<Item>> GetAsync()
        {
            var result = await _sqlConnection.QueryAsync<Item>
                ("GetAllItems",  commandType:
                CommandType.StoredProcedure);
            return result.AsList();
        }

        public async Task<Item> GetAsync(Guid id)
```

```
    {
        return await _sqlConnection.ExecuteScalarAsync<Item>
            ("GetAllItems", new {Id = id.ToString()}, commandType:
            CommandType.StoredProcedure);
    }

    public Item Add(Item order)
    {
        var result = _sqlConnection.ExecuteScalar<Item>
        ("InsertItem", order, commandType:CommandType.StoredProcedure);
        return result;
    }

    public Item Update(Item item)
    {
        var result = _sqlConnection.ExecuteScalar<Item>
            ("UpdateItem", item, commandType:
            CommandType.StoredProcedure);
        return result;
    }

    public Item Delete(Item item)
    {
        throw new NotImplementedException();
    }
    }
}
```

To initialize our concrete class, it is necessary to pass `connectionString` to the SQL database in the constructor of the `ItemRepository` class.

As you can see, the Dapper approach is entirely different from EF Core. It doesn't add any particular overhead to our data source; it merely executes the aforementioned stored procedures by filling the requested parameters.

Summary

This chapter described you how to build a data access layer using EF Core and Dapper. It also showed you how to build unit tests using the in-memory database, and how to execute migrations with EF Core. I want to reiterate that the choice between EF Core and Dapper depends on different parameters: what kind of service we are building, the skills of our team members, and the type of infrastructure we're using.

The topics covered in this chapter provide the necessary knowledge to access data sources in .NET Core, using a code-first approach and also the stored-procedure approach. The chapter covered the use of technologies such as EF Core and Dapper. Additionally, it showed you how to test the data access layer using the in-memory approach.

In the next chapter, we will demonstrate how to implement handlers and the logic of our services.

Implementing the Domain Logic 9

This chapter focuses on the logic layer of the catalog web service. As previously discussed, the logic will be encapsulated in the `Catalog.Domain` project. The chapter shows how to implement the application logic using the service classes approach. The aim of these classes is to perform the mapping logic between the requests and the effective entities used on the data source layer and to provide all the additional logic needed by our application. Moreover, we will also see how to test the implemented code in order to verify the behaviors.

This chapter will cover the following topics:

- How to implement the service classes for our application
- How to implement request DTOs and the related validation system
- How to apply tests to verify the implemented logic

 The code in the following chapter is available in the following GitHub repository: `https://github.com/PacktPublishing/Hands-On-RESTful-Web-Services-with-ASP.NET-Core-3`.

Implementing service classes

Let's proceed with the concrete part of the chapter by implementing the service classes. This layer of abstraction will define the methods that query the data layer, including the `IItemRepository` interface, and map the resulting data.

As mentioned previously, our service implementation will use DTO classes in order to pass the data through the stack. First of all, let's define the request classes needed by our service. To do that, we can start by creating a new `Requests/Item` folder structure in the `Catalog.Domain` project, and by adding a new `AddItemRequest.cs` file in the folder:

```
using System;
using Catalog.Domain.Entities;

namespace Catalog.Domain.Requests.Item
{
    public class AddItemRequest
    {
        public string Name { get; set; }
        public string Description { get; set; }
        public string LabelName { get; set; }
        public Price Price { get; set; }
        public string PictureUri { get; set; }
        public DateTimeOffset ReleaseDate { get; set; }
        public string Format { get; set; }
        public int AvailableStock { get; set; }
        public Guid GenreId { get; set; }
        public Guid ArtistId { get; set; }
    }
}
```

The preceding code defines the add item request. The class is very similar to the `Item` entity class, except that the `Id` field, the `Artist` field, and the `Genre` field are not present. Furthermore, the `Id` field will be generated by the EF Core implementation, and the `Artist` and `Genre` fields are handled by the ORM in order to represent the relationship between the entities.

In the same way, we can proceed by defining the `EditItemRequest` class in the same folder:

```
using System;
using Catalog.Domain.Entities;

namespace Catalog.Domain.Requests.Item
{
    public class EditItemRequest
```

```
    {
        public Guid Id { get; set; }
        public string Name { get; set; }
        public string Description { get; set; }
        public string LabelName { get; set; }
        public Price Price { get; set; }
        public string PictureUri { get; set; }
        public DateTimeOffset ReleaseDate { get; set; }
        public string Format { get; set; }
        public int AvailableStock { get; set; }
        public Guid GenreId { get; set; }
        public Guid ArtistId { get; set; }
    }
}
```

Also in the preceding snippet, the class contains the same fields used by the Item entity, except for the Artist and Genre fields, for the same reason described earlier. As you can understand from the class name, it represents the update item operation. The same approach can be taken for the get item operation shown as follows:

```
using System;

namespace Catalog.Domain.Requests.Item
{
    public class GetItemRequest
    {
        public Guid Id { get; set; }
    }
}
```

It may seem a little bit redundant, defining a request class for a single field. Despite that, we should consider that the HTTP requests received by our service may vary over time. Therefore, this approach guarantees us being able to evolve our requests without adding tons of parameters to the methods of the service class. On top of that, representing our incoming requests as classes provides an easy way to version the different request types evolving over time.

Let's continue by also defining the response classes used by our service classes. Also, in the case of the response classes, it is essential to understand that this approach guarantees us a way to avoid exposing all the fields to the client of our web service. As a first step, we need to define a new Responses folder in the Catalog.Domain project, and create the following classes:

```
// /Responses/Item/PriceResponse.cs
namespace Catalog.Domain.Responses
{
```

```
        public class PriceResponse
        {
            public decimal Amount { get; set; }
            public string Currency { get; set; }
        }
    }


// /Response/Item/ArtistResponse.cs
using System;

namespace Catalog.Domain.Responses
{
    public class ArtistResponse
    {
        public Guid ArtistId { get; set; }
        public string ArtistName { get; set; }
    }
}


// /Response/Item/GenreResponse.cs
using System;

namespace Catalog.Domain.Responses
{
    public class GenreResponse
    {
        public Guid GenreId { get; set; }
        public string GenreDescription { get; set; }
    }
}
```

For brevity, I've defined the implementation of the `PriceResponse`, `GenreResponse`, and `ArtistResponse` classes in a unique snippet of code. Those classes define the field used by the same entity classes we use on the database side. On top of that, we will also define an `ItemReposonse` class, which represents the response of our service:

```
using System;

namespace Catalog.Domain.Responses
{
    public class ItemResponse
    {
        public Guid Id { get; set; }
        public string Name { get; set; }
        public string Description { get; set; }
        public string LabelName { get; set; }
        public PriceResponse Price { get; set; }
        public string PictureUri { get; set; }
```

```
        public DateTimeOffset ReleaseDate { get; set; }
        public string Format { get; set; }
        public int AvailableStock { get; set; }
        public Guid GenreId { get; set; }
        public GenreResponse Genre { get; set; }
        public Guid ArtistId { get; set; }
        public ArtistResponse Artist { get; set; }
    }
}
```

The `ItemResponse` class refers to the other response classes in order to avoid a mismatch between the response data contained in the related entities. Furthermore, the `IItemRepository` implementation will load all the data of the related entities using the `Include` extension method we looked at in the previous chapter, and, as we will see later, the data will be mapped into the response types.

The service class interface

Since we have defined all the requests and response types needed by our service, we are now able to proceed by defining the `IItemService` interface and its implementation. As a first step, we can create a new `Services` folder in the `Catalog.Domain` project and proceed by defining the following `IItemService` interface:

```
using System.Collections.Generic;
using System.Threading.Tasks;
using Catalog.Domain.Requests.Item;
using Catalog.Domain.Responses;

namespace Catalog.Domain.Services
{
    public interface IItemService
    {
        Task<IEnumerable<ItemResponse>> GetItemsAsync();
        Task<ItemResponse> GetItemAsync(GetItemRequest request);
        Task<ItemResponse> AddItemAsync(AddItemRequest request);
        Task<ItemResponse> EditItemAsync(EditItemRequest request);
        Task<ItemResponse> DeleteItemAsync(DeleteItemRequest request);
    }
}
```

The preceding definition exposes the methods needed by our application. First of all, we should notice that all the functions return a `Task<T>` generic type. We can also see that all the methods end with the `Async` prefix, which suggests that the implementation will be asynchronous.

Implementing the mapping layer

This subsection and the following one describe the implementation of two mapping approaches we can use in our application: the *manual approach* and the *reflection approach*.

The *manual approach* involves the definition and implementation of our own mapper classes:

```
using Catalog.Domain.Entities;
using Catalog.Domain.Requests.Item;
using Catalog.Domain.Responses;

namespace Catalog.Domain.Mappers
{
    public interface IItemMapper
    {
        Item Map(AddItemRequest request);
        Item Map(EditItemRequest request);
        ItemResponse Map(Item item);
    }
}
```

The preceding code defines an `IItemMapper` interface, which provides two methods to map `AddItemRequest` and `EditItemRequest` in the `Item` type. In addition, it also defines the mapping method signature to convert an `Item` type into an `ItemResponse` instance. This strategy can be implemented with the following `ItemMapper` class:

```
using Catalog.Domain.Entities;
using Catalog.Domain.Requests.Item;

namespace Catalog.Domain.Mappers
{
    public class ItemMapper : IItemMapper
    {
        public Item Map(AddItemRequest request)
        {
            if (request == null) return null;

            var item = new Item
            {
```

```
            Name = request.Name,
            Description = request.Description,
            LabelName = request.LabelName,
            PictureUri = request.PictureUri,
            ReleaseDate = request.ReleaseDate,
            Format = request.Format,
            AvailableStock = request.AvailableStock,
            GenreId = request.GenreId,
            ArtistId = request.ArtistId,
        };

        if (request.Price != null)
        {
            item.Price = new Price { Currency = request.Price.Currency,
             Amount = request.Price.Amount };
        }

        return item;
    }

    public Item Map(EditItemRequest request)
    {
        if (request == null) return null;

        var item = new Item
        {
            Id = request.Id,
            Name = request.Name,
            ...
            Format = request.Format,
            AvailableStock = request.AvailableStock,
            GenreId = request.GenreId,
            ArtistId = request.ArtistId,
        };

        if (request.Price != null)
        {
            item.Price = new Price { Currency = request.Price.Currency,
             Amount = request.Price.Amount };
        }

        return item;
    }
  }
}
```

Please notice that, for brevity, I've omitted all the fields of the entity defined in the mapping, you can find the full mapper class file in the following repository `https://github.com/PacktPublishing/Hands-On-RESTful-Web-Services-with-ASP.NET-Core-3/tree/master/Chapter09/Catalog`. Both the `IItemMapper` interface and the `ItemMapper` class are located in a `Mappers` folder in the `Catalog.Domain` project. The `ItemMapper` implementation requires a bit of overhead in terms of development, but it performs exactly what you need without any runtime costs, such as reflection. On top of that, the logic is encapsulated in separate classes. The same approach can be applied to the `ItemResponse` mapping – in this case, we will also need to create some isolated mappers for the `Artist` and the `Genre` entities:

```
using Catalog.Domain.Entities;
using Catalog.Domain.Responses;

namespace Catalog.Domain.Mappers
{
    public interface IArtistMapper
    {
        ArtistResponse Map(Artist artist);
    }

    public class ArtistMapper : IArtistMapper
    {
        public ArtistResponse Map(Artist artist)
        {
            if (artist == null) return null;

            return new ArtistResponse
            {
                ArtistId = artist.ArtistId,
                ArtistName = artist.ArtistName
            };
        }
    }
}
```

For brevity reasons, I've included the interface and the concrete implementation in a unique snippet of code. `IArtistMapper` exposes a method called `Map`, which initializes a new `ArtistResponse` given an `Artist` entity class. This approach will be the same for the `Genre` entity:

```
using Catalog.Domain.Entities;
using Catalog.Domain.Responses;

namespace Catalog.Domain.Mappers
{
```

```
public interface IGenreMapper
{
    GenreResponse Map(Genre genre);
}
public class GenreMapper : IGenreMapper
{
    public GenreResponse Map(Genre genre)
    {
        if (genre == null) return null;

        return new GenreResponse
          {
              GenreId = genre.GenreId,
              GenreDescription = genre.GenreDescription
          };
    }
}
}
```

Also, in this case, we define `Genre` as `GenreResponse` mapping. Both these mapping classes can be used independently or referred by other mappers. Once we have implemented the `Artist` and `Genre` mapping logic, we can refer them into `IItemMapper` in order to define the implementation of the `ItemReponse Map(Item item)` mapping method:

```
using Catalog.Domain.Entities;
using Catalog.Domain.Responses;

namespace Catalog.Domain.Mappers
{
    public class ItemMapper : IItemMapper
    {
        private readonly IArtistMapper _artistMapper;
        private readonly IGenreMapper _genreMapper;

        public ItemMapper(IArtistMapper artistMapper, IGenreMapper
            genreMapper)
        {
            _artistMapper = artistMapper;
            _genreMapper = genreMapper;
        }
        ...

        public ItemResponse Map(Item item)
          {
              if (request == null) return null;
              var response = new ItemResponse
```

```
        {
            Id = request.Id,
            Name = request.Name,
            ...
            GenreId = request.GenreId,
            Genre = _genreMapper.Map(request.Genre),
            ArtistId = request.ArtistId,
            Artist = _artistMapper.Map(request.Artist),
        };

        if (request.Price != null)
        {
            response.Price = new PriceResponse { Currency =
              request.Price.Currency, Amount = request.Price.Amount };
        }

        return response;
    }
  }
}
```

We have changed the `ItemMapper` implementation class and we have combined the dependencies with the `IArtistMapper` and `IGenreMapper` interfaces. Furthermore, we can use the `Map` method we've just defined to create `ItemResponse` instances based on the `Item` entities. You may have noticed that I haven't implemented the mapping class for `PriceResponse`. This is because an entity such as `Price` is unlikely to change. Another crucial part to notice is that we are missing the initialization of the dependency injection between the mapper interfaces and their implementation; this part will be covered later in this chapter.

Finally, I want to specify that this is not the only way to implement the mapping layer in our application. In fact, there are also other patterns, for example, using extension methods. Let's take as an example, `Artist` to `ArtistResponse` mapping:

```
public static class MappingExtensions
{
    public static ArtistResponse MapToResponse(this Artist artist)
    {
        return new ArtistResponse
        {
            ArtistId = artist.ArtistId,
            ArtistName = artist.ArtistName
        };
    }
}
```

The preceding code defines a new `MappingExtensions` static class, which can be used as a container for all the extension methods we need for the mapping logic. Furthermore, it is possible to define a `MapToResponse` extension method that can be applied to the `Artist` entity in the following way:

```
ArtistResponse artistResponse = artistEntity.MapToResponse();
```

The extension methods approach can be applied to all the entities of the domain model. Although it seems a lot more immediate, it doesn't highlight the dependency between the services classes and the mapping logic. Therefore, I prefer implementing mapping through the use of separate classes because it provides a better way to understand the dependency flow of the application.

Mapping logic using Automapper

An alternative way is to implement the mapping using the `Automapper` NuGet package. As mentioned in `Chapter 5`, *Web Service Stack in ASP.NET Core*, this approach uses the reflection system provided by .NET in order to match and to map the fields of our classes. It is possible to add the `Automapper` package to the `Catalog.Domain` project using the following CLI instruction:

```
dotnet add package Automapper
```

Automapper uses a profile-based structure in order to define the mapping behaviors of our classes. Let's proceed by defining a new `CatalogProfile` class in the `Mappers` folder:

```
using AutoMapper;
using Catalog.Domain.Entities;
using Catalog.Domain.Requests.Item;
using Catalog.Domain.Responses.Item;

namespace Catalog.Domain.Mapper
{
    public class CatalogProfile : Profile
    {
        public CatalogProfile()
        {
            CreateMap<ItemResponse, Item>().ReverseMap();
            CreateMap<GenreResponse, Genre>().ReverseMap();
            CreateMap<ArtistResponse, Artist>().ReverseMap();
            CreateMap<Price, PriceResponse>().ReverseMap();
            CreateMap<AddItemRequest, Item>().ReverseMap();
            CreateMap<EditItemRequest, Item>().ReverseMap();
        }
```

```
    }
  }
```

The preceding profile will be used by the dependency injection engine to define the lists of mapping behaviors. The `CreateMap` method provided by the `Profile` base class matches two generic types: `TSource` and `TDestination`. It will be possible to also perform the reverse process by chaining the `ReverseMap()` extension method. This can be applied for every request and response type we define in the application. In order to use the mapping logic in our methods, it is necessary to inject the `IMapper` type into the target class and execute the `Map` method in the following way:

```
_mapper.Map<ItemResponse>(new Item());
```

It is important to notice that the `Map` method will throw a runtime exception in the following cases:

- The type of the source and the destination of the mapping don't correspond
- The corresponding source and destination mapping is not explicitly defined in a profile
- There are some unmapped members in the entities (this prevents accidental `null` fields in the destination of the mapping)

Finally, Automapper also requires initialization using the dependency injection of .NET Core. We will see how to add `Automapper` in the DI engine later in this chapter.

The service class implementation

Once the mapper layer is completed, we can proceed by implementing the service layer. Let's start by defining the `ItemService.cs` file in the `Services` folder of the `Catalog.Domain` project. The following code describes the implementation of the constructor method and the reading operations:

```
using System;
using System.Collections.Generic;
using System.Linq;
using System.Threading;
using System.Threading.Tasks;
using Catalog.Domain.Mappers;
using Catalog.Domain.Repositories;
using Catalog.Domain.Requests.Item;
using Catalog.Domain.Responses;

namespace Catalog.Domain.Services
```

```
{
    public class ItemService : IItemService
    {
        private readonly IItemRepository _itemRepository;
        private readonly IItemMapper _itemMapper;

        public ItemService(IItemRepository itemRepository,
         IItemMapper itemMapper)
        {
            _itemRepository = itemRepository;
            _itemMapper = itemMapper;
        }

        public async Task<IEnumerable<ItemResponse>> GetItemsAsync()
        {
            var result = await _itemRepository.GetAsync();

            return result.Select(x => _itemMapper.Map(x));
        }

        public async Task<ItemResponse> GetItemAsync(GetItemRequest
         request)
        {
            if (request?.Id == null) throw new ArgumentNullException();

            var entity = await _itemRepository.GetAsync(request.Id);

            return _itemMapper.Map(entity);
        }
    }
}
```

First of all, we can see that the class refers to both the IItemRepository and the IItemMapper interfaces, which are injected using the constructor injection technique. The snippet also describes the implementation of the GetItemsAsync and GetItemAsync functions. Both methods use the IItemRepository interface to retrieve data from the data source, and the IItemMapper interface to perform the mapping between the Item entity and ItemResponse. The same approach can be taken by the writing operations, which are implemented with the following:

```
namespace Catalog.Domain.Services
{
    public class ItemService : IItemService
    {
        ...

        public async Task<ItemResponse> AddItemAsync(AddItemRequest
```

```
   request)
{
    var item = _itemMapper.Map(request);
    var result = _itemRepository.Add(item);

    await _itemRepository.UnitOfWork.SaveChangesAsync();

    return _itemMapper.Map(result);
}

public async Task<ItemResponse> EditItemAsync(EditItemRequest
 request)
{
    var existingRecord = await
     _itemRepository.GetAsync(request.Id);

    if (existingRecord == null)
    {
        throw new ArgumentException($"Entity with {request.Id}
         is not present");
    }

    var entity = _itemMapper.Map(request);
    var result = _itemRepository.Update(entity);

    await _itemRepository.UnitOfWork.SaveChangesAsync();

    return _itemMapper.Map(result);
}
    }
}
```

Also, in the case of the writing operations, they use the IItemMapper instance to map the request's type with the Item entity type and to retrieve the ItemResponse type. In addition, they perform the operations by calling the IItemRepository instance, and subsequently, they call the SaveChangesAsync method to apply those changes to the database. Once we have implemented the service layer, we can proceed by testing the class and verifying the implementation.

Testing the service layer

This section covers the testing of the service layer part implemented previously. As we did in `Chapter 8`, *Building the Data Access Layer*, we need to set up a mock catalog context that provides the data necessary for testing the service classes. The `Catalog.Infrastructure` project already has its own implementation of the `TestCatalogContext` class and the `ModelBuilderExtensions` class. Furthermore, we can use the same two classes to implement the tests for the service layer. What we need is just a bit of refactoring and optimization on the `Catalog.Infrastructure` project.

Refactoring testing classes

After implementing the `ItemsRepositoryTests` type, in `Chapter 8`, *Building the Data Access Layer*, you might notice that we are using a recurring pattern in the `ItemRepositoryTests` class:

```
...
    var options = new DbContextOptionsBuilder<CatalogContext>()
            .UseInMemoryDatabase(databaseName: "should_get_data")
            .Options;

            await using var context = new TestCatalogContext(options);
            context.Database.EnsureCreated();

            var sut = new ItemRepository(context);

...
```

The preceding snippet has been replicated in every test method written up to now. It is possible to improve our test code by extracting the implementation in a different type. The `xunit` framework provides a way to share test contexts between test methods of the same test class by providing an interface called `IClassFixture`.

`IClassFixture` is a generic type that constitutes a single test context and shares it among all the test methods in the class. Hence, the `xunit` framework cleans up the fixture after all the tests in the class have completed. The `IClassFixture` interface we are going to implement will be used by both the `Catalog.Infrastructure.Tests` project and the `Catalog.Domain.Tests` project. Therefore, we can commonize the implementation in a unique `Catalog.Fixtures` project.

Let's proceed by creating the new project in the `tests` folder:

```
dotnet new xunit -n Catalog.Fixtures -f netcoreapp3.1

dotnet sln ../Catalog.API.sln add
./Catalog.Fixtures/Catalog.Fixtures.csproj
```

The preceding instructions create a new `Catalog.Fixtures` project and add it to the solution. After that, we can proceed by adding the dependencies:

```
dotnet add ./Catalog.Fixtures reference ../src/Catalog.Domain/

dotnet add ./Catalog.Fixtures reference ../src/Catalog.Infrastructure/
```

Finally, we can move all the classes previously implemented in the `Catalog.Infrastructure.Tests` project into the new `Catalog.Fixtures` project just created: `TestCatalogContext.cs`, `Extensions/ModelBuilderExtensions.cs`, and all `.json` files.

Let's continue by creating a new `CatalogContextFactory` class, which will be referred by the `IClassFixture` interface:

```
using System;
using Catalog.Domain.Mappers;
using Catalog.Infrastructure;
using Microsoft.EntityFrameworkCore;

namespace Catalog.Fixtures
{
    public class CatalogContextFactory
    {
        public readonly TestCatalogContext ContextInstance;
        public readonly IGenreMapper GenreMapper;
        public readonly IArtistMapper ArtistMapper;
        public readonly IItemMapper ItemMapper;

        public CatalogContextFactory()
        {
            var contextOptions = new
                DbContextOptionsBuilder<CatalogContext>()
                .UseInMemoryDatabase(Guid.NewGuid().ToString())
                .EnableSensitiveDataLogging()
                .Options;

            EnsureCreation(contextOptions);
            ContextInstance = new TestCatalogContext(contextOptions);
            GenreMapper = new GenreMapper();
```

```
            ArtistMapper = new ArtistMapper();
            ItemMapper = new ItemMapper(ArtistMapper, GenreMapper);
        }

        private void EnsureCreation(DbContextOptions<CatalogContext>
         contextOptions)
        {
            using var context = new TestCatalogContext(contextOptions);
            context.Database.EnsureCreated();
        }
    }
}
```

The CatalogContextFactory class defines a new instance of
TestCatalogContext using the previously assigned contextOptions object. It is
necessary to notice that we are
building ContextOptions using Guid.NewGuid().ToString() property as a database
name in order to provide a new, clean in-memory instance for each test class. In addition,
the class also initializes the three attributes of type IGenreMapper, IArtistMapper, and
IItemMapper which will be used by the service layer tests in order to perform the mapping
of the fields.

It is, therefore, possible to access the instance of the factory class in our tests by using the
following constructor injection approach:

```
using System;
using System.Linq;
using System.Threading.Tasks;
using Catalog.Domain.Entities;
using Catalog.Fixtures;
using Catalog.Infrastructure.Repositories;
using Newtonsoft.Json;
using Shouldly;
using Xunit;

namespace Catalog.Infrastructure.Tests
{
    public class ItemRepositoryTests :
        IClassFixture<CatalogContextFactory>
    {
        private readonly ItemRepository _sut;
        private readonly TestCatalogContext _context;

        public ItemRepositoryTests(CatalogContextFactory
catalogContextFactory)
        {
            _context = catalogContextFactory.ContextInstance;
```

```
        _sut = new ItemRepository(_context);
    }
...
```

The `IClassFixture` interface contains the reference to the factory class just created. The dependency will be resolved at runtime through the constructor of the test class. Note that the entire instance is shared between each unique test class. Therefore, each test method in the test class will share the same database snapshot with the other method.

Finally, we can refactor the `ItemRepositoryTests` class in order to use the new `CatalogContextFactory` implementation. For example, if we take as reference the `should_add_new_item` test method, we can proceed in the following way:

```csharp
public class ItemRepositoryTests : IClassFixture<CatalogContextFactory>
{
    private readonly ItemRepository _sut;
    private readonly TestCatalogContext _context;

    public ItemRepositoryTests(CatalogContextFactory
        catalogContextFactory)
    {
        _context = catalogContextFactory.ContextInstance;
        _sut = new ItemRepository(_context);
    }

    [Fact]
    public async Task should_add_new_item()
    {
        var testItem = new Item
        {
            Name = "Test album",
            Price = new Price { Amount = 13, Currency = "EUR" },
            GenreId = new Guid("c04f05c0-f6ad-44d1-a400-
                3375bfb5dfd6"),
            ArtistId = new Guid("f08a333d-30db-4dd1-b8ba-
                3b0473c7cdab"),
            ...
        };

        _sut.Add(testItem);
        await _sut.UnitOfWork.SaveEntitiesAsync();

        _context.Items
            .FirstOrDefault(item => item.Id == testItem.Id)
            .ShouldNotBeNull();
    }
}
```

The _sut class attribute is used to perform the actual operation we want to test. For example, in the test case above, we are verifying the Add method exposed by the ItemRepository class. The _context attribute is used to verify the result. This approach guarantees the reusability of our test code between the different test classes by providing the tests with better maintainability. All the data is provided by the CatalogContextFactory type, which uses the in-memory database technique provided by ASP.NET Core to store data in memory and simulates the data operation on a real database.

As we did for the ItemRepositoryTests class, we will also see how to use the CatalogContextFactory class in the service layer tests.

 The code in this section is available in the following GitHub repository: https://github.com/PacktPublishing/Hands-On-RESTful-Web-Services-with-ASP.NET-Core-3.

Implementing the ItemService tests

Let's continue by implementing the ItemService test part. As a first step, we should proceed by creating a new Catalog.Domain.Tests project in the tests folder using the following CLI instruction:

```
dotnet new xunit -n Catalog.Domain.Tests -f netcoreapp3.1
```

The preceding command creates a new Catalog.Domain.Tests project in the tests folder. Therefore, we can proceed by adding the new project to the solution using the following instruction:

```
dotnet sln ../Catalog.API.sln add Catalog.Domain.Tests
```

Additionally, the test project has some dependencies. Furthermore, we can proceed by adding the reference using the following command to the Catalog.Domain.Tests folder:

```
dotnet add reference ../Catalog.Fixtures
dotnet add reference ../../src/Catalog.Domain
dotnet add package Shouldly
```

After that, we create a new ItemServiceTests.cs file with the following implementation:

```
using System;
using System.Threading;
using System.Threading.Tasks;
```

```
using Catalog.Domain.Entities;
using Catalog.Domain.Mappers;
using Catalog.Domain.Requests.Item;
using Catalog.Domain.Services;
using Catalog.Fixtures;
using Catalog.Infrastructure.Repositories;
using Shouldly;
using Xunit;

namespace Catalog.Domain.Tests.Services
{
    public class ItemServiceTests :
        IClassFixture<CatalogContextFactory>
    {
        private readonly ItemRepository _itemRepository;
        private readonly IItemMapper _mapper;

        public ItemServiceTests(CatalogContextFactory
catalogContextFactory)
        {
            _itemRepository = new
ItemRepository(catalogContextFactory.ContextInstance);
            _mapper = catalogContextFactory.ItemMapper;
        }

        [Fact]
        public async Task getitems_should_return_right_data()
        {
            ItemService sut = new ItemService(_itemRepository, _mapper);

            var result = await sut.GetItemsAsync();
            result.ShouldNotBeNull();
        }

        [Theory]
        [InlineData("b5b05534-9263-448c-a69e-0bbd8b3eb90e")]
        public async Task getitem_should_return_right_data(string guid)
        {
            ItemService sut = new ItemService(_itemRepository, _mapper);

            var result = await sut.GetItemAsync(new GetItemRequest { Id =
new Guid(guid) });

            result.Id.ShouldBe(new Guid(guid));
        }

        [Fact]
        public void getitem_should_thrown_exception_with_null_id()
```

```
        {
            ItemService sut = new ItemService(_itemRepository, _mapper);

            sut.GetItemAsync(null).ShouldThrow<ArgumentNullException>();
        }
    }
}
```

The preceding code tests the implementation of the reading operations of the ItemService class. The ItemServiceTests class uses the CatalogContextFactory type to initialize and get the base data used by the service. Each test method uses the _itemRepository class property and the _mapper instance to initialize a new ItemService and verify the GetItemAsync and the GetItemsAsync methods provided by the service class.

In the same way, we can use the same technique to implement the writing operation tests:

```
    public class ItemServiceTests :
        IClassFixture<CatalogContextFactory>
    {
        private readonly ItemRepository _itemRepository;
        private readonly IItemMapper _mapper;

        public ItemServiceTests(CatalogContextFactory
catalogContextFactory)
        {
            _itemRepository = new
ItemRepository(catalogContextFactory.ContextInstance);
            _mapper = catalogContextFactory.ItemMapper;
        }

        ...

        [Fact]
        public async Task additem_should_add_right_entity()
        {
            var testItem = new AddItemRequest
            {
                Name = "Test album",
                GenreId = new Guid("c04f05c0-f6ad-44d1-a400-3375bfb5dfd6"),
                ArtistId = new Guid("f08a333d-30db-4dd1-
b8ba-3b0473c7cdab"),
                Price = new Price { Amount = 13, Currency = "EUR" }
                ...
            };

            IItemService sut = new ItemService(_itemRepository, _mapper);
```

```
        var result = await sut.AddItemAsync(testItem);

        result.Name.ShouldBe(testItem.Name);
        result.Description.ShouldBe(testItem.Description);
        result.GenreId.ShouldBe(testItem.GenreId);
        result.ArtistId.ShouldBe(testItem.ArtistId);
        result.Price.Amount.ShouldBe(testItem.Price.Amount);
        result.Price.Currency.ShouldBe(testItem.Price.Currency);
    }

    [Fact]
    public async Task edititem_should_add_right_entity()
    {
        var testItem = new EditItemRequest
        {
            Id = new Guid("b5b05534-9263-448c-a69e-0bbd8b3eb90e"),
            Name = "Test album",
            GenreId = new Guid("c04f05c0-f6ad-44d1-a400-3375bfb5dfd6"),
            ArtistId = new Guid("f08a333d-30db-4dd1-
b8ba-3b0473c7cdab"),
            Price = new Price { Amount = 13, Currency = "EUR" }
            ...
        };

        ItemService sut = new ItemService(_itemRepository, _mapper);

        var result = await sut.EditItemAsync(testItem);

        result.Name.ShouldBe(testItem.Name);
        result.Description.ShouldBe(testItem.Description);
        result.GenreId.ShouldBe(testItem.GenreId);
        result.ArtistId.ShouldBe(testItem.ArtistId);
        result.Price.Amount.ShouldBe(testItem.Price.Amount);
        result.Price.Currency.ShouldBe(testItem.Price.Currency);
    }
  }
}
```

The `additem_should_add_the_entity` and
`edititem_should_edit_the_entity` methods are verifying both the `IItemMapper` logic
implementation and also the `IItemService` implementation. This approach can be used to
test the logic of the service classes layer. In this case, the mapping logic is not so complex.
Besides, I suggest also implementing separate tests in the case of a more complex mapping
logic.

Finally, we can run the test cases we've just implemented by executing the `dotnet test` CLI instruction in the solution folder, or by using our preferred IDE test runner. The CLI result should be similar to this:

```
[xUnit.net 00:00:01.92]   Finished:     Catalog.Infrastructure.Tests

  √ Catalog.Domain.Tests.Services.ItemServiceTests.getitems_should_return_right_data [137ms]

  √ Catalog.Domain.Tests.Services.ItemServiceTests.edititem_should_add_right_entity [112ms]

  √ Catalog.Domain.Tests.Services.ItemServiceTests.additem_should_add_right_entity [15ms]

  √ Catalog.Domain.Tests.Services.ItemServiceTests.getitem_should_return_right_data(guid: "b5b05534-9263-448c-a69e-0bbd8b3eb90e") [5ms]

  √ Catalog.Domain.Tests.Services.ItemServiceTests.getitem_should_thrown_exception_with_null_id [4ms]

Test Run Successful.
Total tests: 10
    Passed: 10
```

The preceding report lists all the tests executed by the `dotnet test` command, and it provides an overview of the successful and failed tests. Furthermore, it is also possible to specify the verbosity of the test by appending the `-v` option next to the `dotnet test -v <q[uiet], m[inimal], n[ormal], d[etailed], and diag[nostic]>` command.

Implementing request model validation

The `Catalog.Domain` project also owns the validation logic of our request models. In this section, we will see how to implement the request validation logic part, which will be also used by our controllers in order to validate the incoming data. Here, I usually rely on the `FluentValidation` package, which provides a really readable way to perform validation checks on every type of object and data structure.

In order to add the `FluentValidation` package to our `Catalog.Domain` project, we can execute the following commands in the project folder:

```
dotnet add package FluentValidation
dotnet add package FluentValidation.AspNetCore
```

The `FluentValidation` package exposes the `AbstractValidation` class, which can be extended to implement our custom validation criteria for a request model class:

```
//Requests/Item/Validators/AddItemRequestValidator.cs

using FluentValidation;
```

```
namespace Catalog.Domain.Requests.Item.Validators
{
    public class AddItemRequestValidator :
AbstractValidator<AddItemRequest>
    {
        public AddItemRequestValidator()
        {
            RuleFor(x => x.GenreId).NotEmpty();
            RuleFor(x => x.ArtistId).NotEmpty();
            RuleFor(x => x.Price).NotEmpty();
            RuleFor(x => x.ReleaseDate).NotEmpty();
            RuleFor(x => x.Name).NotEmpty();
            RuleFor(x => x.Price).Must(x => x?.Amount > 0);
            RuleFor(x => x.AvailableStock).Must(x => x > 0);
        }
    }
}
```

//Requests/Item/Validators/EditItemRequestValidator.cs

```
using FluentValidation;

namespace Catalog.Domain.Requests.Item.Validators
{
    public class EditItemRequestValidator :
AbstractValidator<EditItemRequest>
    {
        public EditItemRequestValidator()
        {
            RuleFor(x => x.Id).NotEmpty();
            RuleFor(x => x.GenreId).NotEmpty();
            RuleFor(x => x.ArtistId).NotEmpty();
            RuleFor(x => x.Price).NotEmpty();
            RuleFor(x => x.Price).Must(x => x?.Amount > 0);
            RuleFor(x => x.ReleaseDate).NotEmpty();
            RuleFor(x => x.Name).NotEmpty();
        }
    }
}
```

These validator classes are located in the `Requests/Item/Validators` path. Let's proceed by analyzing some of the validation criteria implemented in the `AddItemRequestValidator` class:

- The `GenreId` and `ArtistId` fields are required because a vinyl always has this kind of information.
- The class uses the same `NotEmpty` method on the `Name`, `ReleaseDate`, and `Price` fields.

- The `Amount` field of the `Price` class should always be greater than 0. The validator class uses the `Must` method to apply this rule.

The same approach is taken for the `EditItemRequestValidator` class, except for the `Id` field, which is defined as required for the updated process of an entity. The fluent way of working is really useful for different reasons: it is ready to read, easy to maintain, and really helpful when we want to test logic.

Testing request model validation

As mentioned, the `FluentValidation` package provides an excellent way to test our validation criteria.

The `AddItemRequestValidator` and `EditItemRequestValidator` classes implement elementary checks. Furthermore, it may be useful to cover them with some tests to document the logic implemented in these classes. `FluentValidation` provides a `TestHelper` class that provides the assertion conditions necessary to verify the behavior of our validation logic.

Let's see how to do some unit tests for the `AddItemRequestValidator` class:

```
using Catalog.Domain.Entities;
using Catalog.Domain.Requests.Item;
using Catalog.Domain.Requests.Item.Validators;
using FluentValidation.TestHelper;
using Xunit;

namespace Catalog.Domain.Tests.Requests.Item.Validators
{
    public class AddItemRequestValidatorTests
    {
        private readonly AddItemRequestValidator _validator;

        public AddItemRequestValidatorTests()
        {
            _validator = new AddItemRequestValidator();
        }

        [Fact]
        public void should_have_error_when_ArtistId_is_null()
        {
            var addItemRequest = new AddItemRequest { Price = new Price()
};

            _validator.ShouldHaveValidationErrorFor(x => x.ArtistId,
```

```
addItemRequest);
        }

        [Fact]
        public void should_have_error_when_GenreId_is_null()
        {
            var addItemRequest = new AddItemRequest { Price = new Price()
};
            _validator.ShouldHaveValidationErrorFor(x => x.GenreId,
addItemRequest);
        }
    }
}
```

The test class defined in the preceding code verifies that AddItemRequestValidator
triggers a validation error if the GenreId or ArtistId fields are null. It uses
the ShouldHaveValidationErrorFor extension method exposed by the TestHelper
class to verify the behavior. The ShouldHaveValidationErrorFor method also exposes
an IEnumerable of ValidationError, which can be used to check the details of each
message of type ValidationError.

Dependencies registration

In this chapter, we have seen how to implement mapper classes, validators, and service
classes. All these types work together using the dependency injection of .NET Core.
Dependency registration usually happens through the use of extension methods that group
the registered classes by following some criteria. In this case, I will group the registered
classes in the following way:

- Services refer to all the service interfaces and classes defined in the
  Catalog.Domain project
- Mappers refer to all the mapper classes defined in the Catalog.Domain project
- Validations refer to all the fluent validation requirements and dependencies used
  by the application

Now that we have defined the logic behind the separation of dependency registration, we
can proceed by defining a new DependencyRegistration static class in the Extensions
folder in the Catalog.Domain project:

```
using System.Reflection;
using Catalog.Domain.Mappers;
using Catalog.Domain.Services;
```

```
using FluentValidation.AspNetCore;
using Microsoft.Extensions.DependencyInjection;

namespace Catalog.Domain.Extensions
{
    public static class DependenciesRegistration
    {
        public static IServiceCollection AddMappers(this IServiceCollection
services)
        {
            services
                .AddSingleton<IArtistMapper, ArtistMapper>()
                .AddSingleton<IGenreMapper, GenreMapper>()
                .AddSingleton<IItemMapper, ItemMapper>();
            return services;
        }

        public static IServiceCollection AddServices(this
IServiceCollection services)
        {
            services
                .AddScoped<IItemService, ItemService>();
            return services;
        }

        public static IMvcBuilder AddValidation(this IMvcBuilder builder)
        {
            builder
                .AddFluentValidation(configuration =>
                    configuration.RegisterValidatorsFromAssembly
                        (Assembly.GetExecutingAssembly()));
            return builder;
        }
    }
}
```

The preceding code defines three extension methods, one for each group: `AddMappers`, `AddServices`, and `AddValidation`.

The `AddMappers` extension method registers the mapper instances using a *singleton* life cycle, therefore, the mappers do not have any kind of dependency and they don't perform any request-related operation. On the other side, the `AddServices` extension method uses a scoped life cycle because the service classes depend on the repositories that perform I/O operations on the database. Finally, the `AddValidation` extension method is chained with `IMvcBuilder` and is strictly dependent on the MVC stack.

Furthermore, it uses the `AddFluentValidation` method provided by the `FluentValidation` package in order to register all the validation classes.

In conclusion, we can register the dependencies of our application in the following way:

```
using Catalog.API.Extensions;
...

namespace Catalog.API
{
    public class Startup
    {
        ...
        public void ConfigureServices(IServiceCollection services)
        {
            services
.AddCatalogContext(Configuration.GetSection("DataSource:ConnectionString").
Value)
                .AddScoped<IItemRepository, ItemRepository>()
                .AddMappers()
                .AddServices()
                .AddControllers()
                .AddValidation();
        }
    ...
```

Lastly, we can now verify the implementations written during this chapter by again running a `dotnet test` command in the solution folder, or by executing the test runner of our preferred IDE.

Summary

The `Catalog.Domain` project now contains the core logic of the entire application. Although the logic implemented in the `Domain` project is still quite simple, later on in this book, it will become more complex.

The topics covered in this chapter included some of the concepts related to the domain logic implementation of a web service: how to implement the service and the mapping classes, how to implement the request validation process using a fluent approach, and finally, how to test our code using some unit testing techniques.

The next chapter will look into all the HTTP parts of the application. Furthermore, we will focus on the `Catalog.API` project, and how to put together the data access, the service, and the API layers.

10
Implementing the RESTful HTTP Layer

In the previous chapter, we learned how to deal with the logic of our web service in the `Catalog.Domain` project. This chapter will walk you through the HTTP part of the web service and all the components inside the `Catalog.API` project.

We will also demonstrate how to implement and test the controller part of a web service. By the end of the chapter, you will be able to implement, test, and validate HTTP routes using ASP.NET Core. We will cover the following topics:

- Implementing the HTTP layer of a service
- Carrying out tests using the tools provided by ASP.NET Core
- Improving the resilience of the HTTP layer

The code presented in this chapter is available from the following GitHub repository: `https://github.com/PacktPublishing/Hands-On-RESTful-Web-Services-with-ASP.NET-Core-3`.

Implementing the item controller

This section focuses on building the routes to read, writing the catalog data, and exposing the functionalities we already built in the domain layer using the HTTP protocol. Our controller will include the verbs listed in the following routing table:

Verb	Path	Description
GET	/api/items	Retrieves all the items present in our catalog
GET	/api/items/{id}	Retrieves the item with the corresponding ID
POST	/api/items/	Creates a new item by taking the body payload of the request
PUT	/api/items/{id}	Updates the item with the corresponding ID

The preceding routes allow web service consumers to get, add, and update the Item entities. Before starting the implementation, let's look at an overview of the solution schema that we are going to implement:

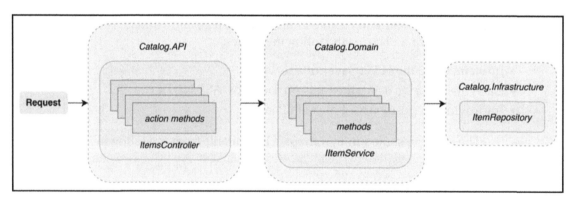

In Chapter 8, *Building the Data Access Layer*, and Chapter 9, *Implementing the Domain Logic*, we implemented and tested, respectively, the Catalog.Infrastructure and Catalog.Domain projects. This chapter focuses on the Catalog.API project. We are going to build and test the action methods that will call the service layer built in the Catalog.Domain project. Let's start by defining a new controller in the Controllers folder of our Catalog.API project, named ItemController:

```
using Microsoft.AspNetCore.Mvc;

namespace Catalog.API.Controllers
{
    [Route("api/items")]
    [ApiController]
```

```
      public class ItemController : ControllerBase
      {
      }
}
```

The `ItemController` class will reflect the routes that we defined earlier. We should note that we decorated the controller class with the `Route` and `ApiController` attributes: the first specifies the base URL of the controller and the second provides some utilities and conventions on the responses type produced by the action methods. The controller will also use the `IItemService` interface to query and write data on our data source. We can use the `IItemService` interface to the `ItemController` class via the constructor injection:

```
using Catalog.Domain.Services;
using Microsoft.AspNetCore.Mvc;

namespace Catalog.API.Controllers
{
    [Route("api/items")]
    [ApiController]
    public class ItemController : ControllerBase
    {
        private readonly IItemService _itemService;

        public ItemController(IItemService itemService)
        {
            _itemService = itemService;
        }
    }
}
```

The preceding code uses dependency injection to add the `IItemService` class as a dependency of the `ItemController` class. Once we have added the `IItemService` interface, we can proceed by implementing the action methods of the controller.

Implementing action methods

We have already dealt with action methods in Chapter 5, *Web Service Stack in ASP.NET Core*. In the following implementation, we will use the IItemService interface in the action methods, as follows:

```
using System;
using System.Threading.Tasks;
using Catalog.Domain.Requests.Item;
using Catalog.Domain.Services;
using Microsoft.AspNetCore.Mvc;

namespace Catalog.API.Controllers
{
    [Route("api/items")]
    [ApiController]
    public class ItemController : ControllerBase
    {
        private readonly IItemService _itemService;

        public ItemController(IItemService itemService)
        {
            _itemService = itemService;
        }
        [HttpGet]
        public async Task<IActionResult> Get()
        {
            var result = await _itemService.GetItemsAsync();
            return Ok(result);
        }

        [HttpGet("{id:guid}")]
        public async Task<IActionResult> GetById(Guid id)
        {
            var result = await _itemService.GetItemAsync(new GetItemRequest
            { Id = id });
            return Ok(result);
        }
    }
}
```

The Get and GetById action methods perform read operations by referring to the IItemService interface and calling the GetItemsAsync and GetItemAsync methods of the underlying service layer, in this case the IItemService interface. Let's proceed by using the same approach to implement the Post and Put action methods of the controller:

```
using System;
```

```
using System.Threading.Tasks;
using Catalog.Domain.Requests.Item;
using Catalog.Domain.Services;
using Microsoft.AspNetCore.Mvc;

namespace Catalog.API.Controllers
{
    [Route("api/items")]
    [ApiController]
    public class ItemController : ControllerBase
    {
        ...
        [HttpPost]
        public async Task<IActionResult> Post(AddItemRequest request)
        {
            var result = await _itemService.AddItemAsync(request);
            return CreatedAtAction(nameof(GetById), new { id = result.Id },
             null);
        }

        [HttpPut("{id:guid}")]
        public async Task<IActionResult> Put(Guid id, EditItemRequest
         request)
        {
            request.Id = id;
            var result = await _itemService.EditItemAsync(request);

            return Ok(result);
        }
    }
}
```

The Post and Put actions use AddItemRequest and EditItemRequest, respectively, to bind data from the HTTP request and pass it through the IItemService interface. Under the hood, the IItemService implementation refers to IItemMapper to get back an entity from the request type and send it through the IItemRepository implementation. With the help of the dependency injection, we can easily loose couple the dependency between the different components. We should also note that the Post action method uses the CreatedAtAction() method exposed by ControllerBase to retrieve the location of the created resource as part of the response. Once we have bound the IItemService APIs into the ItemController action method, we can continue by testing the implementation.

Testing controllers using the WebApplicationFactory<T> class

The ASP.NET Core Framework provides a way to perform *integration tests* using the WebApplicationFactory<T> class. This class allows us to create a new TestServer that emulates a real HTTP server in a separate process. Therefore, it is possible to test our ItemController by calling it through an HttpClient instance provided by the factory. It is essential to note that WebApplicationFactory is a generic class and that it accepts a TEntryPoint type, which is represented by the Startup class of our web service. Before proceeding with the implementation of the test class, let's create a new project in the tests folder that will contain all tests related to the Catalog.API project. Therefore, we can execute the following commands inside the tests folder:

```
dotnet new xunit -n Catalog.API.Tests
cd Catalog.API.Tests
dotnet add reference ../Catalog.Fixtures
dotnet add reference ../../src/Catalog.API
dotnet sln ../../Catalog.API.sln add .
```

The preceding commands add a new Catalog.API.Tests project into the tests folder of the solution, which refers to the Catalog.Fixtures and Catalog.API projects. The project is included in the solution file of the project. The next section describes how to extend the WebApplicationFactory class in order to support the execution of the web service.

Extending the WebApplicationFactory

The WebApplicationFactory class exposes set properties and methods that are useful for configuring the instance of the TestServer and for creating the proper tests fixture for our controllers. In addition, it is possible to extend WebApplicationFactory by overriding the ConfigureWebHost method and substituting the behavior of the *dependency injection services* declared in the original Startup class of the Catalog.API project. The WebApplicationFactory class is part of the Microsoft.AspNetCore.Mvc.Testing package; therefore, it is necessary to add the NuGet package to the Catalog.Fixture project and to the Catalog.API.Tests project by running the following commands in the tests folder of the project:

```
dotnet add Catalog.Fixtures package Microsoft.AspNetCore.Mvc.Testing
dotnet add Catalog.API.Tests package Microsoft.AspNetCore.Mvc.Testing
```

Let's proceed by creating a new `InMemoryWebApplicationFactory` class inside the `Catalog.Fixtures` project. The class will be used by the test classes to instantiate a new `TestServer` object. Therefore, the next step is to create a new `InMemoryWebApplicationFactory` class that extends the `WebApplicationFactory` base class and overrides the `ConfigureWebHost` method to inject the custom *in-memory* database provider:

```
using System;
using Catalog.Infrastructure;
using Microsoft.AspNetCore.Hosting;
using Microsoft.AspNetCore.Mvc.Testing;
using Microsoft.AspNetCore.TestHost;
using Microsoft.EntityFrameworkCore;
using Microsoft.Extensions.DependencyInjection;

namespace Catalog.Fixtures
{
    public class InMemoryApplicationFactory<TStartup>
        : WebApplicationFactory<TStartup> where TStartup : class
    {
        protected override void ConfigureWebHost(IWebHostBuilder builder)
        {
            builder
                .UseEnvironment("Testing")
                .ConfigureTestServices(services =>
                {
                    var options = new
                      DbContextOptionsBuilder<CatalogContext>()
                        .UseInMemoryDatabase(Guid.NewGuid().ToString())
                        .Options;

                    services.AddScoped<CatalogContext>(serviceProvider =>
                      new TestCatalogContext(options));
                    var sp = services.BuildServiceProvider();

                    using var scope = sp.CreateScope();
                    var scopedServices = scope.ServiceProvider;
                    var db = scopedServices.GetRequiredService
                      <CatalogContext>();
                    db.Database.EnsureCreated();
                });
        }
    }
}
```

The preceding `InMemoryApplicationFactory` class implements the `ConfigureWebHost` method, and it initializes an in-memory database using the `UseInMemoryDatabase` extension method. It also inserts a new instance of the `TestCatalogContext` class in the `CatalogContext` service registered using the dependency injection. Therefore, the tests will use the same in-memory database infrastructure we already used for the test cases implemented in the `Catalog.Infrastructure.Tests` and `Catalog.Domain.Tests` projects.

Additionally, the `InMemoryApplicationFactory` implementation creates a new scope that will be used to execute the `EnsureCreated` method. Thus, each new instance of `InMemoryApplicationFactory` will generate the database from the same snapshot of data.

Finally, the entire implementation is executed in the context of the `ConfigureTestServices` method, which provides a way to override the dependency injection services defined in the `Startup` class of the `Catalog.API` project.

 As mentioned in `Chapter 8`, *Building the Data Access Layer*, the in-memory database is not always the preferred alternative, for two reasons. First, it doesn't reflect a real relational database with real constraints on the data. Secondly, it is tricky to deal with in-memory databases when multiple test methods use the same instance, since they may generate inconsistent data. For this reason, we are creating a new instance, using the `UseInMemoryDatabase(Guid.NewGuid().ToString());` statement, for each test class. The `Guid.NewGuid()` instruction guarantees uniqueness between the instances. In real-world applications, another common approach is to create a new instance of a temporary data source and recreate it after each test.

Testing a controller

Once we have implemented the `InMemoryApplicationFactory` class, it is possible to utilize it by implementing the `IClassFixture` interface in our test classes. Therefore, let's start by initializing a new `ItemControllerTests` class in the `Catalog.API.Tests` project:

```
using System.Net.Http;
using System.Text;
using System.Threading.Tasks;
using Newtonsoft.Json;
using Shouldly;
```

```
using Catalog.Domain.Infrastructure.Entities;
using Catalog.Fixtures;
using Xunit;

namespace Catalog.API.Tests.Controllers
{
    public class ItemControllerTests :
IClassFixture<InMemoryApplicationFactory<Startup>>
    {
        private readonly InMemoryApplicationFactory<Startup> _factory;
        public ItemControllerTests(InMemoryApplicationFactory<Startup>
         factory)
        {
            _factory = factory;
        }
        . . . .
    }
}
```

The `ItemControllerTests` class provides remarkable test coverage for the action methods. First of all, the test class implements the generic `IClassFixture` interface provided by the `xUnit.Sdk` package. The `IClassFixture` interface refers to the previously defined `InMemoryApplicationFactory<Startup>` and it injects the new instance of the `factory` class into the constructor of the test classes. Consequently, a new instance of the `factory` will be provided for each test class executed.

Let's take a look at the test methods that cover the get operation of `ItemController`:

```
. .
[Theory]
[InlineData("/api/items/")]
public async Task get_should_return_success(string url)

{
    var client = _factory.CreateClient();
    var response = await client.GetAsync(url);

    response.EnsureSuccessStatusCode();
}

[Fact]
public async Task get_by_id_should_return_item_data()
{
    const string id = "86bff4f7-05a7-46b6-ba73-d43e2c45840f";
    var client = _factory.CreateClient();
    var response = await client.GetAsync($"/api/items/{id}");
```

```
        response.EnsureSuccessStatusCode();
        var responseContent = await response.Content.ReadAsStringAsync();
        var responseEntity = JsonConvert.
         DeserializeObject<Item>(responseContent);

        responseEntity.ShouldNotBeNull();
    }
```

The preceding implementation uses the CreateClient method provided by InMemoryApplicationFactory<Startup> to initialize a new HttpClient instance. Therefore, if we take the get_by_id_should_return_item_data method as an example, it uses the client to call the /api/items/{id} route and checks that the information returned is not null. We can proceed by testing the add item operation by adding the following test methods to the ItemControllerTests class:

```
[Fact]
public async Task add_should_create_new_record()
{
    var request = new AddItemRequest
    {
        Name = "Test album",
        Description = "Description",
        LabelName = "Label name",
        Price = new Price { Amount = 13, Currency = "EUR" },
        PictureUri = "https://mycdn.com/pictures/32423423",
        ReleaseDate = DateTimeOffset.Now,
        AvailableStock = 6,
        GenreId = new Guid("c04f05c0-f6ad-44d1-a400-3375bfb5dfd6"),
        ArtistId = new Guid("f08a333d-30db-4dd1-b8ba-3b0473c7cdab")
    };

    var client = _factory.CreateClient();

    var httpContent = new
StringContent(JsonConvert.SerializeObject(request), Encoding.UTF8,
"application/json");
    var response = await client.PostAsync($"/api/items", httpContent);

    response.EnsureSuccessStatusCode();
    response.Headers.Location.ShouldNotBeNull();
}
```

Consequently, we can choose a similar approach for the `Put` action method implemented in the controller:

```
[Fact]
public async Task update_should_modify_existing_item()
{
    var client = _factory.CreateClient();

    var request = new EditItemRequest
    {
        Id = new Guid("b5b05534-9263-448c-a69e-0bbd8b3eb90e"),
        Name = "Test album",
        Description = "Description updated",
        LabelName = "Label name",
        Price = new Price { Amount = 50, Currency = "EUR" },
        PictureUri = "https://mycdn.com/pictures/32423423",
        ReleaseDate = DateTimeOffset.Now,
        AvailableStock = 6,
        GenreId = new Guid("c04f05c0-f6ad-44d1-a400-3375bfb5dfd6"),
        ArtistId = new Guid("f08a333d-30db-4dd1-b8ba-3b0473c7cdab")
    };

    var httpContent = new
StringContent(JsonConvert.SerializeObject(request), Encoding.UTF8,
"application/json");
    var response = await client.PutAsync($"/api/items/{request.Id}",
httpContent);

    response.EnsureSuccessStatusCode();

    var responseContent = await response.Content.ReadAsStringAsync();
    var responseEntity =
JsonConvert.DeserializeObject<Item>(responseContent);

    responseEntity.Name.ShouldBe(request.Name);
    responseEntity.Description.ShouldBe(request.Description);
    responseEntity.GenreId.ShouldBe(request.GenreId);
    responseEntity.ArtistId.ShouldBe(request.ArtistId);
}
```

The `add_should_create_new_record` test method and the `update_should_modify_existing_item` method adopt the corresponding approach to test the `Post` and `Put` requests and the corresponding action methods. In this case, we are using the same request objects we defined for the `ItemServiceTests` and `ItemRepositoryTests` classes.

We can proceed by executing the previously implemented tests by running the `dotnet test` command in the solution folder, or by using the test runner of our preferred IDE. Later in this next subsection, we will look at how to optimize the initialization of the request and hold the test data at a unique point.

Using `IClassFixture` implies that the same `InMemoryApplicationFactory` instance will be shared by all the test methods. Therefore, we will have the same underlying data for every test method. If we want to keep the tests fully isolated, we can avoid the use of the class fixture and initialize a new `InMemoryApplicationFactory` instance in the constructor of the test class:

```
public class ItemControllerTests
    {
        private readonly InMemoryApplicationFactory<Startup>
    _factory;

        public ItemControllerTests()
        {
            _factory = new
    InMemoryApplicationFactory<Startup>();
        }
        ....
    }
```

This approach also guarantees isolation between every single test method implemented in the test class. Furthermore, the constructor will provide a new instance every time.

Next, let's have a look at how to load test data using xUnit data attributes.

Loading test data using xUnit data attributes

The *xUnit* framework is the preferred choice for testing .NET applications and services. The framework also provides some utilities to extend its capabilities and to implement a more maintainable testing code. It is possible to extend the `DataAttribute` class exposed by the `xUnit.Sdk` namespace to perform custom operations inside our attributes. For example, let's suppose that we create a new custom `DataAttribute` to load test data from a file, as follows:

```
namespace Catalog.API.Tests.Controllers
    {
```

```
    public class ItemControllerTests :
IClassFixture<InMemoryApplicationFactory<Startup>>
    {
        ...

        [Theory]
        [LoadData( "item")]
        public async Task get_by_id_should_return_right_data(Item request)
        {
            var client = _factory.CreateClient();
            var response = await
client.GetAsync($"/api/items/{request.Id}");

            response.EnsureSuccessStatusCode();

            var responseContent =
             await response.Content.ReadAsStringAsync();
            var responseEntity = JsonConvert.DeserializeObject
             <ItemResponse>(responseContent);

            responseEntity.Name.ShouldBe(request.Name);
            responseEntity.Description.ShouldBe(request.Description);
            responseEntity.Price.Amount.ShouldBe(request.Price.Amount);
            responseEntity.Price.Currency.ShouldBe(request.Price.Currency);
            responseEntity.Format.ShouldBe(request.Format);
            responseEntity.PictureUri.ShouldBe(request.PictureUri);
            responseEntity.GenreId.ShouldBe(request.GenreId);
            responseEntity.ArtistId.ShouldBe(request.ArtistId);
        }

        ...

    }
}
```

In this scenario, the implementation decorates the test method using the LoadData attribute, which is reading an item section from a file. Therefore, we will have a JSON file that contains all the test records, and we will use the LoadData attribute to load one of them. To customize the behavior for the ItemControllerTests class, we should create a new class and extend the DataAttribute class provided by xUnit:

```
using System;
using System.Collections.Generic;
using System.IO;
using System.Linq;
using System.Reflection;
using Newtonsoft.Json;
using Newtonsoft.Json.Linq;
```

```
using Xunit.Sdk;

namespace Catalog.Fixtures
{
    public class LoadDataAttribute : DataAttribute
    {
        private readonly string _fileName;
        private readonly string _section;
        public LoadDataAttribute(string section)
        {
            _fileName = "record-data.json";
            _section = section;
        }
        public override IEnumerable<object[]> GetData(MethodInfo
testMethod)
        {
            if (testMethod == null) throw new
ArgumentNullException(nameof(testMethod));

            var path = Path.IsPathRooted(_fileName)
                ? _fileName
                : Path.GetRelativePath(Directory.GetCurrentDirectory(),
_fileName);

            if (!File.Exists(path)) throw new ArgumentException
             ($"File not found: {path}");

            var fileData = File.ReadAllText(_fileName);

            if (string.IsNullOrEmpty(_section)) return
             JsonConvert.DeserializeObject<List<string[]>>(fileData);

            var allData = JObject.Parse(fileData);
            var data = allData[_section];
            return new List<object[]> { new[] {
             data.ToObject(testMethod.GetParameters()
             .First().ParameterType) } };
        }
    }
}
```

The `LoadDataAttribute` class overrides `GetData(MethodInfo testMethod);`, which is supplied by the `DataAttribute` class, and it returns the data utilized by the test methods. The implementation of the `GetData` method reads the content of the file defined by the `_filePath` attribute; it tries to serialize the content of the specified `section` of the file into a generic `object`. Finally, the implementation calls the `ToObject` method to convert the generic `JObject` into the type associated with the first parameter of the test method. The last step in the process is to create a new JSON file called `record-data.json` in the `Catalog.API.Tests` project. The file will contain the test data used by our tests:

```json
{
  "item": {
    "Id": "86bff4f7-05a7-46b6-ba73-d43e2c45840f",
    "Name": "DAMN.",
    "Description": "DAMN. by Kendrick Lamar",
    "LabelName": "TDE, Top Dawg Entertainment",
    "Price": {
      "Amount": 34.5,
      "Currency": "EUR"
    },
    "PictureUri": "https://mycdn.com/pictures/45345345",
    "ReleaseDate": "2017-01-01T00:00:00+00:00",
    "Format": "Vinyl 33g",
    "AvailableStock": 5,
    "GenreId": "c04f05c0-f6ad-44d1-a400-3375bfb5dfd6",
    "Genre": null,
    "ArtistId": "3eb00b42-a9f0-4012-841d-70ebf3ab7474",
    "Artist": null
  },
  "genre": {
    "GenreId": "c04f05c0-f6ad-44d1-a400-3375bfb5dfd6",
    "GenreDescription": "Hip-Hop"
  },
  "artist": {
    "ArtistId": "f08a333d-30db-4dd1-b8ba-3b0473c7cdab",
    "ArtistName": "Anderson Paak."
  }
}
```

The JSON snippet has the following fields: `item`, `artist`, and `genre`. The fields contain data related to the test entities. Therefore, we will use them to deserialize the data into the request models and into the entity types. Consequently, we can apply the `LoadData` attribute to the `ItemControllerTests` class in the following way:

```
using System;
using System.Net;
using System.Net.Http;
```

```
using System.Text;
using System.Threading.Tasks;
using Newtonsoft.Json;
using Shouldly;
using Catalog.Domain.Infrastructure.Entities;
using Catalog.Domain.Requests.Item;
using Catalog.Fixtures;
using Xunit;

namespace Catalog.API.Tests.Controllers
{
    public class ItemControllerTests :
IClassFixture<InMemoryApplicationFactory<Startup>>
    {
        ...
        [Theory]
        [LoadData("item")]
        public async Task get_by_id_should_return_right_data(Item
request){...}

        [Theory]
        [LoadData("item")]
        public async Task add_should_create_new_item(AddItemRequest
request){...}
        [Theory]
        [LoadTestData("item")]
        public async Task
update_should_modify_existing_item(EditItemRequest request){...}
    }
}
```

Now, the test methods accept a `request` parameter of the `Item`, `EditItemRequest`, or `AddItemRequest` type, which will contain the data provided by the `record-data.json` file. Then, the object is serialized into the `request` parameter and sent using the `HttpClient` instance supplied by the `InMemoryApplicationFactory`:

```
[Theory]
[LoadData( "item")]
public async Task add_should_create_new_record(AddItemRequest request)
{
    var client = _factory.CreateClient();

    var httpContent = new
StringContent(JsonConvert.SerializeObject(request), Encoding.UTF8,
"application/json");
    var response = await client.PostAsync($"/api/items", httpContent);
```

```
        response.EnsureSuccessStatusCode();
        response.Headers.Location.ShouldNotBeNull();
}
```

`LoadData` serializes the content defined in the `record-data.json` file into the `AddItemRequest` type. The request is then serialized as `StringContent` and posted using the HTTP client created by the factory. Finally, the method asserts that the resultant code is successful and the `Location` header is not `null`.

We can now verify the behavior of the `ItemController` class by executing the `dotnet test` command in the root of the solution, or by running the test runner provided by our preferred IDE.

In conclusion, now we are able to define the test data in a unique central JSON file. In addition to this, we can add as much data as we want by adding new sections to the JSON file. The next part of this section will focus on improving the resilience of the APIs by adding some existence checks and handling exceptions using filters.

Improving the resilience of the API

The previous sections show a possible implementation of `ItemController` class and how to test it using the tools provided by ASP.NET Core. In this section, we will learn how to improve the resilience of our service by performing some *restriction checks* on the information exposed by the `ItemController`. Additionally, we will look at how to present validation errors and how to paginate returned data. This section will apply the concepts explained in the previous chapters to the web service project.

Existence check

Let's start by implementing the action filter that performs an existence check on the requested data. The filter will be used by the action methods that get or edit a single item. As seen in Chapter 7, *Filter Pipeline*, we are going to implement the following filter:

```
using System;
using System.Threading.Tasks;
using Catalog.Domain.Requests.Item;
using Catalog.Domain.Services;
using Microsoft.AspNetCore.Mvc;
using Microsoft.AspNetCore.Mvc.Filters;

namespace Catalog.API.Filters
```

```
{
    public class ItemExistsAttribute : TypeFilterAttribute
    {
        public ItemExistsAttribute() : base(typeof
            (ItemExistsFilterImpl))
        {
        }
    }

    public class ItemExistsFilterImpl : IAsyncActionFilter
    {
        private readonly IItemService _itemService;

        public ItemExistsFilterImpl(IItemService itemService)
        {
            _itemService = itemService;
        }

        public async Task OnActionExecutionAsync(ActionExecutingContext context,
            ActionExecutionDelegate next)
        {
            if (!(context.ActionArguments["id"] is Guid id))
            {
                context.Result = new BadRequestResult();
                return;
            }

            var result = await _itemService.GetItemAsync(new
GetItemRequest { Id = id });

            if (result == null)
            {
                context.Result = new NotFoundObjectResult($"Item with
id {id} not exist.");
                return;
            }

            await next();
        }
    }
}
```

The action filter resolves the `IItemService` interface in the constructor and uses the injected instance to verify the existence of the entity using the id present in the request. If the request contains a valid `Guid id`, and the id exists in our data source, the `OnActionExecutionAsync` method proceeds by calling the `await next()` method to continue the pipeline. Otherwise, it stops the pipeline and returns a `NotFoundObjectResult` instance. We can apply a filter to the action methods of `ItemController` by adding the `[ItemExists]` attribute:

```
using Catalog.API.Filters;

namespace Catalog.API.Controllers
{
    [Route("api/items")]
    [ApiController]
    public class ItemController : ControllerBase
    {
        ...

        [HttpGet("{id:guid}")]
        [ItemExists]
        public async Task<IActionResult> GetById(Guid id)
        {
            ...
        }
        [HttpPut("{id:guid}")]
        [ItemExists]
        public async Task<IActionResult> Put(Guid id, EditItemCommand request)
        {
            ...
        }
    }
}
```

After applying the `ItemExists` attribute, the API will return 404 if the ID sent by the request doesn't exist. We can also verify the logic implemented in the action filter by injecting a mock instance of the `IItemService` interface and making some assertions about the resulting response. In the following test class, we will use `Moq` to verify the call to the `next()` method. As a first step, we need to add `Moq` to the `Catalog.API.Tests` project by using the following command inside the project folder:

```
dotnet add package Moq
```

Furthermore, we can proceed by defining the `ItemExistsAttributeTests` class:

```
using System;
using System.Collections.Generic;
using System.Threading.Tasks;
using Catalog.API.Filters;
using Catalog.Domain.Requests.Item;
using Catalog.Domain.Responses;
using Catalog.Domain.Services;
using Microsoft.AspNetCore.Http;
using Microsoft.AspNetCore.Mvc;
using Microsoft.AspNetCore.Mvc.Abstractions;
using Microsoft.AspNetCore.Mvc.Filters;
using Microsoft.AspNetCore.Routing;
using Moq;
using Xunit;

namespace Catalog.API.Tests.Filters
{
    public class ItemExistsAttributeTests
    {
        [Fact]
        public async Task should_continue_pipeline_when_id_is_present()
        {
            var id = Guid.NewGuid();
            var itemService = new Mock<IItemService>();

            itemService
                .Setup(x => x.GetItemAsync(It.IsAny<GetItemRequest>()))
                .ReturnsAsync(new ItemResponse { Id = id });

            var filter = new
ItemExistsAttribute.ItemExistsFilterImpl(itemService.Object);

            var actionExecutedContext = new ActionExecutingContext(
                new ActionContext(new DefaultHttpContext(), new
RouteData(), new ActionDescriptor()),
                new List<IFilterMetadata>(),
                new Dictionary<string, object>
                {
                    {"id", id}
                }, new object());

            var nextCallback = new Mock<ActionExecutionDelegate>();
            await filter.OnActionExecutionAsync(actionExecutedContext,
nextCallback.Object);

            nextCallback.Verify(executionDelegate => executionDelegate(),
```

```
Times.Once);
        }
    }
}
```

The preceding `ItemExistsAttributeTests` class mocks the whole `IItemService` interface to simulate the response of the `GetItemAsync` method. Then, it initializes `ItemExistsAttribute` by injecting the mocked `IItemService` interface. Finally, it calls the `OnActionExecutionAsync` method exposed by the `filter` class and it combines the result with the `Verify` method provided by the `Moq` framework to check that the `ItemExistsFilter` class correctly calls the `next()` callback method.

JSON-customized errors

The customization and serialization of the exceptions is a helpful way to simplify *error handling* and improve the monitoring of the web service. These techniques are sometimes necessary for communicating exceptions to a client so that errors can be handled and managed. In general, while the *HTTP status code* provides summary information about the status of the request, the content of the response provides more detailed information about the error.

It is possible to extend the error handling behavior using filters. First of all, let's create a new standard model that represents an error result:

```
namespace Catalog.API.Exceptions
{
    public class JsonErrorPayload
    {
        public int EventId { get; set; }
        public object DetailedMessage { get; set; }
    }
}
```

The preceding class is under the `Filters` folder structure. It contains an `EventId` attribute and a `DetailedMessage` of an `object` type. Secondly, we should continue by implementing a new filter that extends the `IExceptionFilter` interface. The filter will be triggered when an exception is raised, and it will modify the content of the response returned to the client:

```
using System.Net;
using Catalog.API.Exceptions;
using Microsoft.AspNetCore.Hosting;
using Microsoft.AspNetCore.Mvc;
using Microsoft.AspNetCore.Mvc.Filters;
```

```
using Microsoft.Extensions.Hosting;
using Microsoft.Extensions.Logging;

namespace Catalog.API.Filters
{
    public class JsonExceptionAttribute : TypeFilterAttribute
    {
        public JsonExceptionAttribute() :
base(typeof(HttpCustomExceptionFilterImpl))
        {
        }

        private class HttpCustomExceptionFilterImpl : IExceptionFilter
        {
            private readonly IWebHostEnvironment _env;
            private readonly ILogger<HttpCustomExceptionFilterImpl>
_logger;

            public HttpCustomExceptionFilterImpl(IWebHostEnvironment env,
                ILogger<HttpCustomExceptionFilterImpl> logger)
            {
                _env = env;
                _logger = logger;
            }

            public void OnException(ExceptionContext context)
            {
                var eventId = new EventId(context.Exception.HResult);

                _logger.LogError(eventId,
                    context.Exception,
                    context.Exception.Message);

                var json = new JsonErrorPayload { EventId = eventId.Id };

                if (_env.IsDevelopment())
                {
                    json.DetailedMessage = context.Exception;
                }

                var exceptionObject = new ObjectResult(json) { StatusCode =
500 };

                context.Result = exceptionObject;
                context.HttpContext.Response.StatusCode = (int)
HttpStatusCode.InternalServerError;
            }
        }
```

```
        }
    }
```

The preceding code implements the `IExceptionFilter` interface. The class contains the definition of the constructor used to inject some of the dependencies of the filter. It also contains the `OnException` method, which initializes a new `JsonErrorPayload` object populated with the `eventId` field and the content of the message contained in the exception. Depending on the environment, take a look at the `IsDevelopment()` check; it also populates the resulting exception object with a detailed error message. Finally, the `OnException` method uses the `HttpContext`, defined as a parameter, to set the `HttpStatusCode.InternalServerError`, and to add `exceptionObject` previously created as a result of the execution. This approach guarantees to handle exception in a unique way, by centralizing the serialization and the resulting message format of all the errors returned by the web service.

Implementing pagination

Pagination is another essential feature of APIs. `Get` operations usually return a significant number of records and information. Sometimes, it is necessary to implement pagination to avoid a large response size.

> If your APIs are exposed to external clients, it is essential to reduce the response size when possible. Additionally, it could be that the client stores information in the memory of a device, such as a smartphone or an IoT device, that has limited memory.

Let's take a look at how to implement maintainable and reusable pagination in the `ItemController` class. First of all, we need to create a new pagination response model that represents the requested page. We can create a new `PaginatedItemResponseModel.cs` file in the `ResponseModels` folder inside the `Catalog.API` project, using the following content:

```
using System.Collections.Generic;

namespace Catalog.API.ResponseModels
{
    public class PaginatedItemsResponseModel<TEntity> where TEntity : class
    {
        public PaginatedItemsResponseModel(int pageIndex, int pageSize,
long total, IEnumerable<TEntity> data)
        {
            PageIndex = pageIndex;
            PageSize = pageSize;
```

```
                    Total = total;
                    Data = data;
                }

        public int PageIndex { get; }
        public int PageSize { get; }
        public long Total { get; }
        public IEnumerable<TEntity> Data { get; }
        }
    }
```

The `PaginatedItemsResponseModel` function accepts a generic model, and it represents a paginated response type. It also implements some properties related to the page, such as `PageIndex`, `PageSize`, and `Total`. Additionally, it includes an `IEnumerable` interface that represents the records returned by the response. The next step is to change the `Get` action method that is already present in the `ItemController` class, as shown here:

```
using Catalog.API.ResponseModels;
...
    public class ItemController : ControllerBase
    {
        ...

        [HttpGet]
        public async Task<IActionResult> Get(int pageSize = 10, int
pageIndex = 0)
        {
            var result = await _itemService.GetItemsAsync();

            var totalItems = result.Count();

            var itemsOnPage = result
                .OrderBy(c => c.Name)
                .Skip(pageSize * pageIndex)
                .Take(pageSize);

            var model = new PaginatedItemsResponseModel<ItemResponse>(
                pageIndex, pageSize, totalItems, itemsOnPage);

            return Ok(model);
        }
        ...
    }
}
```

We changed the `Get` action method to implement pagination. First of all, note that the method receives some parameters related to pagination: the `pageSize` and `pageIndex` parameters. Secondly, it executes `IItemService` to get the related records and performs a LINQ query to take only the elements of the selected page. Finally, it instantiates a new `PaginatedItemsResponseModel<ItemResponse>` with the metadata related to the page and the data, and returns the instance.

We can cover the implementation using the unit tests by changing the already existing `ItemsControllerTests` file:

```
using Catalog.API.ResponseModels;
...
    public class ItemControllerTests :
IClassFixture<InMemoryApplicationFactory<Startup>>
    {
        ...

        [Theory]
        [InlineData("/api/items/?pageSize=1&pageIndex=0", 1,0)]
        [InlineData("/api/items/?pageSize=2&pageIndex=0", 2,0)]
        [InlineData("/api/items/?pageSize=1&pageIndex=1", 1,1)]
        public async Task get_should_return_paginated_data(string url, int
pageSize, int pageIndex)

        {
            var client = _factory.CreateClient();
            var response = await client.GetAsync(url);

            response.EnsureSuccessStatusCode();

            var responseContent = await
response.Content.ReadAsStringAsync();
            var responseEntity =
JsonConvert.DeserializeObject<PaginatedItemsResponseModel<ItemResponse>>(re
sponseContent);

            responseEntity.PageIndex.ShouldBe(pageIndex);
            responseEntity.PageSize.ShouldBe(pageSize);
            responseEntity.Data.Count().ShouldBe(pageSize);
        }
        ...
    }
}
```

The `should_get_item_using_pagination` test case uses the `InlineData` attribute to test some pagination routes. It calls the `Get` action method, serializes the result into a `PaginatedItemsResponseModel<ItemResponse>`, and, finally, it checks the results.

 Although the pagination implementation technique examined in this chapter provides some performance benefits, it doesn't limit the interaction between our service and the database. To extend the performance benefits to the data source of the service as well, we should consider implementing an ad-hoc query to paginate data directly from our data source.

In the next section, we will continue our journey by extending the APIs in order to also handle related entities. For now, notice that we are exposing the information of the `Item`, `Artist`, and `Genre` entities, without managing the related entities and we are not exposing any route to edit the `Artist` and `Genre` entities.

Exposing related entities

At the moment, the current implementation in the `Catalog.API` project allows us to read, and modify the `Item` entity and its relationship with the `Genre` and `Artist` entities. In this section, we will enable a client to list and add the `Genre` and `Artist` entities. Therefore, we will extend the APIs that allow a client to interact with these entities. This implementation requires us to act on the full stack of the web service; additionally, it involves the `Catalog.Infrastructure`, the `Catalog.Domain`, and the `Catalog.API` projects. Before we begin, let's take a look at the routes we are going to implement:

Verb	Path	Description
GET	/api/artists	Retrieves all the artists present in the database
GET	/api/artist/{id}	Retrieves the artist with the corresponding ID
GET	/api/artist/{id}/items/	Retrieves the items with the corresponding artist ID
POST	/api/artist/	Creates a new artist and retrieves it

In the same way, we will get the corresponding routes for the `Genre` entity as well:

Verb	Path	Description
GET	/api/genre	Retrieves all the genres present in the database
GET	/api/genre/{id}	Retrieves the genre with the corresponding ID

GET	/api/genre/{id}/items/	Retrieves the items with the corresponding genre ID
POST	/api/genre/	Creates a new genre and retrieves it

The routes mentioned in the previous tables provide a way to interact with the `Genre` and `Artist` entities. The implementation of these features will follow the same approach used by the item entity we have seen in the previous sections. Before proceeding, we need to extend the `CatalogContext` class by adding the attributes that represent the `Artist` and `Genre` entities:

```
...
public class CatalogContext : DbContext, IUnitOfWork
{
    public DbSet<Item> Items { get; set; }
    public DbSet<Artist> Artists { get; set; }
    public DbSet<Genre> Genres { get; set; }

    protected override void OnModelCreating(ModelBuilder modelBuilder)
    {
        modelBuilder.ApplyConfiguration(new ItemEntitySchemaDefinition());
        modelBuilder.ApplyConfiguration(new
ArtistEntitySchemaConfiguration());
        modelBuilder.ApplyConfiguration(new
GenreEntitySchemaConfiguration());
        base.OnModelCreating(modelBuilder);
    }
..
```

Now `CatalogContext` also handles the `Artists` and `Genres` entities through the use of the `modelBuilder.ApplyConfiguration` method. In the next subsection, we will extend the implementation of the data access layer through the use of the `Repositories` classes.

Extending the data access layer

In order to extend our APIs with the related entities, we should start from the bottom of our stack. First of all, let's spread the capabilities of the data access layer by adding the following interfaces in the `Repositories` folder of the `Catalog.Domain` project:

```
// Repositories/IArtistsRepository.cs

using System;
using System.Collections.Generic;
using System.Threading.Tasks;
using Catalog.Domain.Entities;
```

```
namespace Catalog.Domain.Repositories
{
    public interface IArtistRepository : IRepository
    {
        Task<IEnumerable<Artist>> GetAsync();
        Task<Artist> GetAsync(Guid id);
        Artist Add(Artist item);
    }
}
```

// Repositories/IGenreRepository.cs

```
using System;
using System.Collections.Generic;
using System.Threading.Tasks;
using Catalog.Domain.Entities;

namespace Catalog.Domain.Infrastructure.Repositories
{
    public interface IGenreRepository : IRepository
    {
        Task<IEnumerable<Genre>> GetAsync();
        Task<Genre> GetAsync(Guid id);
        Genre Add(Genre item);
    }
}
```

Both the IArtistRepository and IGenreRepository interfaces reflect the routes initially defined in this section: the GetAsync method returns the list of the secondary entities, the GetAsync(Guid id) returns the single object, and the Add method allows us to create a new entity. We can now define the actual implementations of the specified interfaces. Likewise, the ItemRepository class implementations will be stored in the Catalog.Infrastructure project:

//Repositories/ArtistRepository.cs

```
using System;
using System.Collections.Generic;
using System.Threading.Tasks;
using Microsoft.EntityFrameworkCore;
using Catalog.Domain.Entities;
using Catalog.Domain.Repositories;

namespace Catalog.Infrastructure.Repositories
{
    public class ArtistRepository : IArtistRepository
    {
```

```
        private readonly CatalogContext _catalogContext;
        public IUnitOfWork UnitOfWork => _catalogContext;

        public ArtistRepository(CatalogContext catalogContext)
        {
            _catalogContext = catalogContext;
        }

        public async Task<IEnumerable<Artist>> GetAsync()
        {
            return await _catalogContext.Artist
                .AsNoTracking()
                .ToListAsync();
        }

        public async Task<Artist> GetAsync(Guid id)
        {
            var artist = await _catalogContext.Artist
                .FindAsync(id);

            if (artist == null) return null;

            _catalogContext.Entry(artist).State = EntityState.Detached;
            return artist;
        }

        public Artist Add(Artist artist)
        {
            return _catalogContext.Artist.Add(artist).Entity;
        }
    }
}
```

The preceding code defines the ArtistRepository type and provides the implementation for the IArtistRepository interface. The class uses CatalogContext as a communication hub between our application and the SQL database. The GetAsync and GetAsync(Guid id) methods use the same pattern already implemented in the ItemRepository class to retrieve the information related to the required entities. Furthermore, the Add method refers to the Artists field exposed by CatalogContext to add a new artist. It is important to note that, in this case, the Add operation doesn't update the data source directly.

Let's proceed by defining the GenreRepository class:

//Repositories/GenreRepository.cs

```
using System;
using System.Collections.Generic;
using System.Threading.Tasks;
using Microsoft.EntityFrameworkCore;
using Catalog.Domain.Entities;
using Catalog.Domain.Repositories;

namespace Catalog.Infrastructure.Repositories
{
    public class GenreRepository : IGenreRepository
    {
        private readonly CatalogContext _catalogContext;
        public IUnitOfWork UnitOfWork => _catalogContext;

        public GenreRepository(CatalogContext catalogContext)
        {
            _catalogContext = catalogContext;
        }

        public async Task<IEnumerable<Genre>> GetAsync()
        {
            return await _catalogContext.Genre
                .AsNoTracking()
                .ToListAsync();
        }

        public async Task<Genre> GetAsync(Guid id)
        {
            var item = await _catalogContext.Genre
                .FindAsync(id);

            if (item == null) return null;

            _catalogContext.Entry(item).State = EntityState.Detached;
            return item;
        }

        public Genre Add(Genre item)
        {
            return _catalogContext.Genre.Add(item).Entity;
        }
    }
}
```

In the same way as `ArtistRepository`, we are implementing the operations for querying and manipulating the `Genre` entities. Although the names of the methods and the implementations are quite similar, I have chosen to keep the repository interfaces separated and redefine each implementation separately. A quicker approach would be to create a generic class that represents the typical behavior of `ItemRepository`, `ArtistRepository`, and `GenreRepository`, but the generic repositories are not always the right choice. In addition to this, building the wrong abstraction is a lot more expensive than duplicating code, and building a unique generic repository for everything means tight coupling the entities.

Extending the test coverage

As we did with the `ItemRepositoryTests` class, we can proceed by testing `ArtistRepository` and `GenreRepository` using the same approach. In Chapter 8, *Building the Data Access Layer*, we defined `TestDataContextFactory`, which is part of the `Catalog.Fixtures` project. We can use this to instantiate an in-memory database for our test purposes:

```
using System;
using System.Linq;
using System.Threading.Tasks;
using Catalog.Domain.Entities;
using Catalog.Fixtures;
using Catalog.Infrastructure.Repositories;
using Shouldly;
using Xunit;

namespace Catalog.Infrastructure.Tests
{
    public class ArtistRepositoryTests :
        IClassFixture<CatalogContextFactory>
    {
        private readonly CatalogContextFactory _factory;

        public ArtistRepositoryTests(CatalogContextFactory factory)
        {
            _factory = factory;
        }

        [Theory]
        [LoadData("artist")]
        public async Task should_return_record_by_id(Artist artist)
        {
            var sut = new ArtistRepository(_factory.ContextInstance);
```

```
        var result = await sut.GetAsync(artist.ArtistId);

        result.ArtistId.ShouldBe(artist.ArtistId);
        result.ArtistName.ShouldBe(artist.ArtistName);
    }

    [Theory]
    [LoadData("artist")]
    public async Task should_add_new_item(Artist artist)
    {
        artist.ArtistId = Guid.NewGuid();
        var sut = new ArtistRepository(_factory.ContextInstance);

        sut.Add(artist);
        await sut.UnitOfWork.SaveEntitiesAsync();

        _factory.ContextInstance.Artist
            .FirstOrDefault(x => x.ArtistId == artist.ArtistId)
            .ShouldNotBeNull();
    }
  }
}
```

The previous code explores a way to implement the tests for the `ArtistRepository` class. The `ArtistRepositoryTests` class extends `IClassFixture<CatalogContextFactory>` to retrieve an instance of the `CatalogContextFactory` type. The test methods use the `ContextInstance` attribute to retrieve a new catalog context and to initialize a new repository.

They proceed by executing the method as a test and checking the results. It is important to notice that every test method uses the `LoadData` attribute in order to load the `artist` section of the `record-data.json` file. For brevity, I've omitted some of the test cases; however, the concept behind them is identical to what we have already seen, and it can be extended to the `GenreRepository` tests.

Extending the IItemRepository interface

Another step we can take to extend our web service project with the related entities is to implement two new methods to retrieve the items related to an artist or a genre in the `IItemRepository` interface: the `GetItemsByArtistIdAsync` and `GetItemsByGenreIdAsync` methods. Both of these methods can be used by the `GET /api/artists/{id}/items` and `GET /api/genre/{id}/items` routes to retrieve the items.

Let's proceed by adding the following methods to the `IItemsRepository` interface and implementing them in the corresponding implementation:

```
//Repositories/IItemRepository.cs
public interface IItemRepository : IRepository
{
    ...
    Task<IEnumerable<Item>> GetItemByArtistIdAsync(Guid id);
    Task<IEnumerable<Item>> GetItemByGenreIdAsync(Guid id);
    ...
}

//Repositories/ItemRepository.cs
public class ItemRepository
    : IItemRepository
{
    ...
    public async Task<IEnumerable<Item>> GetItemByArtistIdAsync(Guid
id)
    {
        var items = await _context
            .Items
            .Where(item => item.ArtistId == id)
            .Include(x => x.Genre)
            .Include(x => x.Artist)
            .ToListAsync();

        return items;
    }

    public async Task<IEnumerable<Item>> GetItemByGenreIdAsync(Guid id)
    {
        var items = await _context.Items
            .Where(item => item.GenreId == id)
            .Include(x => x.Genre)
            .Include(x => x.Artist)
            .ToListAsync();

        return items;
    }
    ...
    }
}
```

This code extends the `IItemRepository` interface and its implementation in order to include the functionalities to query the items using `ArtistId` and `GenreId`. Both methods retrieve data using the `Where` clause and by calling the `Include` statement to include the related entities in the result of the query. Once we have fully extended the repository layer, we can continue by also extending the service classes.

Extending the capabilities of the service layer

The new `Catalog.Infrastructure` functionalities extend the `Catalog.Domain` project and expose `IArtistRepository` and `IGenreRepository` to the controllers of the API project. First of all, we should create a couple of new service classes in the `Catalog.Domain` project in order to query the underlying `Catalog.Infrastructure` layer. Let's start by defining the `IArtistService` and `IGenreService` interfaces in the `Services` folder of the `Catalog.Domain` project:

```
using System.Collections.Generic;
using System.Threading;
using System.Threading.Tasks;
using Catalog.Domain.Requests.Artists;
using Catalog.Domain.Responses;

namespace Catalog.Domain.Services
{
    public interface IArtistService
    {
        Task<IEnumerable<ArtistResponse>> GetArtistsAsync();
        Task<ArtistResponse> GetArtistAsync(GetArtistRequest request);
        Task<IEnumerable<ItemResponse>>
GetItemByArtistIdAsync(GetArtistRequest request);
        Task<ArtistResponse> AddArtistAsync(AddArtistRequest request);
    }

    public interface IGenreService
    {
        Task<IEnumerable<GenreResponse>> GetGenreAsync();
        Task<GenreResponse> GetGenreAsync(GetGenreRequest request);
        Task<IEnumerable<ItemResponse>>
GetItemByGenreIdAsync(GetGenreRequest request);
        Task<GenreResponse> AddGenreAsync(AddGenreRequest request);
    }
}
```

The preceding code snippet contains the declarations of the `IArtistService` and `IGenreService` interfaces. For brevity, I've kept them in the same code snippet. Both interfaces define the methods in the lists, get the details, and then add a related entity. The `GetArtistsAsync()` and `GetGenreAsync()` methods can return the complete list of entities or a single entity, depending on whether the `request` parameter is specified or not. Additionally, it is possible to retrieve a list of `ItemResponse` by artist ID or genre ID using the `GetItemByArtistIdAsync` and `GetItemByGenreIdAsync` methods. Finally, we can add a new artist and genre using the `AddArtistAsync` and `AddGenreAsync` methods.

The preceding implementation also depends on the definition of the following request models:

```
namespace Catalog.Domain.Requests.Artists
{
    public class AddArtistRequest
    {
        public string ArtistName { get; set; }
    }
    public class GetArtistRequest
    {
        public Guid Id { get; set; }
    }
}

namespace Catalog.Domain.Requests.Genre
{
    public class AddGenreRequest
    {
        public string GenreDescription { get; set; }
    }
    public class GetGenreRequest
    {
        public Guid Id { get; set; }
    }
}
```

Here, the request classes define the allowed operation for the `Artist` and `Genre` entities. They are stored in the `Requests/Artist` and `Requests/Genre` folders, respectively. We can continue by implementing the concrete part of the `ArtistService` class, as follows:

```
using System;
using System.Collections.Generic;
using System.Linq;
using System.Threading;
using System.Threading.Tasks;
using Catalog.Domain.Mappers;
```

```
using Catalog.Domain.Repositories;
using Catalog.Domain.Requests.Artists;
using Catalog.Domain.Responses;

namespace Catalog.Domain.Services
{
    public class ArtistService : IArtistService
    {
        private readonly IArtistRepository _artistRepository;
        private readonly IItemRepository _itemRepository;
        private readonly IArtistMapper _artistMapper;
        private readonly IItemMapper _itemMapper;

        public ArtistService(IArtistRepository artistRepository,
IItemRepository itemRepository,
            IArtistMapper artistMapper, IItemMapper itemMapper)
        {
            _artistRepository = artistRepository;
            _itemRepository = itemRepository;
            _artistMapper = artistMapper;
            _itemMapper = itemMapper;
        }
        ...
    }
}
```

The preceding code defines the properties and the constructor of the ArtistService class. The implementation injects the IArtistRepository, IItemRepository, IArtistMapper, and IItemMapper dependencies. The Repositories classes will be used for communicating with the underlying data source of the application. On the other side, the mappers will be called to initialize and map the values sent as responses.

Once we have defined the dependencies of the ArtistService class, we can proceed with the implementation of the core methods:

```
public class ArtistService : IArtistService
{
    ...

    public async Task<IEnumerable<ArtistResponse>> GetArtistsAsync()
    {
        var result = await _artistRepository.GetAsync();

        return result.Select(_artistMapper.Map);
    }
```

```csharp
        public async Task<ArtistResponse> GetArtistAsync(GetArtistRequest
            request)
        {
            if (request?.Id == null) throw new ArgumentNullException();

            var result = await _artistRepository.GetAsync(request.Id);

            return result == null ? null : _artistMapper.Map(result);
        }

        public async Task<IEnumerable<ItemResponse>>
    GetItemByArtistIdAsync(GetArtistRequest request)
        {
            if (request?.Id == null) throw new ArgumentNullException();

            var result = await
    _itemRepository.GetItemByArtistIdAsync(request.Id);

            return result.Select(_itemMapper.Map);
        }

        public async Task<ArtistResponse> AddArtistAsync(AddArtistRequest
    request)
        {
            var item = new Entities.Artist {ArtistName =
    request.ArtistName};

            var result = _artistRepository.Add(item);

            await _artistRepository.UnitOfWork.SaveChangesAsync();

            return _artistMapper.Map(result);
        }
    }
```

The implementation represents the methods already defined in the IArtistService interface. It is quite easy to understand the purpose of the methods by looking at their signatures.

The GetAsync method invokes the IArtistRepository dependency to map and retrieve the result in an ArtistResponse object. GetItemByArtistIdAsync executes the corresponding method with the same name defined in the IItemRepository interface. Finally, AddArtistAsync executes the Add method defined in the IArtistRepository interface and executes the UnitOfWork.SaveChangesAsync method to apply the changes to the data source, and then map the resulting data.

The same approach can be taken by the GenreService implementation class, which will depend on the IGenreRepository and IGenreMapper interfaces.

 You can find the implementation of the GenreService class in the official GitHub repository of the book: https://github.com/PacktPublishing/ Hands-On-RESTful-Web-Services-with-ASP.NET-Core-3.

Finally, we should also remember to include the definition of these interfaces in the AddServices extension method defined in the previous chapter, by incorporating the following changes:

```
using Catalog.Domain.Mappers;
using Catalog.Domain.Services;
using Microsoft.Extensions.DependencyInjection;

namespace Catalog.Domain.Extensions
{
    public static class DependenciesRegistration
    {
        ...

        public static IServiceCollection AddServices(this
IServiceCollection services)
        {
            services
                .AddScoped<IItemService, ItemService>()
                .AddScoped<IArtistService, ArtistService>()
                .AddScoped<IGenreService, GenreService>();
            return services;
        }
    }
}
```

These changes register the IArtistService and IGenreService interfaces in order to be used by the controllers and the other dependencies of the application. In the next section, we will continue the implementation by adding some validation logic to the request models.

Improving the validation mechanism

As we explained in the previous chapter, we are using the FluentValidation package to implement the validation mechanism of the web service. Since we have built the service interfaces to handle the Artist and Genre entities, it is now possible to improve the validation checks already present in the AddItemRequestValidator and EditItemRequestValidator classes. Now, we are going to implement the existence check for the Artist- and Genre-related entities.

Let's start by extending the implementation of the AddItemRequestValidator class:

```csharp
using System;
using FluentValidation;
using System.Threading.Tasks;
using Catalog.Domain.Requests.Artists;
using Catalog.Domain.Requests.Genre;
using Catalog.Domain.Services;

namespace Catalog.Domain.Requests.Item.Validators
{
    public class AddItemRequestValidator :
AbstractValidator<AddItemRequest>
    {
        private readonly IArtistService _artistService;
        private readonly IGenreService _genreService;

        public AddItemRequestValidator(IArtistService artistService,
IGenreService genreService)
        {
            _artistService = artistService;
            _genreService = genreService;
        }
        private async Task<bool> ArtistExists(Guid artistId,
CancellationToken cancellationToken)
        {
            if (string.IsNullOrEmpty(artistId.ToString()))
                return false;

            var artist = await _artistService.GetArtistAsync(new
GetArtistRequest {Id = artistId});

            return artist != null;
        }

        private async Task<bool> GenreExists(Guid genreId,
CancellationToken cancellationToken)
        {
```

```
                  if (string.IsNullOrEmpty(genreId.ToString()))
                      return false;

                  var genre = await _genreService.GetGenreAsync(new
      GetGenreRequest {Id = genreId});

                  return genre != null;
              }
          }
      }
```

The `AddItemRequestValidator` class now injects the `IArtistService` and `IGenreService` interfaces using the constructor injection pattern. In addition to this, the validation class defines two methods, `ArtistExists` and `GenreExists`, which will be used to verify that the `ArtistId` and `GenreId` fields exist in the database by calling the `IArtistService` and `IGenreService` interface methods. Moreover, we can improve the validation rules by checking the existence of the related entities in the following way:

```
using System;
...

namespace Catalog.Domain.Item.Validators
{
    public class AddItemRequestValidator :
AbstractValidator<AddItemRequest>
    {
        ..
        public AddItemRequestValidator(IArtistService artistService,
IGenreService genreService)
        {
            _artistService = artistService;
            _genreService = genreService;
            RuleFor(x => x.ArtistId)
               .NotEmpty()
               .MustAsync(ArtistExists).WithMessage("Artist must exists");
            RuleFor(x => x.GenreId)
               .NotEmpty()
               .MustAsync(GenreExists).WithMessage("Genre must exists");
            ...
        }
    ...
```

The new rules bind the `ArtistId` and `GenreId` fields with the `ArtistExists` and `GenreExists` methods, respectively. The same approach can be taken for the `EditItemRequestValidator` implementation, which will use the same pattern to validate the related entities. Therefore, we now need to extend the test classes in order to verify the new validation rules:

```
...
using FluentValidation.TestHelper;
using Moq;

namespace Catalog.Domain.Tests.Requests.Item.Validators
{
    public class AddItemRequestValidatorTests
    {
        private readonly Mock<IArtistService> _artistServiceMock;
        private readonly Mock<IGenreService> _genreServiceMock;
        private readonly AddItemRequestValidator _validator;

        public AddItemRequestValidatorTests()
        {
            _artistServiceMock = new Mock<IArtistService>();
            _artistServiceMock
                .Setup(x => x.GetArtistAsync(It.IsAny<GetArtistRequest>()))
                .ReturnsAsync(() => new ArtistResponse());

            _genreServiceMock = new Mock<IGenreService>();
            _genreServiceMock
                .Setup(x => x.GetGenreAsync(It.IsAny<GetGenreRequest>()))
                .ReturnsAsync(() => new GenreResponse());

            _validator = new
AddItemRequestValidator(_artistServiceMock.Object,
_genreServiceMock.Object);
        }
        [Fact]
        public void should_have_error_when_ArtistId_doesnt_exist()
        {
            _artistServiceMock
                .Setup(x => x.GetArtistAsync(It.IsAny<GetArtistRequest>()))
                .ReturnsAsync(() => null);

            var addItemRequest = new AddItemRequest { Price = new Price(),
ArtistId = Guid.NewGuid() };

            _validator.ShouldHaveValidationErrorFor(x => x.ArtistId,
addItemRequest);
        }
```

```
        [Fact]
        public void should_have_error_when_GenreId_doesnt_exist()
        {
            _genreServiceMock
                .Setup(x => x.GetGenreAsync(It.IsAny<GetGenreRequest>()))
                .ReturnsAsync(() => null);

            var addItemRequest = new AddItemRequest { Price = new Price(),
    GenreId = Guid.NewGuid() };

            _validator.ShouldHaveValidationErrorFor(x => x.GenreId,
    addItemRequest);
        }
    }
}
```

The preceding code injects the Mock<IArtistService> and Mock<IGenreService>
types into the validator class constructor in order to mock the behavior of the service layer
and verify the logic of the validator class. It also uses
the ShouldHaveValidationErrorFor method to check the expected response. The
ArtistExists and GenreExists methods should throw a validation error in case the ID
of one of the related entities is missing from the data source.

Updating the dependencies in the Startup class

In the previous few sections, we created the IArtistService and IGenreService
interfaces, and their corresponding implementations. Therefore, we want to update the
dependency graph of the application. Although we have already called
the AddMappers and AddServices extension methods of
the DependenciesRegistration static class in the ConfigureService method, we need
to update the dependencies in the following way:

```
    public static class DependenciesRegistration
    {
        ...

        public static IServiceCollection AddServices(this
    IServiceCollection services)
        {
            services
                .AddScoped<IItemService, ItemService>()
                .AddScoped<IArtistService, ArtistService>()
                .AddScoped<IGenreService, GenreService>();
```

```
                return services;
            }
        }
```

We should also add `IArtistRepository` and `IGenreRepository` to the `ConfigureService` method:

```
    ...
    public void ConfigureServices(IServiceCollection services)
    {
        services
            ...
            .AddScoped<IItemRepository, ItemRepository>()
            .AddScoped<IArtistRepository, ArtistRepository>()
            .AddScoped<IGenreRepository, GenreRepository>()
            ....
    }
```

Now, the `ConfigureServices` method of the `Startup` class defines all the required dependencies used by our stack. We are currently able to resolve the dependency chain related to the `ArtistController` and `GenreController` classes, which we will define in the next section.

Adding the related controllers

The `Catalog.Domain` project is now capable of handling requests related to the `Artist` and `Genre` entities through the logic we implemented in the `IArtistService` and `IGenreService` classes. Therefore, we can proceed by creating the controller layer to handle the incoming HTTP requests. Since we have different separate entities, we are going to implement the `ArtistController` and `GenreController` controller classes. Let's first focus on `ArtistController`:

```
    using Catalog.API.Filters;
    using Catalog.Domain.Services;
    using Microsoft.AspNetCore.Mvc;

    namespace Catalog.API.Controllers
    {
        [Route("api/artist")]
        [ApiController]
        [JsonException]
        public class ArtistController : ControllerBase
        {
            private readonly IArtistService _artistService;
```

```
            public ArtistController(IArtistService artistService)
            {
                _artistService = artistService;
            }
        }
    }
```

The above code defines the initial signature of the `ArtistController` class: the implementation injects the `IArtistService` interface from the service layer in order to interact with the information stored in the database. We can proceed further, by defining the implementation of the `Get` and `GetById` action methods:

```
using System;
using System.Linq;
using System.Threading;
using System.Threading.Tasks;
using Catalog.API.ResponseModels;
using Catalog.Domain.Requests.Artists;
using Catalog.Domain.Responses;

namespace Catalog.API.Controllers
{
    ..
    public class ArtistController : ControllerBase
    {
        ...
        [HttpGet]
        public async Task<IActionResult> Get([FromQuery] int pageSize = 10,
[FromQuery] int pageIndex = 0)
        {
            var result = await _artistService.GetArtistsAsync();

            var totalItems = result.ToList().Count;

            var itemsOnPage = result
                .OrderBy(c => c.ArtistName)
                .Skip(pageSize * pageIndex)
                .Take(pageSize);

            var model = new PaginatedItemsResponseModel<ArtistResponse>(
                pageIndex, pageSize, totalItems, itemsOnPage);

            return Ok(model);
        }

        [HttpGet("{id:guid}")]
        public async Task<IActionResult> GetById(Guid id)
        {
```

```
            var result = await _artistService.GetArtistAsync(new
    GetArtistRequest {Id = id});

            return Ok(result);
        }
    }
}
```

The preceding code shows the implementation of `ArtistController`, which corresponds to the `/api/artist` route. `ArtistController` uses `PaginatedItemsResponseModel` to retrieve the information related to all the artists. In the same way, we can use the `IAritstService` interface to execute the other operations and map them with the action methods:

```
...
        [HttpGet("{id:guid}/items")]
        public async Task<IActionResult> GetItemsById(Guid id)
        {
            var result = await _artistService.GetItemByArtistIdAsync(new
    GetArtistRequest { Id = id });

            return Ok(result);
        }

        [HttpPost]
        public async Task<IActionResult> Post(AddArtistRequest request)
        {
            var result = await _artistService.AddArtistAsync(request);

            return CreatedAtAction(nameof(GetById), new { id =
    result.ArtistId }, null);
        }
    }
```

The preceding `ArtistController` class defines the following routes:

Verb	Path	Description
GET	`/api/artist`	Retrieves all the artists present in the database
GET	`/api/artist/{id}`	Retrieves the artist with the corresponding *ID*
GET	`/api/artist/{id}/items/`	Retrieves the items with the corresponding artist *ID*
POST	`/api/artist/`	Creates a new artist and retrieves it

For each route, the *catalog service* will retrieve the corresponding data by executing the `IArtistService` interface methods. The `ArtistService` implementation will dispatch the request to the corresponding method of the repository implementations contained in the `Catalog.Infrastructure` project. Similar to `ItemController`, we can implement any additional validation behavior by using `FluentValidation`. For example, in the case of `AddArtistRequest`, we can proceed with the following implementation:

```
using FluentValidation;

namespace Catalog.Domain.Requests.Artists.Validators
{
    public class AddArtistRequestValidator :
AbstractValidator<AddArtistRequest>
    {
        public AddArtistRequestValidator()
        {
            RuleFor(artist => artist.ArtistName).NotEmpty();
        }
    }
}
```

In the case of `AddArtistRequest`, we want to prevent the user from adding empty `ArtistName` fields. We can create an additional `AddArtistRequestValidator` class under the `Requests/Artist/Validator` path. The validator class contains only one rule related to the non-empty `ArtistName` field.

The same implementation pattern can be also taken by the `GenreController` class. The following code defines the signature of the class implementation:

```
using System;
using System.Linq;
using System.Threading;
using System.Threading.Tasks;
using Catalog.API.Filters;
using Catalog.API.ResponseModels;
using Catalog.Domain.Requests.Genre;
using Catalog.Domain.Responses;
using Catalog.Domain.Services;
using Microsoft.AspNetCore.Mvc;

namespace Catalog.API.Controllers
{
    [Route("api/genre")]
    [ApiController]
    [JsonException]
    public class GenreController : ControllerBase
```

```
    {
        private readonly IGenreService _genreService;

        public GenreController(IGenreService genreService)
        {
            _genreService = genreService;
        }
    }
}
```

The code above injects the `IGenreService` interface using the *constructor injection* practice. Furthermore, we can proceed by creating the corresponding routes we defined for the `ArtistController` class:

```
...

[HttpGet]
public async Task<IActionResult> Get([FromQuery] int pageSize = 10,
[FromQuery] int pageIndex = 0)
{
    var result = await _genreService.GetGenreAsync();

    var totalItems = result.ToList().Count;

    var itemsOnPage = result
        .OrderBy(c => c.GenreDescription)
        .Skip(pageSize * pageIndex)
        .Take(pageSize);

    var model = new PaginatedItemsResponseModel<GenreResponse>(
        pageIndex, pageSize, totalItems, itemsOnPage);

    return Ok(model);
}

[HttpGet("{id:guid}")]
public async Task<IActionResult> GetById(Guid id)
{
    var result = await _genreService.GetGenreAsync(new GetGenreRequest {Id
= id});

    return Ok(result);
}

[HttpGet("{id:guid}/items")]
public async Task<IActionResult> GetItemById(Guid id)
{
    var result = await _genreService.GetItemByGenreIdAsync(new
```

```
GetGenreRequest {Id = id});

    return Ok(result);
}

[HttpPost]
public async Task<IActionResult> Post(AddGenreRequest request)
{
    var result = await _genreService.AddGenreAsync(request);

    return CreatedAtAction(nameof(GetById), new {id = result.GenreId},
null);
}
...
```

The code above defines the `Get`, `GetById`, `GetItemById` and the `Post` action methods implemented in the `GenreController` class. Each action calls the underlying service layer in order to interact with the database. Although the implementation of the action methods is similar to the `ArtistController` class, I still keep the classes separate; therefore, the `Genre` and `Artist` entities can evolve separately without depending on each other.

Extending tests for the ArtistController class

Once we expose the API routes through the `ArtistController` and `GenreController` classes, we are able to proceed by testing the revealed paths using the same approach that we used for `ItemController`. We should continue by creating a new `ArtistControllerTests` class in the `Catalog.API.Tests` project:

```
using System.Collections.Generic;
...

namespace Catalog.API.Tests.Controllers
{
    public class ArtistControllerTests :
IClassFixture<InMemoryApplicationFactory<Startup>>
    {
        public ArtistControllerTests(InMemoryApplicationFactory<Startup>
factory)
        {
            _factory = factory;
        }

        private readonly InMemoryApplicationFactory<Startup> _factory;

        [Theory]
```

```
        [InlineData("/api/artist/")]
        public async Task smoke_test_on_items(string url)

        {
            var client = _factory.CreateClient();
            var response = await client.GetAsync(url);

            response.EnsureSuccessStatusCode();
        }

        [Theory]
        [InlineData("/api/artist/?pageSize=1&pageIndex=0", 1, 0)]
        public async Task get_should_returns_paginated_data(string url, int
pageSize, int pageIndex)

        {
            var client = _factory.CreateClient();
            var response = await client.GetAsync(url);

            response.EnsureSuccessStatusCode();

            var responseContent = await
response.Content.ReadAsStringAsync();
            var responseEntity =
JsonConvert.DeserializeObject<PaginatedItemResponseModel<GenreResponse>>(re
sponseContent);

            responseEntity.PageIndex.ShouldBe(pageIndex);
            responseEntity.PageSize.ShouldBe(pageSize);
            responseEntity.Data.Count().ShouldBe(pageSize);
        }

        [Theory]
        [LoadData("artist")]
        public async Task get_by_id_should_return_right_artist(Artist
request)
        {
            var client = _factory.CreateClient();
            var response = await
client.GetAsync($"/api/artist/{request.ArtistId}");

            response.EnsureSuccessStatusCode();

            var responseContent = await
response.Content.ReadAsStringAsync();
            var responseEntity =
JsonConvert.DeserializeObject<Artist>(responseContent);
```

```
                    responseEntity.ArtistId.ShouldBe(request.ArtistId);
        }
    ...
```

The preceding code describes the test case for the get paginated artist action method and the get by ID action method. Both use the same InMemoryApplicationFactory factory to set up the fake in-memory data source. It is also possible to combine additional tests to verify the add artist process:

```
    ...
        [Fact]
        public async Task add_should_create_new_artist()
        {
            var addArtistRequest = new AddArtistRequest{ ArtistName = "The
Braze" };

            var client = _factory.CreateClient();
            var httpContent = new
StringContent(JsonConvert.SerializeObject(addArtistRequest), Encoding.UTF8,
                "application/json");
            var response = await client.PostAsync("/api/artist",
httpContent);

            response.EnsureSuccessStatusCode();

            var responseHeader = response.Headers.Location;

            response.StatusCode.ShouldBe(HttpStatusCode.Created);
            responseHeader.ToString().ShouldContain("/api/artist/");
        }
    }
}
```

The fixture class initializes a new TestServer instance for each test method and it provides a new HttpClient instance through the CreateClient method to test the routes exposed by the ArtistController class. The tests also use the LoadData attribute to get matching information about the testing records from the record-data.json file. A similar implementation approach can be taken to test the GenreController class action methods.

A final overview

Finally, let's take a look at a quick overview of the code structure we implemented in Chapter 8, *Building the Data Access Layer*, Chapter 9, *Implementing the Domain Logic*, and this chapter. The following architecture schema illustrates the actual construction of the Catalog.API solution:

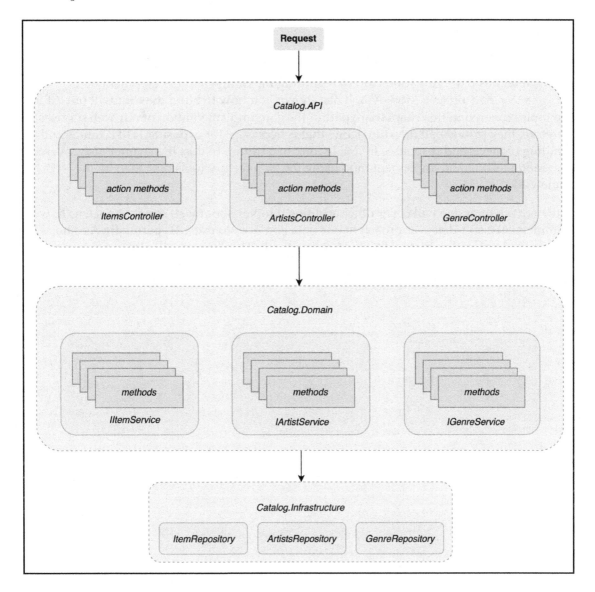

Once the web service instance receives the client request, it dispatches the request to the corresponding action method of the controller. Following this, the action method executes the corresponding function exposed by the service classes defined in the `Catalog.Domain` project, which ships the request to the relevant repository defined in the `Catalog.Infrastructure` project, and then maps the entities with the request and response models.

Summary

This chapter has covered various topics regarding the design and development of the `Catalog.API` project. Moreover, it has shown you how to build the routes of our APIs. The topics covered in this chapter are part of the core implementation of our web services; therefore, they provide all the knowledge that is necessary for exposing HTTP routes and handling requests and responses in .NET Core. In addition to this, the chapter also covered integration testing and implementation using the web factory tools provided by the framework.

In the next chapter, we will cover other additional topics about web services, such as how to implement a soft-delete approach to our data and how to use a **Hypermedia As The Engine Of Application State (HATEOAS)** approach. The chapter will also cover some .NET Core-related topics such as a brief introduction to and the best practices of asynchronous programming in .NET Core.

11
Advanced Concepts of Building an API

The previous chapter went through the implementation of the HTTP layer of the web service. Although the core functionalities of the service are already in place, there are still some refinements to cover. This chapter provides a walk-through of some additional implementations that will be a part of the catalog web service, such as soft deleting resources, the HATEOAS approach, adding a response-time middleware, and some of the best practices for asynchronous code in ASP.NET Core. More specifically, it will cover the following topics:

- Implementing the soft delete technique
- Implementing HATEOAS
- An overview of asynchronous code in ASP.NET Core
- Measuring the response time of APIs using middleware

 The code present in this chapter is available in the following GitHub repository: https://github.com/PacktPublishing/Hands-On-RESTful-Web-Services-with-ASP.NET-Core-3.

Implementing the soft delete procedure

As mentioned in the *Deleting resources* section of Chapter 5, *Web Service Stack in ASP.NET Core*, the soft delete technique is a widespread deletion practice in real-world applications. Furthermore, it is quite uncommon to physically delete entities from our data source.

Deleted data may be relevant for historical purposes and for performing analysis and reports. The soft delete implementation involves all the projects we have seen in the previous three chapters. In order to proceed, let's add a new IsInactive field to our Item entity inside the Catalog.Domain project:

```
namespace Catalog.Domain.Entities
{
    public class Item
    {
        ...
        public bool IsInactive { get; set; }
    }
}
```

Since we changed the schema of the Item entity, we need to perform another EF Core migration by executing the following commands inside the Catalog.API project:

```
dotnet ef migrations add Added_IsInactive_field
dotnet ef database update
```

The result of the execution of the aforementioned command will generate a new migration file inside the Migrations folder and the application of the newly created migration in the database specified in the connection string of the Startup class.

Furthermore, as we saw in Chapter 8, *Building the Data Access Layer*, if we want to connect to the local Docker SQL Server instance, we can specify the following connection string in the appsettings.json file:

```
{
    "Logging": {
        "LogLevel": {
            "Default": "Warning"
        }
    },
    "DataSource": {
        "ConnectionString": "Server=localhost,1433;Initial
Catalog=Store;User Id=catalog_srv;Password=P@ssw0rd"
    }
}
```

The preceding connection string provides the connection to the local instance of SQL Server. In order to run the instance, it is necessary to follow the command we saw in Chapter 8. The following runs the docker instance using the name sql1:

```
docker run -e "ACCEPT_EULA=Y" -e "SA_PASSWORD=<YOUR_SA_PASSWORD>" -p
1433:1433 --name sql1 -d mcr.microsoft.com/mssql/server:2017-latest
```

Furthermore, we can log in into the container using the following command:

```
docker exec -it sql1 "bash"
```

and finally, we can execute the `sqlcmd` in order to log in into the SQL server instance:

```
/opt/mssql-tools/bin/sqlcmd -S localhost -U SA -P '<YOUR_SA_PASSWORD>'

1> CREATE LOGIN catalog_srv WITH PASSWORD = 'P@ssw0rd';
2> CREATE DATABASE Store;
3> GO
1> USE Store;
2> CREATE USER catalog_srv;
3> GO
1> EXEC sp_addrolemember N'db_owner', N'catalog_srv';
2> GO
```

The code above creates the `Store` database with a login user called `catalog_srv`. Later in the book, we will see how to automate this process using the tools provided by Docker. Now, the database schema is updated, and we are able to continue by including the `IsInactive` field in the repository and the service layer of the application.

Updating the IItemRepository implementation

Since we added the new `IsInactive` field in our database, we can proceed by adapting the `IItemRepository` interface to filter our data based on the `IsInactive` field. Therefore, we will proceed by implementing the following changes in order to maintain consistency in our data source:

- The `IItemRepository.GetAsync()` method will filter all the fields by `IsInactive = false`. Consequently, the resulting response will only contain active entities. This kind of approach guarantees that we get a lightweight response when we try to get multiple entities from the database.
- In the same way, `GetItemByArtistIdAsync` and `GetItemByGenreIdAsync` will filter the result by using the `IsInactive = false` flag. Also, in this case, we want to keep the response as light as possible.

- The `IItemRepository.GetAsync(Guid id)` method will retrieve the details of the required entity regardless of the `IsInactive` flag. Moreover, this method is used by the validation checks of the application, therefore, we need to avoid duplicate IDs when we insert new objects, whether they are active or not.

Let's proceed by implementing these specifications mentioned in the `IItemRepository` interface:

```
namespace Catalog.Infrastructure.Repositories
{
    public class ItemRepository
        : IItemRepository
    {

        ...

        public async Task<IEnumerable<Item>> GetAsync()
        {
            return await _context.Items
                .Where(x => !x.IsInactive)
                .AsNoTracking()
                .ToListAsync();
        }

        public async Task<IEnumerable<Item>> GetItemByArtistIdAsync(Guid
    id)
        {
            var items = await _context
                .Items
                .Where(x => !x.IsInactive)
                .Where(item => item.ArtistId == id)
                .Include(x => x.Genre)
                .Include(x => x.Artist)
                .ToListAsync();

            return items;
        }

        public async Task<IEnumerable<Item>> GetItemByGenreIdAsync(Guid id)
        {
            var items = await _context.Items
                .Where(x => !x.IsInactive)
                .Where(item => item.GenreId == id)
                .Include(x => x.Genre)
                .Include(x => x.Artist)
                .ToListAsync();

            return items;
```

```
        }
...
```

This implementation changes the behavior of the `GetAsync`, `GetItemByArtistIdAsync`, and `GetItemByGenreIdAsync` methods by filtering for `IsInactive == false` using the `Where` LINQ clause. On the other hand, `GetAsync(Guid id)` remains the same because, as mentioned in the specifications, we want the get detail operation to always retrieve the information, including cases where the record is not active. Therefore, we can test the resulting implementation by executing the following command in the root of the project:

```
dotnet test
```

All tests should pass because, by default, the `IsInactive` Boolean field is always `false`. To test the `Where(x=>!x.IsInactive)` change, we can add a new record in the `Catalog.API/tests/Catalog.Fixtures/Data/item.json` file by adding a new inactive item:

```json
{
    "Id": "f5da5ce4-091e-492e-a70a-22b073d75a52",
    "Name": "Untitled",
    "Description": "Untitled by Kendrick Lamar",
    "PictureUri": "https://mycdn.com/pictures/32423423",
    "ReleaseDate": "2016-01-01T00:00:00+00:00",
    "Price": {
      "Amount": 23.5,
      "Currency": "EUR"
    },
    "Format": "Vinyl 33g",
    "AvailableStock": 6,
    "GenreId": "c04f05c0-f6ad-44d1-a400-3375bfb5dfd6",
    "Genre": null,
    "ArtistId": "3eb00b42-a9f0-4012-841d-70ebf3ab7474",
    "Artist": null,
    "IsInactive": true
},
```

Therefore, we can verify that the number of records retrieved by the get operation changes by creating a new test and counting the results. For example, if the `item.json` file contains three records and one is inactive, the get operation should retrieve three records. As an alternative, we can double-check by verifying that the `Item.Id` fields of the result do not include an inactive record:

```
namespace Catalog.Infrastructure.Tests
{
    ...
    public class ItemRepositoryTests : IClassFixture<CatalogContextFactory>
    {
        [Theory]
        [InlineData("f5da5ce4-091e-492e-a70a-22b073d75a52")]
        public async Task
getitems_should_not_return_inactive_records(string id)
        {
            var result =
                await _sut.GetAsync();

            result.Any(x => x.Id == new Guid(id)).ShouldBeFalse();
        }
        ...
    }
}
```

I chose to test the deletion behavior by adding a new `getitems_should_not_return_inactive_records` method in the `ItemRepositoryTests` class. The test verifies that when I call the `GetAsync` method of the repository, the result excludes the `Item` entity with the `Id` specified as a parameter of the test. A similar approach can be also taken for the `GetItemByArtistIdAsync` and the `GetItemByGenreIdAsync` methods.

Implementing delete operations

Now that we have implemented the right filtering logic on the repository side, let's proceed by implementing delete operations in the `Catalog.Domain` project by adding a new `DeleteItemAsync` method in the declaration of the `IItemService` interface:

```
namespace Catalog.Domain.Services
{
    public interface IItemService
    {
        ...
        Task<ItemResponse> DeleteItemAsync(DeleteItemRequest request);
```

```
    }
}
```

The `DeleteItemAsync` method refers to a `DeleteItemRequest` type, which can be declared as follows:

```
using System;

namespace Catalog.Domain.Requests.Item
{
    public class DeleteItemRequest
    {
        public Guid Id { get; set; }
    }
}
```

Once we update the `IItemService` interface declaration, we can proceed by adding the implementation to the `ItemService` concrete class:

```
public async Task<ItemResponse> DeleteItemAsync(DeleteItemRequest request)
{
    if (request?.Id == null) throw new ArgumentNullException();

    var result = await _itemRepository.GetAsync(request.Id);
    result.IsInactive = true;

    _itemRepository.Update(result);
    await _itemRepository.UnitOfWork.SaveChangesAsync();

    return _itemMapper.Map(result);
}
```

The `DeleteItemAsync` method receives an `Id` field that is part of the `DeleteItemRequest` class. Besides, it uses the `GetAsync` method to get the details of the entity, and it continues by calling the `Update` method by passing the entity with the `IsInactive` flag set to `true`. The next step is to implement a new action method in the `ItemController` that covers the following HTTP call:

```
DELETE /items/{id}
```

Moreover, we can proceed by changing the `ItemController` as follows:

```
using System;
using System.Threading.Tasks;
using Catalog.API.Filters;
using Catalog.Domain.Requests.Item;
using Microsoft.AspNetCore.Mvc;
```

```
namespace Catalog.API.Controllers
{
    [Route("api/items")]
    [ApiController]
    public class ItemController : ControllerBase
    {
        ...

        [HttpDelete("{id:guid}")]
        [ItemExists]
        public async Task<IActionResult> Delete(Guid id)
        {
            var request = new DeleteItemRequest { Id = id };

            await _itemService.DeleteItemAsync(request);

            return NoContent();
        }
    }
}
```

The Delete action method is decorated with the HttpDelete attribute verb, which means that it is mapped with the HTTP Delete requests. The implementation sets the IsInactive flag through the DeleteItemAsync method, and it returns a NoContent result, which represents an HTTP 204 No Content status code.

We will proceed by testing the changes made to the ItemController class by implementing the following tests:

```
namespace Catalog.API.Tests.Controllers
{
    public class ItemsController :
IClassFixture<InMemoryApplicationFactory<Startup>>
    {
        private readonly InMemoryApplicationFactory<Startup> _factory;

        public ItemsController(InMemoryApplicationFactory<Startup> factory)
        {
            _factory = factory;
        }
        ...

        [Theory]
        [LoadData("item")]
        public async Task
delete_should_returns_no_content_when_called_with_right_id(DeleteItemReques
t
```

```
        request)
        {
            var client = _factory.CreateClient();

            var response = await
    client.DeleteAsync($"/api/items/{request.Id}");

                response.StatusCode.ShouldBe(HttpStatusCode.NoContent);
        }
        [Fact]
        public async Task
    delete_should_returns_not_found_when_called_with_not_existing_id()
        {
            var client = _factory.CreateClient();

            var response = await
    client.DeleteAsync($"/api/items/{Guid.NewGuid()}");

                response.StatusCode.ShouldBe(HttpStatusCode.NotFound);
        }
    }
}
```

This test code covers the following two behaviors:

- The `delete_should_returns_no_content_when_called_with_right_id` test method checks whether the action method correctly returns the HTTP `NoContent` response.
- The `delete_should_returns_not_found_when_called_with_not_existing_id` method checks that the action method returns `HttpStatusCode.NotFound` by passing a non-existent GUID (`Guid.NewGuid`).

In both test cases, we are using the already implemented test infrastructure to verify the new behavior of the web service. In this section, we have seen how to extend our web service in order to support the soft delete operation.

The next section focuses on the implementation of the HATEOAS response approach.

Implementing HATEOAS

We already discussed the theory around the HATEOAS principle in `Chapter 1, REST 101 and Getting Started with ASP.NET Core`. This section explains how to implement the HATEOAS approach for the `ItemController` already present in the `Catalog.API` project. The following snippet of code shows an example of a generic HATEOAS response:

```
{
    "_links": {
        "get": {
            "rel": "ItemsHateoas/Get",
            "href": "https://localhost:5001/api/hateoas/items",
            "method": "GET"
        },
        "get_by_id": {
            "rel": "ItemsHateoas/GetById",
            "href":
"https://localhost:5001/api/hateoas/items/8ff0fe8f-9dbc-451f-7a57-08d652340
f56",
            "method": "GET"
        },
        "create": {
            "rel": "ItemsHateoas/Post",
            "href": "https://localhost:5001/api/hateoas/items",
            "method": "POST"
        },
        "update": {
            "rel": "ItemsHateoas/Put",
            "href":
"https://localhost:5001/api/hateoas/items/8ff0fe8f-9dbc-451f-7a57-08d652340
f56",
            "method": "PUT"
        },
        "delete": {
            "rel": "ItemsHateoas/Delete",
            "href":
"https://localhost:5001/api/hateoas/items/8ff0fe8f-9dbc-451f-7a57-08d652340
f56",
            "method": "DELETE"
        }
    },
    "id": "8ff0fe8f-9dbc-451f-7a57-08d652340f56",
    "name": "Malibu",
    "description": "Malibu. by Anderson Paak",
    "labelName": "Steel Wool/OBE/Art Club",
    "price": {
        "amount": 23.5,
```

```
        "currency": "EUR"
    },
    "pictureUri": "https://mycdn.com/pictures/32423423",
    "releaseDate": "2016-01-01T00:00:00+00:00",
    "format": "Vinyl 43",
    "availableStock": 3,
    "genreId": "7fcdde39-342b-4f80-0db1-08d65233f5a6",
    "genre": null,
    "artistId": "ff1921a8-f49a-4db2-0c2e-08d65233875e",
    "artist": null
}
```

Although this kind of response adds a heavy payload to the effective JSON response, it assists the client by providing the URL for each operation and resource on our data. The HATEOAS principle will be implemented side-by-side with `ItemController`, and it will give all the necessary information to the client to interact with the data owned by the catalog service.

Enriching our model with HATEOAS data

To get HATEOAS working, we will rely on a third-party NuGet package called `RiskFirst.Hateoas`. This package allows us to integrate the HATEOAS principle in our service efficiently. First of all, let's proceed by adding the package to `Catalog.API` by executing the following command in both project folders:

```
dotnet add package RiskFirst.Hateoas
```

Next, create a new entity called the `ItemHateoasResponse` class, which represents the HATEOAS response. This class refers to the already implemented `ItemResponse` class, and it implements the `ILinkContainer` interface exposed by the `RiskFirst.Hateoas` package:

```
using System.Collections.Generic;
using Newtonsoft.Json;
using RiskFirst.Hateoas.Models;
using Catalog.Domain.Responses.Item;

namespace Catalog.API.ResponseModels
{
    public class ItemHateoasResponse : ILinkContainer
    {
        public ItemResponse Data;
        private Dictionary<string, Link> _links;

        [JsonProperty(PropertyName = "_links")]
```

```
public Dictionary<string, Link> Links
{
    get => _links ?? (_links = new Dictionary<string, Link>());
    set => _links = value;
}

public void AddLink(string id, Link link)
{
    Links.Add(id, link);
}
    }
}
```

The `Links` field is a `Dictionary<string, Link>` type and it contains the URLs to the resources related to the response. For example, if we get the response of a specific item, the `Link` attribute will provide the URLs to add, update, and delete the item. The `AddLink` method is used to add new fields to the `Links` dictionary. Therefore, we will continue by using this type of response in a controller in order to provide a HATEOAS-compliant reaction to our client.

Implementing HATEOAS in a controller

The final step is to implement a controller that can handle the `ItemHateoasResponse` response model implemented previously. More specifically, we can proceed by creating a new `ItemHateoasController` class in our `Catalog.API` project. Note that we are building a new controller for demonstration purposes. An alternative would be to edit the already defined `ItemController` to return HATEOAS-compliant responses.

The `ItemHateoasController` class will use the `ILinksService` interface provided by the `RiskFirst.Hateoas` namespace to enrich the `Links` attribute of the `ItemHateoasResponse` model and return it to our client. Let's proceed by implementing the controller:

```
using System;
using System.Collections.Generic;
using System.Linq;
using System.Threading;
using System.Threading.Tasks;
using Catalog.API.Filters;
using Catalog.API.ResponseModels;
using Catalog.Domain.Requests.Item;
using Catalog.Domain.Services;
using Microsoft.AspNetCore.Mvc;
using RiskFirst.Hateoas;
```

```
namespace Catalog.API.Controllers
{
    [Route("api/hateoas/items")]
    [ApiController]
    [JsonException]
    public class ItemsHateoasController : ControllerBase
    {
        private readonly IItemService _itemService;
        private readonly ILinksService _linksService;

        public ItemsHateoasController(ILinksService linkService,
IItemService itemService)
        {
            _linksService = linkService;
            _itemService = itemService;
        }

        [HttpGet(Name = nameof(Get))]
        public async Task<IActionResult> Get([FromQuery] int pageSize = 10,
[FromQuery] int pageIndex = 0)
        {
            var result = await _itemService.GetItemsAsync();

            var totalItems = result.Count();

            var itemsOnPage = result.OrderBy(c => c.Name)
                .Skip(pageSize * pageIndex)
                .Take(pageSize);

            var hateoasResults = new List<ItemHateoasResponse>();

            foreach (var itemResponse in itemsOnPage)
            {
                var hateoasResult = new ItemHateoasResponse { Data =
itemResponse };
                await _linksService.AddLinksAsync(hateoasResult);

                hateoasResults.Add(hateoasResult);
            }

            var model = new
PaginatedItemResponseModel<ItemHateoasResponse>(
                pageIndex, pageSize, totalItems, hateoasResults);

            return Ok(model);
        }
```

```
[HttpGet("{id:guid}", Name = nameof(GetById))]
[ItemExists]
public async Task<IActionResult> GetById(Guid id)
{
    var result = await _itemService.GetItemAsync(new GetItemRequest
{ Id = id });
    var hateoasResult = new ItemHateoasResponse { Data = result };
    await _linksService.AddLinksAsync(hateoasResult);

    return Ok(hateoasResult);
}
```

The Get and GetById action methods are quite similar to the one that is present in ItemController. The only difference is that they return a different response type, which is represented by the ItemHateoasResponse class. Furthermore, the action methods assign the response object to the Data field. Each action method also calls the AddLinksAsync method provided by the ILinksService interface to populate the link attribute. In the same way, we can extend the behavior of the other action methods present in the controller class:

```
    ...

    [HttpPost(Name = nameof(Post))]
    public async Task<IActionResult> Post(AddItemRequest request)
    {
        var result = await _itemService.AddItemAsync(request);
        return CreatedAtAction(nameof(GetById), new { id = result.Id },
null);
    }

    [HttpPut("{id:guid}", Name = nameof(Put))]
    [ItemExists]
    public async Task<IActionResult> Put(Guid id, EditItemRequest
request)
    {
        request.Id = id;
        var result = await _itemService.EditItemAsync(request);

        var hateoasResult = new ItemHateoasResponse { Data = result };
        await _linksService.AddLinksAsync(hateoasResult);

        return Ok(hateoasResult);
    }

    [HttpDelete("{id:guid}", Name = nameof(Delete))]
    [ItemExists]
    public async Task<IActionResult> Delete(Guid id)
```

```
        {
            var request = new DeleteItemRequest { Id = id };
            await _itemService.DeleteItemAsync(request);
            return NoContent();
        }
    ..
```

This is the declaration of the implementation of the create, update, and delete action methods. Also, in this case, we are using the `ItemHateoasResponse` model class to retrieve the response of the action method. We should notice that the action methods declare `Name` in the `[HttpVerb]` attribute decorator, such as `[HttpDelete("{id:guid}", Name = nameof(Delete))]`. Indeed, we will use the `Name` declared by the attribute in the `Startup` class to refer to each route and include it in the `Link` property:

```
namespace Catalog.API
{
    public class Startup
    {
        ...

        public void ConfigureServices(IServiceCollection services)
        {
            ...

            services.AddLinks(config =>
            {
                config.AddPolicy<ItemHateoasResponse>(policy =>
                {
                    policy
.RequireRoutedLink(nameof(ItemsHateoasController.Get),
                        nameof(ItemsHateoasController.Get))
.RequireRoutedLink(nameof(ItemsHateoasController.GetById),
                        nameof(ItemsHateoasController.GetById), _ => new
{id = _.Data.Id})
.RequireRoutedLink(nameof(ItemsHateoasController.Post),
                        nameof(ItemsHateoasController.Post))
.RequireRoutedLink(nameof(ItemsHateoasController.Put),
                        nameof(ItemsHateoasController.Put), x => new {id =
x.Data.Id})
.RequireRoutedLink(nameof(ItemsHateoasController.Delete),
                        nameof(ItemsHateoasController.Delete), x => new
{id = x.Data.Id});
                });
            });
        }
        ...
```

```
        }
    }
```

The `AddLinks` extension method provided by the `RiskFirst.Hateoas` package allows us to define the policies related to a response model. This is the case for the `config.AddPolicy<ItemHateoasResponse>` method, which calls `RequireRoutedLink` for each action method name declared in `ItemsHateoasController`. Note that, similar to the previous cases, we can extract this snippet of code in an external extension method to keep the `Startup` class as clean as possible. Finally, this kind of approach allows us to define different groups of links for different response models. Moreover, it is possible to establish a policy related to a specific response model.

Consequently, we can now run and verify the result by executing the `dotnet run` command in the `Catalog.API` folder. Please note, to run the Docker SQL Server, specify the connection string in `appsetting.json` file. After that, we can run the following `curl` request to verify `ItemsHateoasController`. The resulting JSON response will look as follows:

```
{
    "_links": {
        "get": {
            "rel": "ItemsHateoas/Get",
            "href": "https://localhost:5001/api/hateoas/items",
            "method": "GET"
        },
        "get_by_id": {
            "rel": "ItemsHateoas/GetById",
            "href":
"https://localhost:5001/api/hateoas/items/8ff0fe8f-9dbc-451f-7a57-08d652340
f56",
            "method": "GET"
        },
        "create": {
            "rel": "ItemsHateoas/Post",
            "href": "https://localhost:5001/api/hateoas/items",
            "method": "POST"
        },
        "update": {
            "rel": "ItemsHateoas/Put",
            "href":
"https://localhost:5001/api/hateoas/items/8ff0fe8f-9dbc-451f-7a57-08d652340
f56",
            "method": "PUT"
        },
        "delete": {
```

```
            "rel": "ItemsHateoas/Delete",
            "href":
    "https://localhost:5001/api/hateoas/items/8ff0fe8f-9dbc-451f-7a57-08d652340
    f56",
            "method": "DELETE"
        }
    },
    "id": "8ff0fe8f-9dbc-451f-7a57-08d652340f56",
    "name": "Malibu",

. . .
```

As you can see, in addition to the list of items, `ItemHateoasController` also retrieves an envelope that provides additional information to the client, such as the other routes needed for the get, add, update, and delete operations. Furthermore, this approach gives all the URIs needed by the client, in order to navigate through the information exposed by the web service.

The asynchronous code in ASP.NET Core

In this section, we will discuss the asynchronous code stack of ASP.NET Core. We have already dealt with the asynchronous pattern, and we have already seen that some of the implementations in the previous chapters used asynchronous code extensively.

 Note that the following section is mainly focused on asynchronous code in ASP.NET Core based on .NET Core. Bear in mind that there are some differences between asynchronous programming in .NET Core and .NET Framework. Some of the deadlocking issues that we are used to seeing in .NET Framework are not present in .NET Core.

Before we start digging into the asynchronous code, let's take a look at the differences between synchronous and asynchronous systems in ASP.NET Core.

First of all, when a synchronous API receives a request, a thread from the thread pool will handle the request. The assigned thread is busy until the end of the request life cycle. In most cases, the API performs I/O operations on data or third-party APIs, which means that the thread will be blocked until the end of these operations. More specifically, a blocked thread cannot be used by other operations and requests. For asynchronous code, however, the behavior is entirely different.

The request will be assigned to a thread, but the thread will not be locked, and it can be assigned and used by other operations. If the task is awaited and it doesn't involve CPU-bound work, then the thread can be released to return to the pool to carry out other work.

Task definitions

The `Task` type represents asynchronous tasks. The `Task` class is a representation of a unit of work. We can find similar concepts in other languages. For example, in JavaScript, the concept of `Task` is represented by a `Promise`.

It is common to associate a `Task` type with a thread in our CPU, which is not correct: wrapping a method execution in a `Task` doesn't guarantee that the operation will be executed on another thread.

The `async` and `await` keywords are the easiest way to deal with asynchronous operations in C#: the `async` keyword converts the method into a state machine and it enables the `await` keyword in the implementation of the method. The `await` keyword indicates to the compiler the operations that need to be awaited in order to proceed with the execution of the asynchronous method. Therefore, it is common to find something similar in C# codebases:

```
public async Task<String> GetStringAsync(String url)
{
    var request = await _httpClient.GetAsync(url);
    var responseContent = await request.Content.ReadAsStringAsync();
    return responseContent;
}
```

The preceding snippet is very intuitive: it calls a `url` using the `GetAsync` method of the `_httpClient` instance, and it uses `ReadAsStringAsync` to get the resulting string and store it in the `responseContent` object. It is essential to understand that `async` and `await` are syntactic sugar keywords, and the same result can be achieved in a less readable way by using the `ContinueWith` method:

```
public Task<String> GetStringAsync(String url)
{
    var request =_httpClient.GetAsync(url);
    var responseContentTask = request.ContinueWith(http =>
                      http.Result.Content.ReadAsStringAsync());
    return responseContentTask.Unwrap();
}
```

This code snippet has the same effect as the previous one. The main difference is that this code is less intuitive. Furthermore, in complex operations that execute a lot of nested transactions, we would create a lot of nesting levels.

It is essential to embrace the `async/await` syntax as the primary way of working with asynchronous code. Other languages have taken a similar approach to keep the code more clean and readable. This is the case for ECMAScript, which introduced the `async/await` syntax in ES 2016: `https://github.com/tc39/ecma262/blob/master/README.md`.

The need for asynchronous code in ASP.NET Core

The first thing to underline is that asynchronous code is not about speed. As mentioned before, asynchronous programming is just about not blocking incoming requests. Therefore, the real benefit is about better vertical scalability, instead of increasing the speed of our code. For example, let's suppose that our web services perform some I/O operations such as queries on a database: in case we run our code stack in a synchronous way, the thread used by an incoming request will be blocked and not used by any other request until the read or write (I/O operation) process is completed. By taking an asynchronous approach we are able to release the thread as soon as the read/write operation is executed. Therefore, once the I/O operation is finished, the application will pick up another or the same thread in order to continue the execution of the stack.

The asynchronous code also adds an overhead cost to our system, in fact, it is necessary to add additional logic to coordinate asynchronous operations. For example, let's take a look at the following code:

```
[Route("api/[controller]")]
[ApiController]
public class ValuesController : ControllerBase
{
    // GET api/values
    [HttpGet]
    public async Task<ActionResult<string>> Get()
    {
        return await OperationAsync();
    }


    public async Task<string> OperationAsync()
    {
```

```
        await Task.Delay(100);
        return "Response";
    }
}
```

The aforementioned example defines an action method that calls an asynchronous method. With the help of some external tools, such as ILSpy, it is possible to decompile the C# code and analyze the IL code. The **IL code** is also known as the **intermediate code**, which is the code that is generated by the C# compiler and executed at runtime.

The resulting transformation in the IL code of the previously defined Get method looks as follows:

```
[CompilerGenerated]
private sealed class <Get>d__0 : IAsyncStateMachine
{
    // Fields
    public int <>1__state;
    public AsyncTaskMethodBuilder<ActionResult<string>> <>t__builder;
    public ValuesController <>4__this;
    private string <>s__1;
    private TaskAwaiter<string> <>u__1;

    // Methods
    public <Get>d__0();
    private void MoveNext();
    [DebuggerHidden]
    private void SetStateMachine(IAsyncStateMachine stateMachine);
}
```

As you can see, the method has been transformed into a sealed class that implements the IAsyncStateMachine interface. The MoveNext method continuously checks whether the __state of the state machine is changed and updates the result of the operation. All these operations are performed for each asynchronous operation contained in our code.

What's new in ASP.NET Core?

Since its introduction in the old ASP.NET framework, the async/await code was previously affected by some *deadlock issues*. The old version of ASP.NET uses a class called SynchronizationContext, which essentially provides a way to queue a Task to a context when a method calls other tasks that are nested asynchronous methods and forces them to be executed synchronously using the .Result or .Wait() keywords, therefore, this causes a deadlock of the request context.

For example, let's suppose that the following code is executed on the old version of ASP.NET:

```
public class ValuesController : ApiController
  {
      public string Get()
      {
          return Operation1Async().Result;
      }

      public async Task<string> Operation1Async()
      {
          await Task.Delay(1000);
          return "Test";
      }
  }
```

This leads to a deadlock in the application because the Get() and Operation1Async() methods are using the same context. While the Operation1Async() method captures the context, which will be used to continue running the method, the Get() action method is blocking the context because it is waiting for a result.

For this reason, developers started to fill their asynchronous code with .ConfigureAwait(false) instructions, which primarily provides a way to execute the Task in a different context by avoiding the deadlock issue seen before:

```
public class ValuesController : ApiController
  {
      public string Get()
      {
          return Operation1Async().Result;
      }

      public async Task<string> Operation1Async()
      {
          await Task.Delay(1000)
                    .ConfigureAwait(continueOnCapturedContext: false);
          return "Test";
      }
  }
```

This kind of approach works, but we should consider that by calling Result or .Wait(), we are losing all the benefits provided by the asynchronous programming pattern.

The good news about ASP.NET Core is that it doesn't use `SynchronizationContext`. The *context-less* idea provides lightweight management of the asynchronous code: while ASP.NET queues each asynchronous unit in the request context before assigning it to a thread, ASP.NET Core picks up a thread from the assigned thread pool and attaches it to the asynchronous task.

Moreover, the ASP.NET team has done an excellent job with ASP.NET Core and, as we saw in previous chapters, almost every component that is part of the ASP.NET Core pipeline has both a *synchronous* and an *asynchronous* version. This is the case, for example, for the action filter that we saw in `Chapter 6`, *Filter Pipeline*.

While the `.ConfigureAwait(false)` method is not needed anymore with the new version of .NET Core, we should keep in mind that it is still useful in some codebases. If you are building a .NET library that compiles in .NET Core but also in older version of the .NET Framework, you should still use the `.ConfigureAwait(false)` method in order to avoid deadlocks.

Best practices in asynchronous programming

Let's take a look at some good and bad practices to do with the asynchronous programming model in ASP.NET Core. First of all, the central concept to keep in mind is to avoid mixing between synchronous and asynchronous code. As mentioned previously, ASP.NET Core exposes both the sync and `async` versions of the majority of classes and interfaces. Therefore, before blocking an asynchronous stack with synchronous code, you should explore and check all the alternatives provided by the framework.

The following recommendations come from a high-level perspective of asynchronous programming in .NET. This book is focused on other aspects of the framework. If you want to get more details about how to work with asynchronous programming, I suggest you navigate to the following link: `https://github.com/davidfowl/AspNetCoreDiagnosticScenarios/blob/master/AsyncGuidance.md`. Moreover, if you want a more general overview of concurrency in .NET, I suggest you read the following book: *Concurrency in C# Cookbook* by Stephen Cleary (`https://stephencleary.com/book/`).

Don't use async void methods

A common mistake about asynchronous programming in .NET Core and, more in general, in the whole .NET ecosystem, is to declare a method as `async void`. Indeed, when we declare a method as `async void`, we will not be able to catch exceptions thrown by the method. Furthermore, the `Task` type is used to capture the exceptions of the method and propagate them to the caller. In summary, we should always implement our `async` methods by returning the `Task` type when the method returns `void`, otherwise, we should return the `Task<T>` generic type when the method returns a type. Furthermore, the `Task` type is also useful when we want to notify the status of the operation to the caller: the `Task` type exposes the status of the operation through the following attributes: `Status`, `IsCanceled`, `IsCompleted`, and `IsFaulted`.

Use Task.FromResult over Task.Run

If you have previously worked with .NET Core or .NET Framework, you have probably dealt with both `Task.FromResult` and `Task.Run`. Both can be used to return `Task<T>`. The main difference between them is in their input parameters. Take a look at the following `Task.Run` snippet:

```
public Task<int> AddAsync(int a, int b)
    {
        return Task.Run(() => a + b);
    }
```

The `Task.Run` method will queue the execution as a work item in the thread pool. The work item will immediately complete with the pre-computed value. As a result, we have wasted a thread pool. Furthermore, we should also notice that the initial purpose of `Task.Run` method was intended for the client-side .NET applications: ASP.NET Core is not optimized for the `Task.Run` operations and it shouldn't ever be used to offload the execution of a portion of code. On the opposite side, let's examine another case:

```
public Task<int> AddAsync(int a, int b)
    {
        return Task.FromResult(a + b);
    }
```

In this case, the `Task.FromResult` method will wrap the pre-computed result without wasting a thread pool which means that we will not have the overhead provided by the execution of the `Task.Run` operation.

Enable cancellation

Another important topic is to enable the cancellation of asynchronous operations. If we take a look at the service layer that we implemented in Chapter 8, and Chapter 9, we can see that in some cases we have the possibility of passing CancellationToken as a parameter. The CancellationToken provides a light way to notify all asynchronous operations that the consumer wants to cancel the current transaction. Moreover, our code can examine the CancellationToken.IsCancellationRequested property to detect whether the consumer has requested the cancellation of the task. This kind of approach is especial suitable for long-running operations because the consumer of our asynchronous code can request the cancellation of the current performing task at any point in the process.

Asynchronous code in I/O bound operations

When we implement code in an asynchronous way we should ask ourselves if the underlying process involves any kind of I/O operation. If this is the case, we should proceed by using an asynchronous approach for that stack. For example, the Get operation of the ItemRepository class involves a query to the database:

```
namespace Catalog.Infrastructure.Repositories
{
    public class ItemRepository : IItemRepository
    {
        ..
        public async Task<Item> GetAsync(Guid id)
        {
            var item = await _context.Items
                .AsNoTracking()
                .Where(x => x.Id == id)
                .Include(x => x.Genre)
                .Include(x => x.Artist).FirstOrDefaultAsync();

            return item;
        }
        ...
    }
}
```

In this case, we are using the `FirstOrDefaultAsync` method to execute the operation in an asynchronous way. On the opposite side, if we take as an example another operation, such as the `Add` method of the `ItemRepository` we can see that the operation is not asynchronous even if the EF Core framework exposes the `AddAsync` methods:

```
public Item Add(Item order)
{
    return _context.Items
        .Add(order).Entity;
}
```

This is because in the case of the adding operation we are not performing any kind of I/O operation: the entity is added to the `context` attribute and marked with an added status. The proper synchronization with the database happens when we call the `SaveChangesAsync` method which is asynchronous because it involves I/O operations with the database. In conclusion, we should always keep in mind to understand the full context and stack of the operation that we want to execute in an asynchronous manner. In general, every time we have to deal with the file system, a database, and any other network call we should implement our code using an asynchronous stack, otherwise we can keep the code synchronous in order to avoid additional thread overheads.

Measure response time using middleware

A common way to measure the response time of ASP.NET Core actions is by using a *middleware component*. As seen in `Chapter 3`, *Working with the Middleware Pipeline*, these components act at the edge of the ASP.NET Core request life cycle, and they are useful for performing cross-cutting implementations. Measuring the response time of an action method falls into this implementation case. Furthermore, middleware is the first component hit by a request and the last one that can process an outgoing response. This means that we can analyze and include almost the whole life cycle of the request.

Let's take a look at an implementation of `ResponseTimeMiddlewareAsync`:

```
using System.Diagnostics;
using System.Threading.Tasks;
using Microsoft.AspNetCore.Http;

namespace Catalog.API.Infrastructure.Middleware
{
    public class ResponseTimeMiddlewareAsync {
        private const string X_RESPONSE_TIME_MS = "X-Response-Time-ms";
        private readonly RequestDelegate _next;
        public ResponseTimeMiddlewareAsync(RequestDelegate next) {
```

```
            _next = next;
        }
        public Task InvokeAsync(HttpContext context) {

            var watch = new Stopwatch();
            watch.Start();
            context.Response.OnStarting(() => {
                watch.Stop();
                var responseTimeForCompleteRequest =
    watch.ElapsedMilliseconds;
                context.Response.Headers[X_RESPONSE_TIME_MS] =
    responseTimeForCompleteRequest.ToString();
                return Task.CompletedTask;
            });
            return _next(context);
        }
    }
}
```

The previous class defines an `async` middleware to detect the response time of the requests. It follows these steps:

1. It declares a `Stopwatch` instance in the `InvokeAsync` method.
2. It executes the `Start()` method of the `Stopwatch` instance.
3. It defines a new response delegate using the `OnStarting` method. The `OnStarting` method, which allows us to declare a delegate action to be invoked just before the response headers, will be sent to the client.
4. It calls the `Stop()` method and sets the `ElapsedMilliseconds` property as a custom header using the `X-Response-Time-ms` header.

It is possible to include the `ResponseTimeMiddlewareAsync` class in the middleware pipeline by adding the following line in the `Startup` class:

```
...
public void Configure(IApplicationBuilder app, IWebHostingEnvironment env)
{
    ...
    app.UseMiddleware<ResponseTimeMiddlewareAsync>();
    ...
}
...
```

Furthermore, it is also possible to test the middleware by following the same approach we took for testing the controllers by implementing the following:

```csharp
using System.Threading.Tasks;
using Shouldly;
using Catalog.Fixtures;
using Xunit;

namespace Catalog.API.Tests.Middleware
{
    public class ResponseTimeMiddlewareTests :
IClassFixture<InMemoryApplicationFactory<Startup>>
    {
        public
ResponseTimeMiddlewareTests(InMemoryApplicationFactory<Startup> factory)
        {
            _factory = factory;
        }

        private readonly InMemoryApplicationFactory<Startup> _factory;


        [Theory]
        [InlineData("/api/items/?pageSize=1&pageIndex=0")]
        [InlineData("/api/artist/?pageSize=1&pageIndex=0")]
        [InlineData("/api/genre/?pageSize=1&pageIndex=0")]
        public async Task
middleware_should_set_the_correct_response_time_custom_header(string url)
        {
            var client = _factory.CreateClient();
            var response = await client.GetAsync(url);

            response.EnsureSuccessStatusCode();
            response.Headers.GetValues("X-Response-Time-
ms").ShouldNotBeEmpty();
        }
    }
}
```

The ResponseTimeMiddlewareTests class allows us to make an HTTP call by extending the InMemoryApplicationFactory class. We can check whether the X-Response-Time-ms header exists in the response object. It is important to note that the other measurement doesn't include the startup time of the web server or the application pool. Furthermore, it takes some additional time when the webserver is not initialized.

Summary

In this chapter, we covered some different topics about building an API: from the soft deletion of our resources to how to measure the performance of responses. We also had an overview of the asynchronous programming stack of ASP.NET Core and some recommendations as to how to use it. The topics covered in this chapter will be helpful to you at an advanced development stage in order to improve the readability of the returned data and the performance of the web service. In the next chapter, we will see how to run our catalog solution using containerization technologies. The chapter provides an overview of Docker and on the related Docker compose tools.

12
The Containerization of Services

The previous chapter focused on several advanced topics to do with building web services using ASP.NET Core. This chapter offers a quick introduction to containers and how they can be useful for running your application locally in a sandbox environment. This chapter is not designed to cover everything about containers; rather, it's more of a brief introduction to them. We will learn how to run the catalog service on containers.

In this chapter, we will cover the following topics:

- An introduction to containers
- How to run the catalog service on Docker
- An overview of .NET Core Docker images
- Optimizing Docker images

An introduction to containers

Nowadays, distributed systems form the base of every application. In turn, the foundation of distributed systems is containers. The goal of containerization is to run resources in an isolated environment. Containers define boundaries and the separation of concerns between the components of a distributed system. This separation of concerns is a way for us to reuse containers by providing parameterized configurations. Another important feature of web services and web applications is *scalability*. It should be easy to scale up your containers and create new instances.

Docker is a tool that is designed to create, run, and deploy applications using containers. Docker is also referred to as a platform that promotes this technology. Over the last few years, Docker has become somewhat of a buzzword, and it has been adopted by a considerable number of companies, start-ups, and open source projects. Various projects are associated with Docker.

To begin, let's talk about **Moby** (`https://github.com/moby/moby`), which is an open source project created by Docker. As a large number of people and communities started to contribute to the project, Docker decided to develop Moby. All contributions to the Moby project, which can be considered as a sort of research and development department of Docker, are open source.

Moby is a framework that is used to build specific container systems. It provides a library of components that are the fundamentals of a container system:

- OS and container runtime
- Orchestration
- Infrastructure management
- Networking
- Storage
- Security
- Build
- Image distribution

It also provides the tools that are necessary to build up these components to create a runnable artifact for each platform and architecture.

If we are looking for more downstream solutions, we have the Docker **Community Edition (CE)** and Docker **Enterprise Edition (EE)** versions, which are products that use the Moby project. Docker CE is used by small teams and developers to build their system, while business customers use Docker EE. Both are recommended solutions allowing us to use containerization in development and enterprise environments.

This chapter will use Docker CE to containerize the catalog service. Docker CE and Docker EE are available on the Docker website: `https://www.docker.com/`. You can download and install the Community Edition by following the steps provided at `https://www.docker.com/get-started`.

Docker terminology

Before setting up our service to use Docker, let's take a quick look at the terminology behind this technology.

Let's begin by defining a container image, which is the list of all dependencies and artifacts needed to create a container instance. The term *container image* should not be confused with the term *container instance*, which refers to a single instance of a container image.

A core part of a container image is the Dockerfile. The Dockerfile provides the instructions to build a container. For example, in the case of a container that runs a .NET Core solution, it gives the commands to restore the packages and build the solution. Docker also provides a way to tag the container images and group them all in collections known as **repositories**. Repositories are usually covered by a registry, which allows access to a specific repository. The repositories can be public or private, depending on what they are used for. For example, a private company can use a private repository to provide different versions of containers to internal teams. This centralized way of thinking is powerful, and it gives us a way to reuse containers. The main example of a public repository is `https://hub.docker.com/`, which is the world's most extensive library that provides container images:

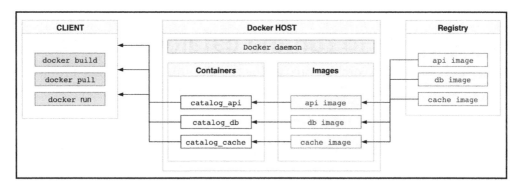

The preceding diagram describes a typical interaction between the components we described in this section. The client usually provides some Docker commands that are parsed and executed in the **Docker HOST**. The **Docker HOST** contains both of the *containers* we are running on the local machine and the images used by those containers. The images are usually taken by a Docker public or private registry, which is generally to the Docker Hub website or a private company repository.

Another essential term to do with Docker is the compose tool. The compose tool is used for defining and running a multi-container application or service. A composer is usually combined with a definition file in a different format, such as a YAML file that defines the structure of the container group.

The compose tool usually runs using the `docker-compose` CLI command. In this chapter, we will use the `docker-compose` command to get our service running in the local environment.

An essential part of a container system is the *orchestrator*. An *orchestrator* simplifies the use of a multi-container system. Moreover, orchestrators are usually applied to complex systems. Examples of container orchestrators include Kubernetes, Azure Service Fabric, and Docker Swarm.

 This book will not cover the use of orchestrators. This chapter gives a high-level overview of the capabilities of Docker and, more generally, containerization. More complex topics to do with Docker require DevOps and system engineering skills.

Let's move on to look at the power of containerization and how to use it to build our applications and services quickly. The next section will apply container principles to the catalog service built in the previous chapter. The following section will also use container technologies extensively to get our examples up and running.

Using Docker to run the catalog service

This section explains how to combine our catalog service with Docker to get it running locally. Let's start by examining the systems behind the catalog service:

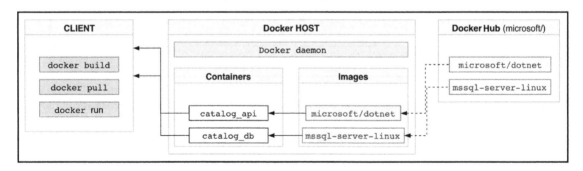

As we can see from the preceding diagram, the web service part runs over the microsoft/dotnet Docker image, and the data source part runs over the Microsoft SQL Server instance using the microsoft/mssql-server-linux Docker image (we already dealt with the containerization of MSSQL in Chapter 8, *Building the Data Access Layer*). Both of the images are downloaded from the public Microsoft repository already present in Docker Hub; let's take a look at how to use docker-compose to define the whole infrastructure of the service.

First of all, let's create a docker-compose.yml file with the following content in the root folder of the project:

```
version: "3.7"
services:
  catalog_api:
    container_name: catalog_api
    build:
      context: .
      dockerfile: containers/api/Dockerfile
    env_file:
      - containers/api/api.env
    networks:
      - my_network
    ports:
      - 5000:5000
      - 5001:5001
    depends_on:
      - catalog_db

  catalog_db:
    image: microsoft/mssql-server-linux
    container_name: catalog_db
    ports:
      - 1433:1433
    env_file:
      - containers/db/db.env
    networks:
      - my_network

networks:
  my_network:
    driver: bridge
```

The preceding file uses the YAML syntax to define two containers. The first is the `catalog_api` container: it will be used to host the core part of the service built on top of the ASP.NET Core framework. The second container is `catalog_db`, which uses a `microsoft/mssql-server-linux` image (the same that we used in Chapter 8, *Building the Data Access Layer*) to set up the MSSQL database.

Furthermore, we should proceed by creating the following folder structure in the root of the project:

```
mkdir containers
mkdir containers/api
mkdir containers/db
```

The preceding folders will contain the files related to the API and the database containers specified in the `docker-compose.yml` file. Let's continue by examining the definition of the `catalog_api` container:

```
catalog_api:
  container_name: catalog_api
  build:
    context: .
    dockerfile: containers/api/Dockerfile
```

The preceding snippet of code specifies the current folder as the build context and the `containers/api/Dockerfile` file to build the Docker image. It also refers to an environment variables file by using the following syntax:

```
...
  env_file:
      - containers/api/api.env
...
```

Finally, it declares the container under a network called `my_network` and exposes port `5000` to the hosting system using the `ports:` directive.

In the same way, the `catalog_db` container declares the same network defined for the `catalog_api` container, and it specifies a different environment variables file using the same approach as seen previously.

At the end of the `docker-compose.yml` file, there is the definition of `my_network`, which uses a bridge driver. The bridge driver is the default option for the network. Two containers under the same bridge network can share traffic.

For more information about the types of drivers provided out of the box, refer to the following link: `https://docs.docker.com/network/`.

Defining environment variables

Docker provides a lot of ways to specify the environment variables of a container. In the `docker-compose.yml` file specified earlier; we use the `env_file` approach. Furthermore, we can proceed by creating the `api/api.env` file in the corresponding path specified in the definition of the `catalog_api` container:

```
ASPNETCORE_URLS=http://*:5000;https://*:5001
ASPNETCORE_ENVIRONMENT=Integration
```

The file syntax expects each line in the file to be in the following format: `VAR=VAL`. In the preceding case, we are defining the environment variables used by ASP.NET Core to run the service: the `ASPNETCORE_URLS` variable specifies the URLs used by the web service and `ASPNETCORE_ENVIRONMENT` specifies the environment name used by the application. In the same way, we should also proceed by defining the `db/db.env` file in the corresponding folder:

```
SA_PASSWORD=P@ssw0rd
ACCEPT_EULA="Y"
```

In this case, the file defines the corresponding variables for the SQL Server container: `SA_PASSWORD` specifies the system administrator account password, the `ACCEPT_EULA` needed by the startup process of SQL Server.

In addition to this, `docker-compose` supports declaring default environment variables in the `.env` file. The file must be placed in the same directory as the `docker-compose.yml` file. The file contains some simple rules for defining environment variables. Let's create a new `.env` file in the root folder of the catalog service directory:

```
COMPOSE_PROJECT_NAME=store
```

The `COMPOSE_PROJECT_NAME` variable is a reserved variable of the `docker-compose` command provided by Docker. It specifies the project name to use to run the containers. Therefore, both the `catalog_api` and `catalog_db` containers will run under the same project, called `store`.

Defining the Dockerfile

Let's proceed by describing the Dockerfile of our compose project. As mentioned previously, the Dockerfile is a simple text file that contains the commands a user could call to assemble an image. Let's examine a possible definition of the Dockerfile contained in the `containers/api/` folder:

```
FROM mcr.microsoft.com/dotnet/core/sdk:3.1.100
COPY . /app
WORKDIR /app
RUN dotnet restore
RUN dotnet build
RUN dotnet tool install --global dotnet-ef
ENV PATH="${PATH}:/root/.dotnet/tools"
RUN chmod +x containers/api/entrypoint.sh
CMD /bin/bash containers/api/entrypoint.sh
```

This code defines specific steps to build the Docker image. The `FROM` directive refers to the base image to use during the build process. This directive is mandatory, and it must be the first instruction of the file. The `COPY` directive copies the project into the `/app` folder, and the `WORKDIR` command sets the `/app` folder as the default working directory. After that, the build script proceeds by executing the `dotnet restore` and `dotnet build` commands. Finally, the Dockerfile adds the `/root/.dotnet/tools` path inside the `PATH` variable and executes the `containers/api/entrypoint.sh` Bash file, which has the following content:

```
#!/bin/bash
set -e
run_cmd="dotnet run --verbose --project
./src/Catalog.API/Catalog.API.csproj"
until dotnet-ef database update --verbose --project
./src/Catalog.API/Catalog.API.csproj ; do
>&2 echo "SQL Server is starting up"
sleep 1
done
>&2 echo "SQL Server is up - executing command"
exec $run_cmd
```

The `entrypoint.sh` entry point file is stored on the same level as the Dockerfile. It runs the main project of the catalog service by performing the `dotnet run` command and, once the database container is ready, it proceeds by executing the `dotnet ef database update` command to create the database schema.

Executing the docker-compose command

To run the catalog service locally, we must complete the compose process from the CLI using the `docker-compose` command. It is possible to get an overview of the commands by running `docker-compose --help`.

The main commands related to the composition of a multi-container application are as follows:

- `docker-compose build`: This builds the services. It executes the build using the Dockerfile associated with the images.
- `docker-compose images`: This lists the current container images.
- `docker-compose up`: This creates and runs the containers.
- `docker-compose config`: This validates and views the `docker-compose.yml` file.

We can proceed by running the catalog service using the following command:

```
docker-compose up --build
```

By specifying the `--build` flag, it is possible to trigger the build before running the containers. Once the build is made, we can just run the `docker-compose up` command until our code changes and we need to rebuild the project.

Although we are now able to run our service using containers, the build and run process is not optimized: we are copying all of the files in the solution into the container; on top of that, we are running the container using the whole SDK of .NET Core, which is not needed if we want to run the project. In the next section, we will see how to optimize the containerization process to be more lightweight.

Optimizing Docker images

Microsoft provides different Docker images to run ASP.NET Core, and, in general, .NET Core applications using Docker. It is essential to understand that a container that executes an ASP.NET Core service doesn't need to provide the SDK as well.

This section presents an overview of the different Docker images available on Docker Hub and how to optimize our deployment using proper Docker images.

An overview of different Docker images

Microsoft provides various images, depending on what it is you're trying to achieve with your application. Let's take a look at the different Docker images supplied in the `microsoft/dotnet` repository in Docker Hub (`https://hub.docker.com/u/microsoft/`):

Image	Description	Size
`mcr.microsoft.com/dotnet/core/sdk:3.1`	This image contains the whole SDK of .NET Core. It provides all of the tools to develop, run, and build your application. It is possible to use development commands such as `dotnet run`, `dotnet ef`, and the whole set of commands provided by the SDK.	690 MB
`mcr.microsoft.com/dotnet/core/runtime:3.1`	This image contains the .NET Core runtime. It provides a way to run .NET Core applications, such as console applications. Since the image contains only the runtime, it is not possible to build the application. The image exposes only the runtime CLI command, `dotnet`.	190 MB
`mcr.microsoft.com/dotnet/core/aspnet:3.1`	This image contains the .NET Core runtime and the ASP.NET Core runtime. It is possible to execute both the .NET Core application and the ASP.NET Core application. As a runtime image, it is not possible to build the application.	205 MB

	This image is a very light one. It contains only the lower-level dependencies (`https://github.com/dotnet/core/blob/master/Documentation/prereqs.md`) that .NET Core needs to run. It doesn't contain the .NET Core runtime or the ASP.NET Core runtime. It is designed for self-hosted applications.	
`mcr.microsoft.com/dotnet/core/runtime-deps:3.1`		110 MB

 Docker images are usually available in three modes: *debian:stretch-slim*, *ubuntu:bionic*, and *alpine*, depending on the OS the image runs on. By default, images run on the Debian OS. It is possible, however, to use another OS, such as *Alpine*, to save some storage. For example, Alpine-based images reduce the size of the `aspnetcore-runtime` image from ~260 MB to ~160 MB.

Multi-stage builds on the catalog service

Let's apply the concept of a *multi-stage* build to the previously defined Docker image. Multi-stage builds are a new feature that requires Docker 17.05 or higher. Multi-stage builds are useful for anyone who has struggled to optimize Dockerfiles while keeping them easy to read and maintain.

Let's explore how it is possible to apply the multi-stage build process by taking a look at the catalog service Dockerfile:

```
FROM microsoft/dotnet
COPY . /app
WORKDIR /app
RUN dotnet restore
RUN dotnet build
RUN chmod +x ./entrypoint.sh
CMD /bin/bash ./entrypoint.sh
```

The previously defined file can be changed in the following way:

```
FROM mcr.microsoft.com/dotnet/core/aspnet:3.1 AS base
WORKDIR /app

FROM mcr.microsoft.com/dotnet/core/sdk:3.1 AS build
WORKDIR /project
```

```
COPY ["src/Catalog.API/Catalog.API.csproj", "src/Catalog.API/"]
COPY . .
WORKDIR "/project/src/Catalog.API"
RUN dotnet build "Catalog.API.csproj" -c Release -o /app/build

FROM build AS publish
RUN dotnet publish "Catalog.API.csproj" -c Release -o /app/publish

FROM base AS final
WORKDIR /app
COPY --from=publish /app/publish .
ENTRYPOINT ["dotnet", "Catalog.API.dll"]
```

As you can see, the Dockerfile now executes three different steps (the first two steps are described together because they use the same Docker image):

- The `builder` step uses the `mcr.microsoft.com/dotnet/core/sdk` image to copy the files and trigger the build of the project using the `dotnet build` command.
- The `publish` step uses the same image to trigger the `dotnet publish` command for the `Catalog.API` project.
- The `final` step, as the name suggests, executes the published package in the runtime environment using the `mcr.microsoft.com/dotnet/core/aspnet:3.1` image. Finally, it runs the service using the `ENTRYPOINT` command.

It is important to note that this change optimizes the resulting image produced by the Dockerfile. After this change, we don't need the `entrypoint.sh` file anymore because the Dockerfile directly triggers the execution of the service using the `dotnet Catalog.API.dll` command.

Using a multi-stage build approach, we should also notice that we cannot trigger the execution of the database migrations because the runtime Docker image doesn't use the **Entity Framework Core (EF Core)** tools. Consequently, we need to find another way to trigger the migrations. One possible option is to unleash the migrations from the `Startup` file of our service. Furthermore, EF Core provides a way to apply migrations at runtime by using the following syntax in the `Configure` method:

```
using Polly;
using Microsoft.Data.SqlClient;
...
    public class Startup
    {
        ...
```

```
        public void Configure(IApplicationBuilder app, IWebHostEnvironment
env)
        {
            if (env.IsDevelopment()) app.UseDeveloperExceptionPage();

            ExecuteMigrations(app, env);
            ...
        }

        private void ExecuteMigrations(IApplicationBuilder app,
         IWebHostEnvironment env)
        {
            if (env.EnvironmentName == "Testing") return;
            var retry = Policy.Handle<SqlException>()
                .WaitAndRetry(new TimeSpan[]
                {
                    TimeSpan.FromSeconds(2),
                    TimeSpan.FromSeconds(6),
                    TimeSpan.FromSeconds(12)
                });
            retry.Execute(() =>
    app.ApplicationServices.GetService<CatalogContext>().Database.Migrate());
        }
    }
}
```

The preceding code ensures the execution of the database migrations through the execution of the `app.ApplicationServices.GetService<CatalogContext>().Database.Migrate()` instruction. Because of the startup times of the `msssql` container, we need to implement a retry policy by handling `SqlException` and retrying with an exponential time approach. The preceding implementation uses `Polly` to define and execute a retry policy. Furthermore, we need to add the `Polly` dependency by executing the following command in the `Catalog.API` project:

```
dotnet add package Polly
```

Retry policies are really useful in the distributed systems world, to successfully handle failure. `Polly` and the implementation of resilience policies in a web service will be discussed in the next chapter as part of communication over HTTP between multiple services.

In a real-world application, it is quite unusual to execute migrations during the deployment phase of the service. The database schema rarely changes, and it is essential to separate the implementations related to the service with the changes made in the database schema. For demonstration reasons, we are executing the migrations of the database in every deployment by overwriting the database changes to take the most straightforward approach.

Summary

In this chapter, we provided a quick overview of the capabilities of Docker and how to use it to improve isolation, maintainability, and service reliability. We looked at the different Docker images supplied by Microsoft and how to use them combined with a multi-step build approach.

The topics covered in this chapter provide an easy way to run our service locally, in an isolated environment, and spread the same environment configuration into staging and production environments.

In the next chapter, we are going to improve our knowledge of how to share information between multiple services. We will also explore some patterns to do with multi-service systems. The concepts related to Docker that we explored in this chapter will also be used in the next chapter to provide a smooth deployment experience.

13
Service Ecosystem Patterns

In the previous chapter, we provided an overview of the containerization process and how to use containers to run a service. We also learned how to host the catalog service on containers using Docker and how to use the multistage build approach to create and run our container images.

This chapter focuses on some patterns that are used when multiple services are part of the same ecosystem. Then, we will look at the implementation of the communication between those services. We will also learn how to build a resilient connection between various web services that are part of the same system in order to avoid some of the common pitfalls related to data exchange.

In this chapter, we will cover the following topics:

- An introduction to the cart service
- Implementing resilient communication using an HTTP client
- An introduction to event buses
- How to perform event bus communication using RabbitMQ

By the end of this chapter, you will have a general understanding of how to improve resilience using `Polly` and how to use an event bus to exchange information between two systems.

An introduction to the cart service

While the `Catalog.API` project handles the catalog items of our store, we don't have anything that handles the cart features. In this section, we will discover a new .NET Core solution that implements a cart service to do this for us. Furthermore, we will introduce a new implementation approach: the **mediator pattern**. Before we walk through the implementation of this new service, let's take a look at an overview of the project structure, which provides the catalog service and cart service solutions:

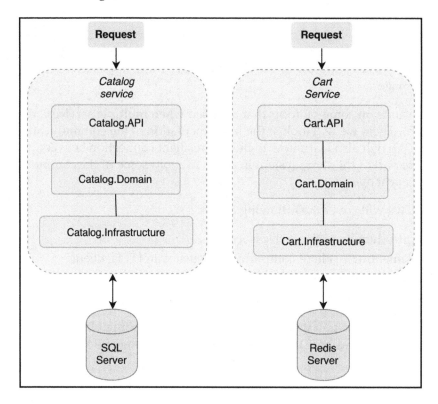

The preceding schema describes the project structure of the catalog service and the cart service. As we already know, the catalog service implements the `API`, `Domain`, and `Infrastructure` projects in order to separate the different layers of the implementation and that it uses SQL Server, combined with Entity Framework Core, as the main data source. However, although the cart service follows a similar project structure, it uses a slightly different implementation pattern and stores cart data in Redis. Therefore, Redis, which is mainly used for caching purposes, offers a very lightweight/high-performance key-value data store that can be also used as a database.

The cart service solution has the following structure:

- The `Cart.API` project contains the controller, which handles the incoming HTTP request from the client. It also includes the error processing aggregation point and the `Startup` class, which initializes the dependency injection engine.
- The `Cart.Domain` project contains the mediator logic and the handlers that dispatch the operations to the underlying layers. Furthermore, it also includes the entities that are used by the application.
- The `Cart.Infrastructure` project is the bridge between the web services and their dependencies, such as the data store and other third-party services.

This chapter won't look at the development process of the cart service in detail: some of the technical aspects have already been discussed, namely, in `Chapter 8`, *Building the Data Access Layer*, `Chapter 9`, *Implementing the Domain Logic*, and `Chapter 10`, *Implementing the RESTful HTTP Layer*. The introduction to the cart service will be useful for you to determine the different communication techniques between multiple web services. Although this chapter will cover some of the key parts of the implementation, such as the handlers, in order to proceed, you need to download the cart service source code from `https://github.com/PacktPublishing/Hands-On-RESTful-Web-Services-with-ASP.NET-Core-3`.

The theory behind the mediator pattern

The mediator pattern is a way to encapsulate logic behind a unique entry point. It uses the concept of requests, responses, commands, or events to abstract the implementations behind a single entry point. This way of implementing the application logic helps the developers in your team keep the logic separated from the web part of the application. To understand how the mediator pattern works, let's take a look at its components.

The preceding schema describes a simple implementation of the mediator pattern. The consumer of the mediator calls the `Send` method by referring to the `IMediator` interface. The mediator implementation passes a specific type of the `IRequest` interface. Therefore, the `Mediator` instance dispatches the messages to the destination handler, which is represented by the `IMessageHandler` implementation, using the concrete implementation of the `IRequest` interface. In the next chapter, we will learn how to use an `IMediator` interface to dispatch messages to specific handlers.

Furthermore, we will use the mediator pattern with the command approach. There are slightly different ways to implement the mediator pattern. The project that we'll be covering in this chapter uses a very popular mediator NuGet packaged called **MediatR**. MediatR is an all-in-one implementation of the mediator pattern that covers in-process messaging. You can find more information about the MediatR project on GitHub: `https://github.com/jbogard/MediatR`.

For the purpose of the *cart service* implementation, we're going to use the following components, all of which have been exposed by the MediatR library:

- The `IMediator` interface is the main entry point of the mediator pattern. It exposes a `Send` method, which is used to dispatch a command or a request to a specific handler in order to obtain a result.
- The `IRequestHandler` interface is a generic interface that's used to define the implementation of a handler. Each `IRequestHandler` type requires an `IRequest` type, which represents the request that's sent through the `IMediator` interface.
- The `IRequest` interface defines the request or the command type that's used to execute a specific handler.

Now that we have more information about how the mediator pattern works, we can continue with the concrete implementation of the cart service solution. In the next section, we will look at how we can define the domain model of the service and implement the data access layer abstraction over the Redis data store.

The domain model and the data access layer

The domain model of the cart service represents the entities that we require to describe the cart session of a user. Specifically, the domain model of the cart service implements three different entity classes: `Cart`, `CartItem`, and `CartUser`. Like the catalog service, all the entities are stored in the `Cart.Domain` project, which will be referred to by the `Cart.Infrastructure` and `Cart.API` projects.

Let's start with the `CartSession` class, which represents a single cart session:

```
using System;
using System.Collections.Generic;

namespace Cart.Domain.Entities
{
    public class CartSession
    {
```

```
            public string Id { get; set; }
            public IList<CartItem> Items { get; set; }
            public CartUser User { get; set; }
            public DateTimeOffset ValidityDate { get; set; }
        }
    }
```

The `CartSession` entity represents a single cart instance that's been created by a user. Therefore, it refers to the `CartUser` class, which contains the user's information. Besides, the `CartSession` entity also provides the `IList<CartItems>` field, which represents the items in the cart and the quantity associated with each item. Let's proceed by also defining the `CartItem` class:

```
using System;

namespace Cart.Domain.Entities
{
    public class CartItem
    {
        public Guid CartItemId { get; set; }

        public int Quantity { get; set; }

        public void IncreaseQuantity()
        {
            Quantity = Quantity + 1;
        }

        public void DecreaseQuantity()
        {
            Quantity = Quantity - 1;
        }
    }
}
```

The `CartItem` class implements a `CartItemId` field and a `Quantity` field. Furthermore, it also provides the `IncreaseQuantity` and `DecreaseQuantity` fields, which are used to increment and decrement the quantity of a specific item, respectively. Finally, it is possible to determine the `CartUser` class, which represents the user related to the cart:

```
namespace Cart.Domain.Entities
{
    public class CartUser
    {
        public string Email { get; set; }
    }
}
```

For demonstration purposes, we are representing `CartUser` with only one property; this will contain the email of the user. The preceding entities are stored in the `Entities` folder, inside the `Cart.Domain` project.

Once we have defined the domain model, we can proceed with the implementation of the data access abstraction. Specifically, the cart service will use the same access pattern we defined previously for the catalog service in order to get information about the cart sessions:

```
// src/Cart.Domain/Repositories/ICartRepository.cs

using System;
using System.Collections.Generic;
using System.Threading.Tasks;
using Cart.Domain.Entities;

namespace Cart.Domain.Repositories
{
    public interface ICartRepository
    {
        IEnumerable<string> GetCarts();
        Task<CartSession> GetAsync(Guid id);
        Task<CartSession> AddOrUpdateAsync(CartSession item);
    }
}
```

The `ICartRepository` method implements methods that retrieve and update our data, the `GetCarts` method retrieves the IDs of the current carts, and the `GetAsync` method gathers information about a specific cart. Finally, the `AddOrUpdateAsync` method allows us to update or add a new cart if it's not present in the data store, while `ICartRepository` defines the operations that are performed by our data store. In the next subsection, we will look at a concrete implementation of the `CartRepository` class.

This domain model has been simplified to provide an example of a possible implementation of the cart. In a real-world application, we should consider other essential information about the state of a cart.

The ICartRepository Redis implementation

The cart service uses Redis (`https://redis.io/`) to store the cart's data. The actual implementation of the `CartRepository` class of the cart service uses a NuGet package powered by Stack Exchange called `StackExchange.Redis`. Furthermore, we will use the `Newtonsoft.Json` package to serialize the objects into Redis using JSON format.

The concrete implementation of the `CartRepository` class will be located in the `Cart.Infrastructure` project, while the `ICartRepository` interface type will be located in the `Cart.Domain` project. Furthermore, the `Cart.Infrastructure` project will also depend on the `StackExchange.Redis` and `Newtonsoft.Json` packages. The `StackExchange.Redis` library provides a low-level abstraction of Redis, so that our .NET applications can read or write data on a Redis instance. Let's take a look at the implementation of the `CartRepository` class:

```
using System;
using System.Collections.Generic;
using System.Linq;
using System.Threading.Tasks;
using Cart.Domain.Entities;
using StackExchange.Redis;
using Cart.Domain.Repositories;
using Cart.Infrastructure.Configurations;
using Microsoft.Extensions.Options;
using Newtonsoft.Json;

namespace Cart.Infrastructure.Repositories
{
    public class CartRepository : ICartRepository
    {
        private readonly IDatabase _database;
        private readonly CartDataSourceSettings _settings;

        public CartRepository(IOptions<CartDataSourceSettings> options)
        {
            _settings = options.Value;

            var configuration = ConfigurationOptions
                .Parse(_settings.RedisConnectionString);

            try
            {
                _database = ConnectionMultiplexer
                    .Connect(configuration).GetDatabase();
            }
            catch (Exception e)
```

```
                {
                    Console.WriteLine(e.ToString());
                }
            }
        ...
        }
    }
```

The CartRepository class uses the StackExchange.Redis library to interact with a Redis instance. It declares an IDatabase property, which represents a connection with the Redis instance, and it uses a custom settings class that defines the connection string associated with the Redis instance. During the initialization of the class, the constructor calls the ConnectionMultiplexer static instance to create a new database connection. Let's proceed by having a look at the ICartRepository interface method's implementations:

...

```
        public IEnumerable<string> GetCarts()
        {
            var keys = _database.Multiplexer.GetServer
                (_settings.RedisConnectionString).Keys();

            return keys?.Select(k => k.ToString());
        }

        public async Task<CartSession> GetAsync(Guid id)
        {
            var data = await _database.StringGetAsync(id.ToString());

            return data.IsNullOrEmpty
                ? null
                : JsonConvert.DeserializeObject
                    <Domain.Entities.CartSession>(data);
        }

        public async Task<CartSession> AddOrUpdateAsync(CartSession
            item)
        {
            var created = await _database.StringSetAsync(item.Id,
                JsonConvert.SerializeObject(item));

            if (!created) return null;

            return await GetAsync(new Guid(item.Id));
        }
    ..
```

The preceding code defines the core methods of the `ICartRepository` interface. The `GetCarts` method gathers all the keys that represent all the cart IDs stored in the Redis instance. The `GetAsync` method retrieves the details of a card by passing the ID of a specific cart and deserializing the resulting content in the `CartSession` entity. Finally, the `AddOrUpdateAsync` method adds or updates the information related to a cart ID by serializing its content and updating the data source using the `StringSetAsync` method, which is provided by the library. We are using Redis because, as an in-memory data structure store, it can retrieve information very quickly. In general, Redis' primary purpose is to act as a caching system, but it can also be used to store information temporarily. Redis is not the best system to prevent data loss, however. All the data is processed in memory and it can only be saved by making a snapshot of the current state of memory. For more information, visit the following website: `https://redis.io/topics/persistence`.

The preceding implementation of `CartRepository` produces two main pitfalls. First of all, Redis is not a database that's designed to scan and retrieve multiple keys. Furthermore, this kind of data store is designed to perform O(1) operations, just like a hash table or a dictionary. Therefore, the `GetCarts` method is very performance inefficient. An alternative and more efficient approach would be to store the list IDs in a specific and unique field and keep them updated every time we add/remove new cart records. Secondly, although the constructor of the `CartRepository` class calls the `ConnectionMultiplexer` static class every time the class is initialized, it is strongly suggested that you initialize the `IConnectionMultiplexer` interface as a singleton instance in order to avoid performance pitfalls.

The next subsection describes the implementation of the handlers that expose the cart operations through the mediator logic. Furthermore, the handlers will call the underlying `ICartRepository` interface in order to perform the I/O process on Redis.

Handlers and routes implementation

The *cart service* implements the handlers that reflect the different actions that occur on cart data in the domain part of our service. As we will see later in this chapter, the handlers are associated with a specific request and are executed by the `IMediator` interface, which is provided by the MediatR library. Also, in this case, these classes are located in the `Cart.Domain` project.

Let's start by taking a look at the implementation of the `CreateCartHandler` class:

//Handlers/Cart/CreateCartHandler.cs

```csharp
using System;
...

namespace Cart.Domain.Handlers.Cart
{
    public class CreateCartHandler : IRequestHandler<CreateCartCommand,
CartExtendedResponse>
    {
        private readonly ICatalogService _catalogService;
        private readonly IMapper _mapper;
        private readonly ICartRepository _repository;

        public CreateCartHandler(ICartRepository repository, IMapper
            mapper, ICatalogService catalogService)
        {
            _repository = repository;
            _mapper = mapper;
            _catalogService = catalogService;
        }

        public async Task<CartExtendedResponse> Handle
            (CreateCartCommand command, CancellationToken
            cancellationToken)
        {
            var entity = new CartSession
            {
                Items = command.ItemsIds.Select(x => new CartItem {
                    CartItemId = new Guid(x), Quantity = 1 }).ToList(),
                    User = new CartUser { Email = command.UserEmail },
                    ValidityDate = DateTimeOffset.Now.AddMonths(2),
                    Id = Guid.NewGuid().ToString()
            };

            var result = await _repository.AddOrUpdateAsync(entity);

            var response = _mapper.Map<CartExtendedResponse>(result);

            var tasks = response.Items
                .Select(async x => await _catalogService
                .EnrichCartItem(x, cancellationToken));

            response.Items = await Task.WhenAll(tasks);

            return response;
```

```
            }
        }
    }
```

The preceding code is the definition of the CreateCartHandler class, which performs the creation cart process. The class uses the constructor injection technique to resolve the dependencies through the dependency injection engine of ASP.NET Core. Furthermore, the handler class depends on the IMapper and ICartRepository interfaces: the IMapper interface is used to map the CartSession instances with the CartExtendedResponse response class, while the ICartRepository interface is used to store the cart data on Redis through the use of the AddOrUpdateAsync method.

The handler assigns a new Guid to the entity and it adds a ValidityDate of 2 months. Furthermore, it also assigns the new cart items list to the cart session by setting a default quantity of 1 for each item. In a similar manner, the GetCartHandler class implements the reading operations based on the Id of the cart:

```
using System.Threading;
...

namespace Cart.Domain.Handlers.Cart
{
    public class GetCartHandler : IRequestHandler<GetCartCommand,
        CartExtendedResponse>
    {
        private readonly ICatalogService _catalogService;
        private readonly IMapper _mapper;
        private readonly ICartRepository _repository;

        public GetCartHandler(ICartRepository repository, IMapper
            mapper, ICatalogService catalogService)
        {
            _repository = repository;
            _mapper = mapper;
            _catalogService = catalogService;
        }

        public async Task<CartExtendedResponse> Handle(GetCartCommand
            command, CancellationToken cancellationToken)
        {
            var result = await _repository.GetAsync(command.Id);
            var extendedResponse = _mapper.Map<CartExtendedResponse>
                (result);

            var tasks = extendedResponse.Items
                .Select(async x => await _catalogService
```

```
                    .EnrichCartItem(x, cancellationToken));

            extendedResponse.Items = await Task.WhenAll(tasks);
            return extendedResponse;
        }
    }
}
```

In this case, the `Handle` method executes the `GetAsync(Guid id)` method that's provided by the underlying repository interface and it maps the response to the `CartExtendedResponse` type. The last handler that's implemented by the `Cart.Domain` project increases or decreases the quantity of an item in a specific cart:

```
using System.Linq;
...

namespace Cart.Domain.Handlers.Cart
{
    public class UpdateCartItemQuantity : IRequestHandler
        <UpdateCartItemQuantityCommand, CartExtendedResponse>
    {
        private readonly ICatalogService _catalogService;
        private readonly IMapper _mapper;
        private readonly ICartRepository _repository;

        public UpdateCartItemQuantity(ICartRepository repository,
            IMapper mapper, ICatalogService catalogService)
        {
            _repository = repository;
            _mapper = mapper;
            _catalogService = catalogService;
        }

        public async Task<CartExtendedResponse>
Handle(UpdateCartItemQuantityCommand command, CancellationToken
cancellationToken)
        {
            var cartDetail = await
                _repository.GetAsync(command.CartId);

            if (command.IsAddOperation)
                cartDetail.Items.FirstOrDefault(x => x.CartItemId ==
                command.CartItemId)?.IncreaseQuantity();
            else
                cartDetail.Items.FirstOrDefault(x => x.CartItemId ==
                command.CartItemId)?.DecreaseQuantity();

            var cartItemsList = cartDetail.Items.ToList();
```

```
cartItemsList.RemoveAll(x => x.Quantity <= 0);

cartDetail.Items = cartItemsList;

await _repository.AddOrUpdateAsync(cartDetail);

var response = _mapper.Map<CartExtendedResponse>
    (cartDetail);
var tasks = response.Items
    .Select(async x => await
    _catalogService.EnrichCartItem(x, cancellationToken));

response.Items = await Task.WhenAll(tasks);

return response;
            }
        }
    }
```

The handler accepts UpdateCartItemQuantityRequest, which defines the CartId, CartItemId, and a Boolean that denotes whether the request is to increase or decrease the quantity of the specified item.

The handler uses the same dependencies that the other handlers do and it performs some additional checks about the removal of the item if the amount is equal to zero. If the quantity associated with CartItemId reaches 0, then the item is removed from the cart session; otherwise, the quantity is updated and the cart proceeds by updating the Redis store and retrieving cartDetail.

Now that our handlers are in place, we will define the controller classes that will expose the HTTP routes for the web service.

Exposing functionalities using CartController

As we've already mentioned, the cart service takes care of the operations that are performed on the cart page of the e-commerce store. Moreover, the service exposes the following route table:

HttpVerb	URL	Description
GET	api/cart/{cartId}	This action retrieves information about a specific cart and its inner products.
POST	api/cart	This action creates a new cart with a list of products specified in the body payload of the request.

PUT	api/cart/{cartId}/items/{id}	This action increases the quantity of the specified item in the specified `cartId` by adding one unit.
DELETE	api/cart/{cartId}/items/{id}	This action decreases the quantity of the specified item in the specified `cartId` by removing one unit.

The preceding table provides some details about the routes we need to define in our controller. Therefore, the following code snippet shows the implementation of this route table while using the `CartController` class in the `Cart.API` project:

```
using System;
using System.Threading.Tasks;
using MediatR;
using Microsoft.AspNetCore.Mvc;
using Cart.API.Infrastructure.Filters;
using Cart.Domain.Commands.Cart;

namespace Cart.API.Controllers
{

    [Route("api/cart")]
    [ApiController]
    [JsonException]
    public class CartController : ControllerBase
    {
        private readonly IMediator _mediator;

        public CartController(IMediator mediator)
        {

            _mediator = mediator;
        }

          [HttpGet("{id:guid}")]
        public async Task<IActionResult> GetById(Guid id)
        {
            var result = await _mediator.Send(new GetCartCommand { Id =
                id });
            return Ok(result);
        }

        [HttpPost]
        public async Task<IActionResult> Post(CreateCartCommand
            request)
        {
            var result = await _mediator.Send(request);
```

```
            return CreatedAtAction(nameof(GetById), new { id =
                result.Id }, null);
        }
    ..
```

As you can see, in a similar way to the previously implemented controllers,
CartController uses dependency injection to resolve its dependencies by initializing the
IMediator interface. Let's proceed by having a look at the implementation of the Put and
Delete action methods:

    ...

```
    [HttpPut("{cartId:guid}/items/{id:guid}")]
    public async Task<IActionResult> Put(Guid cartId, Guid id)
    {
        var result = await _mediator.Send(new
            UpdateCartItemQuantityCommand
        {
            CartId = cartId,
            CartItemId = id,
            IsAddOperation = true
        });
        return Ok(result);
    }
    [HttpDelete("{cartId:guid}/items/{id:guid}")]
    public async Task<IActionResult> Delete(Guid cartId, Guid id)
    {
        var result = await _mediator.Send(new
            UpdateCartItemQuantityCommand
        {
            CartId = cartId,
            CartItemId = id,
            IsAddOperation = false
        });

        return Ok(result);
    }
}
```

The DELETE and PUT methods use the IsAddOperation flag to inform the handler of
whether the requested operation is being used to increase or decrease the quantity.
Therefore, every time we call the routes using the DELETE HTTP verb and the
UPDATE HTTP verb, the service will increase and reduce the amount of the item ID
specified in the URL.

This chapter skips a lot of the validation and REST-compliant features that we covered in Chapter 8, *Building the Data Access Layer*, Chapter 9, *Implementing the Domain Logic*, and Chapter 10, *Implementing the RESTful HTTP Layer*, and then implemented in the Catalog.API project. As we will see from the next section onward, this chapter aims to show you how to share information and events between independent services. Therefore, the cart service will gather information related to the item by calling the catalog service.

Now that we've looked at the implementation stack, we can proceed by implementing the communication between the catalog service and the cart service.

Implementing resilient communication using an HTTP client

In the previous section, we looked at an overview of the cart service's project structure. We learned how the cart service stores information inside a Redis instance and how it retrieves cart-related data for the client.

It is necessary to note that there is a gap between the information stored in the Redis data source and the data that's exposed by the service. Furthermore, by examining the CartItem entity, we can see that it only implements and retrieves CartItemId and Quantity information for the item:

```
namespace Cart.Domain.Entities
{
    public class CartItem
    {
        public string CartItemId { get; set; }

        public int Quantity { get; set; }
        ...
    }
}
```

On the other hand, we can see that CartItemResponse provides a lot of fields related to the item's data:

```
namespace Cart.Domain.Responses.Cart
{
    public class CartItemResponse
    {
```

```
        public string CartItemId { get; set; }

        public string Name { get; set; }

        public string Description { get; set; }

        public string LabelName { get; set; }

        public string Price { get; set; }

        public string PictureUri { get; set; }

        public string GenreDescription { get; set; }

        public string ArtistName { get; set; }

        public int Quantity { get; set; }
    }
}
```

The additional information that's presented by the `CartItemResponse` class is fetched by calling the catalog services. Therefore, the cart service owns the data about the item ID and it can perform a `GET /api/items/{itemId}` request in order to retrieve the item's information. In this section, we will focus on the implementation of an HTTP client to expose the information that's owned by the catalog service.

It is important that you don't replicate information across web services. We need to be able to keep the data sources of web services as separated as possible. Each service owns a single data source and its appropriate information. It is a common practice to share information using HTTP calls to communicate between services. In the following example, we will see how the cart service calls the catalog service directly to retrieve item information. In a real-world application, all the HTTP calls between services are made by passing through a proxy to guarantee the reliability of the service.

Implementing the catalog HTTP client

It is common practice to implement client libraries along with web services. Furthermore, it is the responsibility of a web service to provide a way to communicate with it. For that reason, we can represent the client's implementation using the following schema:

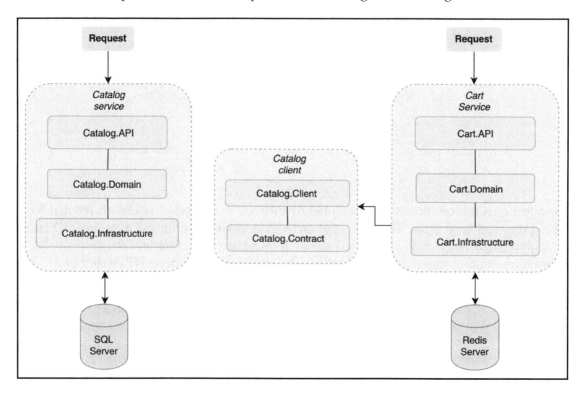

This allows us to publish the catalog service client library in an internal NuGet repository so that we can spread the client to other services. Moreover, the team that owns a specific service should know how it can be implemented and how to expose information in the right way. Let's start by creating two new `classlib` projects in the `Catalog.API` solution, which can be found in the `src` folder:

```
dotnet new classlib -n Catalog.API.Client -f netstandard2.1
dotnet sln ../Catalog.API.sln add Catalog.API.Client

dotnet new classlib -n Catalog.API.Contract -f netstandard2.1
dotnet sln ../Catalog.API.sln add Catalog.API.Contract

dotnet add Catalog.API.Client reference Catalog.API.Contract
```

The `Catalog.API.Client` project will contain all the methods we need to query the catalog service. `Catalog.API.Contract` includes the requests and responses that are used by the client to transfer the data, so we can proceed by copying the classes contained in the `Responses` folder of the `Catalog.Domain` project into the `Catalog.API.Contract` project we created previously. The resulting folder structure will look as follows:

```
.
├─── Item
│       ├─── ArtistResponse.cs
│       ├─── GenreResponse.cs
│       ├─── ItemResponse.cs
│       └─── PriceResponse.cs
├─── Catalog.API.Contract.csproj
├─── bin
└─── obj
```

In order to use the response models in a project, it is necessary to refer to `Catalog.API.Contract`. This practice is usually applied to the request and response classes. By doing this, it is possible to keep the contract of the API in a separate, continuous integration pipeline. As a second step, we need to create a new base client in the `Catalog.API.Client` project. The following `IBaseClient` interface defines the methods that are exposed by the client:

// /Base/IBaseClient.cs

```
using System;
using System.Threading;
using System.Threading.Tasks;

namespace Catalog.API.Client.Base
{
        public interface IBaseClient
        {
            Task<T> GetAsync<T>(Uri uri, CancellationToken
                cancellationToken);
            Uri BuildUri(string format);
        }
}
```

The IBaseClient interface establishes the interface of the client. It exposes two main methods: GetAsync and BuildUri. Both of these methods are implemented in the BaseClient concrete class. The BaseClient class depends on the HttpClient and the string Url of our APIs. The GetAsync method calls the HttpClient and uses the Newtonsoft.Json package to deserialize the response of the client in a generic model, T.

Let's continue by defining the ICatalogItemResource interface and the CatalogItemResource classes. These classes represent the Item resource:

```
// Resources/ICatalogItemResource.cs

using System;
using System.Threading;
using System.Threading.Tasks;
using Catalog.Contract.Item;

namespace Catalog.API.Client.Resources
{
    public interface ICatalogItemResource
    {
        Task<ItemResponse> Get(Guid id, CancellationToken
            cancellationToken = default);
    }
}
```

ICatalogItemResource exposes the Get method by accepting the id and cancellationToken. It returns a Task<ItemResponse> type. Therefore, the CatalogItemResource model is defined in the Catalog.API.Client.Resources project as follows:

```
// Resources/CatalogItemResource.cs

using System;
using System.Threading;
using System.Threading.Tasks;
using Catalog.API.Client.Base;
using Catalog.Domain.Responses;

namespace Catalog.API.Client.Resources
{
    public class CatalogItemResource : ICatalogItemResource
    {
        private readonly IBaseClient _client;

        public CatalogItemResource(IBaseClient client)
        {
```

```
            _client = client;
        }

        private Uri BuildUri(Guid id, string path = "")
        {
            return _client.BuildUri(string.Format("api/items/{0}", id,
                path));
        }

        public async Task<ItemResponse> Get(Guid id, CancellationToken
            cancellationToken)
        {
            var uri = BuildUri(id);
            return await _client.GetAsync<ItemResponse>(uri,
                cancellationToken);
        }
    }
}
```

CatalogItemResource refers to the IBaseClient interface and it implements
the Get method by using the IBaseClient interface. In the same way,
CatalogItemResource is also in charge of providing the paths of the items' resources by
building the Uri of the web service. Besides this, CatalogItemResource uses the
IBaseClient wrapper to perform HTTP operations. Let's dig into the implementation of
the IBaseClass interface:

// /Base/BaseClient.cs

```
using System;
using System.Net.Http;
using System.Threading;
using System.Threading.Tasks;
using Newtonsoft.Json;

namespace Catalog.API.Client.Base
{
    public class BaseClient : IBaseClient
    {
        private readonly HttpClient _client;
        private readonly string _baseUri;

        public BaseClient(HttpClient client, string baseUri)
        {
            _client = client;
            _baseUri = baseUri;
        }
```

```
        public async Task<T> GetAsync<T>(Uri uri, CancellationToken
            cancellationToken)
        {
            var result = await _client.GetAsync(uri,
            cancellationToken);
            result.EnsureSuccessStatusCode();

            return JsonConvert.DeserializeObject<T>(await
            result.Content.ReadAsStringAsync());
        }

        public Uri BuildUri(string format)
        {
            return new UriBuilder(_baseUri)
            {
                Path = format
            }.Uri;
        }
    }
}
```

The preceding code uses the `HttpClient` class that's provided by the framework to implement the `GetAsync<T>` generic method. Therefore, using this generic pattern allows us to deserialize the response using a custom model.

Finally, we can implement the actual client of the service by adding the following components:

// ICatalogClient.cs

```
using Catalog.API.Client.Resources;

namespace Catalog.API.Client
{
    public interface ICatalogClient
    {
        ICatalogItemResource Item { get; }
    }
}
```

// CatalogClient.cs

```
using System.Net.Http;
using Catalog.API.Client.Base;
using Catalog.API.Client.Resources;

namespace Catalog.API.Client
{
```

```
public class CatalogClient : ICatalogClient
{
    public ICatalogItemResource Item { get; }

    public CatalogClient(HttpClient client)
    {
        Item = new CatalogItemResource(new BaseClient(client,
        client.BaseAddress.ToString()));
    }
}
}
```

Finally, it is possible to use `Catalog.API.Client` to instantiate a new HTTP client instance and call the catalog service using a unique and universal contract:

```
var catalogClient = new CatalogClient(new HttpClient());
var result = await catalogClient.Item.Get(new Guid(item.CartItemId),
cancellationToken);
```

Now, we have some standalone DLLs that provide everything we need, so that we can query the catalog web service. In the next section, we will learn how to perform HTTP calls to the catalog service using the client we implemented in this section.

Integrating an HTTP client into the cart service

The next step is to incorporate the HTTP client provided by the catalog service into the cart service. Therefore, we will add a new class whose ownership is to call the catalog service and retrieve the information that's required for the specific cart. Let's start by creating an interface in the `Cart.Domain` project called `ICatalogService`:

```
using System.Threading;
using System.Threading.Tasks;
using Cart.Domain.Responses.Cart;

namespace Cart.Domain.Services
{
    public interface ICatalogService
    {
        Task<CartItemResponse> EnrichCartItem(CartItemResponse item,
            CancellationToken cancellationToken);
    }
}
```

The `ICatalogService` interface is contained in the `Services` folder of the `Cart.Domain` project. It exposes an asynchronous method called `EnrichCartItem`, which accepts `CartItemResponse` and returns the same type. Like we did for the `ICartRepository` interface, we can create the concrete implementation of the `ICatalogService` interface in the `Cart.Infrastructure` project. Therefore, we can use the `ICatalogClient` interface we previously implemented in the *catalog service* to retrieve the catalog information. In a real-world application, these DLLs are usually managed as NuGet packages in the internal repository of the company. In our case, we will copy them and include them in the `Cart.Infrastructure` project, as follows:

```
<Project Sdk="Microsoft.NET.Sdk">

    <PropertyGroup>
        <TargetFramework>netcoreapp3.1</TargetFramework>
    </PropertyGroup>

    . . .

    <ItemGroup>
      <Reference Include="Catalog.API.Client, Version=1.0.0.0,
        Culture=neutral, PublicKeyToken=null">
        <HintPath>ExternalDll\Catalog.API.Client.dll</HintPath>
      </Reference>
      <Reference Include="Catalog.API.Contract, Version=1.0.0.0,
        Culture=neutral, PublicKeyToken=null">
        <HintPath>ExternalDll\Catalog.API.Contract.dll</HintPath>
      </Reference>
    </ItemGroup>
</Project>
```

Let's proceed by creating the `CatalogService` class in the `Cart.Infrastructure` project:

```
using System;
using System.Globalization;
using System.Threading;
using System.Threading.Tasks;
using Cart.Domain.Responses.Cart;
using Cart.Domain.Services;
using Catalog.API.Client;
using Catalog.API.Contract.Item;

namespace Cart.Infrastructure.Services
{
    public class CatalogService : ICatalogService
    {
```

```
private readonly ICatalogClient _catalogClient;

public CatalogService(ICatalogClient catalogClient)
{
    _catalogClient = catalogClient;
}

public async Task<CartItemResponse> EnrichCartItem
(CartItemResponse item, CancellationToken cancellationToken)
{
    try
    {
        var result = await _catalogClient.Item.Get(new
            Guid(item.CartItemId), cancellationToken);
        return Map(item, result);
    }
    catch (Exception)
    {
        return item;
    }
}

private static CartItemResponse Map(CartItemResponse item,
    ItemResponse result)
{
    item.Description = result.Description;
    item.LabelName = result.LabelName;
    item.Name = result.Name;
    item.Price = result.Price.Amount.ToString
        (CultureInfo.InvariantCulture);
    item.ArtistName = result.Artist.ArtistName;
    item.GenreDescription = result.Genre.GenreDescription;
    item.PictureUri = result.PictureUri;

    return item;
}
    }
}
```

CatalogService resolves the ICatalogClient dependency using constructor injection. The class implements the EnrichCartItem function by calling the catalog service client in the following way:

```
var result = await _catalogClient.Item.Get(new Guid(item.CartItemId),
cancellationToken);
```

Now, the method retrieves information related to the catalog item and it maps that data into CartItemResponse using the Map method. As a result, we will have information about each item that's been populated with the new data. It is possible to proceed by referring to the ICatalogService interface in the handlers that have been implemented in Cart.Domain. Let's take GetCartHandler as an example of this:

```
using System.Linq;
...

namespace Cart.Domain.Handlers.Cart
{
    public class GetCartHandler : IRequestHandler<GetCartCommand,
        CartExtendedResponse>
    {
        private readonly ICatalogService _catalogService;
        private readonly IMapper _mapper;
        private readonly ICartRepository _repository;


        public GetCartHandler( ICartRepository repository, IMapper
            mapper, ICatalogService catalogService)
        {
            _repository = repository;
            _mapper = mapper;
            _catalogService = catalogService;
        }

        public async Task<CartExtendedResponse> Handle(GetCartCommand
        command, CancellationToken cancellationToken)
        {
            var result = await _repository.GetAsync(command.Id);
            var extendedResponse = _mapper.Map<CartExtendedResponse>
                (result);

            var tasks = extendedResponse.Items
                .Select(async x => await
                _catalogService.EnrichCartItem(x, cancellationToken));

            extendedResponse.Items = await Task.WhenAll(tasks);
            return extendedResponse;
        }
    }
}
```

We can execute the `_catalogService.EnrichCartItem` method to retrieve the populated data for each `Item` in the `extendedResponse` object. In addition, `GetCartHandler` uses the `Task.WhenAll` method to wait for the tasks to complete and returns their data. To get this process working in the runtime execution, it is necessary to declare the following extension method, which will initialize the dependency and execute it in the `Startup` class of the `Cart.API` project by passing the endpoints of the APIs:

```
using System;
using Microsoft.Extensions.DependencyInjection;
using Cart.Domain.Services;
using Cart.Services;
using Catalog.API.Client;

namespace Cart.Infrastructure
{
    public static class CatalogServiceExtensions
    {
        public static IServiceCollection AddCatalogService(this
        IServiceCollection services, Uri uri)
        {
            services.AddScoped<ICatalogClient>(x => new
                CatalogClient(uri));
            services.AddScoped<ICatalogService, CatalogService>();

            return services;
        }
    }
}
```

`AddCatalogService` will be called in the `CofigureService` method of the `Startup` class. It adds `ICatalogClient` and `ICatlogService` to the dependency injection services by using a scoped life cycle.

Implementing resilience using Polly.NET

In the previous sections, we described how to achieve communication between the catalog service and the cart service. Now, we should be asking ourselves the following questions about the runtime execution and the communication between our services: what happens if the catalog service is down? What happens if the catalog service has a slow response time? The **Polly.NET** package comes in handy for these kinds of issues (`https://github.com/App-vNext/Polly`).

Polly.NET is based on *policies,* where each *policy* can be used individually or combined with others to provide resilience to the client. Out of the box, the library offers some standard resilience policies, such as retry, circuit breaker, and timeout. Let's have a quick look at a sample policy so that we understand how to use them:

```
. . .

    services.AddHttpClient<IMyService, MyService>()
        .AddPolicyHandler(RetryPolicy());
. . .

static IAsyncPolicy<HttpResponseMessage> RetryPolicy()
{
    return HttpPolicyExtensions
        .HandleTransientHttpError()
        .OrResult(msg => msg.StatusCode ==
            System.Net.HttpStatusCode.NotFound)
        .WaitAndRetryAsync(6, retryAttempt =>
            TimeSpan.FromSeconds(Math.Pow(2, retryAttempt)));
}
```

The previous code injects an `HttpClient` instance into `IMyService`. The `HttpClient` instance combines `RetryPolicy` with the `Polly` package. Furthermore, if the HTTP call returns a `404 NotFound` message, it triggers `RetryPolicy`, which retries the request after a specified amount of time that increases exponentially.

Integrating Polly into ICatalogService

Let's look at how we can incorporate Polly.NET into the cart service. As we saw previously, our use case uses the catalog service to gather detailed information about the items in the user's cart and return them to the client. Furthermore, we will implement `CircuitBreakerPolicy` on `ICatalogClient`. `CircuitBreakerPolicy` follows the failing fast approach, which means that, even if the response of the catalog service doesn't arrive, the runtime continues with the execution of the application.

Before starting, let's add some Polly.NET packages to the `Cart.Infrastructure` project by using the `add package` command in the project folder:

```
dotnet add package Polly
```

Let's proceed by creating some policies for `ICatalogClient` by creating a new `CatalogServicePolicies` static class in `Cart.Infrastructure`:

```
using System;
using System.Net;
using System.Net.Http;
using Polly;
using Polly.Extensions.Http;

namespace Cart.Infrastructure.Extensions.Policies
{
    public static class CatalogServicePolicies
    {
        public static IAsyncPolicy<HttpResponseMessage> RetryPolicy()
        {
            return HttpPolicyExtensions
                .HandleTransientHttpError()
                .OrResult(msg => msg.StatusCode ==
                    HttpStatusCode.NotFound)
                .WaitAndRetryAsync(3, retryAttempt =>
                  TimeSpan.FromSeconds(Math.Pow(2, retryAttempt)));
        }

        public static IAsyncPolicy<HttpResponseMessage>
        CircuitBreakerPolicy()
        {
            return HttpPolicyExtensions
                .HandleTransientHttpError()
                .CircuitBreakerAsync(3, TimeSpan.FromMinutes(1));
        }
    }
}
```

The preceding code defines two policies:

- The `RetryPolicy` static method defines the number of retries to carry out before proceeding with the other policies. It uses the `.HandleTransientHttpError` and `.OrResult` methods to detect all the failed conditions that have been returned by the client. Furthermore, it calls the `WaitAndRetryAsync` method, which restricts the `RetryPolicy` to a maximum of three retries. With each retry, it increases the sleep duration.
- The `CircuitBreaker` static method catches all the error conditions by using `.HandleTransientHttpError`. It calls the `.CircuitBreakerAsync` method to define `CircuitBreakerPolicy`. `CircuitBreakerPolicy` will be triggered after three attempts and will be active for 1 minute.

Now, we can inject the definitions of these policies into our `HttpClient` instances, as follows:

```
public static class CatalogServiceExtensions
{
    public static IServiceCollection AddCatalogService(this
    IServiceCollection services, Uri uri)
    {
        services.AddScoped<ICatalogService, CatalogService>();

        services.AddHttpClient<ICatalogClient, CatalogClient>(client =>
            {
                client.BaseAddress = uri;
            })
            .SetHandlerLifetime(TimeSpan.FromMinutes(2))
            .AddPolicyHandler(CatalogServicePolicies.RetryPolicy())
            .AddPolicyHandler(CatalogServicePolicies.
             CircuitBreakerPolicy());
        return services;
    }
}
```

As you can see, we are injecting these policies using the `AddPolicyHandler` method, and we are calling the `CatalogServicePolicies` static class to get them. It is also essential to notice that, before defining the policies, we use the `SetHandlerLifetime` method to determine the lifetime of `HttpClient`. This approach guarantees more resilient communication between the cart service and the catalog service. Furthermore, note that `Polly` policies can be applied to any third-party dependency call, which means that every time we rely on a third-party service, we need to anticipate this kind of approach in order to gracefully handle errors.

Sharing events using an event bus

So far in this chapter, we've seen how we can share information over HTTP by calling other web services. As we've already mentioned, it is important to not replicate information between services and, more importantly, that each service must be the owner of a single data source, which needs to be as isolated as possible. Another technique we can use to share information is pushing data using events. In this section, we will begin by examining one use case that is suitable for an event bus.

Let's suppose that one of the catalog items reaches an available stock amount of zero and enters the sold-out state. We need to propagate this information and tell the cart service that this specific item is sold out. This use case can be implemented using an event bus.

To understand this architecture, take a look at the following schema:

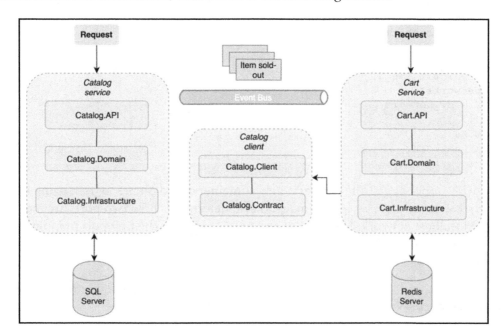

The catalog service triggers an event each time the available stock of an item reaches zero. The cart service listens for this event and then triggers the update of the cart that's stored in the Redis data source. For this purpose, we will use RabbitMQ, which is one of the most common event buses. RabbitMQ provides a .NET package that can be used to implement the communication between two solutions: `https://github.com/rabbitmq/rabbitmq-dotnet-client`.

Setting up a RabbitMQ instance and publishing an event

Event bus communication is composed of two parts: the sender and the receiver. In the case of an event, the actors' names are publishers and subscribers. The previous section described the implementation of the subscriber part. In this case, the catalog service will be the publisher and the cart service will be the subscriber. Before we look at how to implement the publisher part, we need to create a RabbitMQ instance using a Docker container by adding a `docker-compose.yml` file to the catalog service:

```
version: "3.7"
services:
```

```
    . . .
  catalog_esb:
    container_name: catalog_esb
    image: rabbitmq:3-management-alpine
    ports:
      - 5672:5672
      - 15672:15672
    networks:
      - my_network
    . . .
networks:
    my_network:
        driver: bridge
```

The `docker-compose.yml` file defines a new container called `catalog_esb` using the `rabbitmq:3-management-alpine` image. It also determines how two ports are mapped within the localhost network: `5672:5672` and `15672:15672`. The first port mapping is used to expose the RabbitMQ instance, while the second one is used to reveal the management console.

Furthermore, we need to define an extension method that configures RabbitMQ in the catalog web service. We can add the `RabbitMQ.Client` package to the `Catalog.Infrastructure` project using the following command:

```
dotnet add package RabbitMQ.Client
```

Furthermore, we will also need to implement the `ItemSoldOutEvent` type in the `Catalog.Domain` project, under the `Events` folder:

```
namespace Catalog.Domain.Events
{
    public class ItemSoldOutEvent
    {
        public string Id { get; set; }
    }
}
```

The preceding class reflects the event that we've already implemented in the cart project, and it will be used to send the messages through the event bus. The event bus also requires a configuration class that represents the connection parameters to the RabbitMQ instance. The class will be stored in the `Configuration` folder of the `Catalog.Domain` project:

```
namespace Catalog.Domain.Configurations
{
    public class EventBusSettings
    {
```

```
        public string HostName { get; set; }
        public string User { get; set; }
        public string Password { get; set; }
        public string EventQueue { get; set; }
    }
}
```

The `EventBusSettings` type describes the `HostName` of the RabbitMQ instance, the `User` and `Password` of the user, and the `EventQueue` name to use to push messages. Therefore, we can proceed by implementing the extension method that will set up and start the event bus in the `Catalog.Infrastructure` project:

```
using Catalog.Domain.Configurations;
using Microsoft.Extensions.Configuration;
using Microsoft.Extensions.DependencyInjection;
using RabbitMQ.Client;

namespace Catalog.Infrastructure.Extensions
{
    public static class EventsExtensions
    {
        public static IServiceCollection AddEventBus(this
            IServiceCollection services, IConfiguration configuration)
        {
            var config = new EventBusSettings();
            configuration.Bind("EventBus", config);
            services.AddSingleton(config);

            ConnectionFactory factory = new ConnectionFactory
            {
                HostName = config.HostName,
                UserName = config.User,
                Password = config.Password
            };

            services.AddSingleton(factory);
            return services;
        }
    }
}
```

The preceding code defines how we can publish events to RabbitMQ. The extension method performs the following operations:

- It initializes a new EventBusSettings with the EventBus string section passed as a parameter and adds the configuration as a singleton instance to the dependency injection engine of ASP.NET Core.
- It initializes the transport protocol using the RabbitMQ type by initializing a new ConnectionFactory type. ConnectionFactory will provide all the tools related to the publication of messages through RabbitMQ.
- It adds the new ConnectionFactory type into the dependency injection services as a singleton type.

Moreover, it is possible to resolve the ConnectionFactory and EventBusSettings types using the out-of-the-box dependency injection of .NET Core, and proceed by publishing the events using the methods provided by the RabbitMQ.Client packages:

```
using Catalog.Domain.Events;
using RabbitMQ.Client;

namespace Catalog.Domain.Services
{
    public class ItemService : IItemService
    {
        private readonly IItemMapper _itemMapper;
        private readonly IItemRepository _itemRepository;
        private readonly ConnectionFactory _eventBusConnectionFactory;
        private readonly ILogger<ItemService> _logger;
        private readonly EventBusSettings _settings;

        public ItemService(IItemRepository itemRepository, IItemMapper
            itemMapper,
            ConnectionFactory eventBusConnectionFactory,
            ILogger<ItemService> logger, EventBusSettings settings)
        {
            _itemRepository = itemRepository;
            _itemMapper = itemMapper;
            _eventBusConnectionFactory = eventBusConnectionFactory;
            _logger = logger;
            _settings = settings;
        }

        ...

        public async Task<ItemResponse> DeleteItemAsync(DeleteItemRequest
    request,
            CancellationToken cancellationToken = default)
```

```
    {
        if (request?.Id == null) throw new ArgumentNullException();

        var result = await _itemRepository.GetAsync(request.Id);
        result.IsInactive = false;

        _itemRepository.Update(result);
        await _itemRepository.UnitOfWork.
            SaveChangesAsync(cancellationToken);

        SendDeleteMessage(new ItemSoldOutEvent { Id =
request.Id.ToString() });
        return _itemMapper.Map(result);
    }

    private void SendDeleteMessage(ItemSoldOutEvent message)
    {
        try
        {
            var connection = _eventBusConnectionFactory.
                CreateConnection();

            using var channel = connection.CreateModel();
            channel.QueueDeclare(queue: _settings.EventQueue, true,
                false);

            var body = Encoding.UTF8.GetBytes
                (JsonSerializer.Serialize(message));

            channel.ConfirmSelect();
            channel.BasicPublish(exchange: "", routingKey:
                _settings.EventQueue, body: body);
            channel.WaitForConfirmsOrDie();
        }
        catch (Exception e)
        {
            _logger.LogWarning("Unable to initialize the event bus:
                {message}", e.Message);
        }
    }
}
}
```

Here, the `ItemService` class uses dependency injection to inject a new `ConnectionFactory` instance and the `EventBusSettings` into the class. As you may have noticed, the `DeleteItemAsync` method also calls the `SendDeleteMessage` we defined. Furthermore, the `SendDeleteMessage` method uses the `CreateConnection` method in order to create a new connection with RabbitMQ. Then, it continues by creating a new fresh channel using the `CreateModel` method and defining a new queue that has the same name as the queue we defined in the `EventBusSettings` configuration. Finally, it proceeds by serializing the `ItemSoldOut` event and publishing the message using the `EventQueue` field. The whole procedure is wrapped into a try-catch block in order to be ignored in case there is a communication error between the catalog service and the queue. Now that we have set up the sender, we can call the previously defined `AddEventBus` extension method in the `Startup` class of `Catalog.API` in the following way:

```
public void ConfigureServices(IServiceCollection services)
{
        . . .
        services.AddEventBus(Configuration);
}
```

The `AddEventBus` method now uses the `EventBus` section to provide the necessary configuration to the new instance of the `ConnectionFactory` type. Now, we can add the configuration to the `appsettings.json` file:

```
. . .
 "EventBus": {
        "HostName": "catalog_esb",
        "User": "guest",
        "Password": "guest",
        "EventQueue": "ItemSoldOut"
    }
. . .
```

`ConnectionString` specifies the `catalog_esb` instance as the name of the host and the default `username` and `password` provided by RabbitMQ. Furthermore, it also specifies the `ItemSoldOut` endpoint name. Now, every time we delete an item in the catalog service, it will queue a new ItemSoldOut event into RabbitMQ. In the next chapter, we will see how to consume these messages in the cart service. In the next section, we will continue by learning how to set up and configure the cart service Docker image.

Running the cart service using Docker

Let's learn how to run the previously implemented cart service using Docker. As we described in the previous chapter, we are going to define the `docker-compose.yml` file and the Dockerfile in the root of the cart service project. The `docker-compose` file will define two containers: the first hosts the cart service ASP.NET Core instance, while the other represents the Redis instance:

```yaml
version: "3.7"
services:
    cart_api:
        container_name: cart_api
        build:
            context: .
        env_file:
            - .env
        networks:
            - my_network
        ports:
            - 5002:5002
        depends_on:
            - cart_db
    cart_db:
        container_name: cart_db
        networks:
            - my_network
        env_file:
            - .env
        ports:
            - 6378:6378
        image: redis:alpine

networks:
    my_network:
        driver: bridge
```

First, the preceding code defines the `cart_api` container. It is part of `my_network`, which is defined in the same file, and it exposes ports `5002` (HTTP) and `5003` (HTTPS). It also refers to the Dockerfile that's located at the root of the project. Secondly, the `docker-compose.yml` file defines the `cart_db` container, which exposes the default port of Redis (`6378`). The `cart_db` container uses the Alpine version of Redis so that it can save on the container size. The container shares `my_network`.

In this case, we are using a storage system running on a container. Note that this information is not persistent, for two reasons. The first reason is that Redis stores information using a TTL. The default TTL is 24 hours; after that time, the basket information is cleared. It is possible to specify anther TTL when you add a new key to the Redis instance. The second reason is that, once the `cart_db` container is killed, we will lose the information inside it. We are using a Redis instance in the form of a container just for demonstration purposes.

Now, let's look at an overview of the definition of the Dockerfile:

```
FROM mcr.microsoft.com/dotnet/core/aspnet:3.1 AS base
WORKDIR /app
EXPOSE 5002

FROM mcr.microsoft.com/dotnet/core/sdk:3.1 AS build
WORKDIR /project

COPY ["/src/Cart.API/Cart.API.csproj", "/src/Cart.API/"]
RUN dotnet restore "/src/Cart.API/Cart.API.csproj"

COPY . .
WORKDIR "/project/src/Cart.API"
RUN dotnet build "Cart.API.csproj" -c Release -o /app/build

FROM build AS publish
RUN dotnet publish "Cart.API.csproj" -c Release -o /app/publish

FROM base AS final
WORKDIR /app

COPY --from=publish /app/publish .
ENTRYPOINT ["dotnet", "Cart.API.dll"]
```

The Dockerfile fulfills the same instructions as the ones defined for the `Catalog.API` project: it uses the `microsoft/dotnet:sdk` image to build the project and publish it and then it uses the `microsoft/dotnet:3.0-aspnetcore` image to run it. To get the containers working, we need to share information between the `Catalog.API` project and the `Cart.API` project containers. Moreover, it is necessary to initialize the containers in the same project by adding the following `.env` file to the same level that the `docker-compose.yml` file is at:

```
COMPOSE_PROJECT_NAME=store
ASPNETCORE_URLS=http://*:5002
ASPNETCORE_ENVIRONMENT=Integration
```

The COMPOSE_PROJECT_NAME variables set the project name. This value is prepended, along with the service name, to the container upon startup. Finally, it is possible to run both projects by executing the docker-compose up --build command in the Catalog.API and the Cart.API project folders: the docker-compose command in the Catalog.API folder will initialize the catalog_api, catalog_db, and the catalog_esb containers. On the other side, the execution of the docker-compose command in the Cart.API folder will initialize the cart_api and cart_db containers.

Furthermore, it is possible to create a new catalog item by executing the following sequence of HTTP calls:

```
POST /api/genre HTTP/1.1
Host: localhost:5000
Content-Type: application/json
{
  "genreDescription": "R&B"
}

POST /api/artist HTTP/1.1
Host: localhost:5000
Content-Type: application/json
{
    "artistName": "Anderson .Paak"
}
```

These two requests are direct to the localhost:5000 URL, which represents the catalog web service. They return a 201 Created HTTP status code with the ID of each created artist and genre entity. Furthermore, we can proceed by creating a new item in the catalog using the following HTTP request:

```
POST /api/items HTTP/1.1
Host: localhost:5000
Content-Type: application/json
{
  "name": "Test",
  "description": "Description",
  "labelName": "Label",
  "price": {
  "currency": "EUR",
  "amount": 34.3
  },
  "pictureUri": "",
  "releaseDate": "2019-11-21T16:18:42+00:00",
  "format": "",
  "availableStock": 4,
  "genreId":"<genre_id>",
```

```
   "artistId":"<artist_id>"
 }
```

Now, we can proceed by calling the cart API service in order to create a new cart session with the item we just created:

```
POST /api/cart/ HTTP/1.1
Host: localhost:5002
Content-Type: application/json
{
 "ItemsIds": ["<item_id>"],
 "UserEmail":"youremail@gmail.com"
}
```

Finally, we can verify the communication between the catalog service and the cart service by calling the detail of the cart session:

```
GET /api/cart/<cart_id> HTTP/1.1
Host: localhost:5002
cache-control: no-cache
```

The cart service should respond with the details related to the item in the cart by fetching the information that was exposed by the catalog web service. If the catalog web service is down, the cart service will omit all the details of the items by returning only the corresponding ID.

Summary

In this chapter, you have learned how to implement different types of communication in service ecosystems. We looked closely at how to use an HTTP client to share information between services. We also looked at how we can use resilience techniques with `Polly`.

Then, we described how to use an event bus to fire events to a RabbitMQ queue; we used `RabbitMQ.Client` combined with RabbitMQ for this. The topics that were covered in this chapter will be useful when you need to transfer data or perform actions across two or more web services or systems.

In the next chapter, we will learn how to consume `ItemSoldOut` events through the use of the worker services capabilities of ASP.NET Core.

14

Implementing Worker Services Using .NET Core

The latest version of .NET Core includes a simple and convenient way to implement background processes. Moreover, starting from version 3.0, it is possible to create new projects using an out-of-the-box template for worker services. .NET worker services are suitable for multiple use cases. Furthermore, the increasing adoption of cloud technologies and distributed systems also involves event-driven communication between services, which requires the implementation of background processes. This chapter walks through some of the concepts and use cases of the worker services tools provided by ASP.NET Core. We will also have a look at how to integrate the worker service capabilities of ASP.NET Core to consume the ItemSoldOut event queue implemented in the previous chapter.

This chapter covers the following topics:

- Introduction to worker services
- Implementing a worker service using .NET Core
- Deploying and running a worker on Docker
- Extending the background services class

By the end of this chapter, you will be able to implement a worker service and deploy it using Docker container technology.

Introducing worker services

.NET Core worker services can be really useful every time we need to perform a repetitive or background-running operation. In more detail, they can be used in the application layer to enable asynchronous operations and handle the events of an event-based architecture. If every time you need to publish or listen for a message, you need to refresh data based on a schedule, or your application needs to queue a background work item, then you should probably use a worker service. Furthermore, with worker services, it is possible to run multiple background tasks on the same server without consuming a lot of resources.

The foundation of worker services in .NET Core is the `IHostedService` interface. The out-of-the-box worker service template can be used as a guideline to start implementing our worker service project. More importantly, the `IHostedService` interface is implemented by a `BackgroundService` class, which is the base class we should extend to implement our worker service.

Understanding the worker services life cycle

.NET Core uses the definition of the `BackgroundService` class to identify a worker service. The `BackgroundService` class exposes three methods that represent the life cycle stages of the worker service:

```
namespace Microsoft.Extensions.Hosting
{
    public abstract class BackgroundService : IHostedService, IDisposable
    {
        public virtual Task StartAsync(CancellationToken
            cancellationToken);

        protected abstract Task ExecuteAsync(CancellationToken
            stoppingToken);
        public virtual async Task StopAsync(CancellationToken
            cancellationToken);
    }
}
```

The preceding code is the abstract implementation of the `BackgroundService` class. The class implements both the `IHostedService` and `IDisposable` interfaces, and it exposes the following methods:

- The `StartAsync` method represents the first stage of the life cycle of the worker. This method is called when the host is ready to run the worker service. It accepts a `CancellationToken` type parameter, which can be used to cancel the running task.
- The `ExecuteAsync` method contains the core implementation of the `BackgroundService` class. This method is called once the `IHostedService` starts, and it returns a `Task` type that represents the status of the `Task`.
- The `StopAsync` method is called when the hosted application is stopped gracefully.

This section provided an overview of the worker service life cycle methods. In the next section, we will see the hosting models available for the worker services in .NET Core.

Hosting models

The .NET Core worker template is nothing more than a common .NET Core app. Furthermore, we can run the worker template as a common console application. Besides, the worker template also provides the hosting APIs to run the worker as an always-running process. In the case of Windows, it is possible to run the worker using Windows services technology. In the case of Linux, the worker runs using `systemd`.

Furthermore, .NET Core provides two different NuGet packages to specify the host behavior of the worker: the `Microsoft.Extensions.Hosting.WindowsServices` package and the `Microsoft.Extensions.Hosting.Systemd` package, both available on NuGet.

The `Microsoft.Extensions.Hosting.WindowsServices` package provides an extension method called `UseWindowsService()`, which can be applied after the initialization of the host in the `Main` method of the `Program` class. The `UseWindowsService()` method sets `WindowsServiceLifetime` and uses the *Windows event log* as the default logging output.

If we choose to host our worker as a `systemd` service, we need to use the `Microsoft.Extensions.Hosting.Systemd` NuGet package. This package provides the `UseSystemd()` method, which can be applied in the same way as `UseWindowsService()`; in this case, our worker service will use the `SystemdLifetime` class, and it configures the logging to be compliant with the `systemd` format.

 It is important to note that both the `UseWindowsService()` and `UseSystemd()` methods are executed only if the worker service is running respectively as a Windows service and a `systemd` service.

Once we have discovered the different ways to host the worker service, we can proceed by applying these concepts to the concrete of a health-check process. Besides, we will also see how to run the worker on a Docker container.

Implementing a health-checking worker

The following section focuses on the implementation of a worker service. The use case we will cover is a health-checking worker of a generic web service. Furthermore, let's suppose that we want to check the health status of one of our web services regularly. This kind of check is usually performed at the end of the deployment pipeline, or once a service is deployed, to verify that the web service is up and running.

Project structure overview

This section gives you an overview of the worker template project provided out of the box by the .NET Core templating system. We will use this type of project to implement a health-check worker. First of all, let's start by creating a new project using the following CLI command:

```
dotnet new worker -n HealthCheckWorker
```

This command creates a new folder called `HealthCheckWorker` and it creates all of the files needed by a basic worker service project. Let's have a look at the files created by the template `dotnet new worker` command executed previously.

Secondly, we can run the `tree` CLI command (available both on macOS X and Windows), which shows the folder structure of the project previously created:

```
.
├── Program.cs
├── Properties
│     └── launchSettings.json
├── Worker.cs
├── HealthCheckWorker.csproj
├── appsettings.Development.json
├── appsettings.json
├── bin
│     └── Debug
│           └── netcoreapp3.0
└── obj
      ├── Debug
            └── netcoreapp3.0
```

The `Program.cs` file is the entry point of our worker service. As the `webapi` template, the worker template uses the `Program.cs` file to initialize and retrieve a new `IHostBuilder` instance by calling the `Host.CreateDefaultBuilder` and `ConfigureServices` methods. The `Main` static method in the `Program.cs` file initializes a list of workers using the `AddHostedService` extension method:

```csharp
using Microsoft.Extensions.DependencyInjection;
using Microsoft.Extensions.Hosting;

namespace HealthCheckWorker
{
    public class Program
    {
        public static void Main(string[] args)
        {
            CreateHostBuilder(args).Build().Run();
        }

        public static IHostBuilder CreateHostBuilder(string[] args) =>
            Host.CreateDefaultBuilder(args)
                .ConfigureServices((hostContext, services) =>
                {
                    services.AddHostedService<Worker>();
                });
    }
}
```

As previously mentioned, the preceding snippet of code uses `AddHostedService` to initialize the `Worker` class created as a part of the default worker template. It is necessary to notice that, under the hood, `AddHostedService` initializes the class with a `Singleton` life cycle. Therefore, we will have one instance of the worker for the whole execution time of the worker service. In the next section, we will go deep into the life cycle execution of a worker.

 Another major characteristic that distinguishes a worker project from any other .NET Core project is the use of the `Microsoft.NET.Sdk.Worker` SDK. Furthermore, we should also notice that the `*.csproj` file refers to only one additional NuGet package that provides the hosting extension methods used by the `Program` class and the `Main` method: `Microsoft.Extensions.Hosting`.

The next step is to create a new class that represents the configurations of the `HealthCheckWorker` project:

```
namespace HealthCheckWorker
{
    public class HealthCheckSettings
    {
        public string Url { get; set; }
        public int IntervalMs { get; set; }
    }
}
```

`HealthCheckSettings` will contain two attributes: the `Url` and `IntervalMs` attributes. The first attribute contains the HTTP URL of the health check address, specified in `appsettings.json`. The `IntervalMs` attribute represents the frequency life cycle (in milliseconds) of the worker.

Furthermore, it is possible to use the configuration system of .NET Core to bind our configuration object at the execution of the `Main` method of the `Program.cs` file, using the following approach:

```
using Microsoft.Extensions.DependencyInjection;
using Microsoft.Extensions.Hosting;

namespace HealthCheckWorker
{
    public class Program
    {
        public static void Main(string[] args)
        {
            CreateHostBuilder(args).Build().Run();
```

```
        }

    public static IHostBuilder CreateHostBuilder(string[] args) =>
        Host.CreateDefaultBuilder(args)
            .ConfigureServices((hostContext, services) =>
            {
                var healthCheckSettings = hostContext
                    .Configuration
                    .GetSection("HealthCheckSettings")
                services.Configure<HealthCheckSettings>
                    (healthCheckSettings);
                services.AddHostedService<Worker>();
            });
    }
}
```

The preceding code uses hostContext to retrieve the Configuration instance provided by .NET Core. By default, hostContext will be populated with the settings structure written in the appsettings.json file. Moreover, it is possible to use the GetSection method to retrieve the specific configuration section from our appsettings.json file and bind it to the HealthCheckSettings type.

After that, we can proceed with the concrete implementation of the Worker class. Furthermore, we are now able to inject the HealthCheckSettings type instance using the built-in dependency injection of .NET Core. The settings are injected using the IOption interface:

```
public class Worker : BackgroundService
    {
        private readonly ILogger<Worker> _logger;
        private readonly HealthCheckSettings _settings;
        private HttpClient _client;

        public Worker(ILogger<Worker> logger,
        IOptions<HealthCheckSettings> options)
        {
            _logger = logger;
            _settings = options.Value;
        }
...
```

The preceding code defines the attributes of the `Worker` class. As mentioned, the class implements an `_settings` attribute of the `HealthCheckSettings` type initialized using the constructor injection technique. Moreover, we can also see an `HttpClient` attribute, which will be initialized by the `StartAsync` method exposed by the `BackgroundService` class, and it is used in the `ExecuteAsync` method:

```
public class Worker : BackgroundService
{
    . . .

    public override Task StartAsync(CancellationToken cancellationToken)
    {
        _client = new HttpClient();
        return base.StartAsync(cancellationToken);
    }

    protected override async Task ExecuteAsync(CancellationToken
    stoppingToken)
    {
        while (!stoppingToken.IsCancellationRequested)
        {
            var result = await _client.GetAsync(_settings.Url);

            if (result.IsSuccessStatusCode)
                _logger.LogInformation($"The web service is up.
                HTTP {result.StatusCode}");
            await Task.Delay(_settings.IntervalMs, stoppingToken);
        }
    }

    . . .
}
```

After the initialization of the client, the `ExecuteAsync` method implements a `while` loop that will continue until the `stoppingToken` requests the cancellation of the process. The core part of the loop uses the `GetAsync` method of `HttpClient` to check whether the health check route returns an HTTP status message. Finally, the code calls `Task.Delay` with the `IntervalMs` property populated with the `_settings` instance.

As the last step, the `Worker` class overrides the `StopAsync` method exposed by the `BackgroundService` class:

```
public class Worker : BackgroundService
{
    . . .
```

```
public override Task StopAsync(CancellationToken cancellationToken)
{
    _client.Dispose();
    return base.StopAsync(cancellationToken);
}

}
```

The `StopAsync` method executes the `HttpClient` instance disposition by calling the `Dispose()` method, and it calls `base.StopAsync(cancellationToken)` of the base `BackgroundService` class.

 We should notice that the `StartAsync` and `StopAsync` methods always call the parent methods using the `base` keyword. Furthermore, in our case, we need to hold the behavior of the base `BackgroundService` class.

The next part of this chapter will be focused on the execution of the worker on a Docker container. We will see how to configure the `Dockerfile`, and deploy and run the application.

Running a worker service on Docker

This section is focused on the deployment step of the .NET worker template. We will proceed by running our service on a Docker Linux image. As we have already seen in Chapter 12, *The Containerization of Services*, we will use Docker to run the application in a container.

Let's start by configuring the `Dockerfile` in the project folder:

```
FROM mcr.microsoft.com/dotnet/core/runtime:3.0 AS base
WORKDIR /app

# Step 1 - Building the project
FROM mcr.microsoft.com/dotnet/core/sdk:3.0 AS build
WORKDIR /src
COPY ["HealthCheckWorker.csproj", "./"]
RUN dotnet restore "./HealthCheckWorker.csproj"
COPY . .
WORKDIR "/src/."
RUN dotnet build "HealthCheckWorker.csproj" -c Release -o /app/build

# Step 2 - Publish the project
FROM build AS publish
```

```
RUN dotnet publish "HealthCheckWorker.csproj" -c Release -o /app/publish

# Step 3 - Run the project
FROM base AS final
WORKDIR /app
COPY --from=publish /app/publish .
ENTRYPOINT ["dotnet", "HealthCheckWorker.dll"]
```

The preceding code describes the container build and deployment process for our .NET Core worker application. The `Dockerfile` instructions can be grouped into five steps:

1. The first step executes the build of the project using the `dotnet/core/sdk` Docker image:

   - First of all, it sets the working directory as `/src` and copies the files in the project folder.
   - Secondly, it executes the `dotnet restore` and `dotnet build` commands.

2. The second step runs the `dotnet publish` command using the `Release` configuration in the `/app/publish` folder.

3. The third step uses the `dotnet/core/runtime` Docker image to run the result of the previously executed `dotnet publish` using the `dotnet` CLI command.

4. It is possible to build the Docker image using the following command:

   docker build --rm -f "Dockerfile" -t healthcheckworker:latest

5. Furthermore, we can run the previously built image using the following command:

   docker run --rm -d healthcheckworker:latest

The preceding command runs the Docker container and, consequently, the worker service process. The worker service will perform an HTTP GET request to the URL configured in the `appsettings.json` file of the project by applying throttling, also specified in the `appsettings.json` file.

 The previously mentioned `Dockerfile` uses a multi-stage build approach and some other techniques to build the Docker image used to run the project. These concepts, and more, are described in detail in `Chapter 12`, *The Containerization of Services*.

Consuming the sold-out event

The sold-out event we implemented in Chapter 13, *Service Ecosystem Patterns*, provides the information on the items that are not available in the catalog. Furthermore, we can consume this event through the use of the BackgroundService type capabilities we described in this chapter. The cart service will implement a sold-out handler that will handle and remove the item IDs that are not available from the Redis instance.

Creating a sold-out handler

Let's start by creating a handler that manages the sold-out condition of a product in the cart service. First of all, we should proceed by adding the RabbitMQ.Client package to the Cart.Domain project by executing the following command:

```
dotnet add ./src/Cart.Domain package RabbitMQ.Client
```

We can continue by defining a class that represents the sold-out event that's used by the cart service in a new project that will contain all of the events. Therefore, we will proceed by creating a new ItemSoldOutEvent type, which represents a sold-out event:

```
using MediatR;

namespace Cart.Domain.Events
{
    public class ItemSoldOutEvent : IRequest<Unit>
    {
        public string Id { get; set; }
    }
}
```

The ItemSoldOutEvent type contains a reference to Id of the item that's sold out. The type will be used to deserialize the content of the queue into a strongly typed instance and send a message through the MediatR instance. As we did for the configurations of the catalog service, we will also need an analog class that represents the RabbitMQ configurations in the Cart.Infrastructure project:

```
namespace Cart.Infrastructure.Configurations
{
    public class EventBusSettings
    {
        public string HostName { get; set; }
        public string User { get; set; }
        public string Password { get; set; }
        public string EventQueue { get; set; }
```

```
        }
    }
```

The EventBusSettings type defined previously describes HostName of the RabbitMQ instance, User and Password of the user, and the EventQueue name to use to push messages. Furthermore, we can proceed by defining the mediator handler for consuming the ItemSoldOutEvent events by defining a new class in the Cart.Domain project:

```
using System;
using System.Linq;
using System.Threading;
using System.Threading.Tasks;
using Cart.Domain.Entities;
using Cart.Domain.Events;
using Cart.Domain.Repositories;
using MediatR;

namespace Cart.Domain.Handlers.Cart
{
    public class ItemSoldOutEventHandler :
        IRequestHandler<ItemSoldOutEvent>
    {
        private readonly ICartRepository _cartRepository;

        public ItemSoldOutEventHandler(ICartRepository cartRepository)
        {
            _cartRepository = cartRepository;
        }
        public async Task<Unit> Handle(ItemSoldOutEvent @event,
            CancellationToken cancellationToken)
        {
            var cartIds = _cartRepository.GetCarts().ToList();

            var tasks = cartIds.Select(async x =>
            {
                var cart = await _cartRepository.GetAsync(new Guid(x));
                await RemoveItemsInCart(@event.Id, cart);
            });

            await Task.WhenAll(tasks);
            return Unit.Value;
        }

        private async Task RemoveItemsInCart(string itemToRemove,
            CartSession cartSessionSession)
        {
            if (string.IsNullOrEmpty(itemToRemove)) return;
```

```
            var toDelete = cartSessionSession?.Items?.Where(x =>
                x.CartItemId.ToString() ==
                    itemToRemove).ToList();

            if (toDelete == null || toDelete.Count == 0) return;

            foreach (var item in toDelete)
                cartSessionSession.Items?.Remove(item);

            await _cartRepository.AddOrUpdateAsync(cartSessionSession);
        }
    }
}
```

The previous `ItemSoldOutEventHandler` class implements the
`IRequestHandler<T>` interface that's provided by the MediatR package. This interface
contains the `Handle` method, which is the main entry point of the handler. A
new `ItemSoldOutEventHandler` instance will be executed when an event of
the `ItemSoldOutEvent` type is received by the cart
service. `ItemSoldOutEventHandler` depends on `ICartRepository`. Furthermore, the
`RemoveItemsInCart` method retrieves all of the carts stored in our repository, and it
removes the sold-out items every time it receives a message of
the `ItemSoldOutEvent` type.

Testing the sold-out process

It is possible to check the sold-out process by testing `ItemSoldOutHandler`. The handler
will be tested with the same approach we saw for the other handlers:

```
using System;
using System.Linq;
using System.Threading;
using System.Threading.Tasks;
using Cart.Domain.Events;
using Cart.Domain.Handlers.Cart;
using Cart.Fixtures;
using Shouldly;
using Xunit;

namespace Cart.Domain.Tests.Handlers.Events
{
    public class ItemSoldOutEventHandlerTests :
IClassFixture<CartContextFactory>
    {
        private readonly CartContextFactory _contextFactory;
```

```
public ItemSoldOutEventHandlerTests(CartContextFactory
    cartContextFactory)
{
    _contextFactory = cartContextFactory;
}

[Fact]
public async Task should_not_remove_records_whensoldout
    message_contains_not_existing_id()
{
    var repository = _contextFactory.GetCartRepository();
    var itemSoldOutEventHandler = new
        ItemSoldOutEventHandler(repository);
    var found = false;

    await itemSoldOutEventHandler.Handle(new ItemSoldOutEvent {
        Id = Guid.NewGuid().ToString() },
            CancellationToken.None);

    var cartsIds = repository.GetCarts();

    foreach (var cartId in cartsIds)
    {
        var cart = await repository.GetAsync(new Guid(cartId));
        found = cart.Items.Any(i => i.CartItemId.ToString() ==
            "be05537d-5e80-45c1-bd8c-
            aa21c0f1251e");
    }

    found.ShouldBeTrue();
}

...
    }
}
```

The `ItemSoldOutEventHandlerTests` class uses the `CartContextFactory` class to initialize a new repository in each test method using the `_contextFactory.GetCartRepository();` method. Furthermore, the `should_not_remove_records_when_soldout_message_contains_not_existing_id` test method checks that nothing breaks if the `ItemSoldOutEvent` instance has a non-existent ID. On the other hand, the `should_remove_records_when_soldout_messages_contains_existing_ids` test method checks that `ItemSoldOutEventHandler` deletes the item in the basket when the `ItemSoldOutEvent` instance contains an existing ID:

. . .

```
[Fact]
public async Task should_remove_records_whensoldout
    messages_contains_existing_ids()
{
    var itemSoldOutId = "be05537d-5e80-45c1-bd8c-aa21c0f1251e";
    var repository = _contextFactory.GetCartRepository();
    var itemSoldOutEventHandler = new
        ItemSoldOutEventHandler(repository);
    var found = false;

    await itemSoldOutEventHandler.Handle(new ItemSoldOutEvent {
      Id = itemSoldOutId },
        CancellationToken.None);

    foreach (var cartId in repository.GetCarts())
    {
        var cart = await repository.GetAsync(new Guid(cartId));
        found = cart.Items.Any(i => i.CartItemId.ToString() ==
            itemSoldOutId);
    }

    found.ShouldBeFalse();
}
    }
}
```

The second test method provides an existing item ID and verifies the handle method by checking whether the process has effectively removed the items. Now that we have verified the behavior of ItemSoldOutHandler, we can proceed by configuring and registering the event bus instance.

Configuring the background service

Now that we have defined the event bus abstraction, we can proceed by creating a new BackgroundService type that will use the IMediator interface to dispatch the sold-out messages. This book uses RabbitMQ because it is open source and easy to configure but keep in mind that there are tons of products and technologies related to this topic. Before continuing with the implementation of the background service, it is necessary to add some packages to the Cart.Infrastructure project:

```
dotnet add package RabbitMQ.Client
```

Furthermore, we can proceed by creating a new class that extends the
`BackgroundService` type:

```
using System;
using System.Threading;
using System.Threading.Tasks;
using Cart.Domain.Events;
using Cart.Infrastructure.Configurations;
using MediatR;
using Microsoft.Extensions.Hosting;
using Microsoft.Extensions.Logging;
using Microsoft.Extensions.Options;
using Newtonsoft.Json;
using RabbitMQ.Client;
using RabbitMQ.Client.Events;

namespace Cart.Infrastructure.BackgroundServices
{
    public class ItemSoldOutBackgroundService : BackgroundService
    {
        private readonly IMediator _mediator;
        private readonly ILogger<ItemSoldOutBackgroundService> _logger;
        private readonly EventBusSettings _options;
        private readonly IModel _channel;

        public ItemSoldOutBackgroundService( IMediator mediator,
            EventBusSettings options, ConnectionFactory factory,
                ILogger<ItemSoldOutBackgroundService> logger)
        {
            _options = options;
            _logger = logger;
            _mediator = mediator;

            try
            {
                var connection = factory.CreateConnection();
                _channel = connection.CreateModel();
            }
            catch (Exception e)
            {
                _logger.LogWarning("Unable to initialize the event bus:
                    {message}", e.Message);
            }
        }

        ...

    }
}
```

The preceding snippet defines the `ItemSoldOutBackgroundService` type. The class extends the `BackgroundService` base class exposed by the `Microsoft.Extensions.Hosting` namespace. The constructor injects the `IMediator` interface to dispatch the collected events to the `ItemSoldOutEventHandler` type. Furthermore, it also defines the attribute of the `IModel` type that will be populated by the `ConnectionFactory` type injected in the constructor. The `_channel` attribute will be used by the `ExecuteAsync` method provided by the `BackgroundService` class to dispatch the events. Let's proceed by overriding the `ExecuteAsync` method:

```
using MediatR;
using Microsoft.Extensions.Hosting;
using Newtonsoft.Json;
using RabbitMQ.Client;
using RabbitMQ.Client.Events;

namespace Cart.Infrastructure.BackgroundServices
{
    public class ItemSoldOutBackgroundService : BackgroundService
    {
        ...

        protected override Task ExecuteAsync(CancellationToken
            stoppingToken)
        {
            stoppingToken.ThrowIfCancellationRequested();

            var consumer = new EventingBasicConsumer(_channel);
            consumer.Received += async (ch, ea) =>
            {
                var content = System.Text.Encoding.UTF8.
                    GetString(ea.Body);
                var @event = JsonConvert.DeserializeObject
                    <ItemSoldOutEvent>(content);

                await _mediator.Send(@event, stoppingToken);
                _channel.BasicAck(ea.DeliveryTag, false);
            };

            try
            {
                consumer.Model.QueueDeclare(_settings.EventQueue, true,
                    false);
                _channel.BasicConsume(_options.EventQueue, false,
                    consumer);
            }
            catch (Exception e)
```

```
            {
                _logger.LogWarning("Unable to consume the event bus:
                    {message}", e.Message);
            }

            return Task.CompletedTask;
        }
    }
}
```

The preceding snippet uses the `_channel` attribute to initialize a new `EventingBasicConsumer` instance. For each received message, it deserializes the `Body` attribute into an `ItemSoldOutEvent` type and it sends the event to the `IMediator` instance using the `Send` method. Finally, it activates the consuming process by using the `EventQueue` name provided by the `EventBusSettings` type. Also, in this case, the consumption process is wrapped using a try-catch to isolate the process in the event of failure.

Before we can use RabbitMQ, it is necessary to configure the client so that we connect to the right event bus instance. Let's start by creating a new extension method in the `Cart.Infrastructure` project, which can be found under the `Extensions` folder:

```
using Cart.Infrastructure.Configurations;
using Microsoft.Extensions.Configuration;
using Microsoft.Extensions.DependencyInjection;
using RabbitMQ.Client;

namespace Cart.Infrastructure.Extensions
{
    public static class EventsExtensions
    {
        public static IServiceCollection AddEventBus(this
            IServiceCollection services, IConfiguration
         configuration)
        {
            var config = new EventBusSettings();
            configuration.Bind("EventBus", config);
            services.AddSingleton(config);

            ConnectionFactory factory = new ConnectionFactory
            {
                HostName = config.HostName,
                UserName = config.User,
                Password = config.Password
            };
```

```
                services.AddSingleton(factory);

                return services;
            }
        }
    }
```

The previous definition implements an extension method bound with
the ISeviceCollection interface, which is provided by the dependency injection system
of ASP.NET Core. It is used in the Startup class to connect to
RabbitMQ. The AddEventBus method initializes the ConnectionFactory class by passing
the parameter of RabbitMQ.

Finally, we can proceed by activating the background service by adding the following
extension methods to the ConfigureServices method of the Startup class:

```
using System;
...

namespace Cart.API
{
    public class Startup
    {
        public void ConfigureServices(IServiceCollection services)
        {
            services
                ...
                .AddEventBus(Configuration)
                .AddHostedService<ItemSoldOutBackgroundService>();
        }

        ...
    }
}
```

The AddEventBus method adds all of the dependencies needed by the consumption
process of the sold-out events to the dependency injection. Also, the AddHostedService
method registers ItemSoldOutBackgroundService as the IHostedService type.
Finally, to use the event bus, we can proceed by defining the connection information in the
appsettings.json file of the Cart.API project, as follows:

```
{
...
  "EventBus": {
    "HostName": "catalog_esb",
    "User": "guest",
```

```
        "Password": "guest",
        "EventQueue": "ItemSoldOut"
    }
}
```

The connection parameters point to the `catalog_esb` instance defined in the `docker-compose.yml` file defined in the catalog service. Furthermore, the `ItemSoldOutBackgroundService` class will process the message in the `ItemSoldOut` queue and trigger the removal of the items.

Summary

This chapter described how you can use the .NET Core worker template to implement a continuously running task. .NET Core workers are really useful in distributed systems to perform all of the asynchronous and event-based computations without an increase in the load of the server.

The integration with Windows services and `systemd` also provides an efficient way to deploy and to run the worker. This chapter has given you an overview of the .NET Core worker service hosting models, and it showed how to set up and implement a worker service using .NET Core and how to run it on Docker. Finally, we saw how to integrate the `BackgroundService` class capabilities with the previously implemented item sold-out message integration.

The next chapter will cover some of the common security practices provided and implemented by .NET Core.

15
Securing Your Service

In the previous chapters, we saw how to exchange data between multiple services using an event bus and resilient clients and how to consume messages and run background services using ASP.NET Core. This chapter is about securing service data. It covers concepts such as SSL, **cross-origin resource sharing (CORS)**, and HTTP/2, and it walks through the implementation of token-based authentication.

In more detail, this chapter covers the following topics:

- A general overview of SSL
- How to enable CORS in an ASP.NET Core service
- How to enable HTTPS and HTTP/2
- How token-based authentication works
- How to build token-based authentication in ASP.NET Core

By the end of the chapter, you will have a broad understanding of the security features provided by ASP.NET Core, and you will be able to implement token-based authentication in ASP.NET Core.

Overview of secure communication

Security is a crucial aspect of building applications. Web services usually expose information to third-party clients and companies; therefore, it is vital to avoid leaking data. The security layer of a web service is often a tedious part of the development process because it is hard to test and to verify.

Security is important even for web services that are published in the internal network of the company, which, by default, is not accessible from the outside. As software engineers, we should do as much as possible to guarantee a strong level of security when we release a web service. It is also essential to understand that securing a web service is necessary to identify the consumers of your data and to prevent overuse of your web service. The next section will start by describing HTTPS and how to secure your data using HTTPS in a ASP.NET Core web service.

Securing data using HTTPS

A common practice for attackers is to intercept data exchanged between the client and the server. For that reason, it is essential to encrypt communication between them to keep the data secure. SSL uses SSL certificates to set up a trusted connection between the server company and the client. SSL uses *symmetric* and *asymmetric encryption* to encrypt keys used during this communication. Let's see a schema of a typical SSL handshake between client and server:

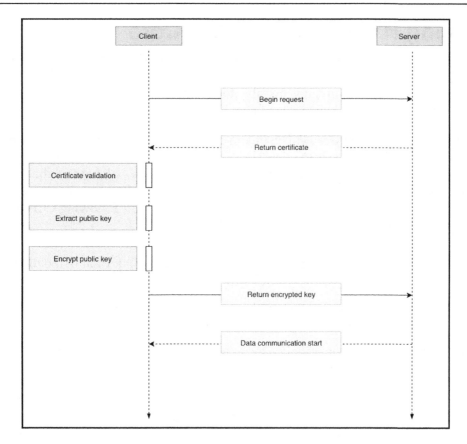

This schema shows the conventional steps of an SSL handshake:

1. The connection starts with the client that initiates the request. Before the start, the server sends an SSL certificate to the client, which ensures that the certificate is valid and trustable.

2. The client proceeds by extracting and encrypting the *public key* included in the SSL certificate.

3. The client sends the encrypted key (private key) to the server, which encodes the data and transmits it back to the client.

4. Data communication starts and the encrypted key is used to encrypt and decrypt data shared by the client and the server.

SSL is the basis of the HTTPS protocol, which is the standard way to transfer encrypted data. The following section describes how to set up and enforce HTTPS in ASP.NET Core.

Enforcing HTTPS in ASP.NET Core

HTTPS is enabled by default on ASP.NET Core. The main middleware related to the HTTPS protocol is the `HttpsRedirection` middleware class, which enforces redirection from HTTP to HTTPS. Therefore, it is possible to call the `UseHttpsRedirection` extension method in the `Startup` class in order to enable the middleware.

Let's see how to enable and force HTTPS in an ASP.NET Core application running in a docker container. The first step is to generate a self-signed certificate used by the ASP.NET Core application that runs in the container. .NET Core provides a global tool that creates a self-signed certificate on your local environment called `dotnet-dev-certs`. We can proceed by installing this tool on our local environment using the following CLI command:

```
dotnet tool install --global dotnet-dev-certs
```

After that, it is possible to create a new certificate using the `.pfx` format in the following command:

```
dotnet dev-certs https -ep <path_to_certificate>/certificate.pfx -p
<certificate_password>
```

The aforementioned instruction specifies the export path using the `-ep` option, with the `-p` password. Furthermore, it is possible to trust the certificate using the `--trust` options.

 It is important to note that the `dotnet-dev-certs` tool works only on Windows and macOS. In the case of Linux, we should proceed by generating the certificate using OpenSSL. The following tutorial (https://www.humankode.com/asp-net-core/develop-locally-with-https-self-signed-certificates-and-asp-net-core) provides more information about the creation of an HTTPS certificate using OpenSSL.

Once we have created a new certificate file, we can proceed by adjusting the `docker-compose.yml` file of the `Catalog.API` and `Cart.API` solutions:

```yaml
version: "3.7"
services:
  catalog_api:
    container_name: catalog_api
    build:
      context: .
      dockerfile: containers/api/Dockerfile
    volumes:
      - ./<path_to_certificate>/:/root/.dotnet/https
    env_file:
      - containers/api/api.env
```

```
networks:
  - my_network
ports:
  - 5000:5000
  - 5001:5001
depends_on:
  - catalog_db
  - catalog_esb
```

...

The aforementioned `docker-compose.yml` definition declares a `volumes` node to create a binding between the local `./certificate/` folder and the `/root/.dotnet/https` folder in the instance of the container. Furthermore, we can proceed by adding the following variables in the `containers/api.env` file:

```
ASPNETCORE_ENVIRONMENT=Integration
ASPNETCORE_URLS=https://*:5001
ASPNETCORE_Kestrel__Certificates__Default__Password=<certificate_password>
ASPNETCORE_Kestrel__Certificates__Default__Path=/root/.dotnet/https/certifi
cate.pfx
```

The file adds two environment variables related to the certificate: `ASPNETCORE_Kestrel__Certificates__Default__Password` provides the certificate password, and `ASPNETCORE_Kestrel__Certificates__Default__Path` defines its path. The new definition of the `docker-compose.yml` file also exposes the `5001` port, and it also adds the `https://*:5001` URL URL to the pool of URLs run by Kestrel. Futhermore, now it is possible to enforce the HTTPS in our `Startup` class by adding the following line in the `Configure` method:

```
app.UseHttpsRedirection();
```

After applying the HTTPS restriction, the client will always be redirected to the HTTPS endpoint of the web service for every request.

HTTP/2 on Kestrel

ASP.NET Core has supported HTTP/2 on Kestrel since version 2.2.0, and it is enabled by default if you are using HTTPS. In addition, another HTTP/2 requirement is support for the **Application-Layer Protocol Negotiation (ALPN)** protocol. The ALPN protocol enhances the handshake process between a client and a server: the client lists all the supported protocols, and the server will confirm which protocol to use for the HTTP transfer. Moreover, this approach allows an eventual fallback to HTTP 1.1 if the client or the server doesn't support HTTP/2.

As the default configuration, both HTTP 1.1 and HTTP/2 run on the same binding, but it is possible to customize and create a dedicated binding for HTTP/2 by extending the Kestrel configuration in the `static void Main` method:

```csharp
using System.Net;
using Microsoft.AspNetCore;
using Microsoft.AspNetCore.Hosting;
using Microsoft.AspNetCore.Server.Kestrel.Core;

namespace Catalog.API
{
    public class Program
    {
        public static void Main(string[] args)
        {
            CreateWebHostBuilder(args).Build().Run();
        }

        public static IWebHostBuilder CreateWebHostBuilder(string[] args)
        {
            return WebHost.CreateDefaultBuilder(args)
                .ConfigureKestrel(options =>
                {
                    options.Listen(IPAddress.Any, 5002, listenOptions =>
                    {
                        listenOptions.Protocols = HttpProtocols.Http2;
                    });
                })
                .UseStartup<Startup>();
        }
    }
}
```

This snippet shows how to set an HTTP/2 binding on port number 5002. This approach forces the HTTP/2 bindings without providing any fallback to HTTP 1.1.

Enabling CORS in ASP.NET Core

Another critical aspect of security is to protect our APIs from CORS calls. By default, it is not possible to use client-side code to call services that are hosted on other domains, because scam websites may use a cross-origin call to get sensitive information about users. This security restriction is called *the same-origin policy*.

The restrictions on the *same-origin policy* act on HTTP calls using the following criteria:

- The request is made from a different domain (for example, the site at `example.com` calls `api.com`).
- The request is enabled from a different subdomain (for example, the website at `example.com` calls `api.example.com`).
- The request is made from a different port (for example, the site at `example.com` calls `example.com:3001`).
- The request is made from a different protocol (for example, the `https://example.com` site calls `http://example.com`).

CORS provides a way to allow a specific domain to make client-side calls to a service hosted within a different domain. This kind of approach becomes very useful when we want to enable a customer or a third-party client to call our service without restrictions. It is also essential to note that CORS can be enabled to allow every domain. This approach must be avoided because it will enable attackers to use our API inappropriately.

ASP.NET Core provides an out-of-the-box way to enable CORS. The framework permits the creation of CORS policies using two approaches: the *middleware approach* and the *attributes approach*. As we saw in `Chapter 3`, *Working with the Middleware Pipeline*, middleware are usually implemented to develop cross-cutting logic that covers the whole web service. On the other hand, *attributes* are used to apply a restriction on a single action. In the same way, this approach is taken for CORS policies.

Implementing CORS using the middleware approach

The *CORS middleware* approach can be used to enable a specific HTTP domain, method, or port to call our service. As with any middleware, it can be defined in the `Startup` class of the service, specifically in the `Configure` method:

```
namespace Catalog.API
{
    public class Startup
    {
        ...
```

```
        public void Configure(IApplicationBuilder app,
        IWebHostingEnvironment env)
        {
            ...
            app.UseCors(cfg =>
            {
                cfg.AllowAnyOrigin();
            });
            ..
        }
    }
}
```

The UseCors middleware extension method accepts an action method to configure the different rules. For example, the previous code executes the AllowAnyOrigin method to allow calls from any website. In the same way, it is possible to define more restricting rules on a specific domain, like this:

```
namespace Catalog.API
{
    public class Startup
    {
        ...
        public void Configure(IApplicationBuilder app,
        IWebHostingEnvironment env)
        {
            ...
            app.UseCors(cfg =>
            {
                cfg.AllowAnyOrigin("https://samuele.dev");
            });
            ...
        }
    }
}
```

In this case, we are blocking all cross-origin requests except those coming from the https:/ /samuele.dev/ website. A more advanced and clean way to define CORS rules is to group them using named policies. It is also possible to use the following approach:

```
namespace Catalog.API
{
    public class Startup
    {
        public void ConfigureServices(IServiceCollection services)
        {
            ...
```

```
        services.AddCors(opt =>
        {
            opt.AddPolicy("BlogDomainPolicy", cfg =>
            { cfg.WithOrigins("https://samuele.dev"); });
        });
        ..
    }

    public void Configure(IApplicationBuilder app,
    IWebHostingEnvironment env)
    {
        ...
        app.UseCors("BlogDomainPolicy");
        ...
    }
  }
}
```

The previous code defines a CORS policy with the name `BlogDomainPolicy` using the `app.AddCors` construct in the `ConfigureServices` method. Once we have described the rules for the policy, we can proceed with using the defined policy in the `Configure` method of the `Startup` class using the `app.UseCors` method. It will enable us to establish different policies and apply them conditionally in the `Startup` class.

Implementing CORS using the attribute approach

In some cases, it may be necessary to define specific policies for some routes or actions. Therefore, it is possible to apply CORS policies using attributes, as follows:

```
namespace Catalog.API.Controllers
{
    [Route("api/items")]
    [ApiController]
    [JsonException]
    [EnableCors("BlogDomainPolicy")]
    public class ItemController : ControllerBase
    {
        ...
    }
}
```

In this case, we are restricting the use of the `BlogDomainPolicy` only to the `ItemController`. Therefore, all of the routes defined under the controller will use the same policy. In the same way, we can add the policy to a specific action method in the controller:

```
namespace Catalog.API.Controllers
{
    [Route("api/items")]
    [ApiController]
    [JsonException]
    [EnableCors("BlogDomainPolicy")]
    public class ItemController : ControllerBase
    {
        ...

        [HttpGet("{id:guid}")]
        [EnableCors("GetByIdActionPolicy")]
        public async Task<IActionResult> GetById(string id)
        {
            ...
        }

        ...
    }
}
```

In that case, the `GetByIdActionPolicy` will act only on the `GetById` action method, while the `BlogDomainPolicy` will act on the whole controller. This approach provides a nice level of granularity; furthermore, it provides a way to specify policies for a single route of the service. The next section describes the characteristics of the token-based authentication approach.

Securing APIs with token-based authentication

Applications have traditionally persisted identity through session cookies, relying on session IDs stored on the server-side. This method brings a few significant problems and pitfalls: it is *not scalable*, because you need a common point where you can store sessions and, every time a user is authenticated; the server will need to create a new record in a data source. Therefore, this approach may become a significant bottleneck for your web service.

Nowadays, token authentication can be helpful to authenticate and authorize users, especially in a distributed system context. The main strength of token-based authentication lies in the fact that the consumer asks for a token to an identity service. Next, the client can store the token locally and use it for authentication and authorization purposes.

Therefore, token authentication is *stateless* and *designed to be scalable*. Let's have a look at the token-authentication process and how it works, to better understand the benefits of this kind of approach:

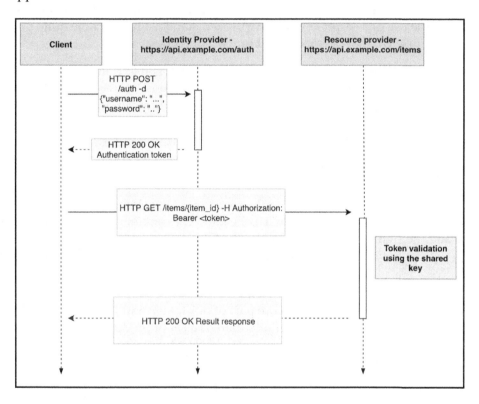

This schema describes a typical workflow when implementing token-based authentication. The schema describes three entities:

- The *client* is the application that is trying to access our resources.
- The *identity provider* is the service that, given a username and a password, provides an encrypted authentication token.
- The *resource provider* is another service called by the *client*. Furthermore, *the resource provider* will accept the encrypted authentication token, and it will provide the information requested by the *client* if it is authorized.

Since token-based authentication has a *stateless* approach, the application doesn't store the authentication tokens. Therefore, it is essential to note that the client must pass the authentication token in every request.

Token-based authentication can be implemented in different ways. **JSON Web Token (JWT)** is a standard, defined in the RFC 7519 (`https://tools.ietf.org/html/rfc7519`) open directive, which describes a way to represent claims between two parties. JWT is defined as a JSON object, which contains the payload, and a signature, which encrypts the data in the token. In other words, it provides a way to encrypt secure data formatted as JSON through the use of a secret key. The JWT token standard has become quite popular in recent years because web services can use it for two purposes:

- **Authorization**: The web service returns a JWT token to transfer information about claims and personal details to signed-in users. Moreover, single sign-on features and token authentication features use this technique to transfer data to the client.
- **Information exchange**: You can use the JWT token standard to prevent data exploitation and to certify the authenticity of the data you have received by signing it with the provided key.

The JWT token anatomy is very similar to the structure of a web request. It is composed of three parts: *header*, *payload*, and *signature*. The header part contains information about the token type and the signing algorithm used by the token:

```
{   "alg": "HS256",    "typ": "JWT" }
```

In that case, we can deduce that the token uses the *HMAC SHA256* algorithm, and it is a JWT token type. The *payload* part is the core part of our token, and it contains the information to be sent to the user. By default, there is a set of predefined information to populate, for example, the `exp` *(expiration time)* field. The following JSON is an example of a payload:

```
{
  "email": "example@handsonaspnetcore.com",
  "nbf": 1546196276,
  "exp": 1546801076,
  "iat": 1546196276
}
```

The `email` field is a claim for the token. `nbf` stands for **not valid before**, and `iat` stands for **issued at**. The three fields represent the time calculated since the UNIX epoch.

Finally, the *signature* part of the token signs the encoded header and the encoded payload with the secret key and the algorithm specified in the header.

The resulting encoded token is similar to the following:

```
eyJhbGciOiJIUzI1NiIsInR5cCI6IkpXVCJ9.eyJlbWFpbCI6InNhdXVlbGUucmVzY2FAZ21haW
wuY29tIiwibmJmIjoxNTQ2MTk2Mjc2LCJleHAiOjE1NDY4MDEwNzYsImlhdCI6MTU0NjE5NjI3N
n0.yQGT1TJYL4U_IqBpoQ6MjUchET06BRE-YJ0sf-MRA
```

It is crucial to note that each point separator (.) in the encoded token represents an encrypted token, as described earlier.

Implementing token-based authentication

In this section, we will see how to perform token-based authentication using ASP.NET Core. Going into more detail, we will dig into the development and testing of the token-based authentication and learn how to store user data in a database using the default identity provider of ASP.NET Core.

Furthermore, we will implement the authentication as part of the *catalog service* solution. It is essential to note that, in real-world applications, the authentication and the whole identity process have a dedicated service with a separate data store.

 For demo purposes, we are going to implement the authentication part inside the *catalog service*. Please consider keeping the identity part of your application in a separate service.

Let's start by adding the packages we need to develop token-based authentication in our `Catalog.Domain` and `Catalog.Infrastructure` projects. Please note that these packages are compatible only with the `netcoreapp3.1` framework, therefore, you need to change the `TargetFramework` variable in the csproj from `netstandard2.1` to `netcoreapp3.1`:

```
dotnet add Catalog.Domain package
Microsoft.AspNetCore.Authentication.JwtBearer
dotnet add Catalog.Infrastructure package
Microsoft.AspNetCore.Identity.EntityFrameworkCore
```

The next step is to define the `User` entity inside the `Catalog.Domain` project:

```
using Microsoft.AspNetCore.Identity;

namespace Catalog.Domain.Entities
{
    public class User : IdentityUser
    {
```

```
        public string Name { get; set; }
    }
}
```

The `User` entity represents a generic user inside the *domain model* of the service. It is important to note that it extends the `IdentityUser` class, which provides some additional fields to the entity. The `IdentityUser` class identifies a storable user entity. Furthermore, the entity can be used to store data through the `Microsoft.AspNetCore.Identity` package.

Let's proceed by declaring the `IUserRepository` interface in the `Catalog.Domain` project:

```
using System.Threading;
using System.Threading.Tasks;
using Catalog.Domain.Entities;

namespace Catalog.Domain.Repositories
{
    public interface IUserRepository
    {
        Task<bool> AuthenticateAsync(string email, string password,
            CancellationToken cancellationToken = default);
        Task<bool> SignUpAsync(User user, string password,
            CancellationToken cancellationToken = default);
        Task<User> GetByEmailAsync(string requestEmail,
            CancellationToken cancellationToken = default);
    }
}
```

This interface represents an intermediary between the *catalog service* and the data layer. Moreover, it can be used to authenticate, register, and retrieve `User` entities. The `IUserRepository` acts like a data store for the user data, and it also performs user-related operations, such as the sign-up process and authentication. It is also important to note that the `AuthenticateAsync` and `SignUpAsync` methods return a boolean that indicates whether the corresponding operation has succeeded.

Defining the service layer

After defining the `User` entity and the `IUserRepository` interface, we can proceed with the definition of the service layer in the `Catalog.Domain` project. Let's start by describing the `IUserService` interface:

```
using System.Threading;
using System.Threading.Tasks;
using Catalog.Domain.Repositories;
using Catalog.Domain.Requests.User;
using Catalog.Domain.Responses;

namespace Catalog.Domain.Services
{
    public interface IUserService
    {
        Task<UserResponse> GetUserAsync(GetUserRequest request,
            CancellationToken cancellationToken = default);
        Task<UserResponse> SignUpAsync(SignUpRequest request,
            CancellationToken cancellationToken = default);
        Task<TokenResponse> SignInAsync(SignInRequest request,
            CancellationToken cancellationToken = default);
    }
}
```

The interface defines the methods necessary for the authentication phase. The `GetUserAsync` method uses the `GetUserRequest` type to retrieve information related to a specific user. The `SignUpAsync` and the `SignInAsync` methods define the sign-up and sign-in process: the sign-up operation returns a new `UserResponse` instance, which determines the information related to the signed user, and the sign-in operation returns the `TokenResponse` instance, which contains the resulting token that will be stored by the client. Therefore, let's proceed by defining the request DTOs used by the service interface:

```
namespace Catalog.Domain.Requests.User
{
    public class GetUserRequest
    {
        public string Email { get; set; }
    }
    public class SignInRequest
    {
        public string Email { get; set; }
        public string Password { get; set; }
    }
    public class SignUpRequest
    {
```

```
            public string Email { get; set; }
            public string Password { get; set; }
            public string Name { get; set; }
        }
    }
```

For brevity, request classes are represented in a unique snippet. The `GetUserRequest` type contains an `Email` field that specifies the email address to retrieve. As we will see later in the chapter, the `GetUser` action method of the controller will need to be authenticated in order to retrieve the user's data.

The `SignInRequest` type defines the `Email` and the `Password` fields used to authenticate the user. Finally, the `SignUpRequest` type also contains the `Name` of the user represented by a string. Please note that for demo purposes, the code only stores the `Name` of the user. In a real-world application, the complexity of the `SignUpRequest` type is likely to increase with more personal information.

Let's proceed by also defining the response type used by the `IUserService` interface:

```
namespace Catalog.Domain.Responses
{
    public class TokenResponse
    {
        public string Token { get; set; }
    }
    public class UserResponse
    {
        public string Name { get; set; }
        public string Email { get; set; }
    }
}
```

The `UserResponse` type is meant to retrieve all the personal information of the user. It is important to note that it obviously omits the `Password` field of the entity for security reasons. On the other hand, the `TokenResponse` type retrieves the `Token` field containing the JWT token resulting from the authentication process.

Therefore, we can continue by describing the implementation of `IUserService` interface: it will contain the logic related to the generation of the token used by ASP.NET Core for authentication, and the get and sign-up operations on user entities. The following code illustrates the dependencies in the implementation:

```
using System;
using System.IdentityModel.Tokens.Jwt;
using System.Security.Claims;
```

```
using System.Text;
using System.Threading;
using System.Threading.Tasks;
using Catalog.Domain.Repositories;
using Catalog.Domain.Requests.User;
using Catalog.Domain.Responses;
using Microsoft.Extensions.Options;
using Microsoft.IdentityModel.Tokens;

namespace Catalog.Domain.Services
{
    public class UserService : IUserService
    {
        private readonly AuthenticationSettings
            _authenticationSettings;
        private readonly IUserRepository _userRepository;

        public UserService(IUserRepository userRepository,
        IOptions<AuthenticationSettings> authenticationSettings)
        {
            _userRepository = userRepository;
            _authenticationSettings = authenticationSettings.Value;
        }
```

As mentioned previously, the `IUserRepository` interface is used as the main entry point
to query and perform operations on our data source.
`IOption<AuthenticationSettings>` type defines the settings needed by the
authentication process:

```
namespace Catalog.Domain.Configurations
{
    public class AuthenticationSettings
    {
        public string Secret { get; set; }
        public int ExpirationDays { get; set; }
    }
}
```

The class is stored in the `Configurations` folder of the `Catalog.Domain` project.
The `AuthenticationSettings` class contains the `Secret` field, which describes a phrase
that is used to encrypt the token's information, and the `ExpirationDays` field provides the
number of days before the omitted tokens expire. Furthermore, we can proceed by defining
the `GetUserAsync` and the `SignUpAsync` methods:

```
. . .
public async Task<UserResponse> GetUserAsync(GetUserRequest request,
    CancellationToken cancellationToken)
```

```
{
    var response = await _userRepository.GetByEmailAsync(request.Email,
        cancellationToken);

    return new UserResponse { Name = response.Name, Email =
        response.Email };
}

public async Task<UserResponse> SignUpAsync(SignUpRequest request,
    CancellationToken cancellationToken)
{
    var user = new Entities.User { Email = request.Email, UserName =
        request.Email, Name = request.Name };

    bool result = await _userRepository.SignUpAsync(user,
        request.Password, cancellationToken);

    return !result ? null : new UserResponse { Name = request.Name,
        Email = request.Email };
}
...
```

The `GetUserAsync` method uses the request provided by the high-level layer to execute the `GetByEmailAsync` method of the `IUserRepository` interface. It also maps the response and retrieves a new instance of the `UserReponse` type.

On the other hand, the `SignUpAsync` method initializes a new `User` instance with the corresponding values, and it performs the `SignUpAsync` method provided by the `IUserRepository` interface. Finally, if the user is created, the `SignUpAsync` method retrieves a new `UserResponse` instance. Let's continue by completing the implementation of the `IUserService` by defining the `SignInAsync` method:

```
...
public async Task<TokenResponse> SignInAsync(SignInRequest request,
CancellationToken cancellationToken)
{
    bool response = await _userRepository.
        AuthenticateAsync(request.Email, request.Password,
        cancellationToken);

    return response == false ? null : new TokenResponse { Token =
        GenerateSecurityToken(request)                k . };

}

private string GenerateSecurityToken(SignInRequest request)
{
```

```
    var tokenHandler = new JwtSecurityTokenHandler();
    var key = Encoding.ASCII.GetBytes(_authenticationSettings.Secret);

    var tokenDescriptor = new SecurityTokenDescriptor
    {
        Subject = new ClaimsIdentity(new[]
        {
            new Claim(ClaimTypes.Email, request.Email)
        }),
        Expires =
        DateTime.UtcNow.AddDays
        (_authenticationSettings.ExpirationDays),
        SigningCredentials = new SigningCredentials(new
        SymmetricSecurityKey(key),
            SecurityAlgorithms.HmacSha256Signature)
    };

    var token = tokenHandler.CreateToken(tokenDescriptor);
    return tokenHandler.WriteToken(token);
}
...
```

As a first step, the `SignInAsync` method calls the underlying `AuthenticateAsync` method provided by `IUserRepository` by giving the `Email` and the `Password` sent by the client. The statement returns a boolean variable that indicates whether the user is authenticated. If the user is authenticated, the method retrieves a new instance of the `TokenResponse` class by calling the `GenerateSecurityToken` method.

The `GenerateSecurityToken` method defines a new instance of the `JwtSecurityTokenHandler` type, which provides some utilities for generating and creates tokens through the use of the `CreateToken` and the `WriteToken` methods.

Furthermore, it defines a new instance of the `SecurityTokenDescriptor` type, which declares the `Expire` time and the `SigningCredentials` fields by signing the `Secret` field of the `AuthorizationSettings` instance.

Applying authentication on the controller

The next steps consist of registering dependencies in the dependency injection engine and in using the resulting dependency, for example, the `IUserService` instance, in the controller layer. Therefore, this section focuses on the `Catalog.API` and `Catalog.Infrastructure` projects.

Let's start by defining a new extension method in the `Catalog.Infrastructure` project, which adds the authentication part:

```
using System.Text;
using Catalog.Domain.Configurations;
using Microsoft.AspNetCore.Authentication.JwtBearer;
using Microsoft.Extensions.Configuration;
using Microsoft.Extensions.DependencyInjection;
using Microsoft.IdentityModel.Tokens;
namespace Catalog.Infrastructure.Extensions
{
    public static class AuthenticationExtensions
    {
        public static IServiceCollection AddTokenAuthentication(this
            IServiceCollection services, IConfiguration configuration)
        {
            var settings = configuration.GetSection
                ("AuthenticationSettings");
            var settingsTyped = settings.Get<AuthenticationSettings>();

            services.Configure<AuthenticationSettings>(settings);
            var key = Encoding.ASCII.GetBytes(settingsTyped.Secret);
            services.AddAuthentication(x =>
                {
                    x.DefaultAuthenticateScheme =
                        JwtBearerDefaults.AuthenticationScheme;
                    x.DefaultChallengeScheme =
                        JwtBearerDefaults.AuthenticationScheme;
                })
                .AddJwtBearer(x =>
                {
                    x.TokenValidationParameters = new
                        TokenValidationParameters
                        {
                            IssuerSigningKey = new
                                SymmetricSecurityKey(key),
                            ValidateIssuer = false,
                            ValidateAudience = false
                        };
                });
            return services;
        }
    }
}
```

The core part of the preceding code is the execution of two methods: AddAuthentication and AddJwtBearer. Both extension methods add the middlewares and the services used by the authentication process. In more detail, AddAuthentication specifies DefaultAuthenticationScheme and DefaultChallengeScheme by applying the JWT bearer authentication scheme.

At the same time, the AddJwtBearer method defines the options related to token authentication, such as the TokenValidationParameters field, which includes the SigningKey used to validate the token parameter.

Furthermore, the IssuerSigningKey must be the same as the key used to generate the token. Otherwise, the validation will fail. It is important to note that the ValidateIssuer and the ValidateAudience fields are false. Therefore, ASP.NET Core will not validate the issuer or the audience URL. Although this approach works fine for testing environments, I strongly suggest using the following setup for production cases:

```
.AddJwtBearer(x =>
{
    x.TokenValidationParameters = new TokenValidationParameters
    {
        IssuerSigningKey = new SymmetricSecurityKey(key),
        ValidateIssuer = true,
        ValidateAudience = true,
        ValidIssuer = "yourhostname",
        ValidAudience = "yourhostname"
    };
});
```

In this case, the validation of the issuer and the audience will happen; therefore it will check that the token issuer and the audience of the token match those specified in the configurations. The AddTokenAuthentication extension method also owns the registration of the AuthenticationSettings used by the UserService class. Therefore, let's have a look at the AuthenticationSettings values defined in the appsettings.json file:

```
...
"AuthenticationSettings": {
    "Secret": "My Super long secret",
    "ExpirationDays": "7"
}
...
```

After that, we can proceed by adding the authentication implementation to the Startup class in the Catalog.API project:

```
namespace Catalog.API
{
    public class Startup
    {
        public Startup(IConfiguration configuration,
        IWebHostingEnvironment environment)
        {
            Configuration = configuration;
            CurrentEnvironment = environment;
        }

        ...
        public void ConfigureServices(IServiceCollection services)
        {
            ...
            services
                .AddTokenAuthentication(Configuration)
            ...
        }

        public void Configure(IApplicationBuilder app,
        IHostingEnvironment env)
        {
            ...
            app.UseAuthentication();
            app.UseAuthorization();
            app.UseEndpoints(endpoints =>
            {
                endpoints.MapControllers();
            });
        }
    }
}
```

The Startup class is the core component that initializes the authentication process. In the ConfigureServices method, it configures and initializes the AuthorizationSettings class by reading from the appsettings.json file. Next, it calls the AddAuthentication extension method by passing the AuthorizationSettings type instance. It is also essential to note that the Configure method adds authentication middleware by calling the UseAuthentication method.

Finally, we can proceed by adding the `UserController` and exposing authentication routes:

```
using System.Linq;
using System.Security.Claims;
using System.Threading.Tasks;
using Catalog.API.Filters;
using Catalog.Domain.Requests.User;
using Catalog.Domain.Services;
using Microsoft.AspNetCore.Authorization;
using Microsoft.AspNetCore.Mvc;

namespace Catalog.API.Controllers
{
    [Authorize]
    [ApiController]
    [Route("api/user")]
    [JsonException]
    public class UserController : ControllerBase
    {
        private readonly IUserService _userService;

        public UserController(IUserService userService)
        {
            _userService = userService;
        }

        [HttpGet]
        public async Task<IActionResult> Get()
        {
            var claim = HttpContext.User.Claims.FirstOrDefault(x =>
                x.Type == ClaimTypes.Email);

            if (claim == null) return Unauthorized();

            var token = await _userService.GetUserAsync(new
                GetUserRequest { Email = claim.Value });
            return Ok(token);
        }

        [AllowAnonymous]
        [HttpPost("auth")]
        public async Task<IActionResult> SignIn(SignInRequest request)
        {
            var token = await _userService.SignInAsync(request);
            if (token == null) return BadRequest();
            return Ok(token);
        }
    }
```

```
[AllowAnonymous]
[HttpPost]
public async Task<IActionResult> SignUp(SignUpRequest request)
{
    var user = await _userService.SignUpAsync(request);
    if (user == null) return BadRequest();
    return CreatedAtAction(nameof(Get), new { }, null);
}
    }
}
```

The preceding code defines the UserController class, which exposes authentication routes. It is important to note that the whole controller is decorated by using the [Authorize] attribute, which means that each route is covered by authentication. Therefore, to access the routes declared within the controller it is necessary to use a valid token in the request. The class defines an action method for each operation defined before in the service layer:

- The Get action method exposes some details regarding the current user, such as the Email field and the Name field. The action method gets user details from the incoming token. The token information is represented by accessing the HttpContext.User property and getting the value of ClaimType.Email.

- The SignIn action method is decorated using [AllowAnonymous] attribute. Furthermore, it is possible to call the action method without being authenticated. The action method binds the request.Email and request.Password fields and sends the request object using IUserService interface. The action method returns the TokenResponse with the generated token.

- The SignUp action method is also decorated using the [AllowAnonymous] attribute. In that case, the action method registers a new user and returns the 201 Created HTTP code if the operation has success.

Our setup is now almost complete. What we need to do is define the last common point between the IUserRepository interface and the underlying data store. For this purpose, we will use again the EF Core framework combined with the Microsoft.AspNetCore.Identity.EntityFrameworkCore package maintained by Microsoft.

Storing data using EF Core

Let's proceed by implementing the data access layer and create a concrete implementation of the IUserRepository interface. The UserRepository class will have to main dependencies, the SignInManager and the UserManager classes, both of which are provided by the Microsoft.AspNetCore.Identity package:

```
using System.Threading;
using System.Threading.Tasks;
using Catalog.Domain.Entities;
using Catalog.Domain.Repositories;
using Microsoft.AspNetCore.Identity;
using Microsoft.EntityFrameworkCore;

namespace Catalog.Infrastructure.Repositories
{
    public class UserRepository : IUserRepository
    {
        private readonly SignInManager<User> _signInManager;
        private readonly UserManager<User> _userManager;

        public UserRepository(UserManager<User> userManager,
            SignInManager<User> signInManager)
        {
            _userManager = userManager;
            _signInManager = signInManager;
        }

        public async Task<bool> AuthenticateAsync(string email,
            string password, CancellationToken cancellationToken)
        {
            var result = await _signInManager.PasswordSignInAsync(
                email, password, false, false);
            return result.Succeeded;
        }

        public async Task<bool> SignUpAsync(User user, string password,
            CancellationToken cancellationToken)
        {
            var result = await _userManager.CreateAsync(user,
                password);
            return result.Succeeded;
        }

        public async Task<User> GetByEmailAsync(string requestEmail,
            CancellationToken cancellationToken)
        {
```

```
                    return await _userManager
                        .Users
                        .FirstOrDefaultAsync(u => u.Email == requestEmail,
                            cancellationToken);
                }
            }
        }
```

As you can see, the resulting code implements the `IUserRepository` interface. The class depends on the `SignInManager<User>` and the `UserManager<User>` types. These types accept a generic entity class that is a representation of the authentication objects. The `SignInManager<T>` generic class provides functionalities with which to interact with the user sign-in process.

It exposes the `PasswordSignInAsync` method used by the `UserRepository.Authenticate` method. On the other hand, the `UserManager<T>` class provides ways to interact with users in a persistent store. Furthermore, `UserRepository` uses the `SignUp` and the `UserRepository.GetByEmail` method to interact with the database.

Declaring the identity database context

Once we have declared the `IUserRepository` implementation, we can proceed by declaring the *identity data context*. The *identity data context* is identified by extending the `IdentityDbContext` class. This type of `DbContext` is used by EF Core to locate and access the data source used as the persistent user store. In order to declare the *identity data context*, it is necessary to extend the `CatalogContext` in the following way:

```
using System.Threading;
using System.Threading.Tasks;
using Microsoft.AspNetCore.Identity.EntityFrameworkCore;
using Microsoft.EntityFrameworkCore;
using Catalog.Domain.Entities;
using Catalog.Domain.Repositories;
using Catalog.SchemaDefinitions;

namespace Catalog.Infrastructure
{
    public class CatalogContext : IdentityDbContext<User>, IUnitOfWork
    {
        ...
        protected override void OnModelCreating(ModelBuilder
            modelBuilder)
        {
```

```
                    modelBuilder.ApplyConfiguration(new
                        ItemEntitySchemaDefinition());
                    modelBuilder.ApplyConfiguration(new
                        GenreEntitySchemaConfiguration());
                    modelBuilder.ApplyConfiguration(new
                        ArtistEntitySchemaConfiguration());
                    base.OnModelCreating(modelBuilder);
                }
            }
        }
```

 It is essential to note that the IdentityDbContext class extends the DbContext class. Furthermore, every property and behavior present in the DbContext class is also inherited by the IdentityDbContext class. Therefore, it is essential to note that the override method, OnModelCreating, must also call the base method.

To provide a way to store user information using EF Core, it is also necessary to add and configure the identity system for the specified User type by calling the AddIdentity extension method. Furthermore, it is also essential to call AddEntityFrameworkStores and refer to the CatalogContext class to add the entity framework implementation. The following code is the previously created AddAuthentication extension method:

```
using System.Text;
using Microsoft.AspNetCore.Authentication.JwtBearer;
using Microsoft.AspNetCore.Identity;
using Microsoft.Extensions.DependencyInjection;
using Microsoft.IdentityModel.Tokens;
using Catalog.Domain;
using Catalog.Domain.Entities;

namespace Catalog.Infrastructure.Extensions
{
    public static class AuthenticationExtensions
    {
        public static IServiceCollection AddTokenAuthentication(this
        IServiceCollection services, AuthenticationSettings settings)
        {
            var key = Encoding.ASCII.GetBytes(settings.Secret);

            services.AddIdentity<User, IdentityRole>()
                .AddEntityFrameworkStores<CatalogContext>();

            ...
            return services;
        }
```

```
        }
    }
```

Finally, we can proceed by initializing IUserRepository with its concrete implementation. Also, in that case, we will declare the dependency injection resolution in the Startup class:

```
public void ConfigureServices(IServiceCollection services)
{
    ...
    services.AddScoped<IUserRepository, UserRepository>();
```

In the same way, we can register IUserService by adding the following row to the AddServices extension method:

```
public static IServiceCollection AddServices(this IServiceCollection
services)
{
    services
        ...
        .AddScoped<IUserService, UserService>();

    return services;
}
```

To sum up, now we have the whole authentication stack in place. The Catalog.API project exposes the HTTP routes through the UserController class. The controller depends on the IUserService interface, which exposes the operation needed by the authentication process.

Consequently, the UserService class depends on the IUserRepository interface, which is the main entry point that calls the API exposed by the EF Core framework. Therefore, we can now proceed by verifying the authentication logic using some tests.

Testing authentication

Testing our code is essential at this point: we should check, document, and verify the behaviors of our system before running the application in a server instance. Furthermore, it is also crucial to test authentication behavior because it is a sensitive part of our service.

Since the UserRepository implementation is the most low-level part of the authentication stack and the first component that relies on EF Core to retrieve, update, and authenticate the user, we can keep it isolated and exclude it from the testing process by mocking the IUserRepository interface.

Both `SignInManager<T>` and the `UserManager<T>` classes represent a core part of our authentication process, and they are part of a third-party package maintained by Microsoft. Furthermore, it is not necessary to cover their implementations with tests.

Let's start by defining a new `UserContextFactory` in the `Catalog.Fixture` project in the `tests` folder:

```
using System.Collections.Generic;
using System.Linq;
using System.Threading;
using Catalog.Domain.Entities;
using Catalog.Domain.Repositories;
using Microsoft.AspNetCore.Identity;
using Moq;

namespace Catalog.Fixtures
{
    public class UsersContextFactory
    {
        private readonly PasswordHasher<User> _passwordHasher;
        private readonly IList<User> _users;

        public UsersContextFactory()
        {
            _passwordHasher = new PasswordHasher<User>();

            _users = new List<User>();

            var user = new User
            {
                Id = "test_id",
                Email = "samuele.resca@example.com",
                Name = "Samuele Resca"
            };
            user.PasswordHash = _passwordHasher.HashPassword(user,
            "P@$$w0rd");

            _users.Add(user);
        }

        public IUserRepository InMemoryUserManager =>
        GetInMemoryUserManager();

        private IUserRepository GetInMemoryUserManager()
        {
            ...
```

```
            }
        }
    }
```

The factory class exposes an IUserRepository instance with some pre-populated data and it depends on the PasswordHasher<T> generic type, which is used by SignUp and in the Authenticate mock methods declaration to *encode-decode* the password by using the HashPassword and VerifyHashedPassword methods.

It is important to note that the IUserRepository interface is mocked through the use of the GetInMemoryUserManager method. Furthermore, it uses List<User> to emulate a data source, and it implements the AuthenticateAsync, GetByEmailAsync, and SignUpAsync methods exposed by the IUserRepository interface using the Moq library:

```
namespace Catalog.Fixtures
{
    public class UsersContextFactory
    {
    . . .

        private IUserRepository GetInMemoryUserManager()
        {
            var fakeUserService = new Mock<IUserRepository>();

            fakeUserService.Setup(x =>
            x.AuthenticateAsync(It.IsAny<string>(),
            It.IsAny<string>(), CancellationToken.None))
                .ReturnsAsync((string email, string password,
                CancellationToken token) =>
                {
                    var user = _users.FirstOrDefault(x =>
                    x.Email == email);

                    if (user == null) return false;

                    var result = _passwordHasher.
                        VerifyHashedPassword(user,
                    user.PasswordHash, password);
                    return result == PasswordVerificationResult.
                        Success;
                });
            fakeUserService.Setup(x =>
            x.GetByEmailAsync(It.IsAny<string>(),
                CancellationToken.None))
                .ReturnsAsync((string email, CancellationToken token)
            =>
                _users.First(x => x.Email == email));
            fakeUserService.Setup(x => x.SignUpAsync(It.IsAny<User>(),
```

```
        It.IsAny<string>(), CancellationToken.None))
            .ReturnsAsync((User user, string password,
            CancellationToken token) =>
            {
                user.PasswordHash =
                    _passwordHasher.HashPassword(user,
                password);
                _users.Add(user);
                return true;
            });
        return fakeUserService.Object;
    }
  }
}
```

The preceding code returns a mocked `IUserRepository` instance by providing a fake behavior for the methods of the interface. Consequently, it is possible to verify the `IUserService` class by implementing the following test class:

```
using System.Threading.Tasks;
...
namespace Catalog.Domain.Tests.Services
{
    public class UserServiceTests : IClassFixture<UsersContextFactory>
    {
        private readonly IUserService _userService;

        public UserServiceTests(UsersContextFactory
            usersContextFactory)
        {
            _userService = new UserService(usersContextFactory.
            InMemoryUserManager, Options.Create(
            new AuthenticationSettings { Secret =
            "Very Secret key-word to match", ExpirationDays = 7 }));
        }
        [Fact]
        public async Task
        signin_with_invalid_user_should_return_a_valid_token_response()
        {
            var result =
                await _userService.SignInAsync(new SignInRequest {
                Email = "invalid.user", Password = "invalid_password" });
            result.ShouldBeNull();
        }
        [Fact]
        public async Task
        signin_with_valid_user_should_return_a_valid_token_response()
        {
```

```
                var result =
                    await _userService.SignInAsync(new SignInRequest {
                    Email = "samuele.resca@example.com",
                    Password = "P@$$w0rd" });
                result.Token.ShouldNotBeEmpty();
            }
            ...
        }
    }
```

The test class implements two different tests:
`signin_with_invalid_user_should_return_a_valid_token_response` and
`signin_with_valid_user_should_return_a_valid_token_response`. In both cases,
the tests will use `UserContextFactory` to resolve the dependency of the class. We will
also use the `Option.Create` method provided by ASP.NET Core to generate
`AuthenticationSettings` options. In this case, we are testing the entire stack that has
been implemented in the handler layer.

It is essential to note that we are excluding the whole underlying part related to the
management and storage of the users' information. We can expand the scope of our tests by
including the controller part. Going into more detail, we can implement the test to check
the functionalities implemented in the `UserController` class. To do that, we will inject a
fake `IUserRepository` implementation at `TStartup` time, using the `services.Replace`
instruction:

```
using System;
...

namespace Catalog.Fixtures
{
    public class InMemoryApplicationFactory<TStartup>
        : WebApplicationFactory<TStartup> where TStartup : class
    {
        protected override void ConfigureWebHost(IWebHostBuilder
            builder)
        {
            builder
                .UseEnvironment("Testing")
                .ConfigureTestServices(services =>
                {
                    ...

                    services.Replace(ServiceDescriptor.Scoped(_ => new
                    UsersContextFactory().InMemoryUserManager));

                    var sp = services.BuildServiceProvider();
```

```
                    using var scope = sp.CreateScope();
                    var scopedServices = scope.ServiceProvider;
                    var db = scopedServices.GetRequiredService
                    <CatalogContext>();
                    db.Database.EnsureCreated();
                });
        }
    }
}
```

We can act on the `InMemoryApplicationFactory<TStartup>` class to replace the `IUserService` with a new instance of the mocked class by initializing the `UsersContextFactory` class. After that, it will be possible to test the `UserController` class action by resolving the `InMemoryApplicationFactory<TStartup>` factory class:

```
using System.Net;
...
namespace Catalog.API.Tests.Controllers
{
    public class UserControllerTests :
    IClassFixture<InMemoryApplicationFactory<Startup>>
    {
        private readonly InMemoryApplicationFactory<Startup> _factory;

        public UserControllerTests(InMemoryApplicationFactory<Startup>
        factory)

        {
            _factory = factory;
        }

        [Theory]
        [InlineData("/api/user/auth")]
        public async Task sign_in_should_retrieve_a_token(string url)
        {
            var client = _factory.CreateClient();
            var request = new SignInRequest { Email =
            "samuele.resca@example.com", Password = "P@$$w0rd" };
            var httpContent =
                new StringContent(JsonConvert.SerializeObject(request),
                Encoding.UTF8, "application/json");

            var response = await client.PostAsync(url, httpContent);
            string responseContent = await
            response.Content.ReadAsStringAsync();

            response.EnsureSuccessStatusCode();
```

```
            response.StatusCode.ShouldBe(HttpStatusCode.OK);
            responseContent.ShouldNotBeEmpty();
        }

        [Theory]
        [InlineData("/api/user/auth")]
        public async
        Task sign_in_should_retrieve_bad_request_with_invalid_password
        (string url)
        {
            var client = _factory.CreateClient();
            var request = new SignInRequest { Email =
            "samuele.resca@example.com", Password = "NotValidPWD" };
            var httpContent =
                new StringContent(JsonConvert.SerializeObject(request),
                Encoding.UTF8, "application/json");

            var response = await client.PostAsync(url, httpContent);
            string responseContent = await
            response.Content.ReadAsStringAsync();
            response.StatusCode.ShouldBe(HttpStatusCode.BadRequest);
            responseContent.ShouldNotBeEmpty();
        }
            ...

        }
    }
}
```

The previous code verifies the routes defined in the UserController class, and it also performs an integration test by checking the authentication process. The sign_in_should_retrieve_a_token test method calls the /api/user/auth address using the HTTP POST verb to verify the implementation of the sign-in procedure.

Additionally, it also validates the operation in case the user's password is wrong. Furthermore, we can also provide more tests to verify the whole process of authentication, from the sign-in phase to the call to retrieve the authenticated user data:

```
    ...

    [Theory]
    [InlineData("/api/user")]
    public async Task
    get_with_authorized_user_should_retrieve_the_right_user(string url)
    {
        var client = _factory.CreateClient();

        var signInRequest = new SignInRequest { Email =
```

```
"samuele.resca@example.com", Password = "P@$$w0rd" };
var httpContent = new StringContent(JsonConvert.SerializeObject
(signInRequest), Encoding.UTF8, "application/json");

var response = await client.PostAsync(url + "/auth", httpContent);
string responseContent = await
    response.Content.ReadAsStringAsync();

response.EnsureSuccessStatusCode();

var tokenResponse = JsonConvert.DeserializeObject<TokenResponse>
(responseContent);

client.DefaultRequestHeaders.Authorization =
    new AuthenticationHeaderValue("Bearer", tokenResponse.Token);

var restrictedResponse = await client.GetAsync(url);

restrictedResponse.EnsureSuccessStatusCode();
restrictedResponse.StatusCode.ShouldBe(HttpStatusCode.OK);
}
...
```

Going into more detail,
the `get_with_authorized_user_should_retrieve_the_right_user` test executes the
following operations:

1. It performs a POST request to the following route/`auth` in order to authenticate
   the user.
2. It deserializes the result of the POST request, and it gets the token field.
3. It adds an authentication header by passing the token, and it performs a request
   to the /`api/user` route.
4. It checks that the result status code is HTTP 200 OK.

In this way, we are testing both the `UsersController` class and the underlying handlers
used in each action method. It is also possible to test the authentication process by running
the catalog web service using the `docker-compose up --build` command. First of all, we
need to create a new user by adding some necessary information, such as the email and the
name of the user:

```
curl -X POST \
  https://localhost:5001/api/users \
  -H 'Content-Type: application/json' \
  -d '{
    "email": "newuser@example.com",
```

```
        "password": "<my_secret_password>",
        "name": "Your name"
    }'
```

The previous HTTP call (written as a `curl` call) creates a new user with the specified credentials. We can proceed by generating the token using our credentials:

```
curl -X POST \
    https://localhost:5001/api/users/auth \
    -H 'Content-Type: application/json' \
    -d '{
        "email": "newuser@example.com",
        "password": "<my_secret_password>"
    }'
```

Finally, we can continue by calling the secret endpoint using the following call:

```
curl -X GET https://localhost:5001/api/users -H 'Authorization: Bearer
<my_token>'
```

The aforementioned `curl` command calls the `https://localhost:5001/api/users/` address by passing the token in the `Authorization` header of the request.

Summary

In this chapter, we learned how to secure a web service using some standard practices. HTTPS is now a standard and must-have feature if you want to secure data. Furthermore, we saw how token-based authentication provides a useful way to secure data and information that are exposed.

The topics covered in this chapter provide a way to secure information exposed by the web service, and explored the implementation of token-based authentication in distributed systems.

In the next chapter, we will see how to cache responses in ASP.NET Core and look at how a caching mechanism works in general.

Section 4: Advanced Concepts for Building Services

4

In this section, we will explain some of the more advanced topics regarding web services. You will learn about caching, monitoring, and logging; deploying on Azure; documenting APIs using Swagger; and using external tools such as Postman.

This section includes the following chapters:

- Chapter 16, *Caching Web Service Responses*
- Chapter 17, *Logging and Health Checking*
- Chapter 18, *Deploying Services on Azure*
- Chapter 19, *Documenting Your API Using Swagger*
- Chapter 20, *Testing Services Using Postman*

16
Caching Web Service Responses

In this chapter, we will explore the caching patterns of ASP.NET Core, as well as the caching strategies and the tools that are provided by the framework to help developers to implement them. The cache may become useful in order to avoid additional computation on the server, and consequently retrieve the fastest response to the client of a web service. Furthermore, we will look at a concrete cache implementation of the catalog web service.

In this chapter, we will cover the following topics:

- Introduction to the HTTP caching system
- Implementing response caching in ASP.NET Core
- Implementing a distributed cache

By the end of this chapter, you will have a general understanding of caching mechanisms and the know-how needed in order to implement a distributed cache in ASP.NET Core using `Redis`.

Introduction to the HTTP caching system

Caching is an essential part of web service development. The primary purpose of web service caching is to improve the performance of our system and reduce the overload of the webserver. Furthermore, fetching something over the network is slow and expensive, and so it is necessary to implement a caching system to improve the responsiveness of our web service and to avoid unnecessary additional computation. In this section, we will focus on some of the features that are defined in the HTTP 1.1 caching specification.

These caching specifications are sent by the webserver to the client. Whoever has ownership of the client needs to read the caching specifications and respond appropriately. In general, there are two common use cases for caching responses: the first one is when a web service exposes very *dynamic content*. In this case, the data changes a lot, and the *caching time* can be reduced or avoided at all. The second case is when our service may serve some *static content*. In that case, we can set a high caching time for the content that doesn't change a lot.

The HTTP caching specification

The HTTP 1.1 caching specification (`https://tools.ietf.org/html/rfc7234`) describes how caches should behave over HTTP. The main header related to HTTP caching is the `Cache-Control` header. This header is used to specify directives in the request and response. It is also essential to note that the `Cache-Control` directives that are defined in the request and the response are independent. The following diagram shows a typical request-response workflow:

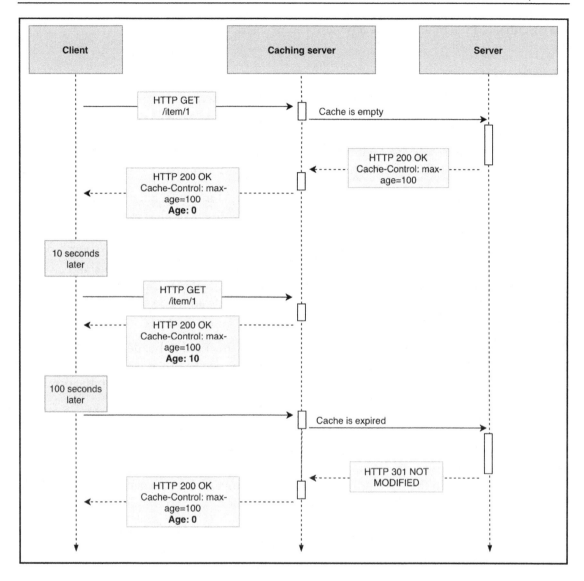

The schema describes the interaction between a generic client and a server with a caching layer between them.

First, the client requests a resource from the server, and the *caching layer* forwards it to the server. The server produces the data for the client and sends the response back; at this point, the caching server caches the response in the *caching layer*. Therefore, if the client performs another call to the same content, the request will not hit the server, but the cache system will provide the cached response.

It is essential to note that the *cache layer* adds some headers to the response:

```
Cache-Control: max-age=100
Age:0
```

Both of these are HTTP headers related to the caching directives. `Cache-Control` adds the `max-age` directive to indicate that the freshness lifetime of the content is equal to 100. The `Age` header specifies the age of the cached content. When `Age` reaches the `Cache-Control: max-age` value, the *caching layer* will forward the request to the server in order to serve the fresh data. Both of the values of the headers are specified in *seconds*.

The `Cache-Control` header can be used to specify the caching mechanism. By default, it is possible to disable the cache by specifying the `no-cache` directive, that is, `Cache-Control: no-cache`. Another crucial aspect of the `Cache-Control` header is the public and private directives, such as `Cache-Control: public,max-age=100`. The `public` instruction means that the cached response can also be stored in a shared cache, and any other client can access that information. On the other hand, when a response is private, this means that it probably contains sensitive information and it cannot be shared with other clients.

The caching specification also defines the `Vary` header. This kind of header is used to indicate which fields influence the cache variation. More specifically, it is used to decide whether a cached response can be used rather than requesting a fresh one from the original server:

```
Vary: *
Vary: User-Agent
```

In the first line of the preceding code, each variation in the request is treated as a single and uncacheable request. In the second line, the request is processed as uncacheable, but the `User-Agent` header is added.

The `Expires` header has the same purpose as the `max-age` directive: to give the cache expiration time. The only reason they differ is that the `max-age` instruction focuses on a fixed date time. For example, we can set the following value:

```
Expires: Wed, 21 Oct 2015 07:28:00 GMT
```

It is essential to note that the `max-age` directive overrides the `Expires` header. Therefore, if both of them are present in the same response, the `Expires` header is ignored. In the next section, we will learn how to implement response caching using ASP.NET Core tools.

Implementing response caching in ASP.NET Core

ASP.NET Core implements a declarative way to manage caching directives in the responses of our web service. Furthermore, it provides an attribute that can be used for caching purposes. The attribute implementation is also compatible with the HTTP 1.1 caching specification, therefore, it becomes easy to implement these caching standards using ASP.NET Core's out-of-the-box implementations, and we don't have to worry about the details of each request. We can specify the caching behavior using the [ResponseCache] attribute that's exposed by ASP.NET Core:

```
namespace Catalog.API.Controllers
{
    [Route("api/items")]
    [ApiController]
    [Authorize]
    public class ItemController : ControllerBase
    {
        private readonly IItemService _itemService;
        private readonly IEndpointInstance _messageEndpoint;

        public ItemController(IItemService itemService,
        IEndpointInstance messageEndpoint)
        {
            _itemService = itemService;
            _messageEndpoint = messageEndpoint;
        }

        ...

        [HttpGet("{id:guid}")]
        [ItemExists]
        [ResponseCache(Duration = 100, VaryByQueryKeys = new []{"*"})]
        public async Task<IActionResult> GetById(Guid id)
        {
            var result = await _itemService.GetItemAsync(new
                GetItemRequest { Id = id });
            return Ok(result);
        }
        ...
    }
}
```

For example, in this case, the code defines a caching directive on the `GetById` action method of the `ItemController` class. The `ResponseCache` attribute sets a `Duration` field and a `VaryByQueryKeys` field: the first one corresponds to the `max-age` instruction while the second one reflects the `Vary` HTTP header.

 So far, we have only added the `Cache-Control` directive to the server responses. Therefore, we are *not* implementing any caching. The caching directives can be used by a third-party system or application, such as the client of our service, to cache information.

In addition to the `ResponseCache` attribute, it is necessary to put caching middleware in front of the web service. `ResponseCachingMiddleware` is the default middleware provided by ASP.NET Core. It is compliant with the HTTP 1.1 caching specification (`https://tools.ietf.org/html/rfc7234`). Therefore, if we think about the `ResponseCachingMiddleware` type, it is possible to change the previous schema in the following way:

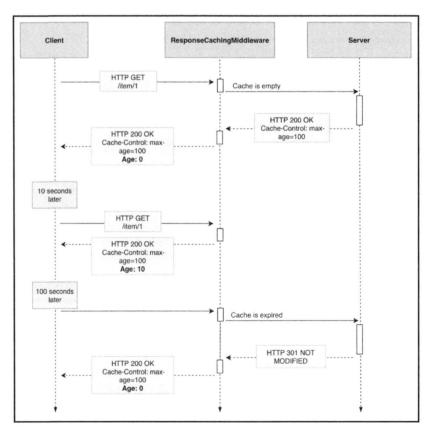

The `ResponseCachingMiddleware` class can be initialized using the
`AddResponseCaching` extension method provided by the
`Microsoft.Extensions.DependencyInjection` package. In addition, we can add
the `ResponseCachingMiddleware` middleware in the middleware pipeline by executing
the `UseResponseCaching` extension method in the `Configure` method of the `Startup`
class. The `ResponseCachingMiddleware` type checks whether a response is cacheable and
stores responses and serves answers from the cache. We can add
`ResponseCachingMiddleware` to the service pipeline by editing the `Startup` class in the
`Catalog.API` project:

```
public class Startup
    {
        ...
        public void ConfigureServices(IServiceCollection services)
        {
            services
                ...
                .AddResponseCaching();
        }

        public void Configure(IApplicationBuilder app,
        IHostingEnvironment env)
        {
            ...
            app.UseHsts();
            app.UseMiddleware<ResponseTimeMiddlewareAsync>();
            app.UseHttpsRedirection();
            app.UseAuthentication();
            app.UseResponseCaching();
            app.UseEndpoints(endpoints =>
                {
                    endpoints.MapControllers();
                });
        }
    }
```

The preceding code adds the caching middleware, but it is not enough to initialize a
caching mechanism. Therefore, if we try to call the route decorated with the
`ResponseCache` attribute using the `curl` command, we will receive the following
response:

```
curl --verbose -X GET
http://localhost:5000/api/items/08164f57-1e80-4d2a-739a-08d6731ac140
Note: Unnecessary use of -X or --request, GET is already inferred.
* Trying ::1...
* TCP_NODELAY set
```

```
* Connected to localhost (::1) port 5000 (#0)
> GET /api/items/08164f57-1e80-4d2a-739a-08d6731ac140 HTTP/1.1
> Host: localhost:5000
> User-Agent: curl/7.54.0
> Accept: */*
>
< HTTP/1.1 200 OK
< Date: Sat, 05 Jan 2019 16:55:21 GMT
< Content-Type: application/json; charset=utf-8
< Server: Kestrel
< Cache-Control: public,max-age=100
< Transfer-Encoding: chunked
< X-Response-Time-ms: 21
<
* Connection #0 to host localhost left intact
```

As you can see, `Cache-Control` tells us that this information can be shared in the cache and that `max-age` is 100 seconds. Therefore, if we call the same route after *N (with N<100)* seconds, we can also see the `Age` header, which contains the time (in seconds) that the object has been in the cache for.

Moreover, if we call the same route after *N seconds* (with *N >= 100*), we will hit the server and cache a new response in the memory. It is also necessary to note that we can cancel the cache middleware by appending a query string parameter to the calling URL. This is because we specified the `Vary` header using the following field:

```
VaryByQueryKeys = new [] {"*"}
```

> It may be the case that defining the `ResponseCache` attribute uses the `VaryByQueryKeys` field. In that case, the attribute will not be able to detect the query string variation. Furthermore, the routes that are covered by the `ResponseCache` attribute will retrieve the following exception: `"ClassName":"System.InvalidOperationException","Message":` `"'VaryByQueryKeys' requires the response cache middleware."`

An important thing to note about the `ResponseCachingMiddleware` class is that it uses the `IMemoryCache` interface to store the content of the response. Hence, if you examine the definition of the class on GitHub (`https://github.com/aspnet/AspNetCore/.../ ResponseCachingMiddleware.cs`), you will see the following constructor:

```
...
        public ResponseCachingMiddleware(
            RequestDelegate next,
            IOptions<ResponseCachingOptions> options,
```

```
            ILoggerFactory loggerFactory,
            ObjectPoolProvider poolProvider)
            : this(
                next,
                options,
                loggerFactory,
                new ResponseCachingPolicyProvider(),
                new MemoryResponseCache(new MemoryCache(new
                    MemoryCacheOptions
                {
                    SizeLimit = options.Value.SizeLimit
                })),
                new ResponseCachingKeyProvider(poolProvider, options))
        { }

    internal ResponseCachingMiddleware(
            RequestDelegate next,
            IOptions<ResponseCachingOptions> options,
            ILoggerFactory loggerFactory,
            IResponseCachingPolicyProvider policyProvider,
            IResponseCache cache,
            IResponseCachingKeyProvider keyProvider)
        {
    ....
```

The preceding method signature defines the constructor of the
ResposeCachingMiddleware class. The constructor uses the this keyword to refer to
another internal constructor overload that's used to initialize the properties of the class. As
you can see, the IResponseCache interface is initialized using the MemoryCache type by
default, which extends the IMemoryCache interface.

The IMemoryCache interface represents the cache stored in the webserver. Additionally, it
is possible to use the IMemoryCache interface as a standalone component by adding the
AddMemoryCache() extension method to the initialization of the services in the Startup
class:

```
        public void ConfigureServices(IServiceCollection services)
        {
            services
                ...
                .AddMemoryCache();
        }
```

This approach allows you to use the `IMemoryCache` interface through the dependency injection engine, which means you can call the `GetOrCreate` and `GetOrCreateAsync` methods to set the cache values in the memory of the webserver. Although the in-memory cache provides a really good abstraction for us to cache data, it does not work in a distributed approach. Therefore, if you want to store and share caches between different web servers, ASP.NET Core provides the tools you'll need to implement a distributed cache. In the next section, we will learn a bit more about how to implement a distributed cache in ASP.NET Core.

Implementing a distributed cache

As we mentioned previously, ASP.NET Core allows us to implement distributed caching. In this section, we will learn how to use `Redis` as a form of cache storage. It is possible to extend the behavior of the caching mechanism of ASP.NET Core by adding and executing the following CLI instruction in the `Catalog.API` project:

```
dotnet add package Microsoft.Extensions.Caching.Redis
```

By doing this, we can connect the `Redis` server and use it by adding the following extension method to the `Startup` class:

```
public class Startup
    {
        ...
        public void ConfigureServices(IServiceCollection services)
        {
            ...
            services
                .AddDistributedRedisCache(
                        options => { options.Configuration =
                        "catalog_cache:6380";
                });
                ...
        }
    }
}
```

Microsoft provides the `AddDistributedRedisCache` extension method, which accepts the options that are used to define the instance of `Redis` so that it can be used as a cache as input. The `AddDistributedRedisCache` extension method is connected to the `catalog_cache Redis` instance. Furthermore, we need to declare the new instance in the `docker-compose.yml` file of the catalog service:

```
...
catalog_cache:
    container_name: catalog_cache
    image: redis:alpine
    networks:
        - my_network

networks:
    my_network:
        driver: bridge
```

The preceding code defines the catalog cache's `Redis` instance. Therefore, the application will be able to use this instance as part of `my_network`. Moreover, we can see what the primary purpose of the package is by having a look at the source of the `AddDistributedRedisCache` extension method:

```
public static class RedisCacheServiceCollectionExtensions
{
  public static IServiceCollection AddDistributedRedisCache(
    this IServiceCollection services,
    Action<RedisCacheOptions> setupAction)
  {
    if (services == null)
      throw new ArgumentNullException(nameof (services));
    if (setupAction == null)
      throw new ArgumentNullException(nameof (setupAction));
    services.AddOptions();
    services.Configure<RedisCacheOptions>(setupAction);
    services.Add(ServiceDescriptor.Singleton<IDistributedCache,
        RedisCache>());
    return services;
  }
}
```

I've omitted some documentation comments for brevity purposes, but you can find the open-source code at the following GitHub link: `https://github.com/aspnet/Extensions/`. `./StackExchangeRedisCacheServiceCollectionExtensions.cs`.

As you can see from the preceding code, the extension methods configure and bind the `RedisCacheOptions` class. Secondly, the preceding snippet adds a new `IDistributedCache` interface to the built-in dependency injection of ASP.NET Core. This interface gives us some useful ways to interact with the `Redis` instance and store the caching information there. Furthermore, the instance is defined as a singleton, which means that all of the components inside the application will use the same instance.

Let's have a look at the `IDistributedCache` interface:

```
public interface IDistributedCache
{
  byte[] Get(string key);

  Task<byte[]> GetAsync(string key, CancellationToken token =
  default (CancellationToken));

  void Set(string key, byte[] value, DistributedCacheEntryOptions
  options);

  Task SetAsync(
    string key,
    byte[] value,
    DistributedCacheEntryOptions options,
    CancellationToken token = default (CancellationToken));

  void Refresh(string key);
  Task RefreshAsync(string key, CancellationToken token =
  default (CancellationToken));
  Task RemoveAsync(string key, CancellationToken token =
  default (CancellationToken));
}
```

In this case, I've omitted the documentation comments for brevity purposes. You can find the complete version at https://github.com/aspnet/Extensions/../IDistributedCache. cs. The interface provides a utility method that we can use to read and write information into the `Redis` instance.

Furthermore, the interface exposes both synchronous and asynchronous methods to do this. Since the interface is part of the dependency injection engine, we can use it in any component, such as the `ItemController` class:

```
namespace Catalog.API.Controllers
{
    [Route("api/items")]
    [ApiController]
    [JsonException]
```

```
[Authorize]
public class ItemController : ControllerBase
{
    private readonly IItemService _itemService;
    private readonly IEndpointInstance _messageEndpoint;
    private readonly IDistributedCache _distributedCache;
    public ItemController(IItemService itemService,
    IEndpointInstance messageEndpoint,
    IDistributedCache distributedCache)
    {
        _itemService = itemService;
        _messageEndpoint = messageEndpoint;
        _distributedCache = distributedCache;
    }
    ...
    ...
```

The ItemController class and any other components in the application can now be resolved and use the IDistributedCache singleton instance by including it in the constructor and action injection.

ASP.NET Core also provides AddDistributedMemoryCache(), which is part of the Microsoft.Extensions.DependencyInjection namespace. Despite its name, it doesn't initialize any distributed cache. Let's have an in-depth look at its implementation:

```
public static IServiceCollection AddDistributedMemoryCache(
  this IServiceCollection services)
{
  if (services == null)
    throw new ArgumentNullException(nameof (services));
  services.AddOptions();
  services.TryAdd(ServiceDescriptor.Singleton<IDistributedCach
  e, MemoryDistributedCache>());
  return services;
}
```

The extension method uses the memory of the webserver to store information. More specifically, the AddDistributedMemoryCache extension method is designed for development/testing environments, and it isn't a real distributed cache.

Finally, we can optimize and refactor the `Startup` class by creating a new configuration class dedicated to the cache. First of all, let's create the following class in the `Configurations` folder of the catalog's domain project:

```
namespace Catalog.Domain.Configurations
{
    public class CacheSettings
    {
        public string ConnectionString { get; set; }
    }
}
```

The class definition contains the `ConnectionString` field of the `Redis` instance. We can proceed by adding the `DistributedCacheExtensions` class to the `Catalog.Infrastructure` project, which can be found inside the `Extensions` folder:

```
using Catalog.Domain.Configurations;
using Microsoft.Extensions.Configuration;
using Microsoft.Extensions.DependencyInjection;
using Newtonsoft.Json;
namespace Catalog.Infrastructure.Extensions
{
    public static class DistributedCacheExtensions
    {
        public static IServiceCollection AddDistributedCache(this
            IServiceCollection services,
            IConfiguration configuration)
        {
            var settings = configuration.GetSection("CacheSettings");
            var settingsTyped = settings.Get<CacheSettings>();
            services.Configure<CacheSettings>(settings);
            services.AddDistributedRedisCache(options => {
            options.Configuration = settingsTyped.ConnectionString; });
            return services;
        }
    }
}
```

The preceding code declares a new `AddDistributedCache` extension method. The method configures the `CacheSettings` node of the `appsettings.json` file by reading and registering the node to the dependency injection engine. Next, it calls the `AddDistributedCache` method to configure the distributed cache so that it can use the provided connection string.

Let's proceed by adding the new `CacheSettings` node to the `appsettings.json` file:

```
...
"CacheSettings": {
  "ConnectionString": "catalog_cache"
}
```

Next, we need to call the `AddDistributedCache` extension method in the `Startup` class:

```
public class Startup
{
    ...
    public void ConfigureServices(IServiceCollection services)
    {
        services
        ...
            .AddDistributedCache(Configuration)
    }
}
```

Now, our application initializes a new `IDistributedCache` instance in the dependency injection engine using the connection string provided by the `appsettings.json` file. In the next section, we will examine an additional level of customization for distributed caches.

Implementing the IDistributedCache interface

It is possible to extend the behavior of the `IDistributedCache` interface by overloading the extension methods. Furthermore, we need to store complex information and not bytes. For example, in the case of the `ItemController` class, we want to pass the `ItemResponse` type to the `Set` method of the `IDistributedCache` interface.

Let's proceed by modifying the `DistributedCacheExtensions` class in the `Catalog.API` project:

```
using System.Threading.Tasks;
using Catalog.Domain.Configurations;
using Microsoft.Extensions.Caching.Distributed;
using Microsoft.Extensions.Configuration;
using Microsoft.Extensions.DependencyInjection;
using Newtonsoft.Json;

namespace Catalog.Infrastructure.Extensions
{
    public static class DistributedCacheExtensions
    {
```

```
private static readonly JsonSerializerSettings
    _serializerSettings = CreateSettings();
...

public static async Task<T> GetObjectAsync<T>(this
    IDistributedCache cache, string key)
{
    var json = await cache.GetStringAsync(key);

    return json == null ? default(T) :

    JsonConvert.DeserializeObject<T>(json,
        _serializerSettings);
}
public static async Task SetObjectAsync(this IDistributedCache
    cache, string key, object value)
{
    var json = JsonConvert.SerializeObject(value,
        _serializerSettings);
    await cache.SetStringAsync(key, json);
}

public static async Task SetObjectAsync(this IDistributedCache
    cache, string key,
object value, DistributedCacheEntryOptions options)
{
    var json = JsonConvert.SerializeObject(value,
        _serializerSettings);
    await cache.SetStringAsync(key, json, options);
}

private static JsonSerializerSettings CreateSettings()
{
    return new JsonSerializerSettings();
}
    }
}
```

The preceding class defines the generic extension methods to get and set a complex object in the Redis cache. It uses the Newtonsoft.Json methods to store objects in JSON format. The class also defines two SetObject<T> methods with different signatures. One provides a default configuration of DistributedCacheEntryOptions, while the other one allows us to override the options inside this configuration. Furthermore, it is possible to use these extension methods in the ItemController class, like so:

```
namespace Catalog.API.Controllers
{
```

```
[Route("api/items")]
[ApiController]
[JsonException]
[Authorize]
public class ItemController : ControllerBase
{
    private readonly IItemService _itemService;
    private readonly IEndpointInstance _messageEndpoint;
    private readonly IDistributedCache _distributedCache;

    public ItemController(IItemService itemService,
    IEndpointInstance messageEndpoint,
        IDistributedCache distributedCache)
    {
        _itemService = itemService;
        _messageEndpoint = messageEndpoint;
        _distributedCache = distributedCache;
    }
    [HttpGet("{id:guid}")]
    [ItemExists]
    [ResponseCache(Duration = 100, VaryByQueryKeys = new[] { "*" })]
    public async Task<IActionResult> GetById(Guid id)
    {
        var key = $"{typeof(ItemController).FullName}.
        {nameof(GetById)}.{id}";
        var cachedResult = await _distributedCache.
            GetObjectAsync<ItemResponse>(key);

        if (cachedResult != null)
        {
            return Ok(cachedResult);
        }
        var result = await _itemService.GetItemAsync(new
            GetItemRequest{ Id = id });
        await _distributedCache.SetObjectAsync(key, result);
        return Ok(result);
    }
}
...
```

The GetById action method uses the IDistributedCache interface to save information about ItemResponse: it defines a key that's composed in the following way:

```
<controller_full_name>.<action_method_name>.<input_id>
```

The action method tries to retrieve this information from the cache; if this information is not present, it performs the request by using the IItemService interface, and it stores the result using the SetObjectAsync method of the IDistributedCache interface.

Although this approach requires a discrete overhead in terms of implementation compared to the `ResponseCache` attribute, the `IDistributedCache` interface relies on an external caching system. Furthermore, it is possible to implement this kind of caching logic by using the filter pipeline stack. Therefore, it is possible to move the caching logic that's implemented in the `ItemController` class into a custom action filter:

```csharp
namespace Catalog.API.Filters
{
    public class RedisCacheFilter : IAsyncActionFilter
    {
        private readonly IDistributedCache _distributedCache;
        private readonly DistributedCacheEntryOptions _options;

        public RedisCacheFilter(IDistributedCache distributedCache,
        int cacheTimeSeconds)
        {
            _distributedCache = distributedCache;
            _options = new DistributedCacheEntryOptions
            {
                SlidingExpiration =
                    TimeSpan.FromSeconds(cacheTimeSeconds)
            };
        }

        public async Task OnActionExecutionAsync(ActionExecutingContext
        context, ActionExecutionDelegate next)
        {
            if (!context.ActionArguments.ContainsKey("id"))
            {
                await next();
            }

            var actionName = (string)
                context.RouteData.Values["action"];
            var controllerName = (string)
                context.RouteData.Values["controller"];

            var id = context.ActionArguments["id"];

            var key = $"{controllerName}.{actionName}.{id}";

            var result = await _distributedCache.
                GetObjectAsync<ItemResponse>(key);

            if (result != null)
            {
                context.Result = new OkObjectResult(result);
```

```
                    return;
            }

        var resultContext = await next();

        if (resultContext.Result is OkObjectResult resultResponse
        && resultResponse.StatusCode == 200)
        {
            await _distributedCache.SetObjectAsync(key,
                resultResponse.Value, _options);
        }
        }
    }
}
```

`RedisCacheFilter` encapsulates the cache logic to avoid replicating it in every action method. It implements the following logic: before the action is executed, it tries to get `ItemResponse` from the cache by composing the key using the controller name, the action name, and the requested `id` value. If the cache key is not populated, it proceeds with the execution of the action method, and if the resulting `StatusCode` is `200`, it continues by storing the result in the `Redis` cache. The next request with the same `id` value will have the cache populated, and the action filter will return the cached object.

It is possible to use the action filter in the following way:

```
[Route("api/items")]
[ApiController]
[JsonException]
public class ItemController : ControllerBase
{
    ...

    [HttpGet("{id:guid}")]
    [ItemExists]
    [TypeFilter(typeof(RedisCacheFilter), Arguments = new object[]
        {20})]
    public async Task<IActionResult> GetById(Guid id)
    {
        ...
    }

    ...
}
```

The action method uses the `TypeFilter` attribute to resolve `RedisCacheFilter`, and it passes the number that represents the cache expiration in seconds as an argument. This implementation strategy is more readable and allows us to avoid code replication between different action methods.

Inject memory cache into the tests

If we try to execute unit tests using `RedisCacheFilter`, we will notice that `get_by_id_should_return_right_data` will fail. This is because the Redis instance is not available in the development environment. Furthermore, we can use the `MemoryDistributedCache` implementation to perform our tests. The `MemoryDistributedCache` implementation is done in the same class that's used by the `AddDistributedMemoryCache` extension method. As we mentioned in the previous chapter, the class doesn't provide a real distributed cache, and it is used for testing purposes.

For that reason, we can add the following line to the `InMemoryApplicationFactory<TStartup>` class, which is contained in the `Catalog.Fixtures` project:

```
namespace Catalog.Fixtures
{
    public class InMemoryApplicationFactory<TStartup>
        : WebApplicationFactory<TStartup> where TStartup : class
    {
        protected override void ConfigureWebHost(IWebHostBuilder
            builder)
        {
            builder.UseEnvironment("Testing")
                .ConfigureTestServices(services =>
                {
                    ...
                    services.AddSingleton<IDistributedCache,
                        MemoryDistributedCache>();
                    ...
                });
        }
    }
}
```

The preceding code replaces the implementation of `IDistributedCache` with an instance of `MemoryDistributedCache`. Therefore, every time our implementation calls the `IDistributedCache` interface, the data is saved in the memory of the testing server.

Summary

In this chapter, we covered some of the main caching scenarios in ASP.NET Core so that you know how the HTTP cache works and how it can be implemented. Furthermore, we learned how to implement a distributed cache using the `IDistributedCache` interface and how to connect the web service to a Redis instance. In the next chapter, we will look at how to deal with logging management and how to perform health checks on the dependencies of the catalog web service.

Logging and Health Checking

17

One of the essential aspects of building web services is logging and health checks. Nowadays, it is preferred to have services with a small scope. This kind of approach provides enormous benefits, but it makes it hard for us to verify whether a service behaves in the right way. Logging helps us to track the actions and the information processed by the web service on the other side, the health check mechanisms provide a way to verify that the service is healthy and all the required dependencies are satisfied. The chapter goes through some of the logging parts of ASP.NET Core, and it shows how to implement health checks using the tools provided by the framework.

In this chapter, we will cover the following topics:

- Logging in ASP.NET Core
- Implementing logging
- Implementing logging providers
- Implementing custom logging in tests
- Web service health check

Logging in ASP.NET Core

We will start this chapter by providing an overview of the different logging components of ASP.NET Core. The framework provides different interfaces that support logging:

- `ILoggerProvider` is used to define a specific type of logging bind with an output channel
- `ILoggerFactory` takes an `ILoggerProvider` interface and initializes it
- The `ILogger` interface is a particular instance of the logging component

The logging interface structure of ASP.NET Core can be described using the following schema:

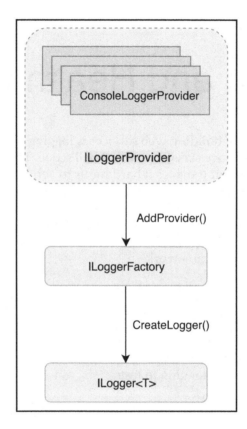

In short, the `ILoggerProvider` interface represents the output of the logs, `ILoggerFactory` creates the right type of instance, and `ILogger` is the actual instance of the logger.

This kind of approach guarantees secure isolation between the `ILogger` interface consumer and the logging provider part. Furthermore, we may choose to add the calls to the `ILogger` interface in the development phase; then, during the release phase, we can decide which provider to use to output our logging data. Moreover, our logging code becomes very flexible, and we can change the output based on the type of environment our service runs in. Let's proceed by learning about the different characteristics of the logging system of ASP.NET Core.

The key characteristics of logging

The ASP.NET Core logging system is characterized by some key attributes that are always present in each log record. Furthermore, it is essential to keep logs as coherent as possible. The crucial components of the ASP.NET Core logging system are the *log category*, the *log level*, the *log event id*, and the *log message*.

The *log category* is specified when the `ILogger<T>` interface is initialized. It is an essential part of the logging process because it identifies the component that is emitting the log record. The *log category* usually corresponds to the type or class that's firing the log records. Let's use the `ItemController` class of the catalog service as an example. The *log category* is defined during the `ILogger` interface injection process:

```
namespace Catalog.API.Controllers
{
    [Route("api/items")]
    [ApiController]
    [JsonException]
    [Authorize]
    public class ItemController : ControllerBase
    {
        private readonly IItemService _itemService;
        private readonly IEndpointInstance _messageEndpoint;
        private readonly ILogger<ItemController> _logger;

        public ItemController(IItemService itemService,
        IEndpointInstance messageEndpoint,
            IDistributedCache distributedCache,
            ILogger<ItemController> logger)
        {
            _itemService = itemService;
            _messageEndpoint = messageEndpoint;
            _logger = logger;
        }

    . . .
```

The `ItemController` class uses the widespread technique of constructor injection to initialize the `ILogger<ItemController>` type. Therefore, the log category is implicitly defined in the signature of the `_logger` property. Although the *log category* helps us identify which component is firing that specific log message, we also need to define the importance of that message.

The *log level* provides information that indicates the severity or importance of the log record. ASP.NET Core provides a helpful extension method that offers some abstraction over the log level:

```
_logger.LogInformation, _logger.LogWarning, _logger.LogError,
_logger.LogCritical
```

Each of these methods is an abstraction that's provided by the `Microsoft.Extensions.Logging` namespace. For example, if we examine the `_logger.LogInformation` method implementation, under the hood, it merely calls the generic `logger.Log` method:

```
public static void LogInformation(
   this ILogger logger,
   EventId eventId,
   Exception exception,
   string message,
   params object[] args)
{
   logger.Log(LogLevel.Information, eventId, exception, message, args);
}
```

The `LogInformation` extension method wraps the `logger.Log` method calls by implicitly defining the level of information provided by the framework. The `LogLevel` attribute is an `enum` structure that's exposed by the `Microsoft.Extension.Logging` namespace, which provides the following out of the box logging levels:

```
namespace Microsoft.Extensions.Logging
{
   public enum LogLevel
   {
      Debug,
      Warning,
      Error,
      Critical,
      None,
   }
}
```

The preceding code describes the different log levels that are provided by the `LogLevel` enumerator. The log levels go from `Trace`, which describes detailed information about the system, to the `Critical` level, which means that the service is unable to work correctly and is shutting down. The `LogLevel` attribute is essential because it is usually used to filter the log messages which tells us of the priority of a logging message.

Once we've identified the level of severity of a specific log message, we need to provide the *log event id*, which helps us identify a specific event in the logging output. While the *log category* usually represents the full path of the class, the *log event id* is useful if we wish to express the method that is currently generating the logging output. Let's use the action methods contained in the `ItemController` class as an example (`Get`, `GetById`, `Create`, `Update`, and `Delete`). It is possible to create a log event class that maps each action method to a specific event id:

```
namespace Catalog.API
{
    public class LoggingEvents
    {
            public const int Get = 1000;
            public const int GetById = 1001;
            public const int Create = 1002;
            public const int Update = 1003;
            public const int Delete = 1004;

    }

}
```

Therefore, we can pass the corresponding log event id when we call the `ILogger` interface in an action method of the `ItemController` class. By doing this, it is possible to identify and group events:

```
_logger.LogInformation(LoggingEvents.GetById, "Getting item");
```

Finally, another essential part of logging records is the message associated with the log record. The logging system of ASP.NET Core also provides a templating system that's analogous to the C# string interpolation feature. Therefore, it is possible to use the templating system in the following way:

```
_logger.LogInformation(LoggingEvents.GetById, "GetById {id} ", id);
```

The preceding code logs a message about *information* severity using the `LoggingEvents.GetById` event id and adds the message `"GetById {id} "`. Now that we have looked at the different logging characteristics provided by ASP.NET Core, we will look at a concrete implementation that's been applied to the *catalog service* project.

Implementing the logging part

In this section, we will learn how to perform logging in the *catalog web service*. Let's start by choosing a layer where we'll execute the logging statements. Since the logic is encapsulated in the `Catalog.Domain` layer project, we will continue by implementing the logging part on the service classes defined in the project. First of all, let's start by defining a new logging class, which contains the corresponding *event id* for each operation:

```
namespace Catalog.Domain.Logging
{
    public class Events
    {
        public const int Get = 1000;
        public const int GetById = 1001;
        public const int Add = 1002;
        public const int Edit = 1003;
        public const int Delete = 1004;
    }
}
```

Once we have established a corresponding *log event id* for each activity, we need to define the logging messages that will be used by the `ILogger` interface. For now, we can determine the following messages:

```
namespace Catalog.Domain.Logging
{
    public class Messages
    {
        public const string NumberOfRecordAffected_modifiedRecords =
            "Number of record affected {records}";
        public const string ChangesApplied_id = "Changes applied to the
            following entity id ({id})";
        public const string TargetEntityChanged_id = "Target entity id
            ({id})";
    }
}
```

The first one refers to the number of records affected by a change, while the second is the entity that's been changed. Finally, the third one provides a message for the target entity of the handler. It is essential to note that both constants follow a naming convention: the first part of their name refers to the content of the message; after the first underscore, we have the parameters that will be replaced by values when we use the logging templating system.

Furthermore, we can proceed by changing the `IItemService` methods by implementing logging. Let's start with the `AddItemAsync` method:

```
using Microsoft.Extensions.Logging;
using Catalog.Domain.Logging;
...

namespace Catalog.Domain.Services
{
    public class ItemService : IItemService
    {
        private readonly IItemMapper _itemMapper;
        private readonly IItemRepository _itemRepository;
        private readonly ILogger<IItemService> _logger;

        public ItemService(IItemRepository itemRepository,
        IItemMapper itemMapper, ILogger<IItemService> logger)
        {
            _itemRepository = itemRepository;
            _itemMapper = itemMapper;
            _logger = logger;
        }
        ...

        public async Task<ItemResponse> AddItemAsync(AddItemRequest
            request)
        {
            var item = _itemMapper.Map(request);
            var result = _itemRepository.Add(item);

            var modifiedRecords = await _itemRepository.
                UnitOfWork.SaveChangesAsync();
            _logger.LogInformation(Events.Add, Messages.
            NumberOfRecordAffected_modifiedRecords, modifiedRecords);
            _logger.LogInformation(Events.Add, Messages.
            ChangesApplied_id, result?.Id);

            return _itemMapper.Map(result);
        }

        ...
    }
}
```

The preceding code tracks the information about the number of affected records and the id of the added record. We can do the same with the other methods of the `ItemService` class. In the case of read-only operations, we can add the id of the target record; for example, in the case of the `GetItemAsync` method:

```
public class ItemService : IItemService
{
    ...

    public async Task<ItemResponse> GetItemAsync(GetItemRequest
        request)
    {
        if (request?.Id == null) throw new ArgumentNullException();
        var entity = await _itemRepository.GetAsync(request.Id);
        _logger.LogInformation(Events.GetById,
            Messages.TargetEntityChanged_id, entity?.Id);
        return _itemMapper.Map(entity);
    }
}
```

The preceding code logs the information related to the id that was retrieved by the service by using the `Event.GetById` field. It uses the `Messages` type to specify the event message. In the next section, we will learn how to log exceptions by enhancing the exception handling implementation of logs.

Exception logging

What if part of the service throws an exception? Handling exceptions is a crucial part of the development process of services. As we saw in Chapter 7, *Filter Pipeline*, it is possible to use them to catch exceptions using a filter. Filters are one of the crucial parts of the MVC stack: they act before and after action methods, and they can be used to log exceptions in a single implementation. Let's have a look at `JsonExceptionAttribute` in `Catalog.API` again:

```
using System.Net;
using Microsoft.AspNetCore.Hosting;
using Microsoft.AspNetCore.Mvc;
using Microsoft.AspNetCore.Mvc.Filters;
using Microsoft.Extensions.Logging;
using Catalog.API.Exceptions;

namespace Catalog.API.Filters
{
    public class JsonExceptionAttribute : TypeFilterAttribute
    {
```

```
        public JsonExceptionAttribute() :
base(typeof(HttpCustomExceptionFilterImpl))
        {
        }

        public class HttpCustomExceptionFilterImpl : IExceptionFilter
        {
            private readonly IHostingEnvironment _env;
            private readonly ILogger _logger;

            public HttpCustomExceptionFilterImpl(IHostingEnvironment
                env,
                ILogger<HttpCustomExceptionFilterImpl> logger)
            {
                _env = env;
                _logger = logger;
            }

            public void OnException(ExceptionContext context)
            {
                var eventId = new EventId(context.Exception.HResult);

                _logger.LogError(eventId, context.Exception,
                    context.Exception.Message);

                var json = new JsonErrorPayload
                {
                    EventId = eventId.Id
                };

                json.DetailedMessage = context.Exception;

                var exceptionObject = new ObjectResult(json) {
                    StatusCode = 500 };

                context.Result = exceptionObject;
                context.HttpContext.Response.StatusCode = (int)
                HttpStatusCode.InternalServerError;
            }
        }
    }
}
```

The class tracks and returns exceptions using the analog pattern, which can be seen in the implementation of the handler: the ILogger<T> interface is injected into the constructor using dependency injection and the _logger.LogError method.

In the next section, we will learn how to verify logging in our test using Moq.

Verifying logging using Moq

Let's learn how to verify our implemented logging. The dependency injection system of the `ILogger` interface helps us to mock the logging mechanism and validate the resulting implementation. It is essential to note that our handlers are using the extension methods of the `ILogger` interface. Let's use the ASP.NET Core implementation of the `LogInformation` extension method in the `Microsoft.Extensions.Logging` namespace as an example:

```
using Microsoft.Extensions.Logging.Internal;
using System;

namespace Microsoft.Extensions.Logging
{
  /// <summary>ILogger extension methods for common scenarios.</summary>
  public static class LoggerExtensions
  {
      public static void LogInformation(this ILogger logger,
         Exception exception, string message, params object[] args)
      {
          logger.Log(LogLevel.Information, exception, message,
              args);
      }
  }
}
```

Extension methods are *not* a mock-oriented construct. They are static methods and, by definition, it is not possible to mock a static construct in C#'s runtime. Thus, we need to provide an *abstraction* over the `ILogger` factory that allows us to inject and mock the interface that's used in our tests.

 In general, it isn't possible to test static methods. Moreover, mock libraries typically create mocks by dynamically creating classes at runtime. Typically, they override the behavior of types by extending them. Since the static methods cannot be overridden, it isn't possible to mock them. Therefore, when we need to mock a static element, it is suggested that we abstract them and encapsulate them into classes.

Let's look at the declaration of the `LoggerAbstraction` class in the `Catalog.Fixture` project:

```
using System;
using Microsoft.Extensions.Logging;

namespace Catalog.Fixtures
{
```

```
public abstract class LoggerAbstraction<T> : ILogger<T>
{
    public IDisposable BeginScope<TState>(TState state) => throw
        new NotImplementedException();

    public bool IsEnabled(LogLevel logLevel) => true;

    public void Log<TState>(LogLevel logLevel, EventId eventId,
        TState state, Exception exception, Func<TState, Exception,
         string> formatter)
        => Log(logLevel, exception, formatter(state, exception));

    public abstract void Log(LogLevel logLevel, Exception ex,
        string information);
    }
}
```

LoggerAbstraction is a generic class that implements the ILogger<T> interface. More specifically, the abstract class defines the Log<TState> method by executing an overloaded version of the void Log method. Both the Log method and the LoggerAbstraction class are abstract, which means we can mock their behavior. Thus, it is possible to mock the behavior of the logging class, as shown in the following modified version of the ItemServiceTests class:

```
namespace Catalog.Domain.Tests.Services
{
    public class ItemServiceTests : IClassFixture<CatalogContextFactory>
    {
        private readonly ItemRepository _itemRepository;
        private readonly IItemMapper _mapper;
        private readonly Mock<LoggerAbstraction<IItemService>> _logger;
            public ItemServiceTests(CatalogContextFactory
                catalogContextFactory, ITestOutputHelper outputHelper)
        {
            _itemRepository = new ItemRepository
            (catalogContextFactory.ContextInstance);
            _mapper = catalogContextFactory.ItemMapper;
            _logger = new Mock<LoggerAbstraction<IItemService>>();
            _logger.Setup(x => x.Log(It.IsAny<LogLevel>(), It.IsAny
                <Exception>(), It.IsAny<string>()))
                    .Callback((LogLevel logLevel, Exception exception,
                        string information) =>
                        outputHelper.WriteLine($"{logLevel}:
                            {information}"));
        }

        ...
```

```
[Theory]
[LoadData("item")]
public async Task additem_should_log_information(AddItemRequest
    request)
{
    var sut = new ItemService(_itemRepository, _mapper,
        _logger.Object);

    await sut.AddItemAsync(request);

    _logger
      .Verify(x => x.Log(It.IsAny<LogLevel>(), It.IsAny
        <Exception>(), It.IsAny<string>()), Times.AtMost(2));
}
...

}
}
```

The `ItemServiceTests` class initializes the `LoggerAbstraction<IItemService>` type as a class attribute. The constructor of the class uses `ITestOutputHelper` to mock the logging system that's used by the service layer:

```
_logger.Setup(x => x.Log(It.IsAny<LogLevel>(),It.IsAny<Exception>(),
    It.IsAny<string>()))
        .Callback((LogLevel logLevel, Exception exception, string
            information) =>
                outputHelper.WriteLine($"{logLevel}:
                    {information}"));
```

`ITestOutputHelper` is an interface that's exposed by the `Xunit.Abstractions` namespace and resolved by the `Xunit` runtime. It allows us to write in the test console of the test runner. Finally, the test class implements the `additem_should_log_information` test method. The test method calls the `AddItemAsync` method that we implemented in the `ItemService` class. Finally, it is possible to verify the `ILogger` interface using the following snippet:

```
_logger
  .Verify(x => x.Log(It.IsAny<LogLevel>(),It.IsAny<Exception>(),
    It.IsAny<string>()), Times.AtMost(2));
```

The preceding snippet verifies that the `Log` method is called two times. It also outputs the resulting log as part of the logging system that's defined by the `ITestOutputHelper` interface. Now that we have implemented the logging mechanism in the service layer of the `Catalog.Domain` project, we will examine and implement the necessary logging providers.

Implementing logging providers

So far, we have defined *what* to log in our application; in this section, we will illustrate *how* to do this. In ASP.NET Core, the logging provider is initialized using dependency injection. Moreover, it is possible to conditionally initialize it, depending on the environment or other startup options.

ASP.NET Core provides some *built-in* logging providers, as shown in the following table:

Providers	Namespace	Description
Console	Microsoft.Extensions.Logging.Console	Sets the console of the running application as the output of the logs.
Debug	Microsoft.Extensions.Logging.Debug	Writes messages in the debug output window when a debugger is attached.
EventSource	Microsoft.Extensions.Logging.EventSource	Sets the Windows ETW as the main log's output.
EventLog	Microsoft.Extensions.Logging.EventLog	Sets the Windows event log as the main log's output.
TraceSource	Microsoft.Extensions.Logging.TraceSource	To use this provider, ASP.NET Core needs to run on the .NET Framework. The application will use the listeners that are provided by the trace source.

It is crucial to note that all the logging providers are complementary. Furthermore, it is possible to add many of them so that we can perform trace logging in more sources. We can configure the provider in the Startup class and in the Program class. Let's take a look at the Program class of Catalog.API:

```
using Microsoft.AspNetCore;
using Microsoft.AspNetCore.Hosting;

namespace Catalog.API
{
    public class Program
    {
        public static void Main(string[] args)
        {
            CreateWebHostBuilder(args).Build().Run();
        }

        public static IWebHostBuilder CreateWebHostBuilder(string[]
            args)
        {
            return WebHost.CreateDefaultBuilder(args)
                .UseStartup<Startup>();
        }
    }
}
```

Here, the `Program` class uses `WebHost.CreateDefaultBuilder` to create the `WebHostBuilder` instance of the service. If we go further into the method, we will see that it uses the following syntax to define the log's provider:

```
...
.ConfigureLogging((Action<WebHostBuilderContext, ILoggingBuilder>)
((hostingContext, logging) =>
{
  logging.AddConfiguration((IConfiguration)
  hostingContext.Configuration.GetSection("Logging"));
  logging.AddConsole();
  logging.AddDebug();
  logging.AddEventSourceLogger();
}))
```

As you can see, the `Program` class defines three built-in providers by default. Also, it uses the `Configuration` instance to pass the configurations that are described in the `appsettings.json` file.

Moreover, it is possible to override the default provider by explicitly calling the `ConfigureLogging` extension method in the `Program` class:

```
...
    public class Program
    {
        ...
        public static IWebHostBuilder CreateWebHostBuilder(string[]
            args)
        {
            return WebHost.CreateDefaultBuilder(args)
                .ConfigureLogging(builder =>
                {
                    builder.[...]
                })
                .UseStartup<Startup>();
        }
    }
```

The preceding snippet is useful if we want to add a custom logging provider to our application. ASP.NET Core also provides us with a convenient way to configure the logging provider in the `Startup` class: it is possible to use the `AddLogging` extension method in `ConfigureServices`:

```
    public class Startup
    {
        ...
        public void ConfigureServices(IServiceCollection services)
```

```
        {
            ...
            services.AddLogging(builder => builder.AddConsole());
        }

    ...
    }
}
```

The preceding snippet initializes the logging services on the execution of
ConfigureServices in the Startup class. The initialization of the logging provider at
the Startup level is useful when we want to initialize the log provider in terms of the
environment or a specific configuration flag. Let's proceed by learning how to implement a
custom logging provider.

Implementing a custom log provider in tests

As we already have seen, the logging system of ASP.NET Core is designed for maximum
extensibility. In this section, we will learn how to implement a custom logging provider
that we can use in our tests. All the test classes that are present in the
Catalog.API.Tests project use InMemoryApplicationFactory<T> to run a web server
and provide HttpClient to call the API. As you may have noticed, the tests don't return
an explicit error when one of the tests fails. For example, let's examine the following test
method in the ItemControllerTests class:

```
public class ItemController :
IClassFixture<InMemoryApplicationFactory<Startup>>
    {
        ...
        [Fact]
        public async Task update_should_returns_not_found
            _when_item_is_not_present()
        {
            var client = _factory.CreateClient();

            var httpContent = new StringContent(jsonPayload.ToString(),
            Encoding.UTF8, "application/json");
            var response = await client.PutAsync($"/api/items/
              {Guid.NewGuid()}", httpContent);

            response.StatusCode.ShouldBe(HttpStatusCode.NotFound);
        }
    ..
    }
```

If for any reason, the call returns an error, we will receive the following message on the test side:

```
...
Shouldly.ShouldAssertException : response.StatusCode
  should be
HttpStatusCode.NotFound
  but was
HttpStatusCode.InternalServerError
...
```

Here, we don't know *why* the API has returned an `InternalServerError`. Here, we can use the `ITestOutputHelper` interface provided by `Xunit` to create a new logger provider and use it in our tests. To declare a logger in ASP.NET Core, we need the following structure and components:

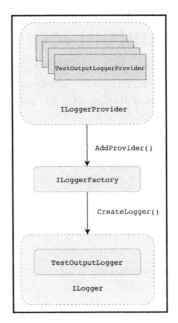

The preceding schema describes two main components:
the `TestOutputLoggerProvider` type and the `TestOutputLogger` type. The `TestOutputLoggerProvider` type's purpose is to manage a list of logger instances. The `TestOutputLogger` class describes the actual implementation of the logging mechanism. Let's start by defining the custom `ILogger` component:

```
using System;
using Microsoft.Extensions.Logging;
```

```
using Xunit.Abstractions;

namespace Catalog.Fixtures
{
    public class TestOutputLogger : ILogger
    {
        private readonly ITestOutputHelper _output;

        public TestOutputLogger(ITestOutputHelper output) =>
            _output = output;

        public IDisposable BeginScope<TState>(TState state) => null;

        public bool IsEnabled(LogLevel logLevel) =>
            logLevel == LogLevel.Error;

        public void Log<TState>(LogLevel logLevel, EventId eventId,
            TState state, Exception exception, Func<TState,
            Exception, string> formatter)
        {
            if (!IsEnabled(logLevel))
                return;

            _output.WriteLine($"{logLevel.ToString()} -
                {exception.Message} - {exception.StackTrace}");
        }
    }
}
```

ITestOutputClass implements the methods provided by the ILogger interface. First of all, it declares an ITestOutputHelper field in the constructor. Then, it uses the _output attribute inside the concrete implementation of the Log method by calling the _output.WriteLine method. The class also implements the IsEnabled method to check whether the log level corresponds to the LogLevel.Error field. If the log record doesn't do this, LogLevel.Error is written in the console's output. To finalize this implementation, we need a logger provider to initialize the custom logger. Let's continue by creating another class called TestOutputLoggerProvider, which extends the ILoggerProvider interface:

```
using System.Collections.Concurrent;
using Microsoft.Extensions.Logging;
using Xunit.Abstractions;
namespace Catalog.Fixtures
{
    public class TestOutputLoggerProvider : ILoggerProvider
    {
```

```
        private readonly ConcurrentDictionary<string, TestOutputLogger>
            _loggers = new ConcurrentDictionary
            <string, TestOutputLogger>();
        private readonly ITestOutputHelper _testOutputHelper;
        public TestOutputLoggerProvider(ITestOutputHelper
            testOutputHelper) => _testOutputHelper = testOutputHelper;

        public ILogger CreateLogger(string categoryName) =>
            _loggers.GetOrAdd(categoryName, name =>  new
            TestOutputLogger(_testOutputHelper));

        public void Dispose() => _loggers.Clear();
    }
}
```

`TestOutputLoggerProvider` defines a `ConcurrentDictionary`, which contains a pair of `string` and `TestOutputLogger`; it also accepts the `ITestOutputHelper` interface as an interface, which is used in the `CreateLogger` method to add the logger to the logging pipeline. By doing this, we can integrate the custom logger into our tests. We will use the `InMemoryApplicationFactory<T>` class, which is implemented in the `Catalog.Fixtures` project, to add the custom logger, as follows:

```
using Xunit.Abstractions;
...

namespace Catalog.Fixtures
{
    public class InMemoryApplicationFactory<TStartup>
        : WebApplicationFactory<TStartup> where TStartup : class
    {
        private ITestOutputHelper _testOutputHelper;
        public void SetTestOutputHelper(ITestOutputHelper
            testOutputHelper)
        {
            _testOutputHelper = testOutputHelper;
        }
        protected override void ConfigureWebHost(IWebHostBuilder
            builder)
        {
            builder
                .UseEnvironment("Testing")
                .ConfigureTestServices(services =>
                {
                    ...
                    if (_testOutputHelper != null)
                    {
                        services.AddLogging(cfg => cfg.AddProvider(new
```

```
                                TestOutputLoggerProvider(_testOutputHelper)));
                        }
                            ...
                    });
                }
            }
        }
```

The preceding class declares a new ITestOutputHelper attribute type and defines a setter. It is possible to add our custom logger by calling the AddProvider extension method inside the ConfigureTestService class by creating a new instance of TestOutputLoggerProvider. After making these changes, we can proceed by integrating the custom logger into the ItemControllerTests class:

```
...
namespace Catalog.API.Tests.Controllers
{
    public class ItemControllerTests :
        IClassFixture<InMemoryApplicationFactory<Startup>>
    {
        private readonly InMemoryApplicationFactory<Startup> _factory;
        public ItemControllerTests(InMemoryApplicationFactory<Startup>
        factory, ITestOutputHelper outputHelper)
        {
            _factory = factory;
            _factory.SetTestOutputHelper(outputHelper);
        }
...
```

As you can see, ItemControllerTests calls _factory.SetTestOutputHelper in the constructor by setting the injected ITestOutputHelper interface. Now, we'll get detailed error messages every time a test throws an error. It is essential to note that the ITestOutputHelper interface is assigned in the test class, which means this is the only point where it is possible to obtain the interface using dependency injection. In the next section, we will learn how to implement health checks related to web service dependencies.

Web service health check

Another essential feature that's always present in web services is the *health checking process* for dependencies. In general, the health check processes are used by the CI/CD pipeline to check whether a service is healthy after its deployment or to perform the feature check-in a monitoring dashboard. Health checks are usually performed by calling HTTP routes to detect whether there are any ongoing issues in the web service.

Note that these services expose the health check routes. The monitoring of these health checks is implemented in an independent and separate application. Furthermore, this practice allows us to keep the services independent from the monitoring logic.

ASP.NET Core provides some out-of-the-box implementations to help developers add health check processes to their services. These features are implemented using a *middleware-oriented approach*. Furthermore, the health checks are exposed as HTTP endpoints, and they can be used to check the status of third-party services, databases, and data storage systems. Thus, we can test the dependencies of the service to confirm their availability and functionality.

The health checks feature was introduced with the *ASP.NET Core 2.2.0-preview1* version in August 2018. This feature introduced the `IHealthCheck` interface. In the future, it will be integrated with the `Polly` library to provide better resilience when users perform logging checks.

Implementing health checks on databases

Databases are usually one of the main dependencies of a web service. Therefore, it is always essential to check the connection between the service and the database. Let's start by learning how to implement health checks using the `AspNetCore.HealthChecks.SqlServer` (https://www.nuget.org/packages/AspNetCore.HealthChecks.SqlServer/) and `Microsoft.Extensions.Diagnostics.HealthChecks.EntityFrameworkCore` (https://www.nuget.org/packages/Microsoft.Extensions.Diagnostics.HealthChecks.EntityFrameworkCore/) packages. We are going to apply these changes to the *catalog service* project. Let's start by adding this package to the `Catalog.API` project:

```
dotnet add package AspNetCore.HealthChecks.SqlServer
```

The `AspNetCore.HealthChecks.SqlServer` package allows us to perform health checks on SQL Server instances. Let's proceed by registering the following services in the `Startup` class:

```
namespace Catalog.API
{
    public class Startup
    {
        ...

        public void ConfigureServices(IServiceCollection services)
```

```
        {
            ...
        services
            .AddHealthChecks()
            .AddSqlServer(Configuration.GetSection
            ("DataSource:ConnectionString").Value);
            ...
        }

        public void Configure(IApplicationBuilder app,
            IWebHostEnvironment env)
        {
            if (!env.IsTesting())
                app.ApplicationServices.GetService<CatalogContext>()
                .Database.Migrate();

            app.UseAuthentication();
            app.UseAuthorization();
            app.UseResponseCaching();
            app.UseHealthChecks("/health");
            ...
        }
    }
}
```

As you can see, the code configures the *health check middleware* using the `AddHealthChecks` extension method, which returns an `IHealthChecksBuilder` interface; it calls the `AddSqlServer` extension method provided by the builder to bind the health check with the SQL Server database. Finally, the code adds the middleware by calling the `UseHealthChecks` method and passing in the health check route. If we can call our service at the `https://<hostname>:<port>/health` route, we will receive the `Healthy/Unhealthy` response, depending on the connection to our data source.

Implementing custom health checks

ASP.NET Core's health check feature is not only suitable for the data source of our service; it can also be used to perform sophisticated and custom health checks. The framework provides the `IHealthCheck` interface so that we can implement our health check. Let's create a new class called `RedisCacheHealthCheck` in the `HealthCheck` folder, inside the `Catalog.API` project:

```
using System;
using System.Threading;
using System.Threading.Tasks;
```

```
using Microsoft.Extensions.Diagnostics.HealthChecks;
using Microsoft.Extensions.Options;
using StackExchange.Redis;
using Catalog.Domain.Settings;

namespace Catalog.API.HealthChecks
{
    public class RedisCacheHealthCheck : IHealthCheck
    {
        private readonly CacheSettings _settings;
        public RedisCacheHealthCheck(IOptions<CacheSettings> settings)
        {
            _settings = settings.Value;
        }

        public async Task<HealthCheckResult>
        CheckHealthAsync(HealthCheckContext context,
            CancellationToken cancellationToken = default)
        {
            try
            {
                var redis = ConnectionMultiplexer.Connect
                (_settings.ConnectionString);
                var db = redis.GetDatabase();

                var result =  await db.PingAsync();
                if (result < TimeSpan.FromSeconds(5))
                {
                    return await Task.FromResult(
                        HealthCheckResult.Healthy());
                }
                return await Task.FromResult(
                    HealthCheckResult.Unhealthy());
            }
            catch (Exception e)
            {
                return await Task.FromResult(
                    HealthCheckResult.Unhealthy(e.Message));
            }
        }
    }
}
```

The `RedisCacheHealthCheck` class uses the `StackExchange.Redis` package to create a connection with the Redis instance specified in the setting's connection string. The core part of this class is the `CheckHealthAsync` method; it returns `HealthCheckResult.Healthy` or `HealthCheckResult.Unhealthy`, depending on the response time of the Redis instance. If a ping takes less than five seconds to come back, it means that the instance is healthy; otherwise, it isn't. The class is part of the ASP.NET Core stack, and it can use the dependency injection engine of the framework to solve dependencies.

Therefore, it is possible to add the class to the health check stack by adding the following snippet to the `ConfigureServices` method of the `Startup` class:

```
. . .
            services
                .AddHealthChecks()
                .AddCheck<RedisCacheHealthCheck>("cache_health_check")
                .AddSqlServer(Configuration.GetSection
                ("DataSource:ConnectionString").Value);
. .
```

This approach will add the check for the SQL Server connection and the custom check we implemented in the `RedisCacheHealthCheck` class to the middleware pipeline. If both of them succeed, the service will be classed as healthy. Futhermore it will be possible to run the catalog containers using the `docker-compose up --build` command and verify the status of the dependencies of the catalog web service by calling the `http://<hostname:port>/health` route.

Summary

In this chapter, we learned how to track the state of our services using logging. We also learned how to customize a logger provider and how to integrate it with an ASP.NET Core application. Furthermore, we dealt with the new health checking feature of ASP.NET Core and learned how to build a custom health check.

Now, you know how to implement logging in an ASP.NET Core application and create a custom logger provider. You will be able to use these skills to keep track of the data that's exposed by your services and monitor the status of your web service instance.

In the next chapter, we will learn how to bring our web service to the cloud using Azure.

18
Deploying Services on Azure

In this chapter, you will learn how to deploy the catalog web service on Microsoft Azure. Although we will be focusing on the Microsoft Azure cloud provider and most of the instructions will be strongly linked to that platform, some of the concepts can be applied to multiple cloud providers: containers are becoming a common way to build and run applications and web services on the cloud, therefore, every cloud provider offers slightly different services and products to host containers. This chapter will not go too deeply into Microsoft Azure; it will provide an overview of **Azure Container Instances (ACI)** and Azure App Service features of the Azure cloud.

In this chapter, we will cover the following topics:

- Getting started with Azure
- Pushing containers into Azure Container Registry
- Configuring ACI
- Configuring app services

Getting started with Azure

As we mentioned previously, Microsoft Azure is the cloud platform built by Microsoft. Azure offers a wide range of IT products, technologies, and integration tools. Virtual machines, serverless technologies, databases, and machine learning pipelines are just some of the products that it provides. In this chapter, we will focus on a few of the services that are presented by Azure, such as **Container Instances**, **App Service**, and **Azure SQL Databases**.

Let's start by creating a subscription. Microsoft allows us to try Azure services out when a new user creates an Azure account for the first time. It is possible to register for a new Microsoft Azure account at `https://azure.microsoft.com/free/`.

The signup process will ask you for some personal details, as well as a valid phone number and valid credit card. By default, Microsoft provides 12 months of popular free services, plus €170 of Azure services for 30 days and 25+ services that are always free. This makes it easy for a new developer or engineer to test/learn how to use some of Azure's new services.

Once you've completed the signup process, you will be able to log in to the Azure portal (`https://portal.azure.com`) using the account you just created.

The Azure CLI is Microsoft's official CLI for managing Azure resources; it is available for almost all OSes and is part of the Azure SDK. The Azure SDK is cross-platform; therefore, it is possible to install it on Windows, macOS, or Linux in three different ways:

Platform	Command	Requirements
Linux	`curl -L https://aka.ms/InstallAzureCli	bash`	You will require some preinstalled software, that is, Python 2.7 or Python 3.x (`https://www.python.org/downloads/`), libffi (`https://sourceware.org/libffi/`), and OpenSSL 1.0.2 (`https://www.openssl.org/source/`). For more information, please go to `https://docs.microsoft.com/en-us/cli/azure/install-azure-cli-linux?view=azure-cli-latest`.
macOS	`brew update && brew install azure-cli`	You will need `brew`, which should already be installed on your machine. For more information about `brew`, please go to `https://brew.sh/`.
Windows	`https://aka.ms/installazurecliwindows`	Microsoft provides an MSI for the Windows platform.

The Azure SDK and its CLI provide all of the command-line tools you'll need to manage Azure services. Let's start by signing in using the CLI. We can do this by executing the following command:

```
az login
```

The preceding command will open a browser window and send you to the sign-in page for the Microsoft Azure portal and save the session into your local environment. In the next section, we will see how to use the CLI to push the container images we built in the previous chapters into the container registry service of Azure.

Pushing containers into Azure Container Registry

In this section, we will focus on deploying our containers into Microsoft Azure. This process involves some resources and services that are provided out of the box by the cloud provider. The following diagram is an overview of the architecture schema that we are going to build:

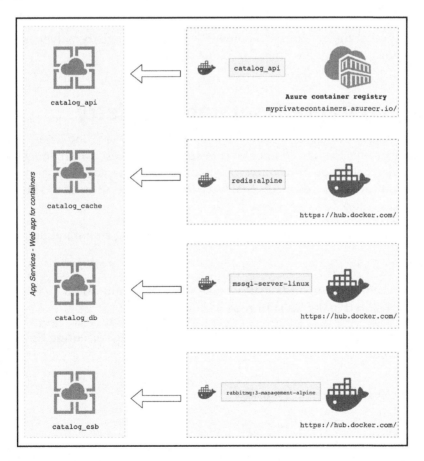

Let's take a look at the different components that are involved in this schema:

- **Azure Container Registry** is a managed Docker Registry service (`https://docs.docker.com/registry/`) based on the open source Docker Registry 2.0. It is possible to use Azure Container Registry to store, manage, and use your private Docker container images. We will use it to save images related to our custom images, such as the `catalog_api` image, and make them available to other cloud services.

- The web app for containers allows us to use our containers and deploy them to **App Service** as a web app. Furthermore, it eliminates time-consuming infrastructure management tasks such as updating, scaling, and in general, managing the infrastructure.

- The other dependencies of the application, such as `catalog_esb` and `catalog_cache`, will take the image from the public Docker Hub (`https://hub.docker.com`).

Let's continue by creating an Azure Container Registry. The registry will be used further in this chapter to push and pull the image of `catalog_api`.

Creating an Azure Container Registry

To create a new Azure Container Registry, we should start by creating a new resource group. Resource groups are a fundamental concept in Azure resource management: they allow us to group a collection of resources for management, deployment, and billing reasons. In general, all of the resources that have the same life cycle should be grouped into the same resource group. Let's get started:

1. First, create a resource group by using the following command on the Azure CLI:

   ```
   az group create --name handsOn --location westeurope
   ```

   The preceding command creates a new resource group called `handsOn` in our account stored in the West Europe region.

2. Next, we will create the Azure Container Registry by executing the following command:

   ```
   az acr create --resource-group handsOn --name
   <container_registry_name> --sku Basic
   ```

The preceding command creates a new Azure Container Registry under the `handsOn` resource group with the name we have chosen. It also defines the **Stock-Keeping Unit (SKU)** for this resource—in our case, the basic one.

 SKU usually refers to a specific variant of a product and all of the attributes that identify that type of product. In the same way, Microsoft Azure uses this term to identify a specific purchasable good or service.

Now that we have created an Azure Container Registry, let's push the `catalog_api` image into the registry. To solve the other dependencies of our container, we will create another `appsettings.json` file dedicated to a `Stage` environment. Therefore, we will set the `ASPNETCORE_ENVIRONMENT` variable to `Stage` to apply the connection string needed by the container. We can proceed by creating the `appsettings.Stage.json` file in the following way:

```
{
    "Logging": {
        "LogLevel": {
            "Default": "Warning"
        }
    },
    "AllowedHosts": "*",
    "DataSource": {
        "ConnectionString": "Server=catalog db.westeurope
        .azurecontainer.io;Database=master;User=sa;
        Password=P@ssw0rd"
    },
    "ESB": {
        "ConnectionString": "host=catalog-esb.westeurope.
        azurecontainer.io;username=guest;password=guest;",
        "EndPointName": "ItemSoldOut"
    },
    "CacheSettings": {
        "ConnectionString": "catalog-cache.westeurope.
        azurecontainer.io:6379,abortConnect=false"
    },
    "AuthenticationSettings": {
        "Secret": "<secret>",
        "ExpirationDays" : "7"
    }
}
```

The preceding `appsettings.json` file definition declares the endpoints for the `catalog_db`, `catalog-esb`, and `catalog-cache` containers. Every endpoint is composed of the name of the container we are going to create, followed by the syntax—`<region_name>.azurecontainer.io`. The first part represents the region, followed by the subdomain of the service we are using, in our case, `azurecontainer.io`. Let's continue by defining the steps to push our local image into the container registry previously created:

1. Let's start by authenticating the Azure CLI in the container registry using the following command:

   ```
   az acr login --name <container_registry_name>
   ```

   This should return a **Login Succeeded** message to the CLI.

2. After that, we can proceed by preparing the Docker image of our service and build the image by triggering the following command in the `Catalog.API` folder:

   ```
   docker-compose build
   ```

   This instruction creates a new Docker image based on the Dockerfile we already have in the project folder. The name of the image will depend on the name specified on the `docker-compose.yml` file and `COMPOSE_PROJECT_NAME` specified in the `.env` file: if the `COMPOSE_PROJECT_NAME` is `store`, then the command will create an image with the `store_catalog_api` name.

3. It is possible to verify the resulting image by executing the `docker images` command:

   ```
   docker images
   REPOSITORY TAG IMAGE ID CREATED SIZE
   catalog_api latest 714e538b7da5 About a minute ago 618MB
   ```

4. It is necessary to get the Azure Container Registry server address so that we can push the local image to the registry. We can proceed by tagging the container that we just created with the server address of the Azure Container Registry we created previously:

   ```
   docker tag catalog_api
   <container_registry_name>.azurecr.io/catalog_api:v1
   docker push <container_registry_name>.azurecr.io/catalog_api:v1
   ```

After tagging the image and using the `docker push` command, Docker will start uploading the container into our Azure container repository. Hence, we will be able to use our container image in all of the services provided by Azure. This upload usually takes some time, depending on the size of the image and the quality of your internet connection. When the upload is completed, it is possible to check the result by browsing the **Container registries** section of the Azure portal (`https://portal.azure.com/`):

In this case, we can see that we have created a container registry called `handsonaspnetcoreacr` under the `handsOn` resource group. Eventually, we can choose to create or manage the container registry directly from the portal. Now that we've pushed the container, we can proceed by configuring ACI.

Configuring Azure Container Instances

The ACI service by Microsoft Azure provides us with a fast and easy way to run containers in the cloud without worrying about the management part of virtual machines or having to learn about new tools. This service is designed to be as quick as possible and ease the process of getting a container up and running in the cloud. Furthermore, it is possible to launch a container by executing a simple Azure CLI command, such as the following:

```
az container create --resource-group myResourceGroup \
                --name cache-container \
                --image redis:alpine \
                --cpu 1 \
                --memory 1 \
                --dns-name-label cache-container \
                --ports 6379
```

The ACI service is the ideal service for testing and running containers in Azure. Hence, the ACI service allows us to lower our infrastructure costs by taking advantage of *per-second billing*. For that reason, the ACI service is also the favorite service for continuous integration and continuous pipeline purposes. The following steps show you how to deploy the catalog service on ACI:

1. Let's start by creating a new resource group so that we can group our containers. Use the following command to do so:

```
az group create --name handsOnContainerServices --location "West Europe"
```

2. We can proceed by getting the registry username and password of the service account of the container registry using the following command:

```
az acr credential show -n <container_registry_name>
```

3. After creating the group, we will need to execute the Azure CLI command using a Bash script from the GitHub repository called aci-deploy.sh:

```bash
#!/bin/bash
# Set the service group name
export resource_group=handsOnContainerServices
# Set the registry address
export registry_address=<registry_address>
# Set the registry username
export registry_username=<registry_username>
# Set the registry password
export registry_password=<registry_password>
# Set the api ASPNETCORE_ENVIRONMENT variables
export environment=Stage
# Set the sql container name
export sql_name=catalog-db
# Set the sql admin password
export sql_admin_pass=P@ssw0rd
# Set the event service bus name
export esb_name=catalog-esb
# Set the event service bus username
export rabbitmq_user=guest
# Set the event service bus password
export rabbitmq_pass=guest
# Set the cache container name
export cache_name=catalog-cache
# Set the service name
export api_name=catalog-api
```

```
az container create --resource-group ${resource_group} \
                    --location westeurope \
                    --name ${sql_name} \
                    --image microsoft/mssql-server-linux \
                    --cpu 1 \
                    --memory 1 \
                    --dns-name-label ${sql_name} \
                    --ports 1433 \
                    --environment-variables ACCEPT_EULA=Y
SA_PASSWORD=${sql_admin_pass}
az container create --resource-group ${resource_group} \
                    --location westeurope \
                    --name ${esb_name} \
                    --image rabbitmq:3-management \
                    --cpu 1 \
                    --memory 1 \
                    --dns-name-label ${esb_name} \
                    --ports 5672 \
                    --environment-variables
RABBITMQ_DEFAULT_USER=${rabbitmq_user}
RABBITMQ_DEFAULT_PASS=${rabbitmq_pass}

az container create --resource-group ${resource_group} \
                    --name ${cache_name} \
                    --image redis:alpine \
                    --cpu 1 \
                    --memory 1 \
                    --dns-name-label ${cache_name} \
                    --ports 6379

az container create --resource-group ${resource_group} \
                    --location westeurope \
                    --name ${api_name} \
                    --image ${registry_address}/catalog_api:v1 \
                    --cpu 1 \
                    --memory 1 \
                    --dns-name-label ${api_name} \
                    --ports 80 \
                    --ip-address public \
                    --environment-variables
ASPNETCORE_ENVIRONMENT=${environment} \
                    --registry-password=${registry_password} \
                    --registry-username=${registry_username}
```

The script mostly runs five different instructions for the creation of new instances of these containers:

- It declares information regarding the containers, such as the resource group, the names to assign to the containers, and some additional environment variables.
- It executes the `az container create` command to create and run `microsoft/mssql-server-linux`.
- It executes the `az container create` instruction to create and run the `rabbitmq:3-management-alpine` image, and it uses the `rabbitmq_user` and `rabbitmq_pass` environment variables to set the default user for the RabbitMQ instance.
- It deploys the Redis cache instance using `redis:alpine`.
- Finally, it executes `az container create` to create and deploy the `catalog_api` image that's already present in the Azure Container Registry repository by specifying the registry URL.

Please note that the execution order follows the same logic of the dependencies of these containers; therefore, the API container is run last. Note that, to keep the demo as simple as possible, the `aci-deploy.sh` script creates the catalog service container using `--ip-address public`, which means that our container can be accessed by anyone. Directly exposing an API without any reverse proxy and an API gateway is strongly discouraged in a production environment so that you avoid exposing your containers to the outside world.

Now that we've executed the script, we can see the result by signing into the Azure portal (`https://portal.azure.com/#`) and checking our container in the **Container instances** section:

As you can see, there are four container instances up and running. All of them are running on DNS using the `--dns-name-label` parameter and can access each other through their addresses. Hence, it is possible to call the container API using the address that was generated by our shell script. We can also check the statistics and the properties associated with the container by clicking on the name of the container:

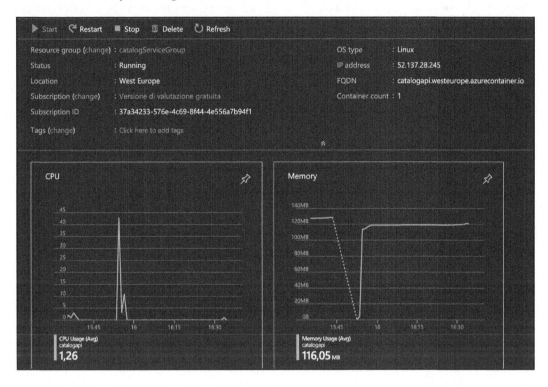

Finally, we can call the health check HTTP route from our browser to verify that all of the dependencies are correct:

```
http://catalog-api.westeurope.azurecontainer.io/health
```

The preceding process describes how to deploy the catalog service into the ACI product. Although ACI are powerful and easy to deploy, they lack some minimal out-of-the-box features, such as SSH, monitoring, and configuration management. Therefore, it becomes hard to manage container instances in a production environment. In the next section, we will focus on a different hosting process that uses app service technologies to host the application called app services. This way of working is more focused on the hosting of web applications and web services; therefore, it provides a set of tools and features for the monitoring and the configuration of the application.

Configuring app services

An alternative to ACI is app services. Microsoft Azure recently released a new feature so that we can deploy Docker images using **app services**. This kind of approach is useful when you want to keep the same environment for your development machine and production environment. In contrast to ACI, app services provides us with a managed way to run our containers. It comes with some out-of-the-box features, such as SSL encryption, monitoring, configuration management, remote debugging, and application scaling settings. On top of that, app services is strongly integrated with other Azure products. Therefore, it is possible to plug other services into `catalog-srv` easily. For example, we may choose to run our Azure SQL Database solution to set up a fully-managed SQL database for the catalog service. Azure SQL provides the broadest SQL Server engine compatibility; it simplifies the maintenance process using the SQL tools you prefer.

 As we mentioned previously, it is not easy to integrate persistence data storage using Docker without using persistent volumes. For that reason, in this section, we will look at an alternative way to store data.

Let's proceed by creating a new Azure SQL database by using the `azuresql-deploy.sh` script in the root folder of the project:

```bash
#!/bin/bash

# Set an admin login and password for your database
export user_admin=catalog_srv
export user_pass=P@ssw0rd
# The logical server name has to be unique in the system
export server_name=storecatalogapi
export database_name=catalog
# The resource group name
export resourceGroup=handsOnAppService
# The ip address range that you want to allow to access your DB
export startip=0.0.0.0
export endip=0.0.0.0

# Create a resource group
az group create \
    --name ${resourceGroup} \
    --location westeurope

# Create a logical server in the resource group
az sql server create \
    --name ${server_name} \
    --resource-group ${resourceGroup} \
```

```
    --location westeurope  \
    --admin-user ${user_admin} \
    --admin-password ${user_pass}

# Configure a firewall rule and open to local Azure services
az sql server firewall-rule create \
    --resource-group ${resourceGroup} \
    --server ${server_name} \
    -n AllowYourIp \
    --start-ip-address ${startip} \
    --end-ip-address ${endip}

# Create a database in the server
az sql db create \
    --resource-group ${resourceGroup} \
    --server ${server_name} \
    --name ${database_name} \
    --service-objective S0 \
     --zone-redundant false
```

In the preceding script, the `azuresql-deploy.sh` file creates the logical server that hosts the `store` database and the effective database that contains the catalog information. First of all, the script proceeds by creating the resource group; then, it continues by creating the Azure SQL elements. Since `start-ip` and `end-ip`, which are specified in the firewall rules, are both `0.0.0.0`, all of the Azure services that are part of that account can connect to the database.

By doing this, it is possible to connect the previously created `catalog-srv` app service to the database.

Creating an app service using a container image

Let's walk through how to create an app service using the previously published image, which is already present in Azure Container Registry, that is, `<registry_name>.azurecr.io/catalog_api:v1`. As a first step, we need to create an app service plan using the following command:

```
az appservice plan create --name catalogServicePlan --resource-group
<service_group_name> --sku FREE --is-linux
```

The app service plan is required for the creation of the app service: it defines a set of computing resources that are used to run all of the app services that are part of the same plan. For this example, we will use the most basic service plan, which can be specified using the following flag: `--sku FREE`. This plan supports up to 10 instances and it does not provide any additional autoscale capability.

Now that we've created all of the requirements, we can proceed by executing the `appservice-deploy.sh` file, which is located in the root of the project:

```bash
#!/bin/bash
# Set the service group name
export resource_group=handsOnAppService
# Set the plan
export plan=catalogServicePlan
# Set the service name
export app_service_name=catalog-srv
# Set the api ASPNETCORE_ENVIRONMENT variables
export environment=StageAppServices
# Defines the ACR registry URL
export registry_address=<registry_address>.azurecr.io

# Create the app service
az webapp create --resource-group ${resource_group} \
                        --plan ${plan} \
                        --name ${app_service_name} \
                        --deployment-container-image-name
${registry_address}/catalog_api:v1
# Set the ASPNETCORE_ENVIRONMENT variable
az webapp config appsettings set -g ${resource_group} \
                        -n ${app_service_name} \
                        --settings
ASPNETCORE_ENVIRONMENT=${environment}
```

The preceding script creates the web app using the `az webapp create` instruction, and after the creation of the app service, it proceeds by executing the `az webapp config appsettings set` command to set the right ASP.NET Core environment value. Once the script has been executed, we can continue by checking the status of the app service in the portal:

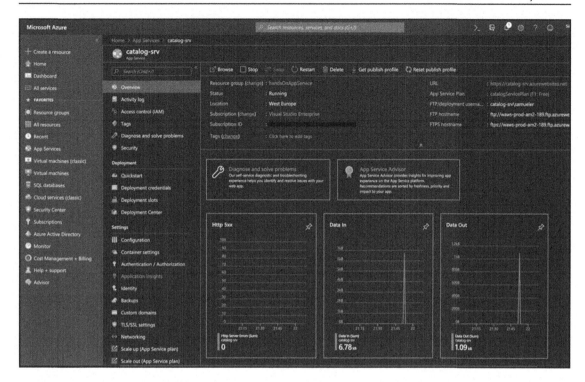

Furthermore, we can verify the status of the service by calling the health check URL: `http://catalog-api.westeurope.azurecontainer.io/health`.

Summary

In this chapter, we have seen how we can host and run the catalog service project in Microsoft Azure. We also learned how to create a private Azure Container Registry and how to store the Docker image of the catalog service. Then, we showed you some of the patterns you can use to get a custom container into the cloud and how to run them using different services offered by the Microsoft Azure cloud provider. Finally, we looked at two different approaches to hosting the catalog service: using the ACI product and Azure App Service and storing the data using the Azure SQL service.

In the next chapter, we will learn how to document APIs using the OpenAPI Specification by implementing the Swagger framework.

19
Documenting Your API Using Swagger

In this chapter, we will learn how to document our API using the OpenAPI Specification and how to use Swagger tools to parse and generate the documentation. Documenting APIs is particularly significant when our web service is consumed by an external company or a foreign organization team. Moreover, some services can be considerably complex and expose a lot of endpoints. For this reason, some tools related to the .NET ecosystem guarantee up-to-date API documentation. Two main toolchains can be used in this process: NSwag and Swashbuckle. In this book, we will cover and use NSwag to document our APIs.

In this chapter, we will cover the following topics:

- Understanding OpenAPI
- Implementing OpenAPI in ASP.NET Core services

By the end of this chapter, you will be able to automatically generate up-to-date documentation that's compliant with the OpenAPI Specification using Swagger and the NSwag package.

Understanding OpenAPI

The OpenAPI initiative is part of the Linux Foundation and defines the **OpenAPI Specification (OAS)** standard. The OpenAPI Specification aims to provide a language-agnostic interface for REST APIs. This kind of approach guarantees that both humans and client applications understand and discover the capabilities of a web service by referring to a unique entry point. In addition, it provides a high-level abstraction that can also be used for business or design purposes.

Furthermore, its standard way of querying services facilitates every kind of automation – from the autogeneration of a client to the autogeneration of the documentation.

Implementing the Swagger project

Just like the OpenAPI Specification, Swagger was born as a language-agnostic specification for describing REST APIs. It has recently been adopted by the OpenAPI project, which means there are no differences between these two projects.

The main aim of Swagger is to autogenerate and expose a document called `swagger.json`, also known as the **Swagger Specification**. The Swagger Specification is the autogenerated documentation of the API and provides information about every single route that's exposed by the web services. The following code shows the structure of an example `swagger.json` file:

```json
{
  "x-generator": "NSwag v12.0.12.0 (NJsonSchema v9.13.15.0 (Newtonsoft.Json
v12.0.0.0))",
  "swagger": "2.0",
  "host": "localhost:5000",
  "schemes": [
    "http"
  ],
  "consumes": [
    "application/json"
  ],
  "paths": {
    "/api/artist": {
      "get": {
        "tags": [
          "Artist"
        ],
        "operationId": "Artist_Get",
        "parameters": [
          {
            "type": "string",
            "name": "artistId",
            "in": "query"
          }
        ],
        "responses": {
          "200": {
            "schema": {
              "type": "file"
            }
```

```
        }
    }
...
```

The preceding snippet describes some of the routes that are defined in the **catalog service** API. As you can see, at the first level of the JSON, there is some general information about the service, such as the `apiVersion`, `title`, and `basePath` of the service. Furthermore, we can also see a node called `paths`, which contains all the paths of our service. For each route, it describes the different response types, the different HTTP verbs, and all the payload information that's accepted by the service. Since we have a unique standard for describing our APIs, it is also possible to define a unique user interface so that we can query and send information to the service; this is what **Swagger UI** does. Swagger UI is a tool that uses the `swagger.json` file to provide a user-friendly UI:

The preceding screenshot shows an example of a useful UI that we can use to browse the different routes that are exposed by the APIs. Furthermore, it allows the consumer to have an immediate overall view of the data that's provided by the API. Now, let's learn how to implement OpenAPI in ASP.NET Core.

Implementing OpenAPI in ASP.NET Core services

There are two different packages that we can use to implement OpenAPI in ASP.NET Core:

- **Swashbuckle**: https://docs.microsoft.com/en-us/aspnet/core/tutorials/ getting-started-with-swashbuckle?view=aspnetcore-2.2
- **NSwag**: https://docs.microsoft.com/en-us/aspnet/core/tutorials/ getting-started-with-nswag?view=aspnetcore-2.2

Both of these use middleware to generate and serve the swagger.json file and allow the user interface to browse the service definition. In this section, we will discuss how to integrate NSwag into our vinyl catalog service. The following schema shows how NSwag is plugged into our ASP.NET Core service:

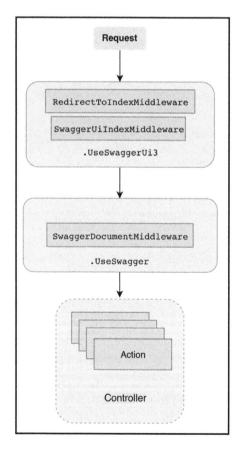

Let's start by adding `NSwag.AspNetCore` to the `Catalog.API` project by using the following command:

```
dotnet add package NSwag.AspNetCore
```

After that, we can proceed by combining the middleware to generate and provide the OpenAPI specification and the middleware to initialize the UI. As we saw in Chapter 3, *Working with the Middleware Pipeline*, we need to use the `Configure` and `ConfigureServices` methods, which are implemented in the `Startup` class:

```
...
    public class Startup
    {
        public void ConfigureServices(IServiceCollection services)
        {
            services
                .AddCatalogContext(Configuration.
                GetSection("DataSource:ConnectionString").Value);

            services
                ..
                .AddOpenApiDocument(settings =>{
                                    settings.Title = "Catalog API";
                                    settings.DocumentName = "v3";
                                    settings.Version = "v3";
                                });
        }

        public void Configure(IApplicationBuilder app,
        IHostingEnvironment env)
        {
            ...
            app
                .UseOpenApi()
                .UseSwaggerUi3();
        }
    }
}
```

`AddOpenApiDocument` adds the services that are required for OpenAPI 3.0 generation. `UseOpenApi` adds the OpenAPI/Swagger generator, which uses API description to perform Swagger generation, and `UseSwaggerUi3` creates and instantiates the middleware that provides the UI of Swagger. Since we integrated the OpenAPI middleware into our service, we can proceed by running our service and browse the `https://localhost/swagger` URL using our preferred browser.

NSwag and Swashbuckle use reflection to browse the action methods inside our controllers. Fortunately, this process is only executed the first time the service runs. Sometimes, complex response types can prevent the `swagger.json` file from being generated. For that reason, it is strongly suggested that you check all the response types that are provided by the action methods of our controllers.

NSwag also provides some useful utilities so that we can perform code generation on our web services, such as the following ones:

- `NSwag.CodeGeneration.CSharp` (https://www.nuget.org/packages/NSwag.CodeGeneration.CSharp/)
- `NSwag.CodeGeneration.TypeScript` (https://www.nuget.org/packages/NSwag.CodeGeneration.TypeScript/)

These allow us to autogenerate client classes for C# and Typescript, respectively.

In this section, we learned how to install and configure NSwag so that we can expose Swagger documentation that's compatible with the OpenAPI Specification. In the next section, we will learn how to explicitly define the conventions for our APIs, as well as how to include additional information in the `swagger.json` contract.

Understanding ASP.NET Core's conventions

The default response type of the Swagger UI produces some incorrect information. If we take a look at the responses section, we will see that the response code is incorrect and that it doesn't correspond with the actual HTTP code that's returned by the web service. When using ASP.NET Core 2.2 or later, it is possible to use conventions to specify the response types:

```
[ApiController]
public class ItemController : ControllerBase
{
    [HttpGet]
    [ApiConventionMethod(typeof(DefaultApiConventions),
    nameof(DefaultApiConventions.Get))]
    public async Task<IActionResult> Get([FromQuery] int pageSize =
    10, [FromQuery] int pageIndex = 0)

    [HttpGet("{id:guid}")]
    [ApiConventionMethod(typeof(DefaultApiConventions),
```

```
    nameof(DefaultApiConventions.Get))]
    public async Task<IActionResult> GetById(Guid id)
    ...
```

For example, the preceding code uses the `ApiConventionMethod` attribute to pass a custom type and a method name. The `ApiConventionMethod` attribute is part of the `Microsoft.AspNetCore.Mvc` namespace and uses the `DefaultApiConventions` static class, which provides a default set of conventions for each action in a generic API. In the same way, we can add that attribute to the writing methods of `ItemController`, such as the `Create`, `Update`, and `Delete` methods:

```
    ...

    [HttpPost]
    [ApiConventionMethod(typeof(DefaultApiConventions),
    nameof(DefaultApiConventions.Create))]
    public async Task<IActionResult> Create(AddItemRequest request)

    [HttpPut("{id:guid}")]
    [ApiConventionMethod(typeof(DefaultApiConventions),
    nameof(DefaultApiConventions.Update))]
    public async Task<IActionResult> Update(Guid id,
    EditItemRequest request)

    [HttpDelete("{id:guid}")]
    [ApiConventionMethod(typeof(DefaultApiConventions),
    nameof(DefaultApiConventions.Delete))]
    public async Task<IActionResult> Delete(Guid id)
  }
}
```

This kind of approach is a shortcut that we can use to declare action method responses without explicitly using the `ProducesResponseType` attribute. Let's take a look at the `DefaultApiConventions` static class, which provides a set of default response types if we declare some static void methods:

```
using Microsoft.AspNetCore.Mvc.ApiExplorer;

namespace Microsoft.AspNetCore.Mvc
{
  public static class DefaultApiConventions
  {
    [ProducesResponseType(200)]
    [ProducesResponseType(404)]
    [ProducesDefaultResponseType]
    [ApiConventionNameMatch(ApiConventionNameMatchBehavior.Prefix)]
    public static void Get([ApiConventionNameMatch
```

```
    (ApiConventionNameMatchBehavior.Suffix), ApiConventionTypeMatch(
    ApiConventionTypeMatchBehavior.Any)] object id)
    {
    }
    ...
  }
}
```

For example, for the Get method, it states the HTTP 200 OK response and HTTP 404 Not found. By doing this, we can easily declare the proper response types for each action. The DefaultApiConventions class is part of the Microsoft.AspNetCore.Mvc namespace.

Custom conventions

The DefaultApiConvention class isn't always suitable for our controllers. Furthermore, it is too generic, and action methods are usually too specific to suit the DefaultApiConvention class. Due to this, ASP.NET Core allows us to create our custom API conventions based on our needs. To declare a new convention, we need to create a new static class with the corresponding static methods, like so:

```
using Microsoft.AspNetCore.Mvc;
using Microsoft.AspNetCore.Mvc.ApiExplorer;

namespace Catalog.API.Conventions
{
    public static class ItemApiConvention
    {

        [ProducesResponseType(200)]
        [ProducesResponseType(404)]
        [ProducesResponseType(400)]
        [ProducesDefaultResponseType]
        [ApiConventionNameMatch(ApiConventionNameMatchBehavior.Prefix)]
        public static void Get([ApiConventionNameMatch
        (ApiConventionNameMatchBehavior.Suffix),
                               ApiConventionTypeMatch
                               (ApiConventionTypeMatchBehavior.Any)]
                                object id)
        {
        }

        ...
    }
}
```

The conventions we've implemented here describe the `Get` action method of `ItemController`. As you can see, this method produces the following HTTP responses: `200`, `404`, and `400`. This approach also allows us to generate and extend the response types that are returned by a route. Furthermore, it is possible to assign and use these conventions by applying the attribute in the following way:

```
[HttpGet]
[ApiConventionMethod(typeof(ItemApiConvention),
nameof(ItemApiConvention.Get))]
public async Task<IActionResult> Get([FromQuery] int pageSize = 10,
[FromQuery] int pageIndex = 0)
{

    ...

}
```

This approach allows us to customize and group API conventions into a unique class and fully-customize the contract of the API. The same approach can be used for the other action methods that are present in the controller classes of your services.

Summary

In this chapter, we have learned how to improve the discoverability of web services by documenting them using the OpenAPI Specification. The OpenAPI technique also provides us with a standard way to generate clients in every language and generate auto-maintainable documentation. Documenting APIs is useful when the service is utilized by third-party teams and consumers, and also provides us with a high-level overview of the information and actions that are exposed by the service.

In the next chapter, we will learn about Postman and how to use it to query, test, and check the responses of a web service.

20
Testing Services Using Postman

Postman is one of the most powerful tools we can use to query APIs and is mainly available to developers and enterprise teams. In this chapter, we will introduce Postman and show you how to use this tool to test and monitor a web service. Postman is described as an API-first solution with the industry's only complete API development environment. Next, we will learn how to use Postman to call a generic HTTP API. Then, we will learn how to import the OpenAPI Specification we generated in the previous chapter into Postman to automatically generate the API calls that are implemented in the catalog service.

In this chapter, we will cover the following topics:

- Overview of Postman
- Importing a collection using OpenAPI

By the end of this chapter, you will have learned how to use Postman to test and verify API responses through the Postman UI and by using the automated testing tools.

Overview of Postman

Postman can be used within a company to share internal APIs and applies the concept of collections so that it can group, index, and query web services. A collection is a group of HTTP calls related to the same service or a collection of services.

The following screenshot shows a conventional UI for Postman. On the left, you can see a list of *collections* that are available in the Postman account, while on the right, you can see the core part of the UI:

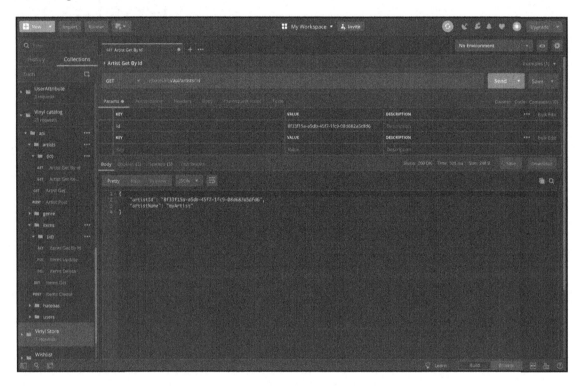

The first half of the UI represents the HTTP request we intend to launch. Each tab at the top of the interface represents an API call; it is possible to type in a URL and specify the HTTP verb on the left. For each request, it is also possible to specify the query parameters, the authorization specification, the headers, the body, and some scripts that we will execute before and after every request.

Here, the request uses the `{{baseUrl}}/api/artists/:id` URL and passes
`id:<guid_value>`. It is important to note that, in Postman, it is possible to specify
environment variables that can be used to parameterize our API queries. In this case, the
`{{baseUrl}}` placeholder is replaced with the values specified in the collection. It is
possible to view the collection variables by clicking on the three dots next to the collection
name, selecting **Edit**, and then navigating to the **Variables** tab:

The second part of the Postman interface is focused on the response of the request. The
main section contains the JSON response of the API:

On the right-hand side, we have the **Status** of the response, the response **Time**, and the
Size of the response. Furthermore, it is possible to switch the format of the response so that
it's either JSON, HTML, or raw text. The response section also provides some detailed
information about the **Headers**, **Cookies**, and **Test Results**.

In the next section, we will learn how to automatically test our API using Postman's tools.

Testing the API using Postman

Postman also provides us with a helpful tool/framework that we can use to test our APIs automatically. The test runtime is based on Node.js; for that reason, we should write a test assertion using JavaScript. The test framework of Postman uses the following workflow to test our code:

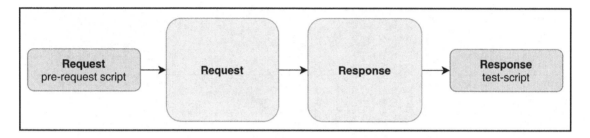

The scripts will execute as follows for every request in a collection:

- A pre-request script will run before every request in the collection. This is considered the setup part of a test case.
- A test script will run after every request in the collection; this is the core part of our test. Furthermore, it provides the core assertions for our test.

Let's use this procedure to implement a simple test for our API:

```
pm.test("response is ok", function () {
    pm.response.to.have.status(200);
});
```

As you can see, the test uses the pm global object to describe a test, and it adds a callback function to make some assertions. In this case, it checks whether the API has a status of 200 OK. The following implementation can be added to a request by typing the preceding code into the **Tests** tab of the request, as shown in the following screenshot:

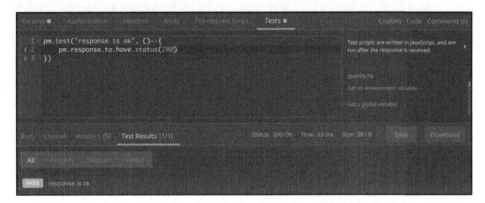

After that, we will be able to check the result in the response part of Postman:

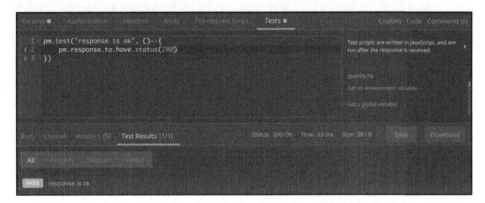

The test results section that's shown in the preceding screenshot contains four different subtabs, all of which group the tests by the results. If an error occurs, the UI provides details of the error.

Using the runner to test the APIs

The Postman team built a runner tool that automatically tests and runs your APIs so that you can – quite literally – sit back and watch your API test itself. Furthermore, you can use scripts to build integration test suites, pass data between API requests, and build workflows that mirror your actual API use cases.

The runner feature requires at least one test to be associated with the request so that it can assert the result. It is possible to access the runner interface of Postman by clicking on the **Runner** button (shown in the yellow rectangle in the following screenshot), which can be found in the top-left corner of the screen, and selecting the collection you want to run:

Postman also allows us to integrate these functionalities using the CLI. The development team published an npm package to execute the runner in a localhost environment. It is possible to install this package on your local machine using the following command:

```
npm install -g newman
```

After that, it is possible to execute the runner on a specific collection by passing the JSON file that represents the collection and then executing the preceding command. It is possible to export a collection by clicking on the three points next to the collection and clicking on the **Export** option:

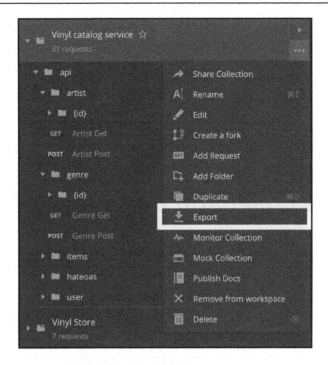

Then, we can proceed by executing this command on the file:

```
newman run examples/sample-collection.json
```

The resulting execution will look something similar to the following:

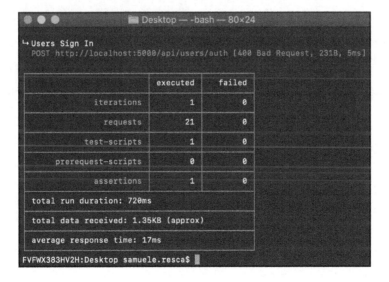

This implementation provides a single and detailed response of each request that was tested and a final report that shows all the information related to the tests. This approach is really useful when we want to integrate Postman's testing capabilities into a continuous integration pipeline. All we need to do is install the `newman` tool on our server and add the path of the collection.

In the next section, we will learn how to use the OpenAPI Specification (described in the previous chapter) to automatically generate a Postman collection.

Importing a collection using OpenAPI

In this section, you will learn how to import a collection using the OpenAPI Specification. Postman uses some of common API description standards, such as OpenAPI v3, Swagger v2 and v1 (as described in the previous chapter), to import the routes of web services. Let's get started:

1. First of all, click on the **Import** (shown in the yellow rectangle) button at the top-left corner of the screen and click on the **Import from Link** tab:

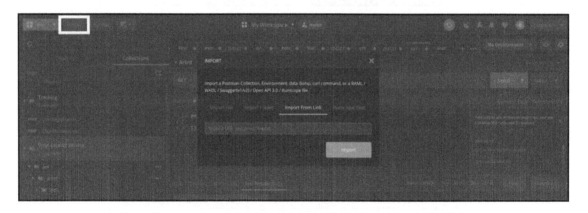

2. Now, we can copy and paste the URL of the document API of the running localhost service, like so:

```
http://localhost:5000/swagger/v3/swagger.json
```

By doing this, the collection will be imported with the same name that we gave our Swagger document. This will contain a selection of all the routes that were described by Swagger.

Summary

In this chapter, we learned how to use Postman to query, test, and monitor web services. Postman's capabilities go beyond this; however, we can also share collections of APIs with other teams and with our consumers. It is an essential tool for any API consumer if they wish to check the results and the information provided by the consumed services.

You now have the necessary knowledge to use the Postman suite to test and verify a web service.

Other Books You May Enjoy

If you enjoyed this book, you may be interested in these other books by Packt:

Hands-On Design Patterns with C# and .NET Core
Gaurav Aroraa, Jeffrey Chilberto

ISBN: 978-1-78913-364-6

- Make your code more flexible by applying SOLID principles
- Follow the test-driven development (TDD) approach in your .NET Core projects
- Get to grips with efficient database migration, data persistence, and testing techniques
- Convert a console application to a web application using the right MVP
- Write asynchronous, multithreaded, and parallel code
- Implement MVVM and work with RxJS and AngularJS to deal with changes in databases
- Explore the features of microservices, serverless programming, and cloud computing

Mastering Visual Studio 2019 - Second Edition
Kunal Chowdhury

ISBN: 978-1-78953-009-4

- Increase your productivity with Visual Studio 2019's new features
- Understand how the installation wizard works and create an offline installation package
- Build stunning applications using WPF, .NET Core, and TypeScript
- Explore NuGet packages in depth
- Accelerate cloud development with Azure
- Debug and test your applications efficiently
- Get to grips with integrating Visual Studio with Git repositories

Leave a review - let other readers know what you think

Please share your thoughts on this book with others by leaving a review on the site that you bought it from. If you purchased the book from Amazon, please leave us an honest review on this book's Amazon page. This is vital so that other potential readers can see and use your unbiased opinion to make purchasing decisions, we can understand what our customers think about our products, and our authors can see your feedback on the title that they have worked with Packt to create. It will only take a few minutes of your time, but is valuable to other potential customers, our authors, and Packt. Thank you!

Index